PRAISE FOR *EDUCATI(* *POLICY RIGHT ON ACCOUNTABILITY, TEACHER PAY, AND SCHOOL CHOICE*

"*Education Restated: Getting Policy Right on Accountability, Teacher Pay, and School Choice* is driven by a fundamental commitment to equity: doing more for the students and families who have the greatest needs but are given the fewest opportunities. Regenstein has a great grasp of the current policy and the political landscape and endeavors to find feasible ways for competing factions to come together around their common commitment to equity. This book challenges a number of sacred cows for reformers and teacher unionists alike, but in a way that invites both groups to rethink current practice in order to do what is right. It also makes clear that we cannot make the progress we want and need unless we devote significantly more resources to early childhood education through 3rd grade. *Education Restated* is both a hopeful book and a realistic book, and one that can provide policymakers and practitioners ways to work together to advance equity."

—**Jo Anderson, Jr.**, founder and former CEO, Consortium for Educational Change; former executive director, Illinois Education Association-NEA; former senior advisor, U.S. Department of Education

"Elliot Regenstein's book is a great place to start if you are ready to get past the same tired education policy conversations to create an educational system worthy of the hopes and dreams of students and families. *Education Restated* is at turns fresh and infuriating—ultimately just the kind of thing we need to be reading and discussing if we are going to co-create innovative education policy solutions that improve the lives of kids."

—**Sandy Boyd**, CEO, Seek Common Ground

"*Education Restated* engages readers from start to finish by reframing, expanding, and simplifying transformational strategies. For example, Regenstein proposes an approach to accountability that honors and leverages school and district context, and boldly explores how race and discipline shape the ecosystem of schools in a way that impacts teacher hiring. Uniquely introspective, *Education Restated* links policy to practice with strategies that can reshape the education system for the better."

—**Dr. Carla Bryant**, executive director, Center for District Innovation and Leadership in Early Education

"No matter what you think you know, *Education Restated: Getting Policy Right on Accountability, Teacher Pay, and School Choice* will change how you view education policy. Instead of simplistic prescriptions, it's full of targeted, practical strategies that will make a real difference."

—**Tim Daly**, CEO, EdNavigator

"Education policy-making often feels like a game of 'Whack-a-Mole,' where one problem is addressed only to see a new issue arise. Drawing upon a background in the education policy, practice, and research fields, *Education Restated* offers a clear-headed, intellectually rigorous, and actionable assessment of the barriers to constructive education policy-making as well as ideas for a way forward for more strategic, collaborative, and successful education systems."

—**David Figlio**, provost and professor of economics and education, University of Rochester; former dean, School of Education and Social Policy, Northwestern University

"Like the polarized society in which it operates, education too often is viewed in binary terms: public or private schools, traditional schools or charter schools, reform or status quo. *Education Restated* examines some of the most contentious education issues, discovering in all of them the potential for collaborative solutions. In his engaging and thought-provoking style, Elliot Regenstein identifies worthy ideas from across the political and public policy spectrums for innovative approaches to accountability, school choice, and teacher quality. This book should be on the reading list of anyone who truly cares about every child receiving a great education."

—**Tom Gentzel**, founder, Gentzel Insights; former executive director and CEO, National School Boards Association

"Elliot Regenstein's *Education Restated* is an accurate appraisal of our education system that analyzes the contemporary configuration, illuminates areas of dissonance, and makes a pragmatic case for how and why we should make a methodological shift to lead us to not just improved student performance but, more importantly, the conditions to foster positive outcomes for both students and educators. As a policymaker and education advocate, I relish in works that provide practical ideas that are thoroughly validated by evidence."

—**Cristina Pacione-Zayas**, Illinois State Senator, Twentieth District

"For almost forty years, the education policy and reform landscape has been dominated by various efforts to drive improvement through some form of accountability, whether it be standards, testing, teacher performance, or even school choice. Individually and collectively, these efforts have failed to produce any meaningful improvement in the lives of students, educators, or the public education system in general. Most of the postmortems on policy failures tend to blame a force or constituency other than that favored by the author. But Elliot Regenstein presents an exceptionally thoughtful and integrative analysis of these efforts—and one that looks at how they fit together in a system oriented toward producing measurable improvement over time. At a moment when the values and existence of public education appear threatened, *Education Restated* provides a constructive and actionable path forward."

—**Robert Pianta**, professor of psychology, Batten Bicentennial
Professor of Early Childhood Education, and dean, School of
Education and Human Development, University of Virginia

"Full of new ways to solve long-standing impasses in education policy, *Education Restated: Getting Policy Right on Accountability, Teacher Pay, and School Choice* is a must-read for anyone who cares about raising the next generation."

—**Dana Suskind**, MD, director of Pediatric Cochlear Implantation
Program and professor of surgery and pediatrics, University
of Chicago; founder and co-director, TMW Center for Early
Learning + Public Health; author of *Parent Nation: Unlocking
Every Child's Potential, Fulfilling Society's Promise*

"Elliot Regenstein takes a rare and much-needed look at education policy that actually makes sense. *Education Restated* is an incredibly smart book but at the same time it's accessible, it's logical, and it doesn't require readers to be education policy experts. If you're intellectually curious, want to see our schools get better, and want an open, balanced, and sophisticated view on how to do so, you'll really love this book."

—**Bradley Tusk**, CEO, Tusk Strategies; co-founder
of the Gotham Book Prize; author of *The Fixer: My
Adventures Saving Startups from Death by Politics*

"For at least the last decade, our nation's education policy-making has been given more to gimmickry and sideshows than to serious concern with the pillars of a system that serves tens of millions of people. Elliot Regenstein is among the most lucid and practical thinkers in our field. *Education Restated* makes the case that a commonsensical approach not only can restore policy-makers' focus on the big issues but also can make critically needed improvements that will have immediate impact at great scale. If the U.S. education system is to be socially just and globally competitive, policymakers and education system leaders should treat this book as a roadmap to progress."

—**John White**, founder and managing principal, Watershed Advisors; former Louisiana State superintendent of education

Education Restated

Education Restated

Getting Policy Right on Accountability, Teacher Pay, and School Choice

Elliot Regenstein

ROWMAN & LITTLEFIELD
Lanham • Boulder • New York • London

Published by Rowman & Littlefield
An imprint of The Rowman & Littlefield Publishing Group, Inc.
4501 Forbes Boulevard, Suite 200, Lanham, Maryland 20706
www.rowman.com

86-90 Paul Street, London EC2A 4NE

British Library Cataloguing in Publication Information Available

Library of Congress Cataloging-in-Publication Data

Names: Regenstein, Elliot (Lawyer), author.
Title: Education restated : getting policy right on accountability, teacher pay, and school choice / Elliot Regenstein.
Description: Lanham : Rowman & Littlefield, [2022] | Includes bibliographical references and index. | Summary: "Education Restated proposes shifts in how we address three areas in education policy: accountability, teacher hiring, and parent choice. In each of these areas policy has been anchored around the wrong core values. By focusing on the right core values, state governments can create promising conditions for education improvement at the local level"-- Provided by publisher.
Identifiers: LCCN 2022019282 (print) | LCCN 2022019283 (ebook) | ISBN 9781475865882 (cloth) | ISBN 9781475865899 (paperback) | ISBN 9781475865905 (ebook)
Subjects: LCSH: Education and state--United States. | Educational accountability--United States. | Teachers--Salaries, etc.--United States. | School choice--United States.
Classification: LCC LC89 .R445 2022 (print) | LCC LC89 (ebook) | DDC 379.73--dc23/eng/20220609
LC record available at https://lccn.loc.gov/2022019282
LC ebook record available at https://lccn.loc.gov/2022019283

To Zoë and Jamie,
even though they like their mom's books better

Contents

Contents

Preface

As the kindergartners line up to leave the room, the teacher hands each one a few squares of toilet paper. It is clear that this is part of their regular routine, and each child quietly accepts the toilet paper as it is handed out. Once each child in the line has their supply, the kindergartners file out into the hall two by two.

Lingering in the back of the room are four adult visitors, three of whom are education policy and foundation types; the fourth is a teacher coach and mentor named Lisa. The three are curious about what they just witnessed and ask Lisa why the teacher was handing out toilet paper. Lisa explains the reasoning as follows:

- This is a K-8 school, which is typical in the city of Chicago.
- In this particular school, toilet paper can't just be left in the bathroom; seventh and eighth graders will shove the rolls into the toilets and then flush them, creating a flooding problem.
- The kindergartners are too shy to ask for toilet paper.
- Therefore, the teacher just gives toilet paper to each child so that if they need it, they have it.

On some level, this approach makes a lot of sense. It's certainly easy for the visitors to tick through some of the other available options to see why they're problematic:

- Stepping up monitoring in the bathrooms would take a lot of staffing capacity, and educators might reasonably prefer preventative approaches to punitive ones. School staff might also prefer to not spend their days lurking awkwardly in the bathroom as a deterrent to mischief.
- Some Chicago high schools have systems where students aren't allowed to use the bathroom between classes (or in the first and last five minutes of class). This is meant to prevent congregating in the bathrooms and

might reduce instances of vandalism. But that might be a hard system to enforce with younger children.

- Separate bathrooms could be created for younger and older kids. But this might be difficult in an old building, and it's not clear students would go only to their assigned bathrooms.
- In many school districts, eighth graders and kindergartners aren't in the same building, and Chicago Public Schools could think about restructuring schools to create a more traditional elementary/middle school configuration. This is obviously a more dramatic change outside the control of the individual school, but is consistent with the practice in other districts and could have benefits beyond allowing the reinstallation of toilet paper dispensers in the student bathrooms.

Yet none of these options even really attempts to solve the real problem, which is that school leaders are living in a world where seventh and eighth graders can be counted on to create havoc in bathrooms.

Schools can take action to address that real problem by providing a supportive environment, structure, and counseling. They can only do so much to mitigate the effects of the world outside, but with the right resources and capacity, they could create a world where the seventh and eighth graders have social equilibrium—and the kindergartners could walk into the bathroom and find toilet paper waiting there for them, as kindergartners do in schools around the country. At least in the ones serving higher-income families.

But this school doesn't have the resources to solve the problem at its root. So instead, kindergartners line up and wait for their teacher to hand them toilet paper before they go into the hall. Maybe later in life they'll go to one of those schools where bathroom stops are only allowed in the middle of class. And the message they'll have gotten from their schooling is this: you can't be trusted to take care of your most basic needs without somehow getting into trouble.

Then when they finish school, they'll be striving for success in the adult world. And as we know, the best sections of the adult world have norms dictated largely by people who grew up taking for granted the availability of toilet paper.

We can do better than this.

Education policy is far from the only discipline where there is a tendency to solve the problem that seems solvable, rather than the one that really matters. This book is about how conversations about three major issues in education policy have not focused deeply enough on the root problems, which has been an impediment to building consensus on solutions. The book proposes approaches to each of these issues meant to draw on the best thinking of rival camps.

Through the administrations of Presidents Bush and Obama, education policy nationally was dominated by an aggressive reform agenda focused on accountability, teacher quality, and charter schools. The period saw the federal government take on a more ambitious role, and states also stepped up their oversight of local schools. The reform movement sparked a self-described "resistance" of educators and activists opposed to the reformers' central tenets.

The 2015 passage of the Every Student Succeeds Act—and the law's implementation during President Trump's administration—saw a retreat from the expansive federal role in education policy. It also saw a loss of steam for the reform movement—even as many of the reform movement's policy building blocks remain in place.

While reformers and resistors disagree about strategies, they do largely agree on the goal of addressing inequalities in education. There are plenty of children who are doing very well in public schools in the United States; the problem is that many children aren't. Both reformers and resistors have articulated some good ideas for the future of education in the United States, but both movements have blind spots that have limited the potential impact of their proposals. With the education system forced to rebuild after the COVID-19 pandemic and a new national focus on systemic inequities, now is the time for some new approaches to education policy.[1]

This book addresses three major policy areas—accountability, teacher quality, and charter schools—that have been the subject of contentious debate in the preceding decades. In each of these areas, it analyzes arguments from both reformers and resistors, making recommendations that are intended to draw on the best thinking of each. In addition to harmonizing ideas within the world of K-12 policy, it also addresses the relationship between K-12 and early childhood.

This book was written out of a belief that there are collaborative solutions out there waiting to be found, and that people of good will from different perspectives can come together to find them. Part of what this book will try to do is surface some of the hidden assumptions that are built into the current system and the "invisible boxes" that constrain our current thinking. If we drill down to the root causes of long-standing problems, we might find some ideas that can establish a new common ground. So if this book helps policy leaders find a new path, or sparks creative thinking that leads to proposals even better than the ones here, it will have succeeded.

As a political society, we are struggling to balance legitimate but competing interests.[2] This book represents one person's attempt to conduct that balancing. Hopefully, you will agree with some of it; it seems very unlikely that you will agree with all of it. But the goal isn't to get you to agree with all of it—it's to help you see these issues with fresh eyes and gain some perspective that you didn't have before. And maybe, just maybe, help you work more effectively with people who disagree with you to make mutual progress toward better outcomes for children.

Moreover, the pandemic has made educators weary. People are worn down, and there have been fierce debates—about COVID mitigations, content, and more—that have tired people out. While this book doesn't go deeply into the most contentious issues of the pandemic, the structural issues it does address help to shape the context for policy discussions on a whole range of practical issues.

You will notice as you go along that this book uses a lot of the first-person plural. When it refers to "we," that's meant to include primarily the author and the reader, with other people thrown in occasionally. Your author was a tour guide in college, and this book is meant to feel like a tour of policy issues; maybe you're seeing them for the first time, maybe you're getting new narratives about a familiar locale, but either way the goal is to have an engaging tour. And the idea of this book is that we're on this journey together.

So, before we leave for the full tour, let me summarize some of the highlights of what we're going to see.

First, as your tour guide it's important for me to emphasize that my viewpoint is that of someone who works on policy and systems. You will not see in-depth discussions of issues that require expertise in classroom teaching, nor will you see a lot of argument about what content children should be taught. Instead, you will see discussions about how teacher assignments should be made and how school success should be measured. Policy is an essential but imperfect tool being deployed in the service of addressing complex and nuanced problems. But it is critical to achieving success at scale for students from families with low incomes.

Reform skeptics have long argued that education reforms don't really change the basic interactions between teachers and students that form the basis of education. By and large, those skeptics have a point. Policy is not likely to be an effective tool for getting teachers to change their classroom behaviors—at least not in the ways policymakers want them to.

But policy has a huge impact in shaping the environment in which teachers and students interact. Indeed, policy has huge impacts not only on which teachers are going to be in which classrooms interacting with which children, but also for helping those of us on the outside understand the impact of those interactions. Those issues are important, and they are the primary focus of this book's recommendations.

Systems thinkers want to fix what's broken. They see that children are not succeeding as they ought to, and they believe something different needs to be done. Over the decades a lot of different things have been done at a policy level.[3] The results for students, however, are not yet satisfactory, particularly for students from low-income families.

Moreover, policymakers are often motivated by a perception that schools are doing poorly—but the results schools get have never been as bad as they've been made out to be. As we will see, a lot of school districts are doing exactly what you might expect them to: providing students with a year's worth of progress every year. Where that's not happening, we need to do something different. But where that is happening, if the children are behind, that's probably not the school's fault.

When schools are succeeding, policymakers need to ask whether they are doing so *because* of their systems context or *despite* their systems context. Some schools will struggle despite every seeming advantage; others will succeed despite every obstacle. But focusing too much on the outliers is a mistake. Policymakers need to look at the overall forces created by their choices—and if those forces are pushing in the wrong direction, they should make policy changes to correct that.

In fact, for the most part, school districts and teachers are making entirely rational choices based on their context. But those choices aren't the ones policymakers wanted them to make. This speaks to the fact that, as commentator Rick Hess likes to say, policymakers can make educators do things, but they can't make them do things well.[4] That's why a lot of the recommendations you're going to see here are about how to build capacity, provide information, process information, or get resources to the places they're needed most. It's not about policymakers providing the right answers; it's about policymakers putting students and teachers in a position to succeed.

Introduction

Let's take a look at what we're planning to visit on our tour. In each of this book's three parts, we'll examine how an important aspect of education policy is shaped by the wrong primary driver. We'll also look at new drivers that are practically and politically feasible but would lead to better outcomes for children. The shifts proposed include:

- changing the primary driver of accountability systems from *test scores* to *success in the early years*;
- changing the primary driver of teacher hiring from *teacher characteristics* to *teacher roles*; and
- changing the primary driver of school choice policy from *political boundaries* to *parent interest*.

Each part takes an in-depth look at one of these shifts.

SHIFTING THE FOCUS OF ACCOUNTABILITY UPSTREAM

The central argument of the part on accountability is that the focus of accountability on the tested years has been a distraction from the best opportunity to improve student outcomes: the years prior to third grade. Almost half of all school districts—including some considered "failing"—can take children who are on track in third grade and keep them on track through high school graduation. But very few school districts can take a cohort of children who are a year behind in third grade and get that cohort caught up by the end of twelfth grade.

One of the greatest flaws in our current accountability regime is that it focuses on only half of the educational spectrum, and not the half with the greatest opportunity for improvement. So this book proposes a new approach to accountability. Like several previous proposals, it urges policymakers to balance test score accountability with a more comprehensive evaluation of the quality of practice—known in some countries as an "inspectorate." This allows for accountability to look at student outcomes and adult job performance, both of which are important measures of school quality. But we will add new dimensions to both halves of that approach:

- With regard to test scores, we'll look at an approach that utilizes growth and proficiency together to identify schools where the students are low performing and not catching up.
- The current focus on proficiency has identified as "failing" some schools where children are way behind but making steady progress. For those schools, the real problem is likely that children are too far behind when they enter at kindergarten. In these schools, what's likely to be needed is an improvement strategy focused on kindergarten readiness, and not necessarily wholesale changes to the school itself.
- In schools where both proficiency and growth are low, an intervention focused on kindergarten readiness won't be enough. These are the schools where more dramatic changes will be needed. But test scores alone don't provide a roadmap for improvement, unlike an inspectorate.
- Having expert reviewers judge the quality of schools through site visits is not a cure-all, but it solves a major problem with test-based accountability that hasn't been widely discussed: test-based accountability focuses only on the years from third grade and up, meaning that the earlier years are essentially excluded from accountability systems. Children in the K-2 years represent almost a third of all elementary school students, and yet their experience is not captured in state accountability systems.
- In early childhood, systems with expert reviewers—known in some K-12 circles as "inspectorates"—are already being used at scale. The implementation of inspectorates in K-12 could be a way to create a more seamless approach to accountability and ensure that all students are included in accountability systems.

The use of growth measures in accountability is already increasing, and voices from across the policy spectrum have called for inspectorate-type approaches to accountability. But those proposals have generally not identified the real problem that schools need to be solving: that children come to school already behind and never get caught up. In fact, existing accountability systems have exacerbated that problem by pressing districts to focus their resources on tests and the tested years. The balanced approach proposed here could help schools focus on what matters most to improved long-term outcomes.

Inspectorates do have the potential to help districts build capacity and to improve instructional practices throughout the system—including the early years. Of course, there are good reasons inspectorates have not already been used at scale. State capacity is limited, and the track record of states supporting school improvement is weak. Here we will take an optimistic but realistic look at what is possible, with proposals for how states might consider implementing an inspectorate-based system—and pair that with the kind of support networks and analytic capacity needed for districts to effectively use the information an inspectorate produces.

The process should start with the state—or states in collaboration—bringing together research experts and practitioners to develop rubrics that will be respected in the field; it should continue with the strategic development of inspection capacity, which should not necessarily be provided directly by state agency employees. We will also examine how the federal government can create the environment in which states can succeed in those efforts—without overstepping its limited institutional role.

In chapter 1, we'll look at the federal government's approach to defining educational quality—with a focus on the Every Student Succeeds Act (ESSA), the current law creating the framework for states to oversee K-12 accountability. We'll look at the important benefits of having federally driven accountability for education outcomes. But we'll also acknowledge the costs of ESSA's accountability regime, including a focus on standardized tests that has adversely impacted instruction. And we'll take a look at how the federal government defines preschool quality in the Head Start program.

In chapter 2, we'll see how ESSA—like the No Child Left Behind Act before it—is distracting us from the years that matter most. Student growth data shows us that if a cohort of children has fallen more than a year behind by second grade, only 20 percent of districts are currently able to get that cohort caught up by the end of high school. So in addition to improving school performance, education policy needs a much stronger focus on what's happening with children before third grade. To date, the available educational opportunities have simply not been sufficient to get children from low-income families on track for success.

In chapter 3, we'll look at how we might reorient school district accountability. The key is to identify schools where both proficiency and growth are low; in these schools, children come in behind and lose ground as they go. These are the schools where the most dramatic action is needed. And in all schools with low proficiency, one of the strategies most likely to succeed is to improve kindergarten readiness—which is often outside the school's jurisdiction. The use of a school inspectorate can also provide schools with actionable information to help them improve, and create continuity in accountability from early childhood through high school.

GETTING THE BEST TEACHERS WHERE
THEY'RE NEEDED MOST

Right now the fixed point in discussions of teacher pay and assignment is seniority; everything else is built around that. Instead, the fixed point should be that districts will ensure that the highest-paid teaching jobs are the ones in schools serving the highest-need students. Additional pay can also be designated for subject shortage areas. After that, seniority can factor into pay and assignments, but it should not trump meeting the needs of students from families with low incomes.

Different teachers play different roles; a high school physics teacher and a kindergarten special education teacher are not fungible, and the candidate pools for those jobs are very different. But historically teacher salary schedules would treat all teaching roles as if they were the same and pay teachers based on their personal characteristics: seniority and education.

Basing teacher pay and assignments on personal characteristics—rather than the role a teacher plays—negatively impacts the schools identified in the accountability part as having limited proficiency and limited growth. If we built teacher pay around roles and properly supported the roles serving children from low-income families, we would create better matches between the students who need the best teachers and the teachers who can actually help them.

Bringing change to the teaching profession has been hard because its members are so often in a defensive crouch seeking to resist the intrusions of management. It's understandable that they feel this way, given the history of how they've been treated.

The work of teachers is often most difficult in underfunded schools where the children are behind and have limited out-of-school supports. It's not a surprise that teacher turnover is high in those schools. It's widely understood that the children with the greatest needs are not well served by novice and underpaid teachers, but existing teacher pay and assignment systems have made it hard to keep top talent in the highest-need schools.

Another important role that is currently underpaid is that of early childhood teachers. Early childhood teachers make less money than elementary school teachers—even though their work should be just as rigorous. An increased focus on improving the child experience in the early childhood years will need to be coupled with an increase in pay for the professionals working with those children.

The best way to change the profession is to change what it values. To date, what it values has been primarily seniority. Higher seniority dictates pay, assignments, and job security. This can be discouraging to young teachers and operationally difficult for districts.

The transition from the existing system to this new system will not be easy and will meet resistance from some teachers. With regard to teachers, though, this pivot does provide an opportunity for unions to embrace their younger members—who have historically gotten short shrift from them. This change isn't bad for all teachers, but it could be bad for some teachers, and we will discuss how policymakers can be cognizant of that dynamic.

It's also important that changes to how teachers are assigned within districts don't give low-resource districts the ability to compete for talent with wealthy districts. For that to happen, the state and federal governments would have to rethink their approach to resource distribution. Those changes are politically hard, but some states have been able to make them; the federal government simplifying and focusing its role would likely help more states to do the same.

In chapter 4, we'll look at the value proposition of the teacher's role. Teaching is a job that appeals to adults who want to work directly with children—but actually working with children can turn out to be difficult in ways that teachers don't expect. Moreover, many teachers—particularly teachers of color—feel isolated and unsupported by their administration and colleagues. Individual schools have a hard time creating successful working cultures when they don't really have control over their personnel, and have strong incentives to avoid being honest about what they need to do to improve. Making the work harder is the fact that policymakers have unrealistic expectations about what schools can accomplish.

In chapter 5, we'll look at why school districts aren't putting their best teachers with the students who need them most. Teacher pay is highly structured and probably always will be. The problem is not the fact that teacher pay is highly structured, the problem is that within that structure the key drivers of increased pay for teachers are seniority and master's degrees—neither of which correlate well with teacher effectiveness.

Attempts to find objective criteria to drive teacher pay that are better correlated with effectiveness have to date been unsuccessful. The nature of teacher pay has led to ongoing struggles in filling certain kinds of teaching jobs, including in schools serving children from low-income families and in a handful of subject areas.

In chapter 6, we'll consider how restructuring teacher pay might get the best teachers in front of the children who most need their help. Right now the highest-paid teachers tend to be those serving the children from the highest-income families in the most successful schools. To actually improve schools serving children from low-income families will require ensuring that the pay for teachers in those schools is at least competitive. Intra-district inequity tends to be caused by seniority-driven placement, which will need to be curtailed for districts to better serve children from low-income families.

While teachers should be empowered in the process of choosing a work location, their empowerment should be balanced against the need to serve children from low-income families effectively. If districts are willing to change how they assign teachers, they will need to be thoughtful about how to work with their teachers to preserve goodwill through the process.

In chapter 7, we'll address another major reason the teacher market is broken: the differences in funding levels between school districts. Districts with limited resources—which often serve children from families with lower incomes—simply can't compete with richer districts for teaching talent. We will look at how states and the federal government distribute funds to districts, and the pressures that have prevented states and the federal government from having a funding approach that is equitable and straightforward. We'll also look at how early childhood teachers get paid, and what will need to be done to strengthen child experiences in the early years.

GIVING PARENTS REAL CHOICES

Parents want many different things out of their children's schools; that's a good thing and one that shouldn't change. So government should work to create accessible options for families that allow them to make the best possible match for their child. Rich families have always been able to do that, frequently by moving into wealthy enclaves with outstanding neighborhood schools. The systems that have been created to give low-income families more options have been incrementally helpful, but not as transformative as they could be.

Indeed, the current system in many states was designed primarily to allow wealthy families to isolate themselves—and to minimize their financial obligation to the rest of the system. Some of the problem is tax and revenue policy; if isolation is a way for rich families to avoid subsidizing the education of others, that's what many of them will do. States don't have to set it up that way, and can have revenue policies that treat low-income districts and schools fairly regardless of where wealthy people live.

Another part of the problem is that district boundaries are too meaningful. In densely populated areas regional approaches to school enrollment have been successful in some instances. Those shouldn't be imposed upon districts, but states can create incentives for collaboration that increase the number of options available. This will also require rethinking inter-district transfer programs, which to date frequently have been an escape valve for wealthy families to escape districts where they are in the minority.

Public charter schools have an important role to play in any regional choice approach. Charter schools offer advantages that traditional schools typically do not: a chance to start fresh with new practices, and a chance to specialize in an educational approach that appeals only to a segment of the market. In a less constrained market, charters can carve out a role that is more complementary of traditional schools and less in competition with them.

Moreover, the fights over funding between traditional public schools and public charter schools have in essence been oriented around the wrong axis. The real problem isn't the allocation of funds between traditional schools and charter schools; it's the inadequate allocation of funds to schools serving primarily children from low-income households—and that allocation problem is one that is both intra-district and inter-district.

Charter schools serving children from low-income families should receive more funds, and charter schools serving higher-income children should receive less; the same should be true of traditional public schools. That approach to funding is needed to create a choice market that offers opportunities to low-income families.

The approach to choice in K-12 can draw on lessons from the early learning system. Currently, in the pre-kindergarten years, families have much more flexibility to choose different options—but they may have fewer options and will likely have limited support and structure to make their choices. Improving early childhood choices—and the connection between those choices and what happens in K-12—will be important to improving long-term outcomes.

The early childhood system is more market-oriented than K-12, but low-income parents do not receive adequate support to participate effectively in the market. The K-12 world would benefit from a greater market orientation, while learning the lesson that adequate supports are necessary to help parents take advantage of flexibility.

There are many aspects of state policy that contribute to the choice environment parents face—including laws regarding funding, district creation and consolidation, inter-district transfers, and charter schools. We will look at recommendations for how states can align all of those policies to create more good options for low-income families—and how the federal government can play an appropriate role in supporting state leadership on this issue.

In chapter 8, we'll look at the diverse possibilities for schooling, and how parents and policymakers think differently about school options. Education is a public good, but it's also a private one—meaning that parents should have options for finding the best match for their child. It's also a positional good, which is to say one in which relative status matters—and government does have a role to play in protecting the positioning of low-income families. Parents will always seek what's best for their own child, so policymakers should structure choice plans to ensure that low-income families have access to good opportunities.

In chapter 9, we'll explore the geography and demography of school choice. To date, parent choice has largely been constrained by political lines. Many school districts have isolated homogenous neighborhoods through the use of attendance boundaries—and in metropolitan areas school district boundaries have frequently had the same impact, with greater force. This chapter will look at how communities have been isolated from each other in ways that curtail educational options.

In chapter 10, we'll discuss charter schools. The inability of the traditional system to create better opportunities for children from low-income families helped lead to the creation of charter schools. The traditional system has seen charters as siphoning money away from traditional schools, but that depends on a belief that the districts had an initial entitlement to that money—which they don't.

In chapter 11, we'll dive into the processes families use to choose schools. It's good for families to have options—but too many options can be overwhelming. Early childhood and K-12 have a mix of decentralized and centralized choice systems, all of which would benefit from better support structures. Parents also need better information to help make their choices.

In chapter 12, we'll see how a more regional approach to school choice might break down some of the existing barriers parents face to finding the right option for their child. Choices should be available over a broader geographic area, with incentives to offer better options for low-income families. Charter schools should be a part of the package.

Early childhood will also be an important part of the design; improving kindergarten readiness is key to improving school performance, and having more schools with students who are already on track will make the available options more attractive. We'll see how both the federal government and states can play a role in facilitating an expanded range of options for families, in both early childhood and K-12.

At the end, we'll conclude by examining some of the trade-offs we've discussed along the way. We'll take a final look at why the proposals included here might have a chance of coming to fruition—or why they might not. And while readers will undoubtedly have their own opinions about each trade-off discussed here, the hope is that this proposed package of trade-offs can provide a useful starting point for policy conversations at the local, state, and federal levels.

So that's what's going to be on the tour. Thank you for coming along; let's get going.

PART I

Shifting the Focus of Accountability

Chapter 1

Federal Accountability for Educational Success

The federal government has chosen to ensure that there is a definition of "success" for which all schools are held accountable. With K-12 schools, the federal government sets parameters within which each state comes up with its own definition. In the federally funded Head Start early childhood program, the federal government sets the definition itself.

This chapter looks at how that accountability works, why the federal government's role is important, and some of the struggles districts and schools have had with implementing federally driven accountability. In subsequent chapters we will dive deeper into the shortcomings of the Every Student Succeeds Act (ESSA) and consider how the federal framework for accountability might be improved.

HOW THE QUALITY OF EDUCATION IS DEFINED UNDER FEDERAL LAW

K-12 School Quality under ESSA

Federal accountability traces its roots back to the Elementary and Secondary Education Act (ESEA), passed in 1965 as part of President Lyndon Johnson's Great Society programs. The goal of ESEA was to support equity for disadvantaged students, and it provided federal dollars to help achieve that goal.[1]

In 2002 the federal government updated the ESEA with the No Child Left Behind (NCLB) Act—marking the culmination of a shift in federal focus toward accountability for performance.[2] NCLB required districts to conduct annual assessments of all students in third through eighth grade, and have an annual exam in high school. Districts and schools that had low proficiency rates could face significant consequences, and the Federal Department of Education made clear that it intended to enforce the law's requirements.[3]

Every element of an accountability system pushes the accountable to do something; the combinations of those pushes have to maintain an appropriate balance for the system to succeed. So a key to the success of any accountability system is counterweighting.[4] In this regard, ESSA builds on a counterweighting that sat at the heart of NCLB—and one that, in principle, is correct.

NCLB accountability for high schools rested on two pillars: high school graduation rates and proficiency on standardized tests. Those two elements stood as important counterweights to each other:

- High school graduation rates are an important child outcome. It is very hard for high school dropouts to succeed in today's economy.[5] But if districts and schools are being measured solely on high school graduation rates, it will give them an incentive to water down the requirements for graduation. The easiest way to improve graduation rates is to make it easier for students to graduate. Doing that improves performance on the metric, but would only exacerbate the problem of students graduating from high school unprepared to succeed in a career path or higher education.[6]
- Proficiency on standardized tests is meant to measure excellence. But if that is your only measure, it gives districts and schools an incentive to make sure that children who aren't achieving excellence aren't included in their count. In effect, schools can push children out to make sure the schools aren't held responsible for their lack of excellence.[7]

From a design standpoint, these two ideas keep each other in balance. Including graduation rates keeps districts and schools from pushing children out; including proficiency measures keeps schools from making graduation too easy. Including only one might push behaviors to swing to one side, so having both is needed to keep the system at the right equilibrium.

It's important to emphasize that these issues are discussed here as system design principles. There are districts and schools that have lowered graduation expectations, and others that have pushed out low-performing students.[8] There are many others that haven't. But the system has to be set up to reduce district and school incentives to do either of those things, and both NCLB and ESSA have correctly identified and addressed that tension. Districts and schools don't always follow the incentives in federal and state policy, but it's still crucial to set the incentives correctly.[9]

While the idea of balancing academic excellence with completion makes sense, the law's approach to measuring academic excellence through proficiency did not. Some states set high standards for proficiency, which meant that the number of "failing schools" quickly rocketed skyward.[10] Other states set low standards for proficiency, which delayed their reckoning—but also created enough inconsistency among states to give plenty of ammunition to the law's critics. In general, state governments found that NCLB taxed their administrative capacity while providing inadequate resources.[11]

ESSA does continue to include student proficiency in the accountability system.[12] There are valid reasons for this, because mastering content is critical to education[13]—and that's what proficiency is supposed to measure. While there are concerns about how proficiency is measured—discussed further below—there is broad agreement that the concept of "content mastery" is an important goal for students.

But one fundamental change in the evolution from NCLB to ESSA is in that the definition of academic excellence now includes student growth, which is a required metric for elementary schools and permitted for high schools.[14] Growth looks at whether students made a year's worth of progress in a year.

Advocates for the use of growth as a measure argue that it is a much better measure of how the *school* is doing.[15] Proficiency is highly correlated with income, and so schools serving high-income children tend to do very well on proficiency measures.[16] But growth is much more a product of how well a child is educated, and thus a fairer basis for measuring school performance.[17]

ESSA also adds accountability for the progress of English learners, to see whether they are making progress toward English language proficiency.[18] States must ensure that children are given annual assessments of English proficiency, and then produce individualized student reports.[19] A 2020 analysis by the Migrant Policy Institute of initial state ESSA plans found that the implementation of the law had not provided the desired clarity about how English Learners are progressing.[20]

Finally, ESSA adds what is commonly referred to as a "fifth indicator"— something the state comes up with that measures school quality or student success.[21] The law establishes the criteria for these indicators, including that they must meaningfully differentiate among schools and be valid and reliable.[22] Suggestions in the law include issues like student or educator engagement, access to advanced coursework, postsecondary readiness, and school climate—but states are allowed to develop their own as long as they meet the statutory requirements.[23]

An important element of NCLB that survived into ESSA is the focus on disaggregated data. Under NCLB, schools and districts couldn't just report aggregated results—they had to provide disaggregated results for different racial groups, students from families with low incomes, English learners, and students with special needs (often referred to as "subgroups").[24] Civil rights groups saw this as a significant advance, as it helped to expose the fact that even at the highest-performing schools there were sometimes children—often

Black and Brown children—who were not achieving at the same level as their classmates.[25]

In sum, federally driven district and school accountability is based on: (1) proficiency; (2) growth—optional for high schools, mandatory for everybody else; (3) for high schools, graduation rate; (4) progress toward English language proficiency for English learners; and (5) something else (the fifth indicator). The law gives states flexibility to determine how much weight to place on each category. Each indicator must carry "substantial weight," and in the aggregate "much greater weight" must be placed on the first four indicators, rather than on the fifth.[26] The terms "substantial weight" and "much greater weight" are not defined.

Preschool Quality under the Head Start Act

ESSA is the federal law that sets a framework for state definitions of educational quality in K-12. When it comes to early childhood, the federal government also has a definition of quality—one embedded in the requirements of the Head Start program, the largest and best-known early childhood program in the country. Head Start funds do not flow through states, but instead go directly to local grantees.[27] The federal government's approach to defining quality looks very different in Head Start, which may offer some useful lessons for K-12.

Head Start was launched as one of President Johnson's Great Society programs in the 1960s, and has evolved considerably since then. It now provides education to more than 650,000 three-and four-year-olds around the country.[28] Younger children (birth to three) are served through the Early Head Start program, which reaches about 10 percent of the eligible population.[29] Eligibility for both of these programs is limited, with a focus on children from low-income families. Head Start providers are expected to utilize state and local learning standards in delivering educational services.[30]

Head Start has long been known for having an extensive and detailed set of requirements for its grantees known as the Performance Standards. In 2011 it streamlined accountability somewhat, including the addition of a process known as the Designation Renewal System[31]—or, less formally, "recompetition." Under recompetition, programs must meet seven conditions to maintain their grant; otherwise, the grant is opened up, and new applicants are allowed to compete for the funds.[32]

One important condition is that Head Start providers must show high ratings on the Classroom Assessment Scoring System (CLASS).[33] The CLASS is an observational tool that includes ratings in Emotional Support, Classroom Organization, and Instructional Support.[34] While K-12 accountability focuses on the measurement of child *outcomes* through test scores, CLASS focuses on the measurement of child *experiences.*

WHY FEDERAL ACCOUNTABILITY IS IMPORTANT

The problem ESSA is trying to solve is one of the central problems of education and a key focus of this book: educational outcomes have historically been more favorable for kids who are rich and/or white, and less favorable for those children who are not.[35] Reasonable people can differ on what causes that problem, what it means, or what to do about it—but the fact of its existence is well established and accepted.

ESSA is the federal government's well-intentioned effort to address that issue. And there's a good reason the federal government has gotten involved. The original federal education law, the ESEA, was born in the civil rights era, when some states were still openly resisting the idea that Black children had an equal right to education. The federal government perceived the need to provide a backstop for Black children and others who were getting the short end of the educational stick. The perception was that education was a national problem that demanded a national solution.

External accountability is driven by a lack of trust.[36] In the 1960s the federal government did not trust that states and locals, left to their own devices, would do right by certain kinds of children—particularly Black and Brown children, or children with low incomes. When the federal government ramped up the pressure on states through NCLB, it was driven by a belief that states hadn't done enough to promote improved outcomes.[37] And some advocates believe that the additional flexibility ESSA has provided will lead to backsliding by states.[38]

Test scores may be imperfect, but the fact that they are the best available measure of student outcomes has secured them a steady place at the heart of accountability systems.[39] This is part of why civil rights groups have pressed for assessment data, even during COVID-19 shutdowns.[40] Some advocates think of standardized test scores as a critical tool for fighting systemic bias.[41] They believe that test scores expose inequities in ways that other measures can't, and that the federal government plays an indispensable role in promoting better student outcomes.

That is not a universally held view within the civil rights community, it must be said. One line of attack on standardized tests is that they are elitist and racist. Critics note that the tests were developed as a sorting mechanism by elites, who then designed them to reward their favored characteristics.[42] The roots of standardized testing do indeed include some ugly racism.[43] Today, critics argue that they exacerbate racial inequality.[44] While there is force to these arguments, it is also important to acknowledge that there are powerful roots to the argument that standardized tests play a role in helping children of color advance.[45]

It has been decades since the 1983 report *A Nation at Risk* catalyzed a wave of reform activity, and that came two decades after the federal government first stepped in to address the issue of educational inequities. The injustice that created the original action imperative for ESEA has evolved, but it hasn't disappeared. Any evaluation of ESSA must start with the importance of its mission. But the urgency of that mission demands that we consider the costs of ESSA—which, in some instances, may stand in the way of that mission's achievement.

THE COSTS OF THE EVERY STUDENT SUCCEEDS ACT

There are a few underlying assumptions that must be true for the ESSA to be a good policy.

1. First, that there is enough disparity in results among students that it is important for the federal government to take some kind of action. As described earlier, this premise is sound and represents a bipartisan consensus that at this point has been in place since the original ESEA.
2. Second, that one form of action the federal government should take is to hold states—and by extension, schools and districts—accountable for how children are doing. This premise follows logically from the previous one. As it turns out, there is a complex relationship between holding states accountable and holding districts and schools accountable; we will bump up against this issue throughout this part of the tour, but for the moment we will accept that in our federalist system there is a defensible logic to this approach.
3. Third, that it is possible for the federal government to define some set of criteria for accountability that are legitimate—that is, those criteria are meaningful enough that they can be used to differentiate among schools.

Note that it is possible to agree with this third premise even while believing that the current criteria are totally wrong. There are many advocates who believe that there are measures that the federal government could use appropriately, even if they believe the current criteria are not those appropriate measures. Agreeing with the first three underlying assumptions here gets you into a conversation about the particulars of a federal education accountability bill, even if it doesn't win your vote for ESSA.

4. Fourth, that the actual criteria articulated in the ESSA—particularly standardized test scores—are good criteria for measuring school and district quality.
5. Fifth, that the law defines appropriate consequences for schools, based on how they are rated by those legitimate criteria.

The rest of this chapter will focus on the final two assumptions and analyze some of the arguments that have been raised to contend that they are not valid. In doing so it draws extensively on the work of experts and advocates from across the political spectrum—and with a focus on whether ESSA's criteria actually improve equitable outcomes for children. It concludes that there are major problems with ESSA and test-based accountability, but that its framework shouldn't necessarily be abandoned altogether.

The next chapter teases out one particular argument for why the focus on standardized test scores in ESSA makes the federal accountability law an incredibly problematic distraction from the most important work needed to achieve equitable outcomes: the work that occurs prior to third grade. The final chapter in this part proposes an approach to federal education accountability that builds on what's good about ESSA, and is more likely to lead to equitable results.

What Do Standardized Test Results Tell Us?

While the next chapter argues that ESSA draws too much attention away from the pre-third grade years, this section focuses on whether ESSA is even doing a good job of providing accountability in the grades it covers. As discussed before, standardized test scores do have some appropriate and potentially valuable uses. But their use in ESSA may push them beyond the boundaries of their usefulness.

The first criticism of standardized tests is that they are not reliable and valid for accountability purposes.[46] Reliability is about whether the tests are accurate enough measures of what they purport to measure and have a reasonable margin of error; validity is about whether the results of the tests are being used for appropriate purposes.[47] Critics of standardized testing are often careful to point out that they are not opposed to assessment—they are opposed to certain kinds of high-stakes assessment, or the misuse of assessment results.[48]

Part of the problem is the challenge of defining "proficiency." The definition can be a slippery one, and reasonable people can disagree about exactly how "proficiency" should be defined.[49] Different definitions of proficiency can lead to very different results, which has major consequences to schools.[50] Indeed, there are a host of complexities to using the percentage of students who are proficient as a measure of school quality.[51]

Federal law gives each state the responsibility for setting its own standards of proficiency. This turns the setting of proficiency standards into a highly political question. If states want to hold schools accountable and demand excellence, they can raise the threshold for proficiency; if they want to make it look like everything is going well, they can lower those cut scores.[52]

While this difference doesn't necessarily matter for purposes of determining which schools within a state would be designated for consequences, it creates a very murky picture of what is happening nationally. It also undermines the idea that proficiency scores are providing some kind of objective truth about school performance.

But let's assume for the moment that proficiency scores could be a reliable measure of whether children have adequately mastered the material they're supposed to learn. Even if those tests tell us that, they do not necessarily tell us how their school contributed to that knowledge.[53] Children don't actually spend that much time in school,[54] and socioeconomic factors have long been known to be a strong predictor of test results.[55] Student mobility—which is heavily correlated with income—has a negative impact on student learning and tends to keep proficiency low.[56] So knowing how *children* are doing is not the same as knowing how *schools* are doing.[57]

Think about it this way. Child A showed up at Lincoln Elementary in first grade, three years behind grade level. Thanks to the heroic efforts of Lincoln's teachers, Child A finishes fourth grade only half a year behind grade level. That's an incredible improvement—but the state assessment will still treat Child A as "not proficient" when grading Lincoln Elementary. Meanwhile, Child B showed up at nearby Roosevelt Elementary at the beginning of third grade, reading at a sixth-grade level. At the end of fourth grade, Child B is still reading at a sixth-grade level, not having progressed very much. But on the state test, Roosevelt will get credit for that child's proficiency.[58]

This was one of the core problems of No Child Left Behind, and it was acknowledged in the passage of the Every Student Succeeds Act. States still have to use proficiency in their accountability metrics, but—as described earlier—they can include *student growth*, which is the term widely used to describe the progress a child has made. This term is not entirely straightforward, as there are multiple ways to measure student progress that each have different implications for school quality measurement.[59] Without minimizing the importance of these complexities, on this tour the term "growth" will be used to mean the level of progress a student has made in the course of a year.

Growth is also affected by out-of-school factors, but it's much more appropriate to rate a school on how it helps students make progress than it is to rate those schools on their students' proficiency. While federal and state law on this issue has evolved at least a little, the cultural understanding of this problem has a long way to go. Parents—particularly parents with the means to choose among school districts—tend to favor school districts with a high percentage of children who are proficient.[60] A whole host of websites and guidance tools have catered to this instinct, an issue we'll see again in chapter 11.[61]

Those parents may think that by sending their kids to a school with high proficiency rates they have ensured that their child will get great teaching. They haven't done that. What they have done, though, is ensure that their child will be surrounded by other children who are succeeding at school, as the state has defined success. That's still meaningful, but it's not the same thing. Proficiency scores play a signaling function, but it's not a signal about how well the professionals did.

The Actual Consequences of Accountability

Another major criticism of ESSA has been based on Campbell's Law—which states that the more you use an indicator for decision-making, the more corruption pressure there will be.[62] NCLB included a whole set of potentially serious consequences for schools that failed to meet proficiency targets. But the consequences spelled out in the law weren't actually used all that often.[63] Instead, in classic Campbell's Law fashion, the real impact of NCLB on the student experience came from the actions educators took to avoid the statutory consequences.

The formal consequences NCLB dictated for schools were generally considered too prescriptive and badly designed. Schools that failed to meet test score benchmarks faced escalating sanctions.[64] States were supposed to provide assistance to struggling schools, and then undertake dramatic restructuring if those efforts were unsuccessful.[65] For the most part states didn't provide nearly enough capacity to help, and then didn't actually force schools to go through dramatic changes.[66] ESSA more or less acknowledged that reality by giving states much greater latitude to define the consequences districts and schools faced for a lack of success.[67]

But during the NCLB era the fear of formal consequences turned out to have a number of important effects on what schools taught, how they taught it, and who they focused on. These Campbell's Law–driven costs haven't been completely eliminated by ESSA, and are still causing impacts in schools today.

How Accountability Affects What Schools Teach

There are all kinds of different subjects children might want to focus on in school. They might want a wide range of arts classes, which have been shown to keep kids engaged and stimulated. They might want great foreign language classes to prepare them for success in an increasingly international world. They might want strong career and technical education, which could help them find meaningful work after high school even if college is not for them. Or they might want any number of other things. Later on we'll dive deeper into what parents want for their children in a school and how the public education system should help them get it.

Whatever subjects children might want to study, federal accountability pushes them to focus on two: reading and math. There are good reasons for that, as reading and math are extremely important.[68] But there's also wide acknowledgment that other things matter, and that the narrow focus of accountability has made it harder for schools to sustain bandwidth for other important activities.[69] Moreover, the accountability pressures may even limit how schools teach reading and math; if teachers know that certain areas are likely to be emphasized on tests, that may be where they put their focus.[70]

How Accountability Affects How Schools Teach

Professor Daniel Koretz's 2017 book *The Testing Charade* catalogs some of the ills that standardized testing has led to, including its impact on teaching. One important aspect of this impact is that the focus on accountability tests may cause schools to emphasize "test prep" teaching strategies. This isn't automatically a bad thing.[71] But it can be a bad thing and can lead to pedagogical methods that are not best practice—including focusing on tricks for succeeding on standardized tests, rather than actually understanding the content.[72]

A more serious problem directly tied to Campbell's Law is corrupted test administration—including scandals that have led to prison terms for professional educators.[73] When the stakes are high enough, educators have felt pressured to engage in conduct that is unethical or illegal, sometimes at large scale and sometimes on their own. Koretz and others appropriately raise the question of how much blame should be laid at the feet of the policymakers who created the stakes.[74]

How Accountability Affects Who Schools Focus On

The next chapter will discuss in much more detail how federal accountability has created too much focus on children in third grade and later. But among third through twelfth graders, a focus on proficiency has already created a focus on what are known as "bubble kids"—children who are right at the threshold of proficiency.[75]

From a federal accountability standpoint, schools had no incentive to focus resources on either (1) children who were safely above the proficiency threshold or (2) children who were too far below that threshold to be caught up in a reasonable time. But those two categories actually include most of the kids in most schools, creating a disconnect between the incentives in the law and the actual mandate of the schools. If a school wanted to improve its performance, its best bet was to direct its energy toward the kids right near the cut line, wherever that was.

Who the bubble kids were varied from state to state, given the different proficiency lines set across the country. But in all states the harm of this narrow focus was exacerbated by the fact that test scores are an unstable measure.[76] All tests have a margin of error; a child who gets a 91 on a test one day could easily get an 89 the next day—and if the cut score is 90, that can make a huge difference. It will always be problematic to try to draw precise distinctions from measurements with a meaningful margin of error.

The problem of "bubble kids" persists into the ESSA era, given the continued focus on proficiency. It has been ameliorated somewhat by the addition of growth as a metric; that can apply to all children.[77] And it's important to say that identifying "bubble kids" as a design problem is very different than saying that schools have actually abandoned their efforts to educate kids who aren't on the bubble; they obviously did not. But just because the misaligned incentive didn't have as damaging an impact as it might have doesn't mean that it should not be corrected.

TRUST AND DISTRUST

ESSA represents an evolution of the external accountability districts and schools have been subject to for decades. And external accountability is important. There is no plausible path to improved educational outcomes that puts complete faith in states and districts; that was true when the federal government passed ESEA in 1965, and it's true today. Much of the rest of this book will reinforce that point even further. But even the best-designed external accountability comes at a cost in trust, and it's important to acknowledge that cost.

Indeed, this highlights the central tension of external accountability. The most successful schools are those that create an environment of trust: the students and parents trust the teachers and administrators, and the teachers and administrators trust each other.[78] The schools that thrive do so because they have internal accountability and take advantage of educators' intrinsic motivation to build capacity at the school.[79]

"Internal accountability" is defined by Michael Fullan and Joanne Quinn as "conditions that increase the likelihood that people will be accountable to themselves and to the group"—that is, their coworkers.[80] It speaks to the relationships among the people actually doing the work of teaching and learning, not the expectations put on those people from the outside.

But those trusting relationships among educators are being developed in an environment shaped by the mistrust of outsiders, particularly policy elites.[81] Test-based accountability is grounded in a distrust of school administrators and teachers.[82] That external accountability generally isn't helping educators do a better job; as we've seen, it can actually make their job harder.[83] And so over time the mistrust has become bi-directional: an *EducationWeek* survey just before the pandemic found that only 1 percent of teachers trusted state legislatures to make education policy, and even fewer trusted governors.[84]

To some degree this is true of any external accountability system, but it seems particularly true of systems based on test-measured proficiency. Because proficiency is so deeply tied to factors outside of a school's control, test-based accountability is seen by school leaders as a form of blaming the victim: policy elites starve neighborhoods and their residents of the resources needed to help children succeed in school, and then blame the schools and teachers in those neighborhoods for poor academic outcomes.[85]

When states have unrealistic expectations, they set schools and teachers up for failure.[86] This understandably makes teachers angry.[87] It's also a practice that's been attacked as racist.[88]

In Part II we'll talk more about the impact accountability has on the teaching profession. But for purposes of looking at accountability, the important point is this: the balance of trust and distrust is inherent in the exercise of external accountability. Schools succeed as environments of trust, but policymakers cannot blindly trust schools to succeed.

The years leading up to NCLB showed policymakers the costs of being too trusting; the years since NCLB have shown educators the costs of not being trusted. So there are times when distrust is needed and appropriate—but there are also times where distrust is misplaced and corrosive.[89] Breaking the cycle of distrust has to start with the leaders in a position of greater authority—which in the case of accountability is the federal and state governments. Striking the right balance going forward will be key to the success of federally driven accountability.

CONCLUSION

For ESSA to be good policy, its criteria for rating schools must be good criteria for measuring school quality—and if those criteria are sound, the consequences dictated by those criteria must be appropriate. On both counts there's a good argument that ESSA is better than NCLB. But as we have seen, the benefits of federal accountability still come at a cost. And the accounting we've done so far only brings us up to the biggest problem of the NCLB/ESSA accountability framework: it focuses all of the energy of school quality measurement and improvement into the years after third grade. For the kids the system is supposed to care about the most, that's simply too late.

Chapter 2

How The Every Student Succeeds Act Distracts Us from Half the System

The Every Student Succeeds Act (ESSA) prioritizes high school graduation. Graduation rates remain a critical part of high school accountability. Moreover—like No Child Left Behind (NCLB) before it—ESSA pushes for high school graduates to be proficient in reading and math, so that they will be prepared to succeed in life beyond high school. Through heated debates about accountability methodology, the goal of having children proficient in reading and math when they graduate from high school is one that has largely been accepted by both educators and policymakers.

From a lifetime earnings perspective, graduating from high school proficient is a good thing.[1] And high school graduation rates have been going up since NCLB was passed.[2] In 2018 the four-year cohort graduation rate was 85.3 percent.[3] Unfortunately, there remain racial gaps in graduation rates. That same year the rates were lower for students who were Black (79%), Hispanic (81%), and American Indian/Alaska Native (74%).[4] And as noted earlier, focusing on graduation rates creates an incentive to make it easier to achieve a diploma—leading to concerns that high school graduates are not adequately prepared for postsecondary work or a career.[5]

Improving high school graduation rates is a major purpose of ESSA, as it should be. But ESSA's approach to accountability focuses on the years from third through twelfth grade. These grades are important, to be sure. But they're only half the story—and not the half that represent the best opportunity to improve the system. This chapter focuses on how students are doing at different points in their educational journey, what implications that should have for the educational system, and how current educational accountability takes account of the early years.

WHAT HAPPENS BETWEEN THIRD
AND TWELFTH GRADE?

The reasonable expectation of schools should be that every year they provide a year's worth of education. If that's not the norm (or at least close to it), then perhaps our definition of "a year's worth of education" isn't quite right. But if the definition is sound, then one year's worth of education should be a baseline expectation. And in fact, third grade scores tend to be very predictive of high school outcomes.[6]

Of course, even if that's the expectation, there will always be variation. Some schools will do better and others worse. So an important follow-up question is, what's the expected range of variation? Are some schools providing two years' worth of growth every year? What is it fair to anticipate?

Thanks to Professor Sean Reardon and the Stanford Education Data Archive (SEDA), we now have some idea of what levels of growth schools can reasonably be expected to produce. The SEDA team provides growth data for schools around the country. The baseline expectation is that schools should provide a year's worth of growth every year; the SEDA shows that about 40 percent of districts provide more growth than that (Figure 2.1):[7]

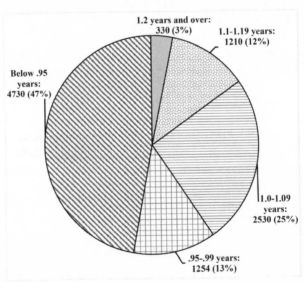

Analysis conducted by Paul Zavitkovsky based on the SEDA national percentiles reported in the New York Times Emily Badger and Kevin Quealy, "How Effective Is Your School District? A New Measure Shows Where Students Learn the Most," The New York Times, last modified December 5, 2017, https://www.nytimes.com/interactive/2017/12/05/upshot/a-better-way-to-compare-public-schools.html?hp&action=click&pgtype=Homepage&clickSource=story-heading&module=second-column-region&region=top-news&WT.nav=top-news&_r=0&mtrref=undefined&gwh=D15E94794A66CF3A2BE1A495D35865B3&gwt=regi&assetType=REGIWALL. This chart first appeared in: Regenstein, "Building a Coherent P-12 Education System in California," 9, n.15.

Obviously, there can be significant variation within districts. But there are a few key lessons we can draw here:

1. First, in 47 percent of districts children are losing a meaningful amount of ground every year they're in school. That's a major problem. A small silver lining is that growth data doesn't correlate with economic status nearly as tightly as proficiency data[8]—meaning that some of those districts with bad growth scores are well-to-do districts with high proficiency scores.
2. On the flip side, in 40 percent of districts children are gaining ground as they go. That's important, and it undermines the narrative that nationally our schools are a disaster. Again, the fact that growth and economic status are less correlated means that there is a critical mass of districts where children from low-income families are actually making good progress on math and reading, even if those districts have low overall proficiency scores.
3. But here's a really important thing that's not well understood. In only 15 percent of districts are children gaining ground at a rate of more than 1.1 years per year. So, if you backmap that, it means that only 15 percent of districts can take a cohort that's a year behind at the end of *second grade* and get it caught up by the end of high school.[9]

Clearly, it would be great to increase the percentage of districts that are capable of taking a cohort that is behind and getting it caught up. Indeed, much of this book is about policies that are supposed to help do that—and there are thousands of books, articles, analyses, blog posts, podcasts, and more that provide insights on improving school performance. Improving the ability of schools to help students progress academically is a critical societal goal.

But take a step back for a moment. Right now, if a school district is producing 1.1 years of growth per year, that puts it in the top 15 percent of schools across the country. If we got every single school district in the country to produce at that level, it would be a phenomenal achievement absolutely without precedent in the history of education reform. Even the most cockeyed optimist would probably say that it's not possible. But even if we could accomplish that ridiculously ambitious goal, *it would still mean that a cohort of kids more than a year behind at the end of second grade would not be caught up by the end of high school.*

In short, if we want to improve high school outcomes, we have to do two major things. One is to improve the performance of those schools and districts where kids are currently losing ground, so that students are more consistently making a year of progress every year. And the other is to dramatically ramp up our efforts to help kids progress in the years *before* required testing starts, because otherwise the teachers and schools in the later years have no real chance.[10]

HOW ARE KIDS DOING WHEN THEY GET TO ELEMENTARY SCHOOL?

The previous analysis talks about what needs to happen in the ten years starting with third grade. Because federally mandated standardized testing doesn't start until third grade, we don't have great data on where exactly kids are at the end of second grade. Moreover, as we've seen, state accountability testing varies too much from state to state; states use a wide range of different assessments and set their own cut scores. But based on the national data we have about where kids are in fourth grade, there is reason to be concerned.

The best national data we have comes from the National Assessment of Educational Progress (NAEP), a non-accountability test administered to a sample of children from across the country. The NAEP is administered to fourth graders, eighth graders, and twelfth graders.[11] NAEP reports results at three levels: Advanced, Proficient, and Basic.[12]

In both math and reading, before the pandemic a high percentage of children did not reach proficiency—or even NAEP's "Basic" level (Table 2.1):

Table 2.1 NAEP 4th Grade Proficiency

	Math	Reading
Percentage of 4th graders who are not proficient	59%	65%
Percentage of 4th graders who do not meet the "Basic" level	19%	34%

NAEP Report Card: Mathematics: National Achievement-Level Results," *The Nation's Report Card*, accessed September 29, 2021, https://www.nationsreportcard.gov/mathematics/nation/achievement/?grade=4.

The racial gaps here are also substantial. In fourth grade math (Table 2.2):[13]

Table 2.2 NAEP 4th Grade Math Proficiency by Race

Race	% who are not proficient	% who do not meet the "basic" level
White	48%	11%
Black	80%	35%
Hispanic	72%	27%
Asian/Pacific Islander	34%	9%
Asian	31%	7%
Native Hawaiian/Other Pacific Islander	82%	36%
American Indian/Alaska Native	76%	33%
Two or More Races	56%	16%

In fourth grade reading (Table 2.3):[14]

Table 2.3 NAEP 4th Grade Reading Proficiency by Race

Race	% who are not proficient	% who do not meet the "basic" level
White	55%	23%
Black	82%	52%
Hispanic	77%	45%
Asian/Pacific Islander	45%	19%
Asian	43%	18%
Native Hawaiian/Other Pacific Islander	75%	42%
American Indian/Alaska Native	81%	50%
Two or More Races	60%	28%

Without getting into a detailed analysis, a top-line conclusion is clear: before the pandemic there were a lot of kids who were behind by fourth grade, many of them pretty far behind. Post-pandemic analyses have only reinforced the point. A 2021 analysis by Curriculum Associates found substantial percentages of third graders were two or more grades behind (Table 2.4):[15]

Table 2.4 Percentage of Students Two or More Years Behind (according to grade-level placement results)

School Characteristic	Math	Reading
Schools >50% Black	55%	59%
Schools >50% Latino	48%	51%
Schools >50% White	29%	28%
Household income less than $50,000	49%	49%
Household income $50,000-$75,000	37%	37%
Household income more than $75,000	25%	26%

Combine that with what we now know about how much schools can do to close that gap, and it reinforces the conclusion that simply improving schools from third through twelfth grade is not going to be enough to achieve the results we want.

WHAT EDUCATIONAL EXPERIENCES ARE KIDS HAVING BEFORE THIRD GRADE?

So, we've established that it's really important to improve how kids are doing by the end of second grade. And fortunately there is a lot of opportunity to do better.

Every state has learning standards for preschool-aged children, and most have learning standards for infants and toddlers.[16] These learning standards define what children should know and be able to do in the years prior to kindergarten entry.[17] This represents a recognition on the part of states that child development in the first five years of life is extremely important. But unlike in K-12 education, there's no guarantee that children will actually be able to access a standards-based education.

Most but not all states offer state-funded preschool programs. Enrollment in state-funded preschool has grown dramatically since 2002, with more than 950,000 spots added[18]—bringing the national total to 1.64 million in the 2019–2020 school year.[19] There is substantial variation in how much states spend on a per-child basis, and in many states the per-child spending is insufficient to offer quality services.[20]

Some states offer preschool to three-year-olds, but publicly funded preschool for four-year-olds is much more common. Of those 1.64 million spots, 1.368 million were for four-year-olds.[21] Nationally 34 percent of four-year-olds are in state-funded preschool, but only 6 percent of three-year-olds.[22]

If done correctly, early childhood education should be fun and engaging while supporting standards-based learning.[23] The best early childhood teaching blurs the distinction between "academic" and "non-academic" skills, recognizing that all child development is integrated.[24] The best early childhood educators take great pride in the fact that early learning is holistic, with strong attention to social and emotional growth.[25] That requires great teaching, which is needed to produce a language-rich environment.[26] Early childhood programs also put a premium on family engagement.[27]

This narrative focuses on three-and four-year-olds, but in fact, the best opportunity to reach children is in the birth to three years.[28] This is basic child development; the ability of human brains to adjust to experiences is greatest at this early age.[29] But enrollment in education-based birth to three programs is far lower than in three to four. The federal Early Head Start program—which is focused on birth to three-year-olds—serves only 3 percent of children from low-income families, and less than 1 percent of the overall birth to three population.[30] And most states don't attempt to provide the birth to three population with standards-based learning.

The evidence base on preschool education is strong—if it's done well.[31] But the preschool programs we've had to date frequently have not been good enough. In too many cases they haven't been designed or funded to the point needed to improve child outcomes. And even then enrollment is limited.

After preschool, kids move on to kindergarten, which is mandatory in nineteen states.[32] While the K-2 years are firmly a part of the public school system, they're also a bit of an outlier within the K-12 system.[33] Accountability doesn't reach them directly, as mandated testing doesn't start until third grade. That means that in some instances schools use these grades as a place to hide their weakest teachers.[34]

One problem is that at a systemic level we have very few scaled measures of how child development is progressing during the preschool years—a problem that continues into K-2. More than thirty states require some form of kindergarten readiness assessment.[35] But those assessments vary across states—and sometimes within them—and data is reported in inconsistent ways.[36] What data we have suggests that most children are not meeting state standards when they enter kindergarten.[37]

Assessment practices in the K-2 years also vary widely by state.[38] In many instances, districts are not obligated to report any data, which is used primarily at the local level for diagnostic purposes.[39] This means that many districts may have some sense of what's happening in their schools during the K-2 years—but at a systemic level, state leaders and the public don't have a good sense of what's going on.

The increased use of kindergarten readiness assessment is starting to allow researchers to analyze what is happening in the K-2 years. For example, in 2021 a University of Virginia study looked at children from different income levels who demonstrated similar levels of literacy in kindergarten, and found that by third grade children from wealthier families were much more likely to be proficient in reading.[40]

The bottom line is that the data shows that kids are falling behind well before third grade, and then we can't catch them up. We can keep them moving forward steadily; that's why third grade scores are so predictive of high school outcomes. But if kids are behind in third grade, chances are they will still be behind at the end of high school. And given how we've set up our education system prior to third grade, it's no surprise that so many of them are behind.

THE OPPORTUNITY

The early years of life are incredibly important to child development and set the stage for everything that comes after. This point is well established in the scientific research and isn't particularly controversial politically.

Moreover, the interaction children have with adults in the early years of life really matters to their development—for good and bad. This, too, is well established in the scientific research, and isn't particularly controversial either.

So there's an incredible opportunity in the early years of life, and almost everybody agrees on that. What's far less clear, though, is exactly what role government plays in ensuring that children have good experiences in those years.[41]

- Advocates for early childhood argue that young families need more support in the early years. On average women have their first baby at age twenty-three,[42] and adults under thirty-five tend to have lower salaries and less wealth than older families.[43] Child care is incredibly expensive for families, with government subsidies not nearly enough to cover the cost.[44] Advocates argue that if government doesn't provide high-quality early childhood education, the children of the lowest-income families will end up entering school far behind grade-level expectations—and then never catch up.
- Opponents of expanded government spending on early childhood point to the track record of government in delivering services and argue that expanding publicly funded programs is unlikely to improve results.[45] They question the ability of government to provide high-quality preschool at scale, arguing that the results of past studies don't justify future investment.[46]

The skeptics make some valid points. There are preschool programs that have been a waste of money—and even the good ones are part of a crazy-quilt system that can be bewildering to parents.[47] It is reasonable to be concerned that government can build early childhood systems efficiently when its track record in doing so is limited.

But there are important reasons that early childhood is a fertile opportunity. First, obviously, from a child development angle the impact is much greater if you invest early. Skill begets skill, and building skills at the beginning of a child's learning journey will carry forward.

From a governmental standpoint, the opportunity is that so much of the infrastructure of early childhood is unbuilt. In K-12, we've already got market saturation; almost all children are already receiving an education in public or private schools. In early childhood, there are large chunks of the population that we're not serving at all. Moreover, the institutions built up around the children who are getting served are much more pliable. While the status quo is always a powerful force, in early childhood there are very few advocates explicitly arguing that it should be preserved.[48]

In short, if we're going to get radical improvement, it's much more likely to come from the early years than the later years. The possibility of incremental change is higher, and the impact of that change is greater. Getting better high school results is absolutely dependent on changing what's happening before third grade. So any education accountability system that's designed to improve high school results has to take account of that.

THE REALITY

Education accountability systems aren't actually looking at what's happening before third grade. To give credit where it's due, ESSA did open the door a little bit. Under NCLB accountability was entirely dictated by test scores, so there wasn't the possibility of state systems taking into account any earlier years. ESSA's "fifth indicator" did raise that possibility, and shortly after ESSA's passage efforts were made to evaluate the possibility of addressing the pre-third grade years.[49]

It didn't happen, though. One of the only states to even make an attempt was Illinois, which officially included space for a K-2 indicator in its ESSA plan—and commissioned a work group to propose an approach to that indicator.[50] That work group issued its report on December 31, 2017.[51] But as of the 2020–2021 school year, the number of schools in Illinois actually held accountable for any K-2 performance remained zero.

To a large extent the omission of the early years from state ESSA plans was entirely predictable given the process states used to develop those plans.[52] The development of states' initial ESSA plans was led by each state education agency, typically with some amount of public engagement. Whatever stakeholder engagement processes had been used to discuss accountability under NCLB generally did not include early childhood leaders.

When discussions about ESSA heated up, those conversations started with the stakeholders who'd already been involved in talking about NCLB. This makes sense, as both NCLB and ESSA have their largest impact on institutional groups like school boards, superintendents, principals, and teachers. Organizations representing those groups—and any relevant reform advocates—are appropriately at the heart of planning for new indicators.

Early childhood could have been a part of those conversations, but it generally wasn't.[53] In many states the early childhood leaders *within the state education agency* had no idea the process was even happening, and weren't invited to participate. Outside of the state education agency early childhood advocacy groups in most states have very limited bandwidth, and might appropriately have been focused on other priorities. So in most states, the ESSA plan was submitted without any serious consideration of how to incorporate the years before third grade into accountability plans.

In fairness, under ESSA there aren't that many great options for including the pre-third grade years in accountability systems.[54] But the omission of those years is important. An accountability system signals priorities, and state accountability systems signal that the priority is the tested years.[55]

That, in the end, is the biggest failure of accountability under ESSA. For each individual student, their best chance of success is to have a great educational experience in their first five years of life and then enter school ready to thrive. After that schools should support their continued growth, particularly in the developmentally critical years prior to third grade. And all of that essential work is completely ignored by state education accountability systems.

Indeed, the message of ESSA and state education accountability systems is to focus on something other than the early years. As long as that accountability pressure exists with no counterweight to address the earlier years, the entire educational accountability regime will be undermining its stated goal.

Chapter 3

The Future of External Accountability

It is absolutely critical that there be external accountability for the performance of schools and districts. Our history shows that without external accountability, many children are unlikely to get the education they deserve. Federal and state governments have developed accountability systems designed to help those children, and there is a reason that many business leaders and civil rights advocates have supported those efforts.

But as we've seen, a key challenge of external accountability will be its tension with internal accountability. The very best schools create an environment based on trust, where adults and children work collaboratively toward shared goals.[1] That culture can't be imposed from the outside—it can only be developed from within. External accountability that undermines those efforts may end up causing more harm than good. The federal government—and states—need to be cognizant of that tension in developing the next generation of accountability systems.

In that next generation of accountability systems, it will be important to apply lessons learned from these last generations. Critical lessons to address include:

- Graduating from high school with the knowledge and skills needed to succeed post-secondary is the key desired outcome of the education system. The journey to that goal is one that takes eighteen years or more.[2] The best opportunity to affect a child's trajectory on that journey is in the first nine years of life. But our current education accountability systems focus only on the second nine.
- Our current accountability systems give schools and districts a rating of how they are doing, but no real guidance on how to do better. Having accountability systems provide guidance would be helpful to inform the development of internal accountability. Moreover, in many schools and

35

districts the external accountability overwhelms the internal accountability, leading to a narrowed curriculum and a diminished experience
for students and teachers.

- Disaggregated data is critical to understand the experience of different
  kinds of students. Schools that may be high-performing overall may
  still not be serving some of its students effectively. If we care about the
  success of every student—which the titles of our federal laws suggest
  we claim to—that kind of detailed information must continue to be
  available.

- Federal and state accountability can be technocratic and may aspire
  to a level of precision that is simply not possible given the available
  data. External accountability isn't necessarily well equipped to make
  fine-grained distinctions that rank districts and schools, and the exercise of attempting those rankings may be damaging to schools in its
  own right.

Importantly, an accountability system is where states define what consti-
tutes a successful school.[3] There are many different possible definitions of
success—an issue we've already touched on and will continue to explore.
But that fact should shape state accountability systems. If the accountability
system is a roadmap for districts and schools on what to do, it should guide
them to the right places—acknowledging that the right place will legitimately
vary from school to school.

The values represented by proficiency and growth measurements are
both the right values. We want schools where the children are experiencing
academic success.[4] We want schools where the children are making good
progress. Even if the specific measurements being used are flawed, the values represented by those indicators are appropriate. The same is very much
true for graduation rates, for improved outcomes for English learners, and
for some of the other priorities that states have addressed with their fifth
indicator.

But we've also seen the problems ESSA's current approach creates. So
what's proposed in the following pages is an approach to changing the consequences that's meant to provide a truer course toward the values ESSA represents. That entails two major complementary shifts. The first would operate
largely within the existing paradigm of ESSA but change the way data is used
to influence school behavior. The second would collect an entirely new set of
data that would give schools actionable information, and provide more support for actions to improve outcomes.

USING PROFICIENCY AND GROWTH
TOGETHER TO DRIVE CONSEQUENCES

Accountability systems define outcomes, measures, and consequences.[5] Ultimately our desired outcome is for students to graduate from high school ready for whatever comes next. Proficiency and growth are two of our critical measures.

States have a tendency to use these measures in complex formulas that produce summative rankings.[6] In some states these rankings are articulated through letter grades.[7] California has a dashboard that provides a range of information about school performance.[8] The variation is substantial, and there are advocacy organizations that then critique these plans based on their own detailed criteria.[9]

All of the formulas and rankings raise the question of consequences—that is, how will the information be used. Current ESSA practice essentially requires coming up with a composite score that combines proficiency and growth. This approach could end up masking weaknesses in one or the other, which could reduce the diagnostic value of each.

Perhaps a better approach would be to balance the two against each other and use them together to diagnose how a school is doing. That might look something like this (Table 3.1):[10]

Table 3.1 Relating Growth to Proficiency in School Quality Measurement

	Strong Student Growth	Weak Student Growth
High Student Performance	These students are thriving, and the schools are helping them do so. Lessons from these schools should be distilled to potentially inform other schools.	These students are doing well, but the situation should be monitored to ensure that they do not fall off track. If growth trends are poor enough supports for the schools may be needed.
Low Student Performance	In this case the schools are doing their job, but the students still need more help. Community-level interventions – including improved early childhood, and wraparound services – are likely the most effective strategy; a diagnostic should be conducted to guide needed supports.	These situations are the most urgent. In these cases community-level interventions are likely to be needed, and should be paired with a diagnostic of school performance that leads to changes in school practice.

This starts to get at what we really need to know about how schools are doing. One of the reasons educators appropriately rebelled against No Child Left Behind (NCLB) Act was the perceived disconnect between the diagnosis and the cure. ESSA may be better, but it doesn't get all the way there. This grid is meant to get closer.

The top left and bottom right corners are meant to reflect long-held goals of accountability systems. If kids are doing well and making strong progress, great—let's learn from that school and see what practices it has that could help other schools do better. If students are far behind academically and making inadequate progress toward their goals, that's a call to action; dramatic intervention is appropriate.

To some degree accountability systems will always have an easier time at the extremes. Getting agreement about which schools are amazing and which are awful feels easier than distinguishing among the B– and C+ schools. This is particularly true given that data can fluctuate from year to year, so that small distinctions among districts in a given year may not be reflective of longer-term patterns. Rather than making too much of artificial or small distinctions, we should keep accountability systems focused on what ultimately matter most: a set of consequences that actually have some hope of improving student outcomes.

That's why the key to the grid in Table 3.1 is the bottom left corner— schools with low proficiency but solid growth. In a world where proficiency is the primary driver, those schools will often be identified as "failing" and face consequences similar to those where both proficiency and growth are low.

But that's a mistake. As we've learned, the right approach in those schools is to focus on the early years before testing starts. Those schools have shown some ability to help kids make the needed progress between third grade and twelfth grade; their real problem is how far behind kids are at school entry, and that's largely out of their control. In fact, when summer learning loss is accounted for the positive impact of these schools may even be understated by existing growth measures.[11]

Relatedly, when it comes to third grade, proficiency acts as an important counterweight to growth. In general, growth is a superior measure of how a school is really doing. But we've also seen that the years before third grade are critically important for child development. In an accountability system based purely on growth, the incentive for schools would actually be to have kids as far behind as possible in third grade; that would give schools the most opportunity to show improvement.

The vast majority of schools wouldn't intentionally do that, of course, but it's bad policy for the state to create any incentive for them to do so.[12] Having third grade proficiency scores as part of the accountability formula helps keep the pressure on to focus on the early years.

While the grid should be used for schools as a whole, it can also be used for subgroups of students. If a particular subgroup is demonstrating different proficiency or growth data than the school as a whole, then a specific strategy may be needed to address that subgroup's performance. The civil rights value of subgroup data should be preserved even with a shift in the overall approach to accountability.

The goal here is to tailor the consequences to the facts on the ground. The accountability hawks who wanted to take dramatic action to help children in the lowest-performing schools have a point—there are some schools that are simply too dysfunctional to help children. In those schools, major changes are needed—for the school, the kids, or both. But the rigid use of proficiency won't let us figure out which schools need that kind of intervention and which ones don't. And a single formula in which proficiency predominates could lead us to the same problem.

Of course, test scores alone give us at best a broad sense of what's going on at a school. To gain a deeper understanding requires an analysis of the school's actual practices. For that, states could turn to a model used in numerous European countries: a school inspectorate.

SCHOOL INSPECTORATES: BENEFITS AND COSTS

The idea of a school inspectorate is that an expert outside evaluator (or team of evaluators) comes to a school and rates it based on direct observation.[13] The evaluators use a rubric and are trained to ensure consistency across schools.[14] These evaluations can provide schools with detailed feedback that they can use to support any improvement processes.[15]

This detailed feedback is a key argument for including inspectorates in accountability systems. Test scores can be useful signals of how students are doing, but they offer no insights to educators on how to improve performance. The goal of an inspectorate is to close that gap, and to use the accountability system to provide meaningful feedback to the accountable.[16]

ESSA's criteria for accountability metrics essentially preclude the use of inspectorate results; there might be creative ways to come up with a fifth indicator based on inspectorate results, but the fifth indicator is clearly not designed to promote this practice.[17]

But this concept is already in use at scale in one important accountability system: the Head Start designation renewal system.[18] Programs are evaluated on their Emotional Support, Classroom Organization, and Instructional Support.[19] Historically test scores in K-12 have been treated as the best possible proxy for the quality of teacher-student interaction—but no proxy can be as effective as direct measurement.

The idea of including inspectorates in education accountability systems is not a new one.[20] But for the most part, advocacy for the idea of an inspectorate has ignored what we've seen is a critical advantage: it's a measure that's not just limited to third grade and up. One benefit of inspectorate-driven accountability is that it can address all of the years of school—not just the tested years. Right now accountability systems essentially ignore the years prior to third grade, and with an inspectorate that's no longer necessary.

There are good reasons why inspectorates haven't taken hold. Among the reasons are the following: (1) the fact that under federal law it's really difficult (if not impossible) to use inspectorate results for accountability in compliance with the relevant laws; and (2) an inspectorate is far more labor-intensive than just analyzing test scores, which means it's potentially a burden on limited state capacity. Both of those are potentially major stumbling blocks, which we'll address in turn.

Reorienting the Federal Approach to Inspectorates

The Every Student Succeed Act (ESSA) opened up new possibilities for metrics of school success, but did not go so far as to contemplate the possibility of a school inspectorate. The next time the law is reauthorized, it should be amended to allow that possibility.

An inspectorate would be an awkward fit within the "fifth indicator" authorized by ESSA. The final indicator of school quality or student success must allow for meaningful differentiation among schools—and be valid, comparable, and used for any entire gradespan across the state.[21] An inspectorate could meet those requirements, although only if it was used consistently for every single school statewide and broken down by grade span.

The more challenging issue is that an inspectorate does not provide data that can easily be broken down on a per-student basis or organized by subgroup. Department of Education regulations require that all indicators be disaggregated by student subgroup.[22] There is probably some way to attribute inspectorate results to the students in a school that could create technical compliance with this requirement, but it's clearly an awkward fit.

The safer course would be a statutory amendment specifically authorizing the use of an inspectorate, whose results could be used for some percentage of a school's accountability rating. States would not be required to use an inspectorate if they didn't want to.

Moreover, given the capacity challenges of launching an inspectorate, the statutory change should also allow states to use inspectorate results for some percentage of districts and schools, but not necessarily all. In allocating weight among the different elements of ESSA ratings—assessment results, graduation rates (in high school), English language proficiency among

English learners, and the "fifth indicator"—the state could allow for two different allocations: one for inspected schools, one for all others.

ESSA's goals of uniformity and consistency are admirable, as is its emphasis on subgroup data. Those elements should largely be preserved, but an exception should be made for inspectorate processes that measure the quality of school performance. Importantly, those inspectorate results should not be exempted from the ESSA requirement that indicators must allow for meaningful differentiation in school performance;[23] that requirement will help to ensure that inspectorate results will not simply allow the state to say that everything is going fine in the schools it inspects.

Building State Capacity for Inspectorates

There are two major problems facing states that want to launch an inspectorate. First, the inspectors need to have a working definition of what makes for a good school—and that requires a rubric (or rubrics) that states don't have. The second is that actually conducting the inspections requires skilled staff that the state doesn't currently have. For states to develop inspectorate systems will require addressing both issues.

Developing Rubrics Presents an Opportunity for Engagement

One concern about an inspectorate approach is that no single rubric could properly be used to evaluate the hundreds or thousands of schools in any state. The "CLASS" rubric looks at classroom practice, which is complicated enough; when you expand outward to school management, the challenges only multiply.

There are certainly some research-based practices that the state might expect of every school, such as the five "essential elements" identified by the University of Chicago Consortium on School Research: leadership, parent–community ties, professional capacity among the faculty and staff, a student-centered learning climate, and ambitious instruction.[24]

But it's also reasonable to think that the diverse array of schools in a given state might make different choices about how to operate based on local conditions—and that on some issues divergent approaches might in fact be best practice given community circumstances. That presents an opportunity.

First, under any circumstances the development of a rubric should be a collaborative process that draws on the best thinking of the field.[25] One way to mitigate the inherent distrust of external accountability is to engage the accountable in developing the rubrics. Administrators, principals, and teachers should all be actively involved in the rubric development process, so that the final product reflects the best thinking of the field—not expectations being imposed on the field from above.[26] That increased credibility will serve the process well in the long term and create better alignment between external accountability and internal accountability.

It also opens the possibility that there could be more than one approved rubric at the state level. Perhaps there are some components of the rubric that could have different criteria for different kind of schools, trying to strike a balance between rigor and flexibility.[27] Each state could take its own approach.

But given that reasonable people can disagree about what makes for a successful school, the state's rubrics should allow for that reasonable disagreement. This would add some administrative burden, to be sure, and that would have to be balanced against the benefits of flexibility. Different states could seek different trade-offs, and ideally learn over time about what works best.[28]

Building the Capacity for an Inspectorate

One of the biggest concerns with the idea of a state-level accountability inspectorate is the fact that states currently have nothing resembling the capacity needed to actually implement such an inspectorate.[29] And there are a number of potential pitfalls along the way:

- It's really hard to get capacity at the state level for anything. State government agency capacity has proven to be a popular target for cutbacks, given that the bureaucracy doesn't have a lot of political champions.[30] That trend is not showing signs of reversing itself any time soon. This problem is most likely to be solved by the federal government, as we'll discuss a little bit later.
- If the state is looking to hire up to perform accountability reviews, the most obvious candidates for those jobs will likely be retired superintendents and principals—many of whom will be looking for part-time jobs they can take to supplement their pensions. These candidates will have a strong knowledge of how schools do and do not actually work, but may not be inclined to provide the "tough love" that a rigorous inspection would actually call for.
- The inspectorate process could be conducted largely by private vendors on state contracts. That offers some advantages in flexibility, and could also lead to the establishment of multi-state inspectorate organizations that develop real expertise in the subject. But that will resurface all of the struggles the education sector has had with developing entrepreneurial capacity.[31]

In some instances states seeking additional capacity have partnered with external organizations.[32] That's not inevitably a bad thing but presents its own management challenges.[33] It also requires careful attention to the need for institutional memory, which can disappear quickly if nested entirely with outside partners.[34]

In creating an inspectorate, states will likely be tempted to leverage the existing infrastructure for accreditation, which provides feedback to schools through intensive reviews.[35] Accreditation has important similarities to what an accountability inspectorate might ultimately look like, although to date it has been much less professional than the models developed in other countries.[36] Lessons could also be drawn for accountability systems that already use site visits in non-ESSA contexts, which are starting to emerge.[37]

Inspectorates are not guaranteed to succeed. If the rubrics are not well designed, they may not produce useful information.[38] Schools may try to mislead inspectors.[39] Maintaining inter-rater reliability among inspectors will require constant vigilance.[40] States must be cognizant of these ongoing challenges if an inspectorate is to thrive.

Developing an inspectorate has the best chance of succeeding if states start small, do it well, and then build up capacity. That likely means starting the inspectorate with a few well-trained inspectors who are prepared to provide thorough and thoughtful feedback. States rolling out inspectorates may want to limit the number of inspections conducted in the early years—perhaps focusing on schools with low proficiency and low growth, where the need is likely greatest. If the program produces useful results, it will have a chance to expand.

It's also the case that this work need not be launched state by state. Having a competitive market for inspectors (and firms of inspectors) might be valuable, and different inspectors could offer different expertise. It will be important for each state to have a clear plan for oversight, which will require some amount of internal capacity. But the scaled conduct of the inspections themselves may well work better with more flexible staffing—and with organizations that can build up expertise across states. Indeed, there is deep skepticism that state education agencies are capable of staffing up to manage initiatives like this one, so it may make more sense for states to manage inspectorates run by others than build up capacity themselves.[41]

Regardless of how state capacity is shaped, it needs to be paid for. The expense need not be prohibitive.[42] But it is likely that in most states it would be hard to pry loose the money without federal support. If federal policymakers are persuaded that an inspectorate could be helpful to states in helping to measure school quality, they could provide funding to help states launch inspectorate initiatives.

Not all states will want to launch an inspectorate, and they shouldn't be made to. But for the ones that do, one way to approach the distribution of funds would be to borrow the model used for State Advisory Council startup grants under the American Recovery and Reinvestment Act (ARRA) of 2009. Shortly before the passage of ARRA, the renewal of the Head Start Act required states to develop early childhood advisory councils—and it authorized the use of federal funds to help those councils get up and running.[43] While no funds were appropriated by the Head Start Act, the ARRA provided $100 million for states to establish their councils.[44]

Because the grants were not meant to be competitive, the Administration for Children and Families (ACF) notified each state of its allocation—which was based largely on population (with a statutory minimum). The statute gave states broad discretion as to how they wanted to use the funds, and states had to prepare applications describing how they planned to use their allocation; as long as the application fell within the statutory parameters, ACF approved the applications. There was a small matching requirement, and several states chose not to apply; their funds were then reallocated to other states.[45]

This approach might work well to help states launch inspectorates. The federal government could clearly define the parameters of its investment; states could then choose whether or not to draw down the money. The initial federal investment could be relatively small, and it could evolve over time as states learn lessons and shift their implementation.

Before the federal government invests in state inspectorates, it should do a cost-benefit analysis to determine whether it thinks the money spent will be worth it when it comes to impacting student outcomes. That's a plausible theory, but far from a guarantee. And one of the reasons inspectorates might not have the intended impact—or evolve over time based on lessons learned—is that states don't have the capacity to make sense of the information they're collecting. That too is an issue that the federal government would be well advised to address.

MAKING SENSE OF THE DATA

Uses and Misuses of State Analytic Capacity

A state inspectorate would generate all kinds of new information about schools and how they operate. For all of that information to actually impact school practices will likely require substantial analytic capacity.[46] Analytic capacity will also be needed to support the ongoing evolution of the inspectorate process, so that it continues to grow and change in ways responsive to the needs of the field. This kind of analytic process is not generally one that states are currently set up to perform.

Problem definition is critical in this work, to make sure that the focus is on the right questions.[47] For decades one of the reasons that school systems have struggled is that they focus on what they can measure even if it's not what matters most.[48] Just having numbers is not enough—there needs to be a sense-making process to support improved practice.[49] And having improved analytics can support improved ongoing conversations among system leaders and practitioners.[50]

State analytic processes should draw on the experience of practitioners.[51] Information about "what works" has not historically translated into changes in practice.[52] The problem isn't just that the wrong information is being used; it's also that decisions are being made by the wrong people, disconnected from practitioners.[53] Improving information is essential to success, but so is improving the connection between research and practice.[54]

Of course, an outside analyst would say that analytic capacity is unlikely to be expanded significantly and that even if it is, it's not clear that districts will build the systems needed to use the information effectively. Data can be used for problem avoidance as much as for problem-solving.[55] And even in fields with abundant resources and a commitment to analytics, the results are at best uneven.[56]

There are a number of ways in which an attempt to build this capacity could go wrong. One of the most obvious is the potential for it to represent a technocratic takeover. If it's working incorrectly, centralized staff with limited information will try to extrapolate conclusions that are politically expedient—whether they're really supported by the data or not.[57] They will then give direction to local staff who actually have a better understanding of the on-the-ground facts.[58]

If the analytic capacity is working correctly, smart analysts will be sifting through different kinds of information to frame choices for policymakers and districts—with a clear explanation of the likely consequences of each option.[59] Most people in the system have very little experience with this kind of data use and will have a hard time picturing it as a likely outcome.

To be clear, developing analytic capacity at the state level requires not just new kinds of resources—it also requires a culture change. There's a long history of state agencies and school districts seeking to avoid the release of information that will make them look bad.[60] A willingness to engage with challenging data will be a prerequisite for using analytic capacity effectively. For the most part, this hasn't happened; previous state efforts to develop analytic capacity have been hard to sustain, or have reverted to a traditional agency focus on compliance.[61]

Sustaining analytic capacity requires heightened trust: in particular, the trust that the release of difficult information will help lead to improved outcomes, rather than the loss of funding and jobs. That is a level of trust many education professionals have never experienced. And in this approach that trust will have to be maintained even when the analysts get it wrong, which happens a lot even when the smartest analysts are using the best possible information.[62] So to sustain analytic capacity, states will have to create safe space for staff who are willing to speak hard truths and learn from their mistakes.

Fixing the process of decision-making is key to improving educational outcomes.[63] Better data is an essential part of that work, even if data alone will never be enough.[64] The new information derived from an inspectorate could play a valuable role in a continuous improvement process.[65] Analysts should also learn from states with best practices around the country, which might provide useful lessons than can be distilled for use in other contexts.[66]

Staffing State Analytic Capacity

While even the best analysts will be wrong some percentage of the time, an analytic enterprise has the best chance of success if it is staffed by people with real expertise to make sense of the information they're receiving.[67] State agencies often struggle to get people with the right skills for traditional roles.[68] Staffing these new analytic roles would likely be even harder.

One of the most fascinating approaches to building state agency expertise came from a newly elected state superintendent who had previously been a district superintendent. He said that he identified the key functions of his agency, and then called some of the best district superintendents in the state and asked them: "When you have a problem with [issue], who do you call?"

It turned out that on some issues there were a few experts sprinkled around the state who had serious credibility in the field; they were the people who their colleagues trusted. So the state superintendent called those trusted experts and asked them to come work at the state for a couple of years, train the relevant oversight division, put in place the right procedures, and then go back to their districts. He said that a number of the people had taken him up on the offer.[69]

That's not the only way to go about it, but this approach spoke to something powerful: there are people in the field who know how to solve problems, and they're not necessarily the staff at the state agency. So if the state agency is going to turn into a problem-solving engine, it needs to access the best wisdom of the field.[70] Hiring experts out of their districts is one way to go about that.

It's not the only way. Most state education agencies have no history with work of this orientation, which suggests it might be best for them to create a new partner organization or find some other external capacity.[71] Regardless of where the permanent analytic staff is housed, practitioners should be involved to provide ongoing expertise.[72]

This is another area where cross-state partnerships focused on common problems could be the most efficient approach. And there may be other creative ways to go about the work not identified here—including focusing on building capacity at the regional or local level. The specifics are less important than the principle: whatever information the state has, it takes smart people to make sense of it—and there are already smart people out there who can contribute to that effort.

Funding State Analytic Capacity

The federal government should also help to support this work, which would complement its important role in supporting education research. Research is a very different animal than analytic capacity, but the two are complementary, and the federal government should be committed to both. While research studies typically don't provide definitive answers to complex questions, they do provide information that can potentially be useful to addressing those questions.[73] Increasing federal funding for research and evaluation would provide more information for the field on what's actually working, and what is likely to work in the future.[74]

These federal investments should bolster research practice partnerships, ensuring that practitioner voice is a part of the design and conduct of research.[75] Providing data transparency and research is a function for which the federal government is uniquely suited, a point that over the years has garnered bipartisan support.[76]

The federal government over the years also supported increased investment in data systems. Since 2005 the State Longitudinal Data System grant program has distributed federal funds to states to build up their data infrastructure.[77] Since its creation the program has distributed more than $800 million to fifty-five states and territories.[78]

From 2005 to 2011, advocates for improved data capacity focused on building the basics of the systems.[79] But once the basics were in place, the conversation shifted to how that data was going to get used.[80] Federal support for continuous improvement initiatives could further advance that conversation.[81] Direct federal investment could be paired with support for complementary state capacity, which could help states use data more effectively—including research findings.[82]

The federal government has played a critical role in funding state education agency capacity. During the NCLB era, the federal–state partnership had a significant impact on the design and capacity of state education agencies, which largely organized around federal compliance—and were largely funded to fulfill that function.[83] A shift in emphasis by the federal government toward funding analytic capacity would likely go a long way toward helping states make the same shift. And having that analytic capacity can make a significant difference in how effective states can be at implementing better policy.[84]

CONCLUSION

ESSA was wise to open up the possibility of indicators that go beyond test scores. But there's also a legitimate concern that having too many indicators just creates confusion; lots of little indicators that don't have much of an impact will not be powerful enough to drive behavior. This model envisions using growth and proficiency as the primary drivers of determining whether or not schools are on track. Our understanding of the conditions in a school—and what changes are needed for it to improve—can also be shaped by an inspectorate. That can be supplemented further still with other data, including some of the indicators now used in state fifth indicators.

In defining consequences for schools, accountability systems need to be sensitive to the fact that schools play an essential but incomplete role in student outcomes.[85] It is appropriate to hold schools accountable for helping students to progress academically; it is not, however, appropriate to punish schools for serving students from families with low incomes.[86] The most important years of a child's life from a brain development standpoint have already occurred by the time that child starts kindergarten. Accountability systems with too great a focus on proficiency understate the importance of that fact.

This proposed framework still envisions a significant role for test scores, despite all of their many flaws. But student outcomes matter, and test scores remain the best tool we have to measure those outcomes.[87] There will always be proposals to improve the content of the tests, or to give them less frequently.[88] Those may well fit comfortably in this proposed framework as well. And reducing the weighting on test scores could mitigate the legitimate Campbell's Law concerns raised by critics of standardized testing, even if it doesn't eliminate them entirely.

While test scores have their place, they shouldn't be the leading edge of accountability work.[89] So an inspectorate can serve as an appropriate counterweight to test scores.[90] Test scores are the required measure of how children are doing—but inspectorate results would tell us directly how the adults are doing, and can give us valuable information about how schools might improve their practice.[91] If the use of test scores is based on a lack of trust in schools and teachers, then perhaps an inspectorate can be a place to honor the exercise of professional discretion and the wisdom the best educators bring to their craft.

More than that, the rubrics themselves can serve as counterweights to some of the criticisms of test score usage. Rubrics could focus specifically on how schools serve high-mobility students, addressing a major shortcoming of the NCLB/ESSA era. If test scores focus too narrowly on math and reading, the rubrics can provide a counterweight by evaluating schools on the breadth of their curriculum. If there are concerns that high-stakes tests are driving bad teaching practices, the rubrics can provide a pull back toward improved instruction—with the recognition that there is not one single magical approach to instruction that all schools should use.[92]

As state education agencies and school districts know well, there can be a substantial difference between collecting information and using it effectively. Considering how much money the education field spends overall, it spends frighteningly little money on providing the ongoing analytic capacity that would help ensure the big pie is spent correctly.[93]

The proposed approach to using assessment results in accountability could be implemented immediately by states under existing law. The proposed inspectorate likely could not be implemented without a change in federal law—and realistically, it probably will not be possible without federal support. And whether or not states change their approach to accountability, they should consider developing analytic capacity that can be used to make sense of whatever data states have—and to identify areas where better data could make a difference.

Whatever metrics are included in an accountability system, we know that the most critical in-school variable for students is their experience with teachers. Getting the best teachers in classrooms with the students who need them most has been an ongoing challenge for the education system. State accountability systems should set the right incentives for that matching process, but they alone won't be enough. In Part II, we'll turn to that issue and focus more on the policy changes needed to improve the quality of teaching for students from families with low incomes.

PART II

Getting the Best Teachers
Where They're Needed

Chapter 4

The Experience of Teachers

There are robust discussions about how to elevate the role of teachers and attract talent into the profession. Clearly the overall quality of the teaching force impacts all schools, and we will look briefly at some of the ways policymakers impact the teacher market as a whole. But because we're focused on schools serving children from low-income families, our primary focus in this chapter will be on the distribution of teachers within the profession. How can we make it possible for the schools serving children from low-income families to compete for teaching talent?

We'll start this chapter by looking at who teachers are, and at the impact policymakers have on the appeal of the profession. We will then examine the experience teachers have in schools—both with their students and with their adult colleagues. School discipline and instructional leadership can look very different from school to school, and both have major impacts on teachers' day-to-day lives; those impacts can spell the difference between a teacher staying in a school and moving on to something else.

In the final chapters of Part II, we'll examine the reasons that the best teachers don't end up working with the students who most need their help. We'll then consider a potential approach to teacher pay that would increase the odds of the best teachers working in the schools with the greatest needs— and the changes to education funding needed to make that happen.

WHO ARE TEACHERS?

In the K-12 world, there are 3.7 million teachers—3.2 million in the public schools.[1] Another 470,000 teachers work in preschools.[2] That may not seem like a lot in a country with more than 260 million adults in the workforce.[3] But in a diverse economy it actually represents one of the most popular professions.[4]

Teaching is a solidly middle-class profession, other than preschool teachers (Table 4.1):

Table 4.1 Teacher Salaries by Grade Band

Age Band	Median Annual Salary
Preschool teachers	$31,930[i]
All full-time wage and salary workers	$52,156[ii]
Kindergarten and elementary school teachers	$60,660[iii]
Middle school teachers	$60,810[iv]
High school teachers	$62,870[v]

i) "Occupational Outlook Handbook: Preschool Teachers," *U.S. Bureau of Labor Statistics.*

ii) This amount is actually the median weekly income for the third quarter of 2021, multiplied by 52. "Median weekly earnings of full-time wage and salary workers by sex, quarterly averages, seasonally adjusted," *U.S. Bureau of Labor Statistics*, accessed December 5, 2021, https://www.bls.gov/news.release/wkyeng.t01.htm.

iii) "Occupational Outlook Handbook: Kindergarten and Elementary School Teachers," *U.S. Bureau of Statistics*, accessed November 22, 2021, https://www.bls.gov/ooh/education-training-and-library/kindergarten-and-elementary-school-teachers.htm.

iv) "Occupational Outlook Handbook: Middle School Teachers," *U.S. Bureau of Statistics*, accessed November 22, 2021, https://www.bls.gov/ooh/education-training-and-library/middle-school-teachers.htm#tab-1.

v) "Occupational Outlook Handbook: High School Teachers," *U.S. Bureau of Statistics*, accessed November 22, 2021, https://www.bls.gov/ooh/education-training-and-library/high-school-teachers.htm.

Teachers are disproportionately women—nationally, about 76 percent.[5] Male teachers are more common in high school, where they represent 36 percent of teachers; in elementary school, only 11 percent of teachers are male.[6] Among preschool teachers 98.7 percent are women.[7] The younger the child, the more likely their teacher is to be female.

The teaching force is substantially whiter than the country as a whole

Table 4.2 Teacher Racial Demographics

Race	U.S. Population[i]	Teachers[ii]
White, not Hispanic	60%	79%
Black	13%	7%
Hispanic or Latino	19%	9%
Asian	6%	2%
American Indian/Alaska Native	1%	1%
Pacific Islander	>1%	>1%
Two or more races	3%	2%

i) "*Quick Facts Population Table*," *United States Census Bureau*, accessed July 14, 2021, https://www.census.gov/quickfacts/fact/table/US/PST045219.

ii) "Characteristics of Public School Teachers," *National Center for Education Statistics.*

(Table 4.2):

K-12 teaching jobs generally require bachelor's degrees, and more than half of teachers have graduate degrees.[8] This is not the case in preschool, as in many states bachelor's degrees are not required to teach preschool.[9] Teachers in schools serving a high percentage of students in poverty are more likely to lack proper certification, or to not have an educational background in the subject they are teaching.[10] As for charter schools, their teachers are often younger, less experienced, and less likely to have a graduate degree.[11]

The number of education degrees being awarded has continued to decline steadily, with a sharp drop since the Great Recession in 2008–2009.[12] Indeed, from 2010 to 2018 there was a 28 percent reduction in the number of students completing education degrees—and a similar decline in the number of students enrolling.[13]

The shrinking of the overall talent pool has a disproportionate impact on the schools with the most limited resources. Schools serving a high percentage of students from low-income families tend to have higher turnover and a harder time filling vacancies.[14] This is in part because teachers in these schools are paid less than their colleagues in other schools.[15] Their working conditions may also be less favorable.[16]

THE ADULT ECOSYSTEM SURROUNDING SCHOOLS

In 2015 Craig Lindvahl, a newly appointed member of the Illinois State Board of Education, was wrestling with how best to fulfill his new policy-focused role. A former teacher, he said that in his classroom the thing that led to success was love—the love he had for his students and the love they had for learning. (He was too modest to say that his students loved him, but they likely did.)[17] How, as a policymaker, could he legislate love? What he came to understand was that he couldn't regulate love, but what he could do is try to create the conditions in which teachers who have that love can succeed, and be more inclined to remain in the classroom.[18]

For the most part, teachers would not report that policymakers are creating the conditions in which teachers who have that love are able to succeed. Policy-oriented reformers frequently fail to understand the limits of legislative action.[19] They have a tendency to overestimate their ability to improve teaching practice, which most reforms over the years haven't done.[20] Policy changes frequently don't help teachers implement best practice[21]—and can actually end up reducing the ability of the best teachers to use their discretion.[22] In the end, the teaching profession ends up being defined by people who don't really know its work.[23]

Professor Jal Mehta has explained that education reforms are most likely to work when they meet the following conditions:[24]

- They solve a problem teachers think they have rather than a problem reformers wish teachers thought they had;
- They are consistent with prevailing norms and values;
- They are either consistent with what teachers already know how to do or provide the needed tools, infrastructure, and practical guidance needed to enable teachers to achieve the goals they set out; and
- In a locally controlled and decentralized system, they continually win public support for their objectives across many districts and school communities.

Teachers are constantly being barraged by new policy initiatives that do not meet some or all of these criteria—which can wear them down and give them reform fatigue.[25] Policymakers consistently underestimate how hard it will be to implement their policies.[26] History shows that implementation is incredibly hard even when the implementers want policies to work. But unsurprisingly, teachers are resistant to policymaker initiatives.[27] And that resistance reduces the odds of successful implementation even further.[28]

To build a stronger teaching profession will require honoring teacher knowledge and expertise.[29] But that knowledge and expertise can be really different than the knowledge and expertise used by policy leaders and advocates. And policy types are not always good at acknowledging that somebody else knows better than they do. The same can also be true of philanthropic leaders. This can lead them to take a dim view of the people charged with implementing their ideas.[30]

These policy and philanthropic leaders got into their roles by making a set of life choices very different than the life choices made by teachers. They rose through the ranks using a skill set that is distinct from the skill set teachers develop and deploy. It is relatively common for policymakers to assume that teachers will behave as they the policymakers would when confronted with a particular set of choices—and not as the teachers themselves have consistently demonstrated they will actually behave.[31]

The disconnect goes beyond the fact that policymakers and philanthropic leaders may lack the understanding of teacher context—it's also a problem that they're not a member of the same club. If teachers and education leaders want to criticize their preparation programs, or their professional development, or their work conditions, that's fair; that form of complaining is part of the natural bonding that occurs among members of any profession.[32] But when lawyers and policy types disparage those same institutions, they are outsiders, and that puts teachers on the defensive.[33]

ENGAGING WITH CHILDREN

One of the primary draws of teaching is the unique opportunity to interact directly with children—and to have a positive impact on their development.[34] Teachers justifiably describe themselves as part of a noble profession, and no discussion of teaching should lose sight of that nobility. One of the key differences between teaching and almost any other profession is the intensity and duration of interaction with children.

But actually dealing with children turns out to be very difficult in many schools. Children are naturally energetic.[35] Historically one of the struggles of school systems has been to bring order to what otherwise might be a chaotic enterprise.[36] In the early twentieth century school could be a miserable experience, and kids who misbehaved were likely to be pushed out with no expectation of returning.[37] Order remains a priority for many schools today.[38]

Teachers want schools to be safe;[39] so do students.[40] But actually creating that safety can be one of the hardest parts of the work for adults in a school. If adult capacity is inadequate, the experience for everybody in a school building—teachers and students—will suffer.

Because dealing with disciplinary issues is such a critical part of the teacher experience and school climate, understanding its dynamics is important to shaping any proposal aimed at attracting teachers to particular schools—and then retaining them once they get there. On this tour we aren't going to seriously attempt to resolve the complex debates about how discipline ought to work in schools. We will, however, seek at least a basic understanding of how the politics of school discipline might influence teachers' choices about where to work.

The Balancing Act of School Discipline

There is an inherent tension schools live with every day. On the one hand, every individual child needs an opportunity to succeed. At a systemic level, justice demands that we treat all children as social, political, and legal equals;[41] adequate schooling is an essential part of achieving that justice.

On the other hand, one disruptive student—or a small group of disruptive students—can make things very difficult for the other children around them and harm their learning environment.[42] And if teachers feel like they cannot punish students who behave badly, they may feel like their authority is undermined.[43] Violent students are appropriately a serious concern for teachers.[44]

The key to school safety is, unsurprisingly, strong relationships between adults and students.[45] It's understandable that teachers may prefer teaching students who they see as respectful.[46] But building and maintaining strong adult–child relationships can be really hard if there aren't enough teachers, or if the teachers aren't well supported.[47]

Problems with student–teacher interactions tend to be more significant in schools serving primarily students from families with low incomes. The experiences and relationships children have outside of school can have a major impact on child behavior in schools.[48] It is not students' fault that they may be experiencing trauma, and students have the best chance of succeeding if schools are sensitive to that trauma in developing policies on discipline.[49]

Still, students impacted by trauma can cause challenges for teachers. Teachers in high-poverty schools report higher rates of verbal and physical conflict.[50] They are also far more likely to report that student behavior creates an unsafe environment.[51] This reinforces the notion that out-of-school factors can have a major influence on in-school behaviors and that teachers are, in many instances, being counted on to act as social workers in addition to teaching content.

If schools are unable to completely wash their hands of students who present disciplinary problems, they sometimes find other approaches to isolating those students.[52] One strategy some schools have used is to simply shunt children with disciplinary issues into special education classes.[53] Dr. Julia McWilliams tells the story of a school she worked at that just took all of the kids with disciplinary problems and stuck them in a room in the basement.[54] And as she tells it, when those kids were let out of the basement, the rest of the school got more chaotic.[55] This experience was not unique, as schools have found various ways to keep students with behavioral issues away from other students.[56]

Dealing with the behavioral issues of children can put strain on adult relationships within the school. Spending the day in the classroom with children can leave teachers feeling isolated from other adults.[57] Teachers can end up feeling like administrators don't respect them and have their backs, which can lead to them feeling worn out by their dealings with more difficult students.[58]

In fact, a 2021 survey of teachers that asked them to identify their preferred job attributes identified the most important attribute as "a principal who 'supports them with disruptive students.' "[59] Support on discipline issues has also been identified by teachers as one of the most important factors in whether they would continue to work in schools serving children from low-income families.[60]

One argument advocates for charter schools make is that charters may be able to create a more orderly environment.[61] There certainly are charter schools that have done a good job of creating a successful learning environment where discipline issues are well managed.[62] But opponents of charter schools reply that one strategy charter schools may be using is the same strategy neighborhood schools used before compulsory attendance laws: simply getting rid of the most difficult kids.[63] And when charter schools do that the neighborhood school is left with a kid whose underlying behavioral issues remain, and who now knows they're at a school of last resort.[64]

Some schools have a clear theory of action on how to handle disruptive students.[65] Engaging teachers in developing school discipline and behavior policies is one promising capacity-building strategy.[66] But in many schools the ongoing work of striking the balance between the rights of the disruptor and the disrupted can leave teachers feeling dissatisfied.

Ultimately this is a capacity problem. It takes hard work to create a strong environment, and not every administrator has the skill and bandwidth to do that work. Getting to the root causes of behavioral issues is harder than just punishing kids.[67] And school leaders may have strong incentive to sweep disciplinary issues under the rug, as the perception that a school has disciplinary problems can be bad for its enrollment (an issue whose stakes we will discuss in chapter 8).[68]

Teachers understand they will have to deal with stress. But if the interactions with children are no longer rewarding and they don't feel like they're making a difference, they'll leave.[69] Discipline is one of the biggest sources of tension between principals and teachers.[70] And if the overall ecosystem of a school isn't supportive, then it can be hard for teachers to feel like they're making a difference.

Race and Discipline

The scene is the office of the district superintendent in a small city in the south, during the first term of the Obama Administration. The district's student population was largely Black; the white kids had moved out to the suburbs or enrolled in private schools. (We'll talk about that more in Part III.) Everybody in the room was white. The local school board had chosen to not renew the superintendent's contract, and now, as a lame duck, he was ready to unburden himself.

As he told the story, when he'd arrived in town five years earlier he'd discovered that the schools were liberal users of corporal punishment.[71] The teachers felt like they absolutely needed to use the paddle to maintain order. He had tried to get them to stop, but they had resisted; he said the teachers' claim was that if the students knew that the teachers couldn't paddle them, the kids would run wild.

After some discussion they had reached a compromise. One of his goals was to avoid having kids paddled in the classroom. So each school would designate a single paddler for the building; kids who ran afoul of the rules would be sent to that paddler, and the beating would be administered in the privacy of that paddler's office. The teachers maintained their leverage on the students, and the superintendent got paddling out of the classroom. All of the adults won, sort of.

The superintendent said that this policy had been implemented a few days before the school year started. He hadn't heard anything about it until a few days after the start of school, when he got a call from one of his best principals—a Black woman. As he told the story, she called him and said something along the lines of the following: "I am our school's designated paddler. I just got a white kid sent to me with a disciplinary issue. If I paddle him, my career will be over. What do I do?"

And so a mid-course adjustment was made. According to the superintendent, a new policy was implemented (if not publicized): each school would have *two* paddlers—one white, one Black. The white students could get paddled by a white administrator; the Black students could get paddled by a Black administrator. That was one school district's version of racial equity.

The role of race in school disciplinary cultures can be significant even if it's not always quite that violent or explicit. School suspensions disproportionately impact Black students.[72] Racial disparities in discipline can involve both differential selection and differential processing: Black and Brown students may be more likely to be chosen for disciplinary action,[73] and then once they're chosen may face more severe punishments.[74] The official rules of discipline will generally be neutral,[75] but the enforcement can make clear distinctions between white children and the "problem kids"—typically African American males.[76]

Racial differentiation in discipline can shape entire school cultures. If white children know that they're not likely to be punished, they can take more latitude in how they behave—knowing that they'll get away with it.[77] In some instances, that is because they know that if they get in trouble their parents will intervene and get them out of it. But at some point, the mere threat of parental involvement becomes substantial enough that teachers skip the process of going through the motions of discipline, and just let white kids skate.[78] In these situations, the disciplinary process reinforces ideas of privilege, both for the privileged and for the non-privileged.[79]

Not every school is racially diverse—and disciplinary inclinations do not cleave neatly along racial lines. Black teachers may believe strongly that firm punishment is critical to the success of their Black students.[80] The disruption of classrooms can have a negative impact on educational outcomes for Black and Brown children.[81] Racial gaps in discipline can also vary widely across states and districts.[82] So the issues are complex—and acknowledging that racial disparities in discipline are real doesn't answer the question of what to do about them, which is an ongoing source of political disagreement.[83]

It's important to emphasize that systemic issues of racial discipline are larger than any individual teacher or school. Teachers' level of racial bias is similar to that of the population as a whole.[84] There will be instances when administrators try to make teachers the scapegoats for systemic problems that the teachers themselves didn't cause.[85] That's because it's easier for administrators to push the problem downward than to push upward on systems and policymakers.[86] In part because of that dynamic, some teachers will resist diversity training because they think it means that people consider them racist.[87]

It's also important to acknowledge that dealing with disciplinary issues is a major source of stress for teachers, in their interactions with both students and administrators. An increased focus on racial disparities in discipline is important, and it's not right to sweep the issue under the rug. Some districts have already made an effort to start this work.[88]

Actually addressing racial disparities in discipline will require improved capacity at the teacher and school level. When policymakers force changes in the approach to discipline without providing the needed supports, those policy changes will not lead to improvement at the school level.[89] So if policymakers do not provide supports and resources for the important work of reducing racial disparities—whatever their chosen policy—teachers across that spectrum will experience this issue as one more complex dynamic on which they are blamed for larger societal forces, and then are expected to sort out the solutions on their own.

It's Not Just the Big Kids

The children most likely to get expelled from school? Preschoolers.[90] Black preschool children are the most likely to be expelled, and boys are far more likely to be expelled than girls.[91] The long-term negative impacts of these disciplinary actions on the affected children can be substantial, particularly given that preschoolers are at a very sensitive developmental stage.[92]

States have responded by passing laws prohibiting preschool suspension and expulsion.[93] But as with K-12 discipline, the primary issue is capacity. Teachers may not have the skills to manage challenging behaviors; the low salaries and poor work conditions of early childhood settings may leave them with limited bandwidth to manage those behaviors, and teachers have their own implicit biases.[94]

The prevalence of suspensions and expulsions in preschool should actually not be surprising. First, as we've seen, teachers in the early years are paid less and may have minimal supports around them. Second, in early childhood a meaningful percentage of children aren't getting served at all, which affects the calculation individual providers make. If they kick out a kid who's difficult, there might be a kid who's easier to serve waiting to take their place—meaning the provider keeps its enrollment (and its funding), with less work.

The wave of state laws aimed at eliminating the practice of preschool suspension and expulsion will only work if they actually build capacity to help children with behavioral needs at the building and classroom levels. So far the history on that subject is not promising. Policymakers have for many years tried to fight the practice of schools simply pushing out the kids they don't know what to do with—but by trying to fight the practice through mandates rather than capacity-building, they have largely failed.

Conclusion

One of the main reasons people become teachers—and one of the main reasons teachers stay on the job—is the chance to work with children. But working with children is complicated. Those complications may look different for children of different ages, but schools need the capacity to manage all of those complications. In schools with adequate resources, that capacity is often available; in schools with more limited resources, sometimes the complications overwhelm the capacity. And because those low-resource schools are disproportionately the ones serving children from low-income families, it puts those children—and the teachers working with them—at a disadvantage.

THE ADULT ECOSYSTEM OF SCHOOLS

Teachers are heavily shaped by their experience within schools and systems.[95] In discussing school discipline, experience teaches that the problem isn't just the kids—it's how the adults in charge support teachers in dealing with the kids. Strong leadership is the single most important factor to school success.[96] And for many teachers the adult ecosystem of the school turns out to be a source of ongoing frustration.

The Importance of Leadership and School Culture

Instructional leadership is key to school success.[97] If principals can hold teachers to high standards and provide a shared vision for the school, that has a positive impact on student achievement.[98] Strong leadership encompasses a range of behaviors—including instructional leadership, shaping the school climate, supporting professional learning communities, and managing personnel.[99] That's generally more work than any single person is going to be able to do on their own, which is why collaboration between principals and teachers is so critical.[100]

Teacher leadership and principal leadership can be mutually reinforcing.[101] Many teachers want to be a part of school leadership.[102] That requires building trust, which can be difficult in the school environment.[103] Principals do have incentive to trust their teachers, because that can improve teacher performance—which reflects well on them.[104] Sometimes, however, principals struggle to share control with teachers, in part because they worry that too much autonomy will lead to disorderly environments within the building.[105] Another problem for principals in sharing power is that they may feel like they have very little control to begin with.[106]

A key power that principals often lack is the ability to choose their faculty and staff. While principals are responsible for leading a school, in many instances they have very little control over who works there.[107] This can make it difficult to establish the desired school culture. Empowering principals to do their own hiring can be a key step in the establishment of a successful school culture.[108] Empowering them more broadly can go even further toward creating a successful school environment.[109]

Principal judgment matters because teacher hiring is not really an empirical ranking process, it's a matchmaking process. Some teachers might thrive in some school settings, but not in a setting focused on children from low-income families.[110] Different school ecosystems can demand different skills and behaviors, and a teacher who connects with the students in one school will not inevitably connect with the students in another.[111] There is also evidence that students of color can benefit from having teachers that are the same race as theirs.[112]

The best schools operate with a coherent set of drivers and a collaborative culture, but principals can't impose that unilaterally if the conditions around them are unfavorable.[113] The best school cultures—the ones in which teachers are most likely to be happy—will be those in which there is strong internal accountability, which creates greater coherence in systems.[114] Indeed, if teachers and principals have good relationships, it can contribute to teacher retention.[115]

But in schools serving students from families with low incomes, it can be harder to attract and retain qualified teachers due to the working conditions and comparatively low pay.[116] A disproportionate number of teachers in these schools may be novices—and these schools may be ill-positioned to support those novices.[117] These schools can end up populated by the lowest-quality teachers, which has significant impacts on student outcomes.[118] That can lead to organizational dysfunction and ongoing faculty turnover.[119] Staff churn is very damaging in an environment where relationships are of paramount importance.[120]

To some degree, principals and teachers find common cause in their distrust of central offices. In many instances, teachers empathize with their principals, who they understand are also in a difficult position.[121] School leaders may be facing the same difficult work conditions as teachers.[122] And when principals feel abandoned by the district office, they may face a sense of hopelessness and burnout.[123]

It is worth noting here that current external accountability systems don't really tell us much of anything about school culture. An approach to external accountability that included an inspectorate would create greater understanding of school culture and how it impacts student outcomes—and the teacher experience.

Race and Teachers

When schools were segregated, so were teachers.[124] Segregated schools created a Black middle class of teachers.[125] Desegregation of schools had the impact of splitting up Black teaching forces, which could be hard on those teachers—or push them out of the workforce altogether.[126]

For example, when Nashville desegregated in the early 1970s, the district aimed to have Black teachers comprise 20 percent of the faculty in each school—which, in many instances, led to the dissolution of relationships that had been formed in schools with Black-dominated faculties, and to white teachers treating their new Black colleagues badly.[127] In other instances, Black teachers just got fired, because white families didn't want Black teachers and white teachers didn't want Black colleagues.[128]

There is research showing that teachers do not believe students of color can succeed—leading to lower expectations.[129] And research has shown that low teacher expectations can lead to inferior student outcomes.[130]

Black teachers may be more effective at connecting with Black students.[131] Teachers of color may also be more willing than white teachers to address difficult and important civic topics.[132] Maximizing the percentage of students that learn from a teacher who believes in their potential is an essential part of improving school performance. Having teachers who are the same race as their students is not a cure-all on that subject,[133] but there is at least some evidence showing that it can have positive impacts.

This evidence suggests that teachers of color should be treated as valuable assets, but that is often not the case.[134] When schools can find talented teachers of color, those teachers may face unrealistic expectations; they might be marketed as saviors so that systems can avoid dealing with systemic problems.[135] Or they may feel like they have to do extra work as a mentor and supporter to students of color, which can be exhausting.[136]

Black teachers can feel isolated because of their race, which may make them more likely to leave the profession.[137] The lack of a critical mass of teachers of color may be part of what makes it hard for the ones already there to stay in the profession. And the out-of-school environment for teachers also matters; for example, communities without a Black middle class may have a hard time attracting and retaining Black teachers.[138]

There is also a need for teachers who have facility with languages other than English. According to the 2009–2013 American Community Survey conducted by the U.S. Census Bureau, 20 percent of the U.S. population speaks a language other than English at home.[139] But the nation faces a shortage of qualified bilingual teachers, which has a negative impact on children.[140] And when those teachers are on the job, they may face extra burdens, including developing their own materials.[141]

Teacher Autonomy and Support

Teachers want to be respected, and have the chance to grow in their work; this is where their intrinsic motivation lies.[142] Administrative insensitivity is something that deeply bothers teachers.[143] They are often concerned that administrators won't respect them and will treat them as scapegoats when things go wrong.[144] If performance expectations are dictated by others, the message to teachers is that they can't be trusted.[145] So when teachers feel like an uncaring authority is treating them like they're stupid, they get angry.[146] And if teachers feel like they can't achieve the moral rewards they were hoping for, they can become demoralized.[147]

In addition to the concerns about disrespect from higher-ups, teachers care a great deal about the other teachers in their school.[148] We've seen that successful schools will have a sense of mutual obligation among professionals, and teachers will have the opportunity to convene to work on common issues.[149] Teachers need protected time to collaborate, which improves their practice.[150] When teachers feel empowered, that can create a positive impact on learners.[151]

But when there isn't cooperation among teachers, schools can end up as essentially a free-for-all work environment in which all of the adults are out for themselves.[152] It's hard for teachers to maintain their ideals if nobody else around them is doing so.[153] So having a critical mass of engaged teachers is key.[154]

Teachers do not like to lose their autonomy.[155] But there is a tension between autonomy and responsibility—which is to say, sometimes "autonomy" can be code for "you have to do everything yourself."[156] In some cases, teachers would rather have less responsibility and less work.[157]

Whatever level of autonomy teachers have, successful schools know that teaching is not just an individual trait, it's a cultivated skill.[158] Successful teacher professional development is job-embedded and content-specific.[159] It's also systemic, with ongoing collaboration and continued cycles of inquiry to support improvement.[160]

But it is widely agreed that most professional development is terrible.[161] Much of it is in short workshops that don't really influence practice.[162] It's frequently disconnected from the actual curricular materials teachers are using.[163]

And this area of practice has resisted reform for many years. Despite years of lip service to the importance of professional development, performance remains weak.[164] This is in large part because actually doing a good job would require changing existing systems and building greater capacity, which is hard.[165]

CONCLUSION

The challenges facing the teaching profession fall most heavily on the schools serving the lowest-income students. To some degree, this isn't a problem of the teaching profession, per se; those students from families with low incomes are the ones most likely to need extra support, which can change the nature of the teacher's role. To account for that more difficult role, the teachers working with students from families with low incomes should be paid more. But in fact, the opposite is usually true—they're usually paid less. In the coming chapters, we'll look at why that is.

Chapter 5

Why Districts Don't Put Their Best Teachers with Low-Income Students

While teacher salaries are the main expense for districts, just increasing the amount of money districts have by no means guarantees that they will then hire great teachers. Moreover, in larger districts, the methods of assigning teachers often lead to the best-paid and most senior teachers working with the students from the highest-income families. While there isn't a perfect correlation among teacher salary, teacher seniority, and teacher effectiveness, district systems often make it very hard to recruit and retain good teachers in schools serving primarily children from low-income families.

This chapter looks at those systems, and how they limit the talent pool for some of the highest-impact teaching jobs. It starts by looking at why school districts have formal salary schedules. It then looks at the key drivers of increased pay within those schedules—and at failed attempts to change those drivers, which offer lessons for any future attempts at changing teacher pay. It concludes by looking at how early childhood education is funded, and why early childhood teachers are so underpaid.

WHY TEACHER PAY IS SO RIGIDLY STRUCTURED

In the 19th Century schooling didn't look much like it does today. Society was far more rural, and school attendance was voluntary.[1] When the 20th Century dawned children attended school for approximately five years, almost entirely in elementary school.[2] High school was still reserved primarily for bright children whose parents didn't need them to work.[3]

In the late 1800s women were seen as desirable for teaching jobs in part because they didn't have any power, so they would be easier to manage.[4] At the time there were not a lot of other opportunities for women to work outside the home.[5] As of 1870 most teachers in most states were women.[6] By the time the Constitution was amended to guarantee women the right to vote in 1920,[7] women represented approximately 86% of the teaching force.[8]

Lower pay was part of the deal, and female teachers got paid much less than male teachers.[9] The basic model was that men would be in charge, make the decisions, and be paid higher salaries; women would do the front-end labor, cheaply.[10] This had appeal to men who didn't want to pay a lot in taxes to support public schools, as it kept school spending relatively low.[11]

The early 20th century saw a growing education bureaucracy, with larger administrations managing in an increasingly urban society.[12] In cities there were sometimes ongoing battles between the elite of the education profession—who thought they should be able to control the system—and the elected leaders who had historically run the schools, often as a patronage operation.[13] It was easy for teachers to get caught in the middle.[14] When the education elites won and took power, teachers could find themselves resisting the dictates of autocratic superintendents.[15]

Pushes by women for equal pay go back to at least the early twentieth century.[16] It was around the same time that teachers started organizing in earnest.[17] The National Education Association (NEA) was founded in 1857, but was a decorous enterprise that also included administrators and college faculty.[18] When the NEA was founded, women were not allowed to hold positions of authority within the organization, although women fought fiercely for the opportunity.[19]

In contrast, the forming of the Chicago Teachers Federation was driven by women.[20] In 1897 the Chicago Teachers Federation presented a new, more militant face, fighting ferociously for more money and greater independence.[21] The American Federation of Teachers (AFT) emerged in 1916, with the Chicago teachers joining forces with others around the country under the umbrella of the American Federation of Labor.[22]

Up until about 1960, union power was relatively limited. Government unions didn't strike or even bargain collectively, which constrained their influence.[23] Elementary and high school teachers also remained somewhat divided; high school teachers were more likely to be male and generally got paid more, but elementary school teachers wanted in on that.[24] Collectively it was a recipe for inaction, until a 1962 teachers' strike in New York City set the union movement on a new course.[25]

Before the 1960s both national teacher unions had no-strike policies in place.[26] Part of the rationale was that striking was not seen as the kind of thing white-collar professionals would do.[27] But Albert Shanker of the AFT local in New York argued that white-collar professionals wouldn't accept being pushed around by administrators while getting underpaid.[28] Even though strikes were illegal, Shanker and the New York union pushed for a strike as a form of civil disobedience.[29]

It worked. Teacher unions gained members rapidly through the 1960s, with a concomitant rise in power.[30] And in the 1960s and 1970s they solidified their position by fighting for the adoption of public policies that entrenched their power.[31] In many states, they fought successfully for laws requiring teachers to join unions,[32] although in 2018 the Supreme Court ruled that such laws were unconstitutional.[33]

Because unions don't trust the decision-making of administrations, they push for key decisions in districts to be made on objective criteria.[34] There's good reason for that, as there is a history of arbitrary judgments or favoritism in teacher pay.[35] Especially considering the scale of school districts at this point, there are good arguments for having some kind of formal framework for teacher salaries. Teachers have consistently resisted subjective pay schemes,[36] and it is unlikely that opposition will be dropped in the foreseeable future.

THE KEY DRIVERS OF TEACHER COMPENSATION

Objective Criteria That Get Used: Seniority and Credentials

Once you have formal frameworks, you need objective criteria to drive those frameworks. And seniority has always been a convenient one.[37] It is certainly objective, and over time, it becomes self-reinforcing; when seniority has been the driving criterion for so long, changing midstream would feel like an injustice to the people who've achieved high levels of seniority (or are on the cusp of doing so). This is particularly true in a field where defined-benefit pensions are also an important component of overall salary.[38]

So seniority is a major driver of teacher pay.[39] In districts with multiple schools, it can also be the driving factor in teacher assignment.[40] And when districts are laying teachers off, seniority is frequently the driving criterion.[41] This means that when districts have to cut back, the teachers who are most likely to remain on payroll are the most expensive teachers. During the pandemic this also meant significant layoffs for teachers of color.[42]

When there is salary inequality within districts, it is largely driven by age and education.[43] This makes sense given that in most states and communities increases in pay for teachers come from two factors: increases in seniority and the acquisition of new educational credentials.[44] But neither of these drivers are particularly predictive of teacher effectiveness.

Seniority can make a difference in teacher quality, particularly in the first few years of teaching.[45] But it's not possible to say categorically that twenty-year veterans are better than fifth-year teachers. Nonetheless, in most districts that twenty-year veteran will be paid more than the fifth-year teacher as a matter of contractual principle. The disparity between younger teachers and older teachers is exacerbated by the fact that teachers receive defined-benefit pensions.[46]

Teaching has a much flatter pay curve than other professions, meaning that it takes far longer for teachers to reach their peak earnings.[47] Paying younger teachers more and changing the curve over time could have a positive impact on teacher retention.[48] Overall, our approach to teacher pay ends up back-loading teacher pay and influence.[49] This creates a situation in which senior teachers are extremely powerful and may have interests different from those of younger teachers.[50]

The fact that teacher pay is backloaded also creates specific incentives for districts, who can use seniority pay as a way to push expenses into the future; they can agree to contracts with teachers knowing that the bill won't really come due until some new set of board members or new superintendent has taken over. This ability to kick the can down the road can be politically appealing for local board members who don't want to make hard choices.

The problem with misaligned incentives is arguably worse when it comes to educational attainment. Many salary schedules give teachers credit for earning masters degrees or other post-baccalaureate credentials.[51] The research on the impact of master's degrees on teaching quality is withering; there are a few areas where they may make a difference, but mostly they don't.[52]

But this is a hard requirement to get rid of once people start investing money in obtaining master's degrees. Nationally districts are spending billions of dollars a year on this incentive;[53] the teachers receiving it are going to fight to preserve that (as are the education schools receiving the tuition dollars). Systemically, this is a form of sunk-cost fallacy:[54] the fact that we've wasted a lot of money on this incentive in the past is causing us to keep wasting money on it in the future.

Objective Criteria That Sparked Resistance: Attempted Teacher Pay Reforms in the NCLB–ESSA Era

Resistance to performance pay runs throughout the public sector.[55] That hasn't stopped policymakers and district leaders from trying to implement it, even though to date success has been limited.[56] Critics of teacher pay structures have noted, correctly, that there is essentially no connection between how good a teacher is and how much that teacher gets paid. Indeed, neither of the current drivers on salary schedules create pressure on teachers to improve at their craft.

But it's hard to pay teachers for excellence when there isn't real agreement about what excellence looks like.[57] For a performance pay approach to work, there has to be some driver that's agreed upon as the differentiator of teacher pay. Value-added measures that tracked growth on test scores were one measure that got a lot of focus, but didn't hold up as a metric worthy of serving as a driver of teacher pay.[58] As a conceptual matter, it seems possible that a performance pay scheme could be developed that has a positive impact on the profession; as a practical matter, we haven't gotten there and don't seem all that close.

Some arguments against merit pay are based on principle. As the argument goes, merit pay is based on the assumption that if teachers were paid more, they would become more effective teachers.[59] But according to this argument, teachers have deep intrinsic motivation, and merit pay is an extrinsic motivator.[60] Thus, it's not clear that bonuses or other forms of merit pay will actually improve performance.[61]

The second point is almost certainly true. But it's not clear that merit pay is based on the assumption that higher pay would improve teacher effectiveness. In fact, one key argument for merit pay is that it would make the teaching profession more appealing to motivated candidates.[62] A pay system that is flat and not based on performance attracts a different kind of candidate than a system that rewards people for demonstrating their skill.

HOW TEACHER PAY POSITIONS THE FIELD AGAINST COMPETITORS

Of course, even a really good merit pay system—which we don't yet have and might never—just reallocates dollars within an existing pie, but doesn't entirely reposition teaching within the larger job market. Teaching is not alone in that its appeal as a profession is tied to the larger economy.[63] In the 2010s the economy steadily grew[64]—and enrollment in teacher preparation programs declined dramatically.[65]

Advocates for teachers have argued that low pay is a factor in teacher shortages.[66] But one problem with this argument is that there isn't really an overall shortage of teachers; there's a shortage of teachers in some critical areas.[67] Like all professions, teaching operates in a competitive market for talent. But by establishing pay structures that are largely disconnected from market forces, teaching puts itself at a competitive disadvantage.

If teacher salary schedules are based on seniority and education level, then they aren't being based on the specific role a teacher plays within the district. And not all roles are created equally in the marketplace. It is possible for public employee salaries to reflect the competitive pool for talent;

there's a reason that in many states the highest paid public employee is a football coach,[68] and it's that the market for college football coaches pays a lot better than the market for most public roles. But teacher pay has not been structured that way.

What this means is that there are persistent shortages in certain kinds of jobs. There are very few schools that have a hard time hiring general elementary school teachers.[69] But by comparison, there are a lot of schools that have a hard time hiring special education, math, and science teachers.[70] In other fields, a shortage in some areas but not others could lead to differentiation in pay among specialties.[71] That hasn't happened in teaching.

There are valid reasons that pay hasn't been differentiated among different subject areas. For one thing, paying more for math and science teachers would appear to fly directly in the face of a long-standing fight for gender equity. Math and science are two subject areas with a much higher percentage of male teachers than the field as a whole.[72] That raises a fundamental tension. One of the longest-standing discontents within the profession is that female teachers of younger students have been paid less than the male teachers of older students.[73]

Rural areas may have special challenges in recruitment. In major metropolitan areas it's common for teachers to live in one district and work in another. But because of their distance from urban centers, teaching in rural schools requires living in rural areas.[74] That, along with low salaries, can make it hard to fill rural teaching jobs.[75] For many candidates even higher salaries wouldn't be enough to get them to move to (or stay in) rural areas, which is likely to continue to be a problem in an increasingly urbanized society.

Another potential issue is that districts may not have recruiting mechanisms in place to address shortage areas.[76] If a district is getting plenty of applications for elementary school jobs, it may not realize that it needs a totally different approach to hire other kinds of teachers.[77] This may be particularly true when subject area shortages are combined with schools that have been hard to staff, which we will discuss further in the next chapter.

The fact that the same shortage areas have persisted for years speaks to a fundamental failure of the teacher market. To date, that failure has not been enough to inspire serious action to change teacher pay to address shortage areas. Moreover, when districts have additional resources, they often focus on hiring more teachers rather than paying their current teachers more.[78] Spreading their resources thinly reduces their ability to pay more for the spots that are genuinely hard to fill.

CONCLUSION

There are good reasons that school districts pay teachers through formal structures with objective criteria. There are also good reasons that seniority and master's degrees became the dominant objective criteria—and that test scores didn't replace them. But having those factors as the key drivers of teacher pay and assignments has meant that which teachers get paid the most might bear no relationship to the teaching roles that are most important for the district. In the next chapter, we will look at how teacher pay might be reoriented to reflect the value districts place—or should place—sustaining high-performing schools in communities with limited resources.

Chapter 6

Restructuring Teacher Pay to Help the Children Who Need It Most

In Part I, we saw that there are two major problems that need to be addressed to improve student outcomes. One is getting students off to a better start, because so many kids—particularly Black and Brown kids—have fallen far behind by third grade. Another is to improve student growth for those children who are behind. If we're really serious about those problems, we need an approach to teacher pay that will encourage excellent teachers to take them on. But in our current system, the financial incentive is to teach high school students from wealthy families who are already thriving academically.

As we've seen, there are valid reasons why teacher pay practices have evolved the way they have. Attempts to change those practices have to reckon with the underlying forces that created the current system and that remain in place today. And in doing so, it's important to focus on what's most important: improving the ecosystem of the least successful schools—the ones where performance is low and students aren't achieving growth.

Right now, there are too many schools where external policies have created an internal culture with inadequate stability and support. Teacher placement policy surely is far from the only factor at work in creating those conditions. But it is one of them. And it suffers from a fundamental flaw: a pay system based on personal characteristics, rather than role. This chapter looks at the current market for teacher hiring, and how a change in approach to salaries might change that market.

WHERE TEACHERS CURRENTLY WANT TO TEACH

As we've seen, teachers with seniority generally get priority in where they choose to work. And—reflecting a natural human tendency—they tend to gravitate toward the easiest schools to work at.[1] Teachers prefer to teach high-achieving children from wealthier families, and are more likely to leave schools where they can't do that.[2]

It's understandable that this would be the case. As we've seen, schools serving children from low-income families are more likely to have higher rates of confrontation between students and teachers, which makes for difficult working conditions.[3] They may also be subject to harsher evaluations.[4] Overall, the conditions in these schools may be less favorable, for a whole host of reasons.[5]

These conditions contribute to the fact that schools serving children from low-income families have higher rates of teacher turnover, which itself contributes to an undesirable school climate.[6] When teachers leave, these schools have a harder time filling vacancies.[7] They then end up with teachers who have lower qualifications than those in low-poverty schools.[8] Those teachers are more likely to be novices, who, in general, are less effective.[9]

These patterns lead to substantial inequities within districts.[10] The highest-paid teachers are in schools that serve the fewest disadvantaged students.[11] When senior teachers avoid high-poverty schools, those schools end up spending less money on a per-child basis.[12] That disparity is driven by teacher preferences and signed off on by local officials.[13]

It's worth a reminder here that there are schools serving students from families with low incomes that are producing strong levels of student growth, as we discussed. In some of these schools, there are many talented teachers who are doing their best to serve a noble cause.[14] For many low-income schools, the biggest change that's needed is to increase kindergarten readiness—and any lack of kindergarten readiness surely cannot be blamed on the school's faculty. Context is not destiny, and it's important not to paint with too broad a brush.

It's also clear, however, that there are too many schools serving students from families with low incomes where a cocktail of bad working conditions and low pay have made it impossible to attract and retain the best teachers. If the pay improved in these schools, it doesn't guarantee that working conditions would follow. But it's a place to start.

HOW CAN WE MAKE SCHOOLS SERVING LOW-INCOME KIDS MORE ATTRACTIVE TO TEACHERS?

Preserving the Salary Schedule

Teachers in schools serving children from low-income families should be paid more, and the question is exactly how that should happen. One limitation

Part II assumes is that whatever pay scheme districts use to attract teachers to these schools will be part of a salary schedule. While teachers might be willing to populate a salary schedule with criteria other than the ones currently in use—seniority and additional credentials—they're unlikely to abandon the salary schedule altogether.[15]

This is particularly true given that we've now had several generations of administrators who have never been trained to exercise discretion in setting salaries. While more creative proposals for teacher pay are surely welcomed and potentially valuable, it's unlikely that district management systems currently have the capacity to implement them well.

So that means the exercise is to find some drivers that could be used on a salary schedule to better effect than the two we have now. Some teachers may never open their minds to that possibility. But if any were to do so, it is likely that the new drivers of salary would have to include at least some of the positive aspects of the existing drivers: they would have to be objective, transparent, and reasonably accessible to all teachers.

The history of teacher unionism led to a focus on equality within the profession, primarily because male teachers of older students were being paid more than female teachers of younger students.[16] So there is pressure to treat all teaching jobs within a given school district as effectively the same.

When that is the starting premise, how much the district spends on a particular role is dependent on who gets that job, not on how much that role means to the enterprise. This means that school systems have ended up with their most expensive employees in the least important roles—a terrible misallocation of resources. Salary schedules need to stop facilitating that misallocation and start correcting it.

A Salary Schedule Based on Roles

Teachers should be able to choose the schools where they want to work. But districts should have the ability to define why a teacher might want to work in a school. How teachers get paid sends a strong signal about what school districts prioritize.[17] So districts and states should allocate resources to the schools serving the lowest-income students—and/or the schools that need the most help—as a sign that those are the schools that they focus on improving.[18]

Districts and states should allocate funds to schools by formula, weighted for student needs.[19] We know that attracting and retaining teachers in tough environments requires paying them more.[20] We also know that addressing the needs of the lowest-performing schools will require a package of investments that goes beyond teacher salaries, to include other supports.[21] So districts should start their budgeting process by allocating the most money to the schools with the greatest need. Teachers could then choose where they want to work, knowing that the salaries will be higher in the schools where student incomes are lowest.

The Every Student Succeeds Act (ESSA) should actually be forcing conversations about how districts allocate their resources among schools. The ESSA requires districts to report expenditures on a per-school basis.[22] States have not yet fully implemented that provision.[23] But when fully implemented, this requirement should instigate discussions at a local level about how money is allocated among schools[24]—and should provide an entry point to the conversations needed to change teacher pay, at least in districts with multiple schools.

While many districts do not offer incentives to teach in high-needs schools, there are examples of districts that have used incentives to good effect.[25] Charlotte-Mecklenburg schools had a Strategic Staffing Initiative that included financial incentives for teachers.[26] In Long Beach, California, data has been used to match the most expert teachers with the students who have the greatest needs.[27] In 2019 Texas adopted a new incentive structure designed to retain teachers in high-needs schools.[28]

So it's not entirely implausible to think that teachers might be willing to accept a pay structure that prioritizes high-needs schools: a 2018 survey of teachers showed that a whopping 89 percent of teachers favor incentives to teach in hard-to-staff schools.[29] A survey of teachers in low-performing schools indicated that salary was one of the most important factors impacting whether or not they would want to stay in that school.[30]

It's also the case that salary schedules based on role might find traction more quickly in districts that are not unionized. States without mandatory collective bargaining have seen higher premium pay for teachers in high-needs subjects or schools, and lower premiums for master's degrees.[31] Districts that are not required to collectively bargain might be early adopters of new pay systems, and then unionized districts could learn from their experience.

Of course, there are many factors districts will have to take into account in restructuring their pay. As we will see in the next chapter, districts will also have to compete with each other—and state funding policy will impact their ability to do so. Within larger districts there's an ever-present tension between the desire of communities to choose their teachers, and the desire of teachers to choose their schools.[32] That also speaks to the question of what impact a change like this would have on parents, and that's a subject we'll talk about more in Part III.

For now, the bottom line is that it's appropriate for districts to want to make particular schools a more attractive place for teachers to want to work, but actually making those schools more attractive will come at some cost.

Subject Shortage Areas

Having looked at the possibility of salary schedules that prioritize the role of teaching in high-needs schools, it's also worth revisiting the issue of subject shortage areas that we touched on earlier. As we noted, there are certain subject matters that have historically experienced teacher shortages[33]—but providing incentive pay in those subject areas might disproportionately favor male teachers, which creates a political challenge.

Some districts do offer incentives for teachers to teach subject areas in which there's a shortage.[34] And teacher preparation programs are starting to produce comparatively more teachers in shortage areas.[35] If districts are changing to a system of pay based on roles—as they should—then including some resources to address shortage areas makes sense. They will also need to allow time for the transition, as teachers may need new training to be successful in new roles—and potentially to fulfill licensing requirements.

When commodities are scarce, it is normal to have to pay more for them. Teachers in certain subject areas are a comparatively rare commodity, so it makes sense to pay them more money. If over time the shortages are eliminated, then pay scales should be adjusted to account for that. But as long as there are subject area shortages, differential pay should be a core strategy for addressing them.[36]

In doing so districts should also pay close attention to the demographics of their teachers and ensure that differential pay is reinforcing rather than undermining the efforts to diversify the teaching workforce. How districts address subject shortage areas should also be integrated with their approach to addressing schools serving students from families with low incomes.

In identifying shortages, districts should not ignore early childhood education. They may not think of themselves as having a shortage of early childhood teachers, because they may not see paying for early childhood services as their job.[37] But many districts have a shortage of children who come into kindergarten having gotten the support they needed to be successful in the birth to five years. That shortage needs to be front and center in discussions of teacher pay.

HELPING TEACHERS THROUGH A TRANSITION IN PAY SYSTEMS

The Choppy Waters of Transition

Psychologists talk about an "endowment effect," in which people become attached to things or benefits that they already possess.[38] Teachers have gotten used to the world in which they could eventually choose to have high salaries for working with kids from wealthier families. Many teachers will not give that up easily.

Given that the allocation for schools serving high-income students would go way down under this plan, you'd now have the highest-paid and most senior teachers facing a choice: either go to a school serving mostly low-income kids, or take a potentially substantial pay cut. That is not a choice most senior teachers ever thought they would have to make, and it's likely that many of them will resist it vehemently. As we've seen, these teachers have disproportionate sway within teacher unions. And if one goal is for districts to build trust with unions (an issue discussed later in this chapter), taking a meat ax to the salaries of veteran teachers is not a good way to do that.

There is an obvious way out: just keep paying them. A district could create a "hold harmless" for some transitional period, which would reallocate some dollars to prioritized schools while attempting to minimize the negative impact on senior teachers. But that's really expensive, and not all districts will have the financial wherewithal to do that. If the federal government, a state, or a powerful philanthropy wanted to incentivize a changeover in spending, it could potentially provide one-time money to cover hold harmless costs through a transition, if a district committed to maintaining the revamped system for a period of years.

That may not be the only way to accomplish a change like this. Some districts might have the leverage to impose the system more or less unilaterally and just accept that some senior teachers will leave. Some unions might see it as an equity-focused forward-thinking change. And in some cases, a shift like this might be packaged with buyouts for senior teachers who were on the cusp of retiring anyway. Local situations will vary. But there's no question that a change like this could be very difficult even where districts want to do it.

If districts develop salary schedules based on role, they will still need some mechanism for allowing teachers to sort themselves into schools. Those mechanisms could well be based on seniority and/or incumbency.

There are definitely teachers who are most likely to thrive in settings that do not involve working with children from low-income families, and those teachers should have the chance to contribute in schools where their talents will be most useful.[39] And the pool of teachers who can thrive in schools serving primarily students from high-income families with few disciplinary problems is likely deeper than the pool of teachers who can thrive in schools with more challenging conditions. So while the redistribution could end up harming more affluent schools, that won't necessarily be the case.

To maximize the impact of a changeover, the prioritization of schools serving students from families with low incomes should go beyond salary—it should also include layoff prioritization. Part of why turnover is high at low-income schools is that when layoffs occur, they disproportionately impact junior teachers. The students facing the most turmoil outside of school should have the most stability within it. So to reduce teacher turnover in these schools, layoff prioritization should also be based on role, rather than on seniority.

Districts in states without mandatory collective bargaining have already started eliminating "last in, first out" layoffs. While seniority is the sole or preponderant criterion in 80 percent of districts in states with mandatory collective bargaining, in states with permissive collective bargaining the percentage is 34 percent—and in states where collective bargaining is prohibited it's 13 percent.[40] The most significant factor used in those districts other than seniority is performance rating.[41]

How Unions Might Approach Proposed Changes

A proposal like this would potentially put unions in a tricky position. The voices that have historically been most powerful within unions—senior teachers—are potentially the ones most adversely impacted by this change. While some of those senior teachers might support it as a progressive change, that can't be the expectation.

But a focus on higher pay in the highest-needs schools has significant racial equity implications. As we've seen, the teaching field is disproportionately white—and students from families with low incomes are disproportionately Black and Brown. We've also seen that there is benefit to matching students with teachers who have the same background they do. Some states, cities, and districts are undertaking efforts to diversify the teaching field.[42] This change in how teachers are paid at the local level could complement larger efforts to recruit teachers of color.

So unions would have to figure out how they want to handle a situation like this one. Unions frequently argue that the interests of teachers and the interests of students are aligned.[43] That's often true, but it may not be here. What's best for the lowest-income students is to have a fair shot at getting the district's best teachers into their schools. Right now they don't have that, and the reallocation of resources within a district will require upending some long-held union norms.

Moreover, unions have frequently—and correctly—argued that out-of-school factors play a major role in student outcomes. In this case, though, union-negotiated policies end up creating in-school factors that accelerate the negative impact of out-of-school factors facing students from families with low incomes. Union leaders will face countervailing pressures: the pressure to take care of their most senior members and the pressure to support the schools that need it most—and the subset of union teachers who work in those schools. For years union leaders have in effect chosen the former, and while it seems plausible that they might switch to the latter, it still would be very challenging.

The context for these swirling pressures is a new one for union leaders, given a recent change in labor law. Prior to 2018 a union certified to represent a unit of public employees could require "agency fees" from members of that unit, even if that individual did not choose to join the union. The agency fees generally reflected the services the unions performed on the unit's behalf.

As noted before, that's no longer legal. In 2018 the Supreme Court of the United States ruled in the case of *Janus v. American Federation of State, County, and Municipal Employees, Council 31* that unions cannot compel agency fees, meaning that employees who do not want to support the union no longer have to.[44] While some states had already gotten rid of mandatory agency fees, for many teacher unions *Janus* threatens a major source of revenue.

But *Janus* hasn't led to the collapse of unions, because the work unions do is still important to teachers.[45] Teachers strongly value the role unions play, particularly at the local level.[46] Some politicians try to separate union members from union "bosses," but those union leaders are bound together with their members—who by and large are very supportive of their local union leaders.[47]

The fact that teacher union membership is now purely voluntary may also turn out to be a new opportunity. To retain members, teacher unions now have to be responsive to their members. Dialing back the excessive focus on seniority may be one way to be more responsive to members.[48] Yes, seniority matters and older teachers need to be protected.[49] But if unions struggle to make their case to younger members, that may force them to adjust.

How Management Should Approach Proposed Changes with Unions

For all their resources, it can be easy for teacher unions to fall into a scarcity mindset.[50] They don't trust policymakers and managers, and so they behave as if they are under constant threat. Like most organizations, they fear loss more than they want gain;[51] this can keep them in a defensive and oppositional posture.[52]

So in many ways the future of teacher pay be shaped by how politicians and management treat the teachers involved. Teacher union militancy is responsive. When unions feel attacked, they organize and push back—which is exactly what most human beings would do. The fiercest unions are generally the ones trapped in a vicious cycle with unyielding managers. Breaking that cycle and creating mutual trust are hard but important—and will require strong management buy-in. That may not happen much, but it does happen.[53]

Where trust is lacking, agreement can be difficult.[54] If union members don't trust management, any agreement with management may be attacked as a sellout.[55] If union members have been conditioned to expect war, it will take real work to acculturate them to anything else—and that work is risky for union leaders. If union membership wants confrontation, union leaders who don't provide it are likely to be replaced by new leaders who will.

Even the unions that are most powerful today are built on a foundation of defensiveness—they often think of themselves as prey animals, not predators. After *Janus*, management may have more leverage than it's ever had before. How it uses that leverage will play a critical role in shaping the evolution of teacher unionism in the years ahead. Union critics are probably right that unions aren't going to change their behaviors on their own.[56] But that's because they didn't develop those behaviors on their own, either.

Over time, union leaders have been conditioned to not trust management, and both management and unions now have the opportunity to renew themselves.[57] That renewal may not seem particularly likely; unions are large and complex organizations that can struggle to shift positions.[58] But if we're trying to improve teacher quality—and develop schools that operate more effectively—it is directionally essential. An evolution in teacher pay is a challenging but promising opportunity to attempt that renewal.

CONCLUSION

Teacher quality is a critical driver of student outcomes, and right now teacher placement policies contribute to major inequities in our education system.[59] The process of placing teachers in schools is a matching process—and we're doing the matching the wrong way. Districts have negotiated away their ability to define the value proposition of critical teaching roles, and they need to reclaim that ability. Once they have that ability, they should support teacher choice. But the constraints on teacher choice need to be different than they are now.

Districts should start to deal with the market issues caused by the misalignment of constraints on teacher choice. Some roles within the district are more attractive than others. So if pay scales don't allow the district to counterbalance the attractiveness of the role, certain roles will remain the hardest to fill. As it happens, those roles tend to be the ones we said at the beginning of the book would be the top priority: the roles of working with the children who need the most help.

And that's a values issue that overlays the market issue. What's needed is a market-based approach to teacher pay that places an appropriate value on the school ecosystems surrounding children from low-income families, who are disproportionately Black and Brown. If the biggest problem we're trying to solve is inequity in outcomes, we have to address inequity in conditions.

That requires committing to spending money on the entire ecosystem of schools serving children from low-income families, including teacher pay and overall staffing (such as social workers and nurses or extracurriculars). Rewarding teachers with seniority is a legitimate value, but it's not a higher value than that.[60]

Redistributing funds among teachers will not come easily, if it happens at all. The systems currently in place took years to establish, and senior teachers have a legitimate interest in preserving their place within the hierarchy. Districts should approach this work with a spirit of humility and partnership. In some places teachers may be willing to try something new; if those places can be successful, others can follow suit.

These last two chapters have focused on the systems within districts for paying and assigning teachers. But every year thousands of teachers change jobs across districts. The systems within districts matter to teacher assignment—but so do the resource levels of districts competing against each other talent. In the next chapter we'll look at how those resource levels vary.

Chapter 7

How State and Federal Policy Shapes the Market for Teachers

In some states teacher pay is determined by a statewide salary schedule.[1] In most states, though, teacher pay is set locally. This means that teacher salary can be a point of competition among districts. And indeed, geography is a major driver of difference in teacher pay.[2]

Because teacher pay is generally the primary expenditure for individual districts, there is a strong relationship between funding equity among districts and teacher pay.[3] Which is to say that in states that shortchange the districts that serve primarily students from families with low incomes, those districts end up paying their teachers less than the teachers in districts serving richer kids.

If you're trying to help the children who need it most, it will be hard for communities serving primarily children from low-income families to compete with the privileged communities that use local resources to attract great teachers with high salaries.[4] That gap is caused largely by state approaches to school finance. This chapter looks at how state and federal funding influences the ability of school districts to compete for talent—and at the limitations the early childhood sector faces in attracting good teachers.

HOW STATES DISTRIBUTE FUNDS TO SCHOOL DISTRICTS

In the days leading up to May 18, 2005, there was a buzz around the Illinois State Capitol. For years, Illinois' school funding formula had been one of the least equitable in the United States. The state provided comparatively little education funding, leaving locals to pick up the rest of the burden. That burden fell disproportionately on the lowest-income communities, creating huge inequity within the system. Now, it seemed, there was momentum to make a change, with energy growing behind legislation that would increase state funding for schools while providing a property tax offset.

The bill required hiking state income taxes, but proponents had been claiming publicly that it wouldn't raise taxes on the lowest-income Illinoisans. The governor was very clear that he planned to veto it; he had vowed not to sign any bill that raised taxes in any way. But Democratic leaders in the Senate thought they could put together a veto-proof majority, and then carry momentum into the House. On May 18 they were planning a huge rally at the Capitol, with then-Chicago school CEO Arne Duncan making a rare appearance in Springfield.

The proposed legislation was entirely defensible as public policy; it really did increase spending for low-resource districts, and shift more of the burden onto the state. The property tax rates in low-income communities were astronomical. Given that Illinois school funding was at the time among the most inequitable in the country, the merits of the bill were genuine.

The problem was that the public relations campaign surrounding the tax consequences of the bill bore no resemblance to what the bill itself actually did. The bill's proponents had talked a lot about how the legislation would tax the rich and spare the poor, but that wasn't accurate. By shifting the tax burden away from property taxes toward income taxes, it would in fact reduce the tax bill for many Illinoisans—but that depended on the ratio of their income to their property wealth, not the raw amount in either category. Some rich people would come out ahead, others behind—and the same would be true for low-income families.

While the governor was opposed to the bill, he wanted to maintain a friendly relationship with its Senate sponsors. In early May, he dispatched his education staffer to meet with them and tell them they had a problem: the bill they were pushing didn't do what they said it did. The senators were walked through the findings; they were then urged to consider some amendments to make the substance of the bill line up with its public relations campaign, or to consider changing their messaging to line up with what the bill actually did. They expressed appreciation for the outreach, but didn't make any changes.

Meanwhile, Diane Rado—the dogged and thorough education reporter for the Chicago *Tribune*—was interested in data on the effect of the bill. She and the *Tribune* constructed a tool that allowed readers to put in some rough information about their income and property taxes—and then get a calculation of how this legislation would impact their tax bill. And on the morning of May 18, 2005, the front-page story in the *Tribune* described how this legislation would actually impact Illinois taxes.[5]

The rally went on as planned—but after the *Tribune* story, the bill was dead, and everybody knew it. Legislators were skittish about the idea of voting for a major tax increase whose consequences they didn't fully understand, especially when just hours ago they'd thought they did understand them. Arne Duncan and Chicago School Board President Michael Scott came to Springfield and met with the governor and Chicago legislators, and the room was very much against them.[6] It wouldn't be until 2017 that Illinois actually passed school funding reform.[7]

The politics of school funding at the state level are brutal, and there are a few basic problems that pop up in multiple states: funding is inequitable, it irresponsibly pushes expenses into the future, and it shortchanges the early childhood investments that would have the greatest impact. Let's examine each of those in turn.

Funding Formulas Shortchange the School Districts Serving the Most Low-Income Students

One of the distinguishing features of education is that more than any other social good, it is funded at the local level.[8] This is one of the major reasons that inequitable funding is so complicated to address. Each community is expected to fund its own schools, and then the state layers funding over the top of that—with a small dose of federal funding included. Most local education funding comes from property taxes, whereas state education revenue comes primarily from income and sales taxes.[9] All told, about 47 percent of school funding comes from states, 45 percent from communities, and 8 percent from the federal government.[10]

Because property can't move, property taxes have long been seen as a logical tax base for local governments.[11] School districts are the single largest consumer of property tax revenue in the United States.[12] In the 1970s taxpayers rebelled against what they perceived as high property taxes, leading to many state law limitations on how much property tax revenue communities could raise.[13] Some of these constraints continue to operate on school districts.

It is harder for low-income school districts to raise money, and they generally have less of it.[14] The dependence of school funding on property taxes means that low-income communities will have higher property tax rates than high-income communities—which is a disincentive for businesses to locate there.[15] Moreover, discrimination in assessments of property value can lead to communities of color paying more for the same services.[16]

So wealthier communities can raise more money with less effort than lower-wealth communities.[17] State funding formulas generally seek to offset local inequities, at least to some degree.[18] But there is wide variation on how state funding impacts local resource levels.[19] Some states have done a very good job of ensuring that the districts serving the lowest-income students have adequate resources; others have not.[20] These formulas also can be quite complicated, making them hard for legislators to understand.[21]

Given our focus on helping students in low-resource communities, these funding formulas are incredibly important. There are intra-district spending disparities—and we'll talk more about those—but inter-district disparities are a bigger deal.[22] In most states there is substantial inequity between low-income and high-income districts, with state funding formulas not potent enough to overcome those disparities—or making them worse.[23] In many instances, there are substantial disparities among neighboring districts.[24]

Formulas are generally based on student enrollment—with one important exception we'll discuss in a minute—and are often weighted to account for the fact that some students are more expensive to educate.[25] Importantly, how equitable a formula is and how much money states put into it are both meaningful; even a well-designed formula will not provide adequate support if states don't fund it adequately.[26] So in general, reductions in state education funding will hurt low-income districts the most.[27]

The major exception to using enrollment in funding formulas is the "hold harmless." A "hold harmless" basically says that if in the course of a year a district loses enrollment such that the state's funding distribution mechanism would normally warrant cutting its allocation, the state won't actually reduce its funding—it will provide a "hold harmless" for the district.[28]

Of course, while the district losing enrollment is held harmless, some other district that's gaining enrollment is being harmed—because money that could otherwise be sent its way is instead being redirected to pay for students who are no longer there.[29] But politicians are nervous about getting attacked by school districts whose budgets have been cut, and so hold harmlesses persist.

When state legislatures are considering potential changes in funding formulas, the path to a majority in both chambers looks something like this.

- First, there's the question of how to redistribute the pie. Legislative districts where the schools come out ahead are at least good prospects to vote yes. Legislative districts where the schools come out behind are probable no's. There are occasionally legislators who will vote against their legislative district's narrow self-interest for the good of the state. But there aren't that many of those legislators, which is why hold harmless provisions are sometimes used to increase the number of legislative districts where the schools come out at least even.
- Then there's the question of how big the pie is. Obviously, it's much easier to create legislative districts that have increased funding for schools if there's more money total—which means more tax revenue. And as we've noted, if you're trying to help the lowest-wealth districts more state money can help. But raising more revenue usually means raising tax rates, and if you're doing that, then all of a sudden there's

potentially a sizable chunk of the legislature that will vote against the bill on that basis alone.

- Then there's the question of whether anyone actually trusts the numbers. Simple bills with a clear appeal to the legislators' core constituencies are easy; complicated bills of uncertain impact are hard. Will school funding really increase in the legislator's district? What will the tax impact actually be? How will the taxing and spending evolve over time, given population trends and projections for the state economy? It can be very hard to take the leap of faith on a bill with so many hard-to-predict variables.
- But let's say the legislature has run that gauntlet and created a formula that seems to generate more winners than losers, and people believe the numbers. Now remember that if the proposal is designed to improve equity, then by definition the "loser" legislative districts are the wealthiest ones in the state. And while on the legislative floor those legislators may have only one vote, their constituents are disproportionately likely to be among the state's most powerful voices—and the biggest campaign donors.

As bumpy as that road is, states have tried very hard to travel it. A study of school funding reform between 1990 and 2014 found sixty-seven reforms in twenty-seven states.[30] These reforms largely shifted the balance of funding in ways favorable to lower-income schools, but not always.[31] In many ways the study ended up reinforcing the idea that the problems of school funding are very complicated.[32]

Categorical Funding

Whatever primary funding formula states have, they will often also have separate funding streams called "categoricals," which provide funds for some targeted purpose.[33] While the primary funding formula is usually money that districts can use however they want, categoricals cannot be used that flexibly.[34] These are the mandates that local districts must wrestle with in developing their budgets.

While states administer categorical funds, some of them are federally driven.[35] Categoricals make it more difficult for school districts to control how they spend their money.[36] That's their purpose; they are created by the federal government and state to ensure that districts spend money in particular ways, rather than trusting districts to spend money as they see fit.

There may be good reasons for that. States cannot assume that districts will spend money as the state would want. Given what we know of district decision-making processes—and the pressures school districts face—it's potentially appropriate for the federal government and states to ensure that certain kinds of support are provided to students.

Categoricals have a really important political benefit: they're far more politically satisfying than the funding formula. Every categorical has a constituency attached to it, and that constituency is watching that small line item very closely.[37] Raising the right categorical by tens of thousands of dollars might buy more political goodwill than adding millions to the primary formula.[38]

While states have different approaches to special education, in some states it is a separate form of categorical funding. Variation across states in special education funding is substantial, and different state funding formulas may incentivize different behaviors.[39] A 2019 analysis by the Education Commission of the States found seven different state approaches to special education spending.[40] States also have various ways of limiting their exposure, which can push expenses onto districts[41]—potentially with inequitable effects.

Although there are good reasons to have categoricals, they come at some cost. Historically categoricals have tended to be inequitable, favoring wealthier districts.[42] Many categoricals are not designed to prioritize districts serving students from families with low incomes, making them more beneficial to wealthier districts. That can also mean that the wealthiest districts—which are often disproportionately politically powerful—then fight for categorical expansion at the state level, at the expense of formula funding more heavily weighted toward lower-resource districts.

Moreover, having more categorical funding creates more separate funding streams at the local level, which can contribute to central office bureaucracy.[43] This means that categoricals can act to reinforce district cultures of status quo preservation, and may not be helpful to districts in their broader teacher-hiring efforts.

One of the boldest efforts to get rid of categoricals came in 2013 when California established its Local Control Funding Formula (LCFF). The LCFF dramatically reduced the number of categorical programs, consolidating them into formula funds that prioritize districts with more modest resources.[44] So far the LCFF does appear to have increased equity in funding distribution.[45] It also appears to be having a positive impact on academic outcomes.[46] But it still allows districts to shift funds away from the highest-need students.[47]

The complexity of categoricals and special education funding means that in many states policymakers may have only a limited idea of how they work. It's even less likely that policymakers understand the other options available and the potential impact of alternative approaches. Given the significant amount of money many states have tied up in categoricals, at least building that understanding could be a worthwhile first step. State governments—or philanthropic partners—could commission analyses of categorical spending, its equity implications, and its impact on the ability to hire great teachers in the lowest-resource communities.

Teacher Pensions

Constituents want better services and lower taxes, and it can be hard to reconcile those desires. Historically, the way politicians do that is by deficit spending. At the federal government, where budgets do not have to be balanced, it has led to annual budget deficits in each of the past twenty years.[48] But states generally have balanced budget requirements.[49] So what states do is underfund their pension obligations. For state legislators the ability to please constituents today is far more important than any potential adverse impact on the state budget years later.[50]

Even as teacher salaries have remained relatively flat, teacher pension obligations have grown.[51] Teachers typically receive defined benefit pensions, as opposed to defined contribution plans.[52] In defined contribution plans—like a 401(k)—a certain amount of money is invested, and then the market dictates whether the plan is worth more or less over time.[53] But in a defined benefit plan, the retiree will receive a fixed amount of money—and the employer is obligated to come up with it.[54]

States generally create pooled pension funds for teachers, and each year put a certain amount of money into that fund.[55] But shortchanging pension obligations is a time-honored manner for making the state budget seem balanced. Nationally as of 2020 the unfunded pension obligations were about $500 billion.[56] At this point the cost of paying down the unfunded liability is growing rapidly compared to the actual benefits for teachers.[57] And because of how the pension system is structured, this ends up meaning that the lower-income new teachers are subsidizing the higher-income older ones.[58]

In the long term, pensions threaten to eat up an increasing share of state budgets—which in turn could reduce the money available for day-to-day school operations. And that can have a major impact on the schools serving the most students from families with low incomes, given that state funding is most important to those districts. So the equity implications of pension shortfalls are substantial.

The equity implications are compounded by the fact that pension systems themselves tend to benefit teachers in the wealthiest districts. As we've seen, the highest-paid teachers tend to work with the wealthiest students. But the spending gap between low-wealth and high-wealth districts may be even greater when pensions are taken into account.[59]

States and school districts may play a cat-and-mouse game when it comes to pension funding. When states set up the rules for their pension system, they commit to sharing the cost with school districts. Districts usually figure out pretty quickly how to minimize their own share and maximize the state's. For example, if an administrator's pension is based on their final salary—or the average of their final salaries over their past few years—the district and administrator will negotiate for a last-minute pay spike.[60]

For districts this is often a good deal, especially if the state is picking up most of the pension costs; they pay a little bit extra for a finite period of time, and then their employee can retire to a much more generous pension. The two parties involved in negotiating the administrator's pay package are able to foist most of the costs onto somebody else, which for their purposes is extremely convenient. And if states adjust the rules, districts can be counted on how to change their benefit packages to ensure that they are pushing the maximum possible obligation onto the state.

Teacher pensions disproportionately benefit older teachers, and many short-term teachers will never receive pension benefits at all.[61] There's evidence that teachers would rather have their money in salary than in pension benefits.[62] But if states feel political pressure to keep their pension system, they need to restructure them to ensure that they are equitable.

It's not fair for states to push onto districts obligations that the state itself created.[63] But it's also bad policy for the state to allow wealthy districts to create obligations on the state's behalf. The state should make sure going forward that if it is changing its approach to teachers' salaries, it is also changing its approach to teacher pensions in an aligned manner. Otherwise, the pension system will threaten to unravel any efforts the state makes through the funding formula to help districts serving students from families with low incomes.

HOW THE FEDERAL GOVERNMENT COULD REDUCE INTER-DISTRICT DISPARITIES

The federal government's spending may not represent a high percentage of overall education spending, but it has substantial downstream impacts on state and district behavior. When ESSA is reauthorized, there are a few directional changes the federal government could consider that would help to provide resources to lower-resource districts. Those changes would be incrementally helpful to those districts as they compete in the market for teacher talent.

As we have seen, the problem with state funding is that it is inadequate, inequitable, and too complicated.[64] Given that the federal government interacts primarily with states, one way to frame its role is as a potential partner for states trying to solve those problems, as a supporter of state action to make funding more adequate, equitable, and simple. Let's address each of those in turn.

Adequacy

The pandemic led to an enormous infusion of federal money into the education system.[65] At this point, it is not clear whether that level of investment
will be sustained into the future. But even with the federal government's
remarkable expenditures, most of the money in the system is still from state
and local sources. Notably, federal American Rescue Plan funding included
specific requirements meant to protect funding to "high poverty" schools.[66]

The primary source of federal funds for K-12 education is Title I of the
ESSA.[67] Most Title I money has historically flowed to districts, which misses
a chance to leverage state investment.[68] Indeed, Title I money originally
focused on students (and groups of students); in the 1980s the focus shifted
toward schools.[69]

But schools are not the primary partner for the federal government, states
are. A rethinking of federal education funding should put more money into
formulas that pass through states, increasing the federal government's leverage on state formulas. To be clear, the money should continue to flow toward
districts—it should just pass through states first on the way.

In thinking about the federal government's ongoing role, one tension is
whether the federal government should reward states that invest their own
resources in education, or compensate for the ones that don't. The best use of
federal leverage will be the former. If states think the federal government will
cover for their shortcomings, that gives them incentive to back off; if states
know that adding more money to education helps them draw down federal
funds, that gives them incentive to spend more. Thus, the federal government should structure funding to reward states that are willing to invest their
own funds.[70]

There are various potential ways to measure whether or not states are actually doing that. Professor Bruce Baker has identified what's likely to be the
fairest: examining the state level of effort, measured by comparing education spending to the state's available resources.[71] In some low-wealth states
achieving adequacy is highly unlikely without federal support.[72] When states
increase their effort in education funding, the federal government should help
to accelerate its spending.[73]

The federal government should also consider ramping up its spending on
special education. Federal law sets a target of 40 percent federal funding for
special education services; in recent years the actual number has been below
15 percent.[74] When school officials talk about "unfunded mandates," IDEA
(Individuals with Disabilities Education Act) is the most prominent example—and their complaints on this front are legitimate. Relieving the pressure
on state and local budgets caused by federal underfunding of IDEA would
create greater flexibility with other discretionary funds.

As we have seen, early childhood education is a critical part of the system—so the adequacy of pre-kindergarten (pre-K) funding is deeply relevant to the overall success of the system. And in pre-K education the federal government has always been a more prominent player than in K-12.

In the 2019–2020 school year states collectively spent a little over $9 billion on state-funded preschool, which is still less than the $10.75 billion the federal government spends on Head Start.[75] State preschools serve more children than Head Start because they collectively spend less on a per-child basis.[76] But the percentage of the system supported by direct federal investment is far greater in early childhood than in K-12.

Equitable Distribution

The federal government can also play a role in stimulating equitable distribution at the state level. To date, the distribution of federal funds has been complicated and created mixed incentives for states and districts.[77] Moreover, it hasn't always reached the students it was intended to reach.[78]

If federal funding is going to be realigned to focus on state effort, it can also be weighted to account for how state effort impacts the lowest-wealth districts. That is, if states can demonstrate that their funding is being effectively targeted to the lowest-wealth districts—and actually leading to equitable resources for the lowest-income students—that should be rewarded by the federal government as part of the "effort" formula.[79]

In this approach, the federal government would be influencing states in how they set up their education funding formulas. If a state chooses to emphasize equitable spending, the federal government would reward that; if the state didn't want to prioritize equitable spending, that would still be its right.[80]

But it's likely that if the federal government made a change of this kind, some states would make responsive policy changes. States made enormous policy changes in response to Race to the Top, which was a one-time $4.35 billion federal investment.[81] The federal government spends far more than that on Title I every year.[82] If the Title I formula created incentives for states to improve their support for low-income districts, many states would respond.[83] And that would be in addition to the states that have already developed comparatively equitable formulas.[84]

When it comes to early childhood education, the federal government's role has been on serving the lowest-income children through Head Start. Head Start does in fact target the lowest-income children, which has historically made it a force for equity. But because it bypasses states it does nothing to leverage equity in state early childhood funding distribution. Nonetheless, because many state preschool programs have restricted eligibility to lower-income children,[85] early childhood funding is generally more equitable than K-12 funding. Over time, the federal government should continue to emphasize equity in its early childhood spending and evaluate the impact of its efforts.

Simplicity

There are several ways in which the federal government could help create greater simplicity in funding. One of them was identified before: to pass Title I formula funding through the primary state education funding formula. Title I currently has four different funding formulas that serve different purposes.[86] These are layered on top of whatever the state's funding formula is, and are frequently used in ways that lead to fragmentation in student services.[87] Creating one formula that goes directly to states—and creates better incentives for state behavior—would dramatically simplify school funding overall.

The federal government also plays a role in the complexity of categorical funding. The Trump Administration proposed to collapse multiple funding streams while cutting the federal education budget; its efforts were consistently unsuccessful.[88] The pressures that keep categorical spending alive at the state level are very much present at the federal level too.[89]

The challenge with categorical spending is that it usually represents a worthy idea—but what's less clear is whether a small dedicated funding stream (and its concomitant administrative costs) is the best way to advance that idea. Advocacy groups will always want to embed their priorities at the federal level if they can—it's a lot easier than fighting for them separately in every state, or district by district. But it's the federal government's responsibility to consider whether those categoricals are the best use of its limited resources.

While some other categoricals might be better off consolidated, the federal government's role in special education does remain critical.[90] In the next reauthorization of IDEA, the federal government should look at whether it's possible to support states in developing simpler approaches to funding—which in turn could allow for improved efficiency and equity at the local level. The federal government might also think about what district-level supports or incentives would give district leaders the instigation and cover they need to make changes to special education practice, given the capacity that will likely be needed to make meaningful changes in a sensitive area.

State early childhood funding is overly complex, and the federal government does play a role in that.[91] Head Start is a direct federal-to-local program; states may choose to include it in planning for state-funded preschool, but they don't have to—and in some communities, the programs end up competing for enrollment.[92]

When Head Start was founded during the Great Society, there were good reasons for it to bypass states entirely; while some of those reasons still exist, it's also the case that states have come a long way since then. The next reauthorization of Head Start should consider ways in which Head Start could be more thoughtfully integrated into state early childhood funding approaches, without sacrificing the commitment to comprehensive services and serving the neediest children that has characterized the program since its founding.

HOW DOES ALL OF THIS IMPACT TEACHER HIRING?

While intuitively it might make sense to argue that giving more money to districts will help them improve teaching, it's not actually obvious that it will. So it's worth pausing briefly to unpack the theory of action a little bit more.

First, it must be acknowledged that policymakers have struggled to come up with definitions of "good teaching" that can be scaled statewide. Going back to the 1800s, teacher evaluations have been overwhelmingly positive.[93] In its 2009 report *The Widget Effect*, TNTP found that under 1 percent of teachers were given unsatisfactory ratings.[94] That sparked a major investment of federal resources focused on improved teacher evaluation, plus major philanthropic investment in improved evaluation practice.[95] For the most part, though, the reforms have not changed the fact that almost all teachers receive positive evaluations.[96]

But while policymakers have struggled to differentiate among teachers, school districts do it all the time in their hiring processes. Any school district that gets two or more applicants for a job opening is in a position to decide what it is looking for in that job and to weigh different factors in deciding on a hire. This kind of decision-making is one with which districts are familiar.

That's not to say they're great at it, necessarily.[97] Of course, problems with hiring aren't unique to schools; even the most sophisticated businesses can struggle to bring in the right talent.[98] So the assumption can't be that districts with more money will magically become better at hiring the right teacher every time.

But what those districts will be able to do is attract a larger candidate pool with higher-paying jobs. If all other things are equal, an $80,000 a year job will draw more applicants than a $55,000 a year job. Of course, all other things aren't equal, particularly for low-resource school districts. But that's all the more reason they need to have competitive pay to attract a stronger pool of candidates.

Indeed, there's no need for an empirical definition of "the best teachers," as the traits desired will vary from district to district and even position to position. Sometimes districts will make good matches; other times they won't.

But the more candidates districts have, the more likely it is that they will make a good match. And the more money they can offer, the more likely it is that they will have good candidates.

PAY FOR EARLY CHILDHOOD TEACHERS

Many states have invested directly in early childhood, rather than simply trusting that districts will invest in preschool using discretionary funds. In some states pre-K is part of the funding formula.[99] In other states it's effectively a categorical—and because of that, districts would rather see the money end up in the K-12 formula, where they have more control over it.[100]

In general, though, low per-child funding in state preschool programs makes it hard for preschool providers to pay teachers adequately. That's why, as we saw, preschool teachers earn barely more than half the annual salary of kindergarten and elementary school teachers. And going beyond preschool teachers to look at the larger early education and care sector, it's fair to say that early childhood professionals are more likely to be female and of color than the teaching force as a whole—and they get paid very little.[101]

We'll take a deeper look at early childhood funding in chapter 8, but for the moment the important thing to know is this: early childhood funding is largely driven by the federal government and states, and many children don't receive services. Only 47 percent of four-year-olds receive publicly funded preschool or Head Start, and for three-year-olds the percentage is 16 percent.[102] Overall, enrollment for four-year-olds and three-year-olds is substantially lower than the enrollment of five-year-olds.[103] Ramping up service would require a major surge in teacher hiring.

As we've seen, preschool teachers are paid less than kindergarten teachers (and other elementary school teachers).[104] One reason for the difference in pay between K-12 and early childhood can be explained by their differing qualifications. While in a K-12 teacher a bachelor's degree is an assumed starting point, not all states require a bachelor's degree in their state preschool programs.[105] Head Start doesn't require them either; in Fiscal Year 2019, 71 percent of Head Start teachers had one.[106]

Policymakers sometimes draw distinctions between "care" and "education." States have in place a framework for early *education*: Every state has learning standards for three-and four-year-old children, and most states have them for infants and toddlers as well.[107] As with learning standards for older children, skilled teaching is needed to help children meet the standards.

Safe and supportive custodial care is a value, and the federal government and states subsidize it through the Child Care and Development Block Grant.[108] But it's not sufficiently funded to support teachers who can instruct children in accordance with state learning standards. In fact, child care providers in 2019 made a median hourly wage of $11.65—less than half of what preschool teachers make.[109] It's not reasonable to expect that child care programs can provide standards-based education with those wages.

In 2015 the National Academy of Sciences issued a massive report on the early childhood workforce that, among other things, recommended that all lead teachers be required to obtain a bachelor's degree.[110] In 2020 the National Association for the Education of Young Children (NAEYC) released the results of a multi-organization "Power to the Profession" process that called for three levels of early childhood educator designations, with only one requiring a bachelor's degree.[111] The discrepancy between the two set off another round of debates about the value of a bachelor's degree for early childhood teachers.[112]

As the National Academies acknowledged, the research on the impact of bachelor's degrees to date has not shown conclusively that they have a significant impact.[113] The report justifies its recommendations on the grounds that the work of early childhood teaching is no less rigorous than that of elementary school teaching, which does require a bachelor's degree.[114] It acknowledged that in the current market teachers with bachelor's degrees tend to gravitate into jobs with older children, which pay more.[115]

One argument for the bachelor's degree requirement is that early childhood to date has tolerated teaching that isn't sufficiently focused on instruction. For example, Head Start programs nationally have much higher ratings for emotional support and classroom organization than for instructional support.[116] The idea is that the current expectations for teachers are set low enough that it's possible to meet them even without a bachelor's degree, but if the expectations were set where they ought to be then it would be obvious that a bachelor's degree is needed to meet them.[117]

Even if this is true, though, raising standards comes with complications. The current workforce in early childhood is racially diverse; there will be strong pressure to ensure that any changes to existing requirements are respectful of that diversity and seek to preserve it.[118] If new degree requirements are imposed without increasing salaries, then the requirements just serve to place a new burden on professionals who are already making very little money.[119] Adjusting the requirements upward would require a transitional period, with substantial support for professionals currently in the field to meet new requirements.[120]

Education and care aren't really a binary, they're more of a spectrum. For the foreseeable future, there will have to be a role for early childhood professionals who do not have bachelor's degrees. In 2021 the National Head Start Association (NHSA) released a set of proposals for improving the early childhood workforce that explicitly sidestepped the bachelor's degree debate.[121]

But the National Academies, NAEYC, NHSA, and others agree that it will be important for early childhood teaching to be improved in the years ahead. As we have seen, the early years are the best opportunity to improve child outcomes. Just enrolling kids in programs won't accomplish that—those programs have to actually deliver a quality education. Great teaching will be needed to make that happen, and the current system is not well designed to deliver great early childhood teaching at scale.

In measuring existing shortages among educators, it's natural to think in terms of the number of available jobs—with the shortage representing the percentage of available positions that employers are having a hard time filling. But in early childhood, that's potentially the wrong denominator. The current denominator assumes that a large percentage of children will not receive early childhood education at all. As we've seen, that assumption has a damaging effect on the education system.

Addressing math and science shortages could lead to an even wider gap between male and female teachers—but increasing pay in early childhood could close that gap. Indeed, it could be seen as a step toward equity for women, including women of color.[122] Of course, an increase in salaries for early childhood professionals could draw more men into the profession; currently they represent less than 3 percent of early childhood teachers.[123]

The goal of this book is to identify policies that support improved education for the children who need it most. We've seen the data showing that the early years are the best opportunity for states to improve educational outcomes. While other chapters have talked about the need to pay teachers based on their role rather than their characteristics, early childhood teachers have already been paid differently based on their role; so far that's worked out very badly for them.

Increasing teacher pay in the early childhood years won't have a perfect correlation with improved quality—but as long as early childhood teachers are at the absolute bottom of the teacher pay scale, it's unlikely that outcomes for young children will improve the way they need to. This work will likely need to be led by the federal government and states rather than districts, for reasons discussed further in chapter 8.

CONCLUSION

Teacher hiring requires money. If districts with limited local resources don't get help from the state or federal governments, they will be at a disadvantage in competing for teaching talent. Changing the way state and federal funds are distributed is perhaps the most important policy change needed to help get better teachers in the classrooms of low-resource districts.

The main expense of school districts is teacher salaries, so the money being spent in wealthy districts is largely going to ensure that the teachers there are well paid.[124] This creates competition with lower-wealth districts, and makes it harder for those districts to compete for talent.[125] Even if those districts attempted an initiative to increase teacher pay in high-poverty schools, they'd be competing with districts offering even higher pay to teach in low-poverty schools.

State funding formulas are complicated. Between the primary funding formula, categoricals, and pensions, there are inevitably some number of ways in which wealthy school districts are being subsidized at the expense of low-resource districts. Systematically addressing those incentives is hard, and it's unlikely that states will be able to turn all of the levers to favor the districts most in need of help. But looking at every opportunity to do so is a key step toward improving the quality of teaching in those low-resource districts.

States have, in some instances, been able to change their funding formulas to help low-resource communities. If the federal government were to provide greater incentive for states to do so, that would surely help. Discussions of changing federal funding formulas are always politically charged, and there's no guarantee that the federal government will be able to make the proposed formula changes. But the principle of helping the lowest-resource districts is one that has appeal across party lines. And if the federal government could really make that change—and help states to do the same—it would increase the odds that low-resource communities could compete for talented teachers.

The federal government and states also should bolster the market for early childhood teachers—both by hiring more and paying them more. The early years are critical to child development, and the quality of teaching children are receiving in those years is not what it could be. That's a systemic failure, and one that the federal government and states should work to correct. It will undoubtedly be expensive, but it's one of the most promising investments available to policymakers as they think about how to improve student outcomes.

It must be acknowledged that simply sending more money to districts won't inevitably lead to hiring better teachers, or better student outcomes.[126] It is appropriate to focus on how districts are spending money, particularly if they're getting more of it. But the fact that money could be spent more efficiently doesn't change the fact that in some places more is needed—particularly in some low-resource communities and particularly to serve preschool-aged children in those communities.

Federal and state mechanisms for distributing dollars aren't the only thing that matters to hiring great teachers. But without those federal and state resources, districts in low-resource communities may start out at a daunting disadvantage. That needs to be changed.

In Part I, we talked about how the quality of schools is defined—and how to change that definition process to help reflect the reality of schools serving children from low-income families. In Part II, we've talked about the policy changes needed to make those schools a more attractive option for top teachers. In Part III, we'll build on those conversations to talk about how to increase the number of schools that are desirable options for all families, how to help families navigate their options, and how to make more options available.

PART III

Giving Parents Real Choices

Chapter 8

Schools as a Private, Public, and Positional Good

Today and in the future, we should not make policy with the expectation that parents will ever do anything other than what they think is best for their own kid. Every parent will have his or her own definition of what that best thing is. The goal of policy should be to help as many parents get as close as they possibly can to that best thing.

There are many different kinds of schools for parents to choose among, as there should be. But talking about school choice requires us to wrestle with significant questions about what obligation parents have to the larger public.

Our existing structures largely reflect a system created by rich white parents to help them meet their own needs. There is a long history of wealthy white parents seeking to place their children in schools populated primarily by other wealthy white kids. Whether that's done through the drawing of district boundaries, charter or magnet schools, vouchers, or other means, it has the effect of exacerbating racial and financial inequality.

Parents with means have always exercised choice; any proposed approach to parent choice that ignores the reality of how affluent parents behave is highly likely to fail. So the practical question we need to address is this: how can the behavior of rich white parents best be channeled or contextualized so that *all* parents have a real opportunity to do what they think is best for their own kid? The basic structures of choice need to be re-evaluated to determine whether they are supporting or undermining outcomes for children from low-income families.

Many advocates for choice make a strong argument that they are trying to provide low-income families with the same opportunity for choice that wealthy families have always had. Choice is only meaningful if there are multiple good options for all families.

In metropolitan areas the real competition for resources and enrollment has been between schools serving low-income families and those serving wealthier families. The schools serving low-income families have for the most part been losing that battle. Reversing that polarity will create an environment in which discussions of public school choice can genuinely create better options for the families who need them most.

In Part III, we will start in this chapter by looking at how schools compete with each other to attract parents and students. In the next chapter, we will look at how political boundaries shape that competition—both boundaries within districts and boundaries between districts. The following chapter explores the politics of charter schools, an alternative form of public school that is meant to provide families with additional choices. After that is a chapter discussing the process of how families choose schools and the kind of information they need to be successful at the process.

We'll conclude Part III with a chapter that considers how families can genuinely be provided with more meaningful choices. That will require breaking down political barriers, supporting families through the choice process—and including early childhood.

WHAT PARENTS WANT OUT OF SCHOOLS

There are a lot of different things families might want out of their schools.[1] What follows is a non-exhaustive list:

- Families might want their children to go to integrated schools to take advantage of the life lessons that can only be learned from having diverse classmates.[2]
- Or they might want their children to go to schools largely with children who have a similar demographic background, where they might feel at home among familiar faces.[3]
- Families may want their child to go to a neighborhood school to take advantage of the benefits of a local community.[4] For early childhood programs this is a particularly significant factor.[5]
- Or they might want their child to go to a school with a distinctive academic focus, which could be a magnet or charter school.[6]
- Families may want a school with a broad curriculum, including a focus on the arts.[7]
- Other families may want a school that focuses on high-quality career readiness, including technical education.[8]
- Or families may want a curriculum that focuses on democracy and leadership.[9]
- Or they may want a school that focuses on content knowledge and builds an understanding of common cultural currency.[10]

- Or they might want a good football team, a talented marching band, and a lot of school spirit.[11]
- Families may want their children to go to schools that include a real focus on social and emotional learning, with an eye toward support for child development.[12]
- Or they might want schools with a focus on order and discipline, where disruption is infrequent.[13]
- Families may want their children to go to schools that offer personalized learning, where each child can advance at their own pace.[14]
- Or they might feel most comfortable with schools that have a traditional arrangement of age-based grade spans.[15]
- Families may want a school with high test scores that demonstrates academic achievement.[16]
- No, in general families don't seek out schools with low test scores. But some families may not care as much about test scores as a sign of academic quality and may be more focused on school culture or other aspects of a school's experience.[17]

Obviously, there is a spectrum between each of these binaries—and most of these are not mutually exclusive, meaning that different parents will want different combinations of characteristics.[18] But it's fair to say that reasonable parents may want very different things for their children.[19] Indeed, parents with multiple children may want different things for each of their children. That may mean very little in rural areas, where there may be only one school within reasonable driving distance.[20] But in more densely populated areas it should lead to the creation of multiple options for parents.

EDUCATION AS A PUBLIC, PRIVATE, AND POSITIONAL GOOD

Education as a Positional Good

Sigal Ben-Porath and Michael Johanek of the University of Pennsylvania's Graduate School of Education have a very helpful frame for thinking about school choice. They explain that education is simultaneously three things: a private good, a public good, and a positional good.[21] Each of those has different implications.

A private good is something that benefits the recipient.[22] Education clearly meets that standard. On a most basic level, higher levels of education are strongly predictive of higher earnings.[23] While the benefits to individuals of education can and should go far beyond income, that data point alone is sufficient to justify considering education as a private good. And the behavior of parents as consumers has had a major influence on the shape of educational institutions.[24]

A public good benefits the public at large, and education plainly does that as well.[25] Education has positive externalities—which is to say, each of us benefit from other people being educated.[26] In addition to economic benefits, education can lead to stronger and more involved communities.[27] This justifies government investment in education, even though it benefits the users directly.[28]

But education is also a positional good.[29] It is to your benefit that other people are educated—but if they're better educated than you are, that might actually be to your disadvantage in a competitive job market. For this reason, affluent communities may be more supportive of efforts to help other communities if doing so does not threaten their privileged position.[30] In fact, historically some wealthier communities defined their own interests as "public interests" to the exclusion of others.[31] The continuing opposition to racial preferences in publicly funded programs—even in progressive states— suggests that parents will remain skeptical of efforts to provide positional advantages to other groups.[32]

While parents may acknowledge education as a public good, they will treat it as a private and positional one. As we saw earlier in this chapter, parents will have idiosyncratic definitions of "better." But they can be counted on to pursue that definition on behalf of their child.[33] And they can also be counted on to pressure policymakers to ensure that they have access to their definition of "better." The current system emerged from those pressures.

In many ways the real divide in thinking about education as a public good is between policymakers and parents.[34] Both progressive and conservative policymakers and advocates have argued that the purpose of education policy should be to help children from low-income families; they may disagree about strategies and tactics, but they can agree on that goal. But parents are focused on educating *their* child.[35] And no matter what their politics, parents with means will take steps to make sure that they get what they want for their kids.

One of the concerns some policymakers have about the exercise of choice in the education system is that it seems to emphasize education as a positional good more than a public one. If education is for the public good, placing too high a value on parent choice might undermine our goals.[36] Choice systems can end up compounding existing advantages; there are very few instances where poor Black children can choose to go to school with rich white kids.[37]

But the powerful counterargument is that to minimize parent choice puts what's best for children in the hands of government officials, rather than the people who love those children most.[38] Systems that support choice give families the direct ability to find the best option for their child and give consumers more power.[39] It's also framed as an important strategy to support equity; rich parents have always exercised school choice through where they choose to live, and reformers' goal has been to open up more options for other families.[40] And it simply cannot be the case that a neighborhood school can be all things to all children—so having more options in the marketplace increases the odds that parents will find a good match for their child's needs.[41]

The nature of education as a public good demands that we strive for at least some minimum baseline of quality in public schools. And equity does demand that we try to make choices available to all families, not just those with the ones with the resources to pick up and move if they're unhappy with their child's school. Moreover, choice is only meaningful if families have good options to choose among, so ensuring that those options are available is in the public interest. In Parts I and II, we've talked about the accountability systems and teaching capacity needed to support those good options.

In the next few chapters, we'll look more deeply at how parents choose among schools. In doing so, though, it is important to think of education as representing three different kinds of good. And Ben-Porath and Johanek are correct when they argue that because the system represents a mix of public and private good, it's appropriate for there to be a balance of power between the state and parents in determining where children go to school.[42]

Early Learning as a Positional Good

The case for early childhood education as a public good is compelling. Brain development is most rapid in the earliest years of life—and at that age it takes less effort to impact brain development than it does later in life.[43] The nature of a child's relationships in his or her youngest years has a substantial impact on that brain development.[44] Developing strong skills in the earliest years positions children to be successful as they continue their development.[45]

Despite this science, early education is optional. School is compulsory in the K-12 years—every state requires children to start school at some point between the ages of five and seven, and continue through some point between the ages of sixteen and eighteen.[46] In those years, children have an obligation to show up at school, and schools have an obligation to take them. Neither of those things are true of the earlier years, in which participation in education is voluntary—and parents may want educational options that simply aren't available.

When it comes to early learning, wealthy parents have the ability to pay for preschool, and they do. Fortunately, in most cities admission to preschool is not as hyper-competitive as it is in New York City, where ambitious parents are known to go to great lengths to get their children into the "best" preschools.[47] In general, the more education parents have had, the more likely their child is to attend preschool.[48]

But the availability of publicly funded early education is spotty. Nationally, only about 47 percent of four-year-old children attend publicly funded preschool programs, and only 16 percent of three-year-olds.[49] Another 19 percent of four-year-olds and 35 percent of three-year-olds attend privately funded preschools—but the remaining 34 percent and 49 percent of four- and three-year-olds, respectively, are not enrolled in any program.[50]

The nation's largest preschool program is the federally funded Head Start program. Reaching over 650,000 children across every state, Head Start is known for a holistic focus on child development.[51] Head Start has been shown to have beneficial long-term impacts on both educational and health outcomes.[52]

In the past two decades, state investment in early childhood—particularly state-funded preschool—has grown substantially. Since 2002, states have added 950,000 preschool spots,[53] representing more than half of the 1.64 million preschool spots available in the 2019–2020 school year.[54] The heavy focus is on four-year-olds, who fill 1.368 million of those 1.64 million spots (roughly five of every six).[55]

But the results vary substantially across states.[56] In Washington, DC and Vermont, more than 75 percent of four-year-olds and 50 percent of three-year-olds are being served.[57] Another six states—Wisconsin, Florida, Oklahoma, West Virginia, Iowa, and Georgia—are serving more than half of their four-year-olds.[58] No other states are serving even a quarter of their three-year-olds, although Illinois (22%) and New Jersey (21%) at least come close.[59] This reinforces the idea of early learning as a positional good: for parents in some states it's simply an accepted part of the educational experience, and in other states parents are completely on their own.

State preschool has fared well in some states because it can be a signature initiative that governors push. In some cases, they're persuaded by the research; in other cases, they might just think it's good politics; and in some instances, it's been a way to push for increased education spending that doesn't go to teacher unions (or even school districts). Unlike K-12 education, early childhood allows politicians to talk about expansion and serving new constituents; that's a political asset.

One reason that states have invested directly in early childhood education is that school districts mostly do not. There are a host of reasons that districts do not spend a lot of money on early childhood:

- Preschool is optional, not mandatory, and school districts will appropriate focus first on that which they are obligated to do.[60] Given the number of things districts are already required to do, this is a legitimate problem.

Moreover, there will sometimes be advocates who argue that districts shouldn't expand into preschool until they've "fixed" whatever they're doing in K-12. As we've seen, this is tantamount to arguing that nobody should repair the leak in the boat until they've finished bailing out all of the water.[61] But it's still an argument that sometimes gets traction politically.

- Related to preschool's status as an optional service, it often lacks an established constituency within the district. The district leaders responsible for the politics of the budget will be looking first to satisfy existing vested interests—many of whom make compelling cases for additional resources.[62] By contrast, the parents who need early childhood services may not have any relationship with the district, let alone an understanding of how to advocate effectively for new resources.[63]

- It takes a long time for preschool to have an impact. Let's say a superintendent comes in and in their first year launches an ambitious new preschool program for four-year-old children. As an aside, that's not even necessarily a good idea—successfully rolling out a preschool program should involve a community planning process—but let's say it happens.

  So if the new preschool program is in the first year of the superintendent's term, the first cohort will take its third grade standardized tests in the superintendent's fifth year. But by then, the superintendent is probably closer to the end of their term than the beginning.[64] Given the duration of superintendent tenures, new superintendents are more likely to want to make changes that have a chance at a faster impact.[65] If education leaders are under pressure to improve test scores immediately, they may make decisions that benefit the school at the expense of the children.[66]

- Then there's the issue of student mobility. In low-income districts, more than a third of the children enrolled in kindergarten may have moved to another district by the time they get to third grade.[67] Given what we know about the importance of the pre-kindergarten years and the impact of mobility on student outcomes, it would be really helpful for those children to receive high-quality preschool. But school districts understandably don't want to spend their limited resources on an optional service for kids who are about to move somewhere else anyway.

- Then there's the fact that preschool is potentially expensive. Each new classroom of preschoolers will generally require a teacher and a teacher's aide, plus other supports; in districts with a space crunch, that's another potential expense. In the 2019–2020 school year, publicly funded preschool cost $6,329 per child, and that includes programs of widely varying quality.[68]

- Finally, even if the school district wants to get involved, the early childhood community doesn't always want the school district to get involved.[69] For private early childhood providers, four-year-olds are essential to their business model; it's much more expensive to provide care to infants and toddlers, given the need for lower adult–child ratios.[70] If the school districts start offering free preschool, parents will understandably take advantage of it—but then the private child care providers might not be able to make ends meet.[71] So unless new school district offerings for four-year-old preschool will include offering spaces through local private providers—or are accompanied by additional funding for infant and toddler care—the existing child care community may be forced to publicly oppose school district plans for preschool expansion.

Given all of that, it's not surprising that so many school districts don't invest their discretionary funds in early childhood.

This is not to say that *local* funds are never invested in early childhood. There have been multiple local initiatives focused on early childhood; New York City, San Antonio, Denver, Seattle, San Francisco, and Chicago are among the most notable, and there are others.[72] But in most of the highest-profile local early childhood efforts, one of three things has happened:

- The funding was approved by a local referendum that was submitted to voters. Early childhood services are popular with the public.[73] Most of the obstacles previously listed apply to school districts, not individual voters. When voters are asked directly, they are more likely to support early childhood.
- A leading mayor has made it part of their political agenda. The most prominent example of this was New York City Mayor Bill de Blasio, who implemented pre-K in a city with mayoral control of the schools.[74]
- A philanthropic partnership has led to leveraging the local funding.

To be clear, districts are the service provider for a lot of early childhood services funded by other governments—including Head Start and state-funded preschool. In some cases where state funds are inadequate, districts will provide supplemental funding to preschool services. But in general, the incentives operating on school districts to date have limited their interest in early childhood investment. And the local variation contributes further to the nature of early childhood education as a positional good.

COMPETITION AMONG SCHOOLS

Because education is a positional good, schools end up competing with each other. They seek to position themselves in the marketplace through professional talent and student enrollment, which are interrelated—improvement in one helps support improvement in the other. We have seen that schools can choose to differentiate themselves in numerous ways, and will see in future chapters that the process of choosing schools can be a difficult one for parents. For the moment, though, let's do a brief introduction to the nature of competition among schools.

First, as noted previously, it's important to acknowledge that the most intimate competition among schools is in geographic areas where there are at least two schools that it would be feasible for any individual child to attend. That is not always the case. Almost a third of students live in a "town" or "rural" setting, where there may not be multiple options within driving or busing difference.[75] If parents have to work in these areas, then school choice might not be a realistic option.

In some of these areas school choice might be feasible. Almost half of those "town" or "rural" students live in "fringe" areas that are closer to urbanized areas, and some of those "town" settings have multiple schools. But there is a segment of the population that lives in areas where the low population density makes school choice extremely difficult.[76]

Historically, choice in denser area was deeply tied to geography. Children attended the school in their neighborhood, so parents chose their school by choosing where to live. When neighborhoods would market themselves the local school was sometimes a major selling point.[77]

The rise of magnet schools and then charter schools decoupled to some degree the relationship between geography and choice.[78] Magnet schools could bring together students from multiple neighborhoods, potentially to create diverse school environments.[79] Charter schools can also draw from a broad geography, sometimes cutting across district lines.[80] These approaches create new options for students beyond their neighborhood school.

New options create competition. Some advocates for choice argue that competition can create improved outcomes with greater efficiency.[81] But at the individual school level, it can be very hard to compete with other schools in the same district. We saw earlier that districts don't ensure that the schools serving the lowest-income children have the resources to hire and retain the best teachers; in the same vein, districts often don't give those schools the capacities needed to adjust their behaviors to increase enrollment.

For individual schools, not controlling their own budget, staffing, or program, makes it difficult for them to position themselves in a competitive market.[82] For competition to bring change requires the competitors to have the capacity to adjust and do things differently.[83] In some instances, districts have that capacity but have stripped it from individual schools—then left those schools to compete without the benefit of the tools needed to do so.[84] And even when competitors respond to each other, their focus may be more on marketing than on actually improving educational quality.[85]

Moreover, the stakes of competition look very different for individual schools than they do for districts and charters. For districts and charters, the stakes are usually quite clear: increased enrollment means more money from the state, and decreased enrollment means less money from the state. But for individual schools the stakes are different. Greater enrollment may mean more money for the district—but because districts have different methodologies for allocating funds, increased enrollment at the school level may provide no direct benefit to that school.

Enrollment can be an important factor in the most desperate version of competition among schools, the competition to avoid closure.[86] In some large cities—including Chicago and Philadelphia—large-scale school closures have forced a scramble among existing schools to avoid being eliminated altogether.[87] These changes can be disruptive for families, who have no guarantee that students will end up in a better school after closure.[88]

There are surely times when schools do in fact need to be closed for financial reasons, particularly if they have lost enrollment.[89] And members of a community may reasonably disagree as to whether they want to keep the neighborhood school open, or close it and try a fresh start.

But the act of school closure can create distrust in neighborhoods of the central authority responsible for the closings.[90] From the school's perspective, it will feel like the district created the conditions in which it had no real chance of success, and then punished it for not succeeding.[91] In other instances, population loss in a neighborhood can drive down enrollment, and that may have been far out of a school's control.[92]

Community leaders may also feel like their schools are being judged on the wrong criteria. People from outside a community might judge the quality of schools based on criteria like test scores—but to those communities the value of the school goes far beyond that.[93] Moreover, as we saw in Part I, proficiency on standardized tests is not necessarily a strong gauge of a school's academic success, let alone its larger value to the community.

Neighborhood schools have surely been starved and abused in many cities, but that doesn't inevitably mean they've done a bad job. So if a neighborhood feels like its school was set up to fail, that feels like a reminder that education is a positional good—with their neighborhood in an unfavorable position.

Proponents of competition will rightly point out that the districts could have set themselves up so that schools could be more nimble in their competition.

But it's fair to say that hasn't been a widespread district response. To the extent districts are good at competing, it tends to be at ensuring that they are offering attractive options to the wealthy parents they need to keep their tax base intact, as we will see in subsequent chapters.[94]

Competition is and will remain a fact of life for schools and for districts. Because education is a private and positional good in which having diverse options can be good for families, that competition can be expected to continue. But because education is a public good in which we should place a high value on serving the children with the fewest advantages, the rules of the competition need to be shaped so that those children have the best possible opportunities. In the chapters ahead, we will see what that might look like.

CONCLUSION

Parents may want very different things from schools. Because education is in part a private good, parents have the ability to choose from among different options. Because education is also a public good, the government helps to frame those choices. And because education is a positional good, historically the wealthy have been able to take best advantage of existing choice systems. In the competition among schools, having access to wealthy white students has tended to be a self-perpetuating advantage.

In the next chapter, we'll take a deeper look at the way that choices in housing have shaped the education system. The history of school segregation has long historical roots in the United States and has evolved over the years in response to judicial and political pressures. In the chapter after that, we'll examine in more detail the emergence of charter schools and the role they play in the larger choice ecosystem. After that, we'll look at the process of parental choice, before concluding Part III with some recommendations for future policy change—and an assessment of the roles different levels of government should play in executing those changes.

Chapter 9

The Geography and Demography
of School Choice

Political boundaries have always defined school attendance. Sometimes those political boundaries are drawn within a given jurisdiction—such as the attendance boundaries within a school district. Other times the political boundaries are between jurisdictions, such as the boundaries among the more than 13,000 school districts in the United States.[1] Those lines have different meanings, which we will explore.

Schooling is a market, and parents make decisions about where children will go.[2] Families with means have always utilized the power of exit: if they don't like their school, they'll leave.[3] State laws can also authorize families to transfer across districts without changing their residency, either through inter-district transfers or open enrollment.[4] Open enrollment has been a tool for Black parents to attempt enrollment in predominantly white schools;[5] it has also been a mechanism for white parents to remove their children from diversifying schools.[6]

One prominent form of school choice is charter schools. Charter schools, as their name suggests, are "chartered" by an oversight authority—which is not necessarily a school district.[7] The ability to charter schools is created by state law, and state policies vary considerably.[8] But every charter school has an authorizer that is responsible for the performance of that charter school.[9]

While charters are public schools, some choice programs allow students to receive public funds that support enrollment in private schools. Vouchers—or newer variants like education savings accounts—are funds that are provided by states directly to parents or private schools, allowing parents to use public funds to enroll in non-public schools.[10] These programs may or may not place any restrictions on the private schools that end up enrolling students using these funds; the approaches have varied from program to program.[11]

These forms of competition exist primarily in urban areas; in rural areas, there is not enough population density to sustain competition.[12] But over time the population of the United States has steadily urbanized, to the point that now more than 80 percent of the population lives in urban areas.[13] Thus, for most school districts competition from other providers is a major form of accountability. This chapter looks at how attendance boundaries operate to constrain parent choice—both within districts, and then across them.

THE IMPACT OF ATTENDANCE
BOUNDARIES WITHIN DISTRICTS

Any school district with more than one school in a given grade span must decide how it plans to set attendance boundaries among those schools. This process has historically created enclaves for wealthy white students, who may go to a homogenous school not that far away from homogenous schools serving children from low-income families of color.[14] That has the positional effect of reinforcing racial and economic hierarchies within education. This approach may be deeply problematic as a matter of policy and justice, but it persists for a very powerful reason: it's actually a rational response to the pressures school districts face.

Why Districts Keep Discriminating by Race and Income

School districts are in a competitive market. Because their funding is dependent on enrollment, it's to their advantage to keep around the parents in the best position to provide financial support. By definition, that is wealthy parents—who are disproportionately white. Those parents are also the most likely to have children who are proficient on standardized tests, which as we've seen has historically been used as a key marker of district success.

Within a metropolitan area wealthy parents will likely have the choice of multiple school districts. By definition, the fact of their wealth gives them a greater ability to choose where they live.[15] So more than most parents, they are likely to be able to realize their goal of putting their children in a neighborhood school that meets their desires.

In 2011 the Fordham Institute identified what it called "private public schools"—schools that were technically public, but which had so few children from low-income families that they were effectively private.[16] The existence and persistence of these schools create a market force that many other school districts to some degree find themselves responding to.[17]

As we've seen, it's not fair to make assumptions about exactly what any given family is going to want based on its demographic characteristics. But in the aggregate, there's no question that a significant number of rich families want their kids to go to school with the children of other rich families. And given that, school districts make every effort to give their customers what they want: schools that give wealthy families the option of enrolling their child in a school with plenty of kids from similar backgrounds.[18] As we saw in Part II, those schools also tend to attract the best teachers.

Districts are deeply motivated by the fear that if they don't provide private public options, their wealthy constituents will pick up and leave.[19] Historically there have been plenty of examples of districts that attempted school integration, only to see white families head for the suburbs or private schools.[20] This is generally easier where districts are smaller, rather than countywide[21]—which is the case across the north and Midwest.[22] When this happens, districts have less money in their budget without any reduction in their obligation to the highest-needs children.

It's also important to point out that the pressures on districts come from all points on the political spectrum. It's true that Democrats are more likely than Republicans to say that school segregation is an important issue.[23] But the separation of wealthy families into exclusive schools occurs in liberal cities and metropolitan areas.[24] How families think about education as a public good does not always drive how they act with regard to the private good of their own child's education.

History Perpetuates Itself

Prior to the Supreme Court's landmark *Brown v. Board of Education* decision, a fundamental premise of the education system in many states—including northern states—was that white students and students of color should not attend school together and that schools for white children should be superior.[25] The Supreme Court's decision in *Brown* didn't throw out the existing system so that everybody could start over; it instead called for major shifts within a largely built-up landscape. That proved to be extremely difficult.

The market forces that created the pre-*Brown* education landscape didn't just disappear when *Brown* was decided. *Brown* was arguably based on the idea of education as a private and positional good, where the positional imbalance was so egregious that Black families had to be given better choices as market consumers.[26] And districts continued to stratify their schools in the post-*Brown* era.[27] Over time school district efforts have helped to preserve neighborhood characteristics, for better or worse; most of the neighborhoods that were low-income in the 1930s remain low-income today.[28]

The preservation of neighborhoods has not been solely a function of school district decision-making. Indeed, the historical focus of districts on neighborhood schools has created a strong tie between school policy and housing policy.[29] In some cities Black enclaves emerged, both because Blacks wanted to live together in community and because whites wanted to keep them out of their own neighborhoods.[30] Post-World War II federal housing law explicitly supported segregation, and the administration of that law reinforced segregation–even after the Supreme Court's decision in *Brown*.[31]

The construction of postwar public housing led to a surge in low-income populations in some neighborhoods, which in turn led to school overcrowding.[32] And as public housing was taken down years later, the schools built to serve those neighborhoods were then far too large for the remaining enrollment.[33] Moreover, exclusionary zoning laws promoted segregation and kept low-income housing out of primarily white suburbs.[34]

Whoever controls the levers of local government has powerful tools at their disposal to shape housing patterns.[35] But historically, when official means weren't available, neighborhoods would enter into restrictive covenants or neighborhood association agreements designed to keep neighborhoods white, with banks and insurance companies providing reinforcement.[36]

Once neighborhoods are segregated, it's relatively straightforward to place schools tactically in ways that reinforce racial boundaries.[37] Pervasive residential segregation in the postwar period coincided with a surge in school construction.[38] Residential segregation gives districts the ability to design attendance zones that lead to homogenous schools.[39] Accordingly, attendance boundaries can have the effect of reinforcing concentrated poverty.[40] As a complement, boundaries can also create small pockets of privilege within a larger city.[41]

These residentially driven inequities in education are one of the reasons for the push to create charter schools, magnet schools, and other schools of choice that can decouple neighborhoods from schools.[42] Some states also have laws meant to allow families to choose any school within the district where they live.[43]

Children going to school in neighborhoods other than their own can expose them to very different social norms, and crossing into new territory can teach children new lessons.[44] So there can be real benefits to having children go to schools in different neighborhoods. This is not always true, though; in gang territory, crossing certain lines can prove to be dangerous for students.[45]

While choice options have changed the geography of school attendance, most students attend a zoned school rather than a school of choice.[46] We'll discuss that issue further in coming chapters. But in the late 1960s and early 1970s—long before the rise of charter schools—the federal courts attempted to force integration, often by requiring students to attend schools in neighborhoods other than their own.[47] This initiative was widely known as "busing," which was a term created by opponents of integration to make their opposition seem less racially charged.[48]

While the south had a long history of explicit racial segregation, in the north that segregation was often de facto—not legally required but the established product of years of government policy and family choice.[49] Because residential neighborhoods were segregated, integration could be resisted in the name of "neighborhood schools."[50] And even modest efforts at integration faced fierce backlash, which ultimately reduced the inspiration of school districts to even try.[51]

At the time, federal courts were in some cases pressing districts to implement race-based desegregation plans. Now, Supreme Court law actually limits the ability of districts to undertake race-based desegregation even when they want to. In 2007 the Supreme Court issued an opinion in the case of *Parents Involved in Community Schools v. Seattle School District No. 1* that restricted the ability of districts to use race as a factor in determining enrollment.[52]

While Seattle justified its race-conscious planning as necessary to rectify past injustices, the Court rejected its argument; Chief Justice John Roberts concluded, "The way to stop discrimination on the basis of race is to stop discriminating on the basis of race."[53] Districts can potentially use non-racial demographic factors; the concurring opinion of Justice Kennedy—whose vote was needed to achieve a 5–4 majority in the resolution—explicitly stated that other demographic factors could still be used in assignment policy.[54]

Parents Involved doesn't preclude districts from voluntary desegregation, but it did prove to be discouraging to some districts that were interested.[55] Louisville—whose desegregation plan was also at issue in the *Parents Involved* case—retrenched to sustain a desegregation plan even after *Parents Involved* held that it could not use race as a factor in doing so.[56] While the public support for continuing the work was in many ways admirable, in 2021 an investigation by the *Louisville Courier-Journal* found that the plan ended up displacing a large number of Black children, and that children in Black neighborhoods had fewer options than white children.[57] So the execution of the plan may not have achieved its stated goals.

Measuring Intra-district Fiscal Inequities

Historically data on intra-district fiscal inequity has actually been very limited. Prior to ESSA, districts typically took their total spending and just reported per-school averages—which could mask the substantial differences within districts.[58] The Every Student Succeeds Act forced greater transparency on this issue, which has allowed for better analysis.[59] The new reporting requirement hasn't yet sparked significant action, but at least the seeds have been planted.[60]

What data is emerging reinforces the notion that districts are channeling money to their wealthiest students. In 2013 California's Local Control Funding Formula provided funding to districts based on their low-income student population.[61] But once those funds got to the districts, the districts had the power to allocate them, and accordingly they got allocated to the schools serving the wealthiest students.[62] And the amount of money formally allocated among schools may understate the gap, given that schools serving wealthy children often have involved parent groups that provide additional private resources.[63]

There are districts that have made intentional efforts to create schools that are socioeconomically diverse.[64] But overall, intra-district inequity remains a meaningful problem, in part for the reasons discussed in chapter 8.

Attendance Boundaries and Early Childhood

In developing a strategy for using early learning to improve overall achievement, districts will need to wrestle with the fact that early childhood programs are not subject to the same attendance boundaries as K-12 schools. Non-school providers of Head Start and child care may end up paying no attention to attendance boundaries at all. The rules for school-based state preschool may vary from state to state and may allow for neighborhood preferences.[65]

If districts are reworking their student attendance boundaries, it's important for them to figure early childhood into their plans. Because early childhood programs don't have the same attendance boundaries as schools, an individual early childhood program might send its graduates to multiple elementary schools—and elementary schools might receive kindergartners from a host of early childhood programs. Understanding how these patterns work may be critical for districts seeking to improve the early experiences of their students.

DISTRICT BOUNDARIES AS A FORTRESS WALL

The United States has a long-standing tradition of local control in education.[66] "Local control" is another way of saying "distrust": Americans don't trust the federal and state government to do what's best for their communities, so they want to keep control to themselves.[67] As we've already seen, there are good reasons for this distrust; on certain issues, communities are genuinely better positioned than states and the federal government to make decisions.

But the term can also be one of privilege.[68] School districts have often been the vehicle to reinforce education's nature as a positional good; wealthy families served by prosperous districts will get their needs met, but as we've seen, communities with limited resources will need help from the outside in order to be successful.[69] The federal government and states have at times exhibited an appropriately healthy distrust for the dynamics local control can create.

What we'll do next is trace the history of how district boundaries became so important to resource allocation, and what that's meant. We'll look at how district boundary lines are used by the wealthy to avoid responsibility for the non-wealthy, and the lengths to which districts go to enforce that exclusion. But we will also see that district lines can be permeable if states want them to be, which opens up some interesting options for how to help children from low-income families.

Suburbanization and *Milliken*

After World War II many Black families migrated from the south to the north and west.[70] At the same time, white families were moving out of the cities and into suburbs that excluded families of color.[71] Segregation of schools was the norm in both the south and the north; in the south, it was frequently a product of explicit laws mandating the separation, whereas in the north, it came from a mix of policies and legally enforced private practices.[72]

For example, Black families that wanted to move to the suburbs could not get the federal loans that in 1950 were underwriting half of the nation's mortgages—and supporting the development of white-dominated suburbs.[73] Public housing was segregated by law.[74] The suburbs became a powerful political constituency in their own right, and suburban leaders sought to protect their investment in their homes.[75] Segregation was a key strategy for doing so.[76]

Those forces of segregation were consumer-driven, and the consumers were not strictly self-identified segregationists. Parents at the top of the societal pyramid will want their children to go to school with other children from the top of the societal pyramid, because that's how private and positional goods tend to work.[77]

Parental decisions about their child's schooling aren't necessarily motivated by explicit racial animus or any malice toward low-income families. They're motivated by a parental desire to do what they see as best for their children, which in their minds is to surround them with other talented students who just happen to look like they do.

So the motivations for isolation are complex and include both racial and economic factors.[78] But in some cases white families simply haven't wanted their children to go to school with Black children.[79] Historically, many white communities excluded Black families even when those families had the financial wherewithal to live there.[80] In many cases if a Black family moved into a neighborhood, realtors would urge other white families to leave—allowing them to then sell the houses to Black families, who paid a premium because their options were otherwise limited.[81]

The period from 1968 to 1972 was one that saw a particularly aggressive role for the federal courts in seeking integration.[82] The Supreme Court's 1968 decision in *Green v. County School Board of New Kent County* accelerated the push on schools to integrate, and in the south the levels of interracial contact in schools changed dramatically in just a few years.[83]

But the ability of white suburbs to resist integration was reinforced by the 1974 Supreme Court decision in *Milliken v. Bradley*, which limited the ability of federal courts to order remedies to segregation that cut across district lines.[84]

Milliken came at a time when school desegregation litigation was still very active in federal courts, and it greatly constrained the ability of federal courts to issue areawide remedies.[85] *Milliken* allowed the forces of segregation the space they needed to establish enclaves of privilege, and then ensured that those enclaves would be allowed to persist.[86] This reinforced the idea of education as a positional good, with school district boundaries an important mechanism for reinforcing existing positions.

The legal framework allowing for segregation led to significant segregation in practice. A 2019 study by EdBuild found more than 1,000 instances nationwide of district boundaries that preserved substantial differences in racial demographics—and per-pupil spending.[87] Reports in 2021 from the Urban Institute and Bellwether both found meaningful relationships between school attendance boundaries and housing policy.[88] A 2020 EdBuild report highlighted district boundaries with the most significant economic impact, which are primarily in the Deep South and the Rust Belt.[89] At this point, most segregation occurs across district lines, rather than within districts.[90]

These lines help to enforce a substantial school spending gap. Another 2019 EdBuild report found that districts serving primarily white students have roughly the same overall enrollment as districts serving primarily students of color—and that the districts serving primarily white students spend about $23 billion more per year (about $2,200 more per student).[91] These districts have greater wealth to access, and therefore more money to spend on their schools.[92] As we saw in chapter 7, that has a major impact on the buyer's market for teachers.

To be clear, suburbs as a category are socioeconomically diverse.[93] While the suburbs include wealthy areas, they are also increasingly home to immigrants and low-income families.[94] And the suburbs remain an attractive destination for young families with school-age children.[95] But the fact that the suburbs overall are becoming more diverse does not mean that individual school districts are becoming more diverse.[96] District boundaries are, as we have seen, still widely used to enforce segregation. And even those districts that are integrated may struggle to support their diverse population.[97]

The lines between wealthy districts and their less-fortunate neighbors are vigorously policed, as suburban school districts can go to great lengths to enforce residency requirements.[98] They hire investigators to follow children who they suspect have not established legal residence, which has in some cases led to the arrest and imprisonment of parents who send their child to a school in a district other than the one they live in.[99] Districts may set up anonymous tip lines so that parents can call to report on residency fraud.[100]

These districts are treating education very much like a private and positional good, not a public one. They are protectors of a precious commodity—the education provided in their schools—and will use dramatic means to defend that commodity.[101]

In sum, school district boundaries allow the wealthy to hoard resources for themselves—which they then use to attract the best teachers. This creates a landscape in which the children who come from the greatest wealth end up with the most support on their educational journey, whereas the lowest-income children have the least. District boundaries aren't what created the societal forces driving that inequality, but they have been a valuable tool in preserving the exclusivity of wealthy districts.

If at First You Don't, Secede

In the north and Midwest, school districts are often quite small.[102] For example, a 2016 report in Illinois found that of the state's 859 school districts, 294 served 599 or fewer students.[103] Of those 859 districts, 212 districts controlled only a single school building; another 152 districts had only two buildings.[104] That is local control taken to a relative extreme. And the more fragmented school districts are in a suburban area, the greater the economic segregation.[105]

The overall trend since World War II has been toward school district consolidation. In 1939–1940 there were 117,108 school districts nationwide; by 1960 the number was down to 40,520, and by 1970 had halved again to 17,995.[106] The pace of consolidation slowed substantially at that point, and the most recent national total is a little over 13,000.[107] Coincidentally or not, this slowdown occurred in the wake of the *Milliken* decision.[108]

In the south, countywide districts have been the norm.[109] This is because, after the Civil War, white leaders did not want to allow Blacks to self-govern—so they created jurisdictions large enough to ensure white control.[110] But more recently, wealthy white residents of countywide districts have decided that they no longer want to subsidize the education of lower-income families in their county—nor do they want to run the risk of having their schools subject to the control of a board populated by representatives of those lower-income families. And so they have chosen to secede.

What that means is that small havens of wealthy white families are creating small independent districts that allow them to exercise greater control over their schools. A 2019 EdBuild report found that efforts to secede had accelerated in the preceding years.[111] The new districts are whiter and wealthier than the ones they leave behind.[112]

In Jefferson County, Alabama, white areas have been walling themselves off, creating a handful of wealthy and successful districts—and leaving multiple under-resourced districts with almost no white students.[113] In North Carolina, special legislation was passed to allow white enclaves in the Charlotte suburbs to separate from a larger district.[114] In Tennessee the largely Black Memphis school district dissolved, in order to be absorbed by the Shelby County system—which then splintered into seven different districts after suburban municipalities sought to withdraw.[115]

The secession phenomenon is not unique to the south, but in the south, secession has been used to accelerate the racial divide among school districts.[116]

State law sets the parameters for secession, and different states have made very different policy choices. Some states don't allow secession at all; others allow it but limit the circumstances in which they can occur—including requiring that it be approved not only by the portion of the district seeking to secede, but by the rest of the district as well.[117] Some states require the consideration of socioeconomic factors in the withdrawal process, or consideration of the funding impact secession would have.[118]

Cutting Across the Boundaries

School district boundaries are created by state law. So even if *Milliken* restricts the ability of federal courts to order integration across district lines, states themselves can allow for inter-district enrollment.[119] Inter-district enrollment programs can allow children from city centers to enroll in suburban schools, which can give students from low-income neighborhoods a chance at greater opportunity.[120] And some states have moved toward broader inter-district enrollment, with promising results.[121] These efforts have shown potentially beneficial results for students afforded the opportunity.[122]

But inter-district enrollment processes don't inevitably help students from families with low incomes. Inter-district transfer programs generally give discretion to the receiving district over whether to participate.[123] This discretion may be necessary to the survival of the program; without it, suburban parents might seek to close down inter-district transfers altogether.[124]

Allowing districts discretion means that predominantly white districts near predominantly Black districts will simply keep the wall up if they so choose.[125] Indeed, some districts refuse to participate in inter-district enrollment plans even after their enrollment has dropped;[126] this suggests they may be worried about the kinds of students who would enroll if they opened up the doors. In other cases, inter-district programs end up creating a matchmaking process in which wealthy white parents who want to escape lower-income districts can enroll in a higher-resourced district nearby—and force the low-income district they're escaping to send money along with the kids.[127]

So states set the meaning of school district boundaries and define how permeable they are. When it comes to early childhood, though, the boundaries are much more fluid. Because the programs themselves aren't necessarily delivered by school districts, those district lines may be much less meaningful. There are certainly many district-administered preschool programs that are restricted based on geography. It's also the case that in most states there isn't universally available free kindergarten for parents of all incomes—so the available programs may have restricted eligibility or availability. But parents do not face the same restrictions with their pre-kindergartners that they do in the K-12 system.

CONCLUSION

Within every demographic group—by race and income—there is diversity of opinion as to what is best for their children. But historically the geography of school choice has been driven by rich white people who do not see it as their job to support the education of poor children of color.[128]

In some cases wealthy white parents want their kids to go to integrated schools, but not necessarily have to share a classroom with children from different backgrounds. In other cases they want to live in integrated districts, but not send their kids to integrated schools. And in some cases they move to districts where the legal force of the district's boundaries ensures the homogeneity of schools. What this leaves us with is a system in which Black students are more than twice as likely as white students to attend high-poverty schools.[129]

Clearly, the primary system of allocating educational goods by neighborhood has created major disparities between economic and racial groups. And the political forces that created that system are powerful and bipartisan. So it makes sense that advocates for children from low-income families would seek some kind of workaround. In the next chapter we'll take a look at the landscape of charter schools, which in the past few decades have emerged as an alternative to the system of traditional neighborhood schools.

Chapter 10

The Workaround

Public Charter Schools

Charter schools are an innovation that have become a study in contradictions. Their roots include a focus on empowering union teachers, and their growth has been fueled in part by advocates seeking to disempower teacher unions. They are public schools that are routinely attacked for undermining public schools. They are criticized in some instances for excluding low-income children and children of color—and in other instances, for serving only low-income children and children of color. Many charter advocates are motivated by a desire to escape the bureaucracy of the traditional school system, and yet in many ways, the charter sector has come to mimic that traditional system.

President Bush and President Obama both expressed their support for charter schools.[1] And during their administrations, the market share of charter schools roughly sextupled; from 2000 to 2017 the percentage of students attending charter schools grew from 1 to 6 percent.[2] But they have taken on an outsized importance because they tend to cluster in major media markets, and they make for good press because of the divides they expose. Indeed, they are one of the signature issues that have divided the Reformers from the Resistance. This chapter examines the politics of charter schools and their role within the larger education system.

THE GEOGRAPHY AND DEMOGRAPHY OF CHARTER SCHOOLS

How Charter Schools Are Established

Charter schools are created by state law, and there is wide variety in how state law allows for the establishment of charters.[3] In general, state laws establish a set of authorizers, who in turn establish the charter schools themselves.[4] State law defines the powers of authorizers, including the parameters they are required to set for the schools they authorize.[5] The authorizer gives each of its schools a charter, which defines the terms of its operation and the expectations the school is supposed to meet.[6] The power to shut down underperforming schools is a significant accountability tool that authorizers wield.[7]

Authorizers are a diverse group.[8] School districts are one important authorizer, and indeed 48 percent of charter schools are authorized by school districts.[9] The most significant authorizers of charter schools are school districts and state education agencies.[10] But depending on state law authorizers can also include mayors, universities, or other kinds of organizations.[11] Those authorizers are themselves held accountable by the states, which have widely varied policies for doing so.[12] Given this variation, the quality of authorizing can be very uneven.[13]

While most charter schools are still individually operated, the past twenty years have seen significant growth in large charter networks. The most recent data shows roughly a third of charter schools operated by charter management organizations or education management organizations (which are for-profit).[14] These organizations can function essentially as non-geographic school districts.[15] They often have a particular model of schooling that they are seeking to scale.[16] These larger charter networks may be seen as actually replicating the larger public system rather than providing a distinctive alternative.[17]

State law generally exempts charter schools from certain statutory requirements that traditional schools are expected to follow.[18] But charter schools are still subject to some amount of regulation, and some charter school advocates believe that they still face too much bureaucratic oversight.[19] The tension of autonomy and quality assurance can put authorizers in a difficult position—especially in those states where authorizers have financial incentives to keep schools afloat even when they're not getting the job done.[20]

Critics charge that states' oversight of charter schools can be subject to "regulatory capture"—which is to say that the government agencies responsible for overseeing charter schools abandon their monitoring responsibilities to become cheerleaders for the sector.[21] Charter advocates have indeed focused a lot of policy attention on state government, including state legislatures.[22] This makes sense considering that charter schools are created by state law—and in some states, there isn't even a law allowing charter schools.[23]

In some states, authorizers can place charter schools in districts even when the districts don't want them.[24] Charter advocates see this power as critical to break up local monopolies on the delivery of education.[25] One of the primary arguments for charter schools is that they can represent something of a fresh start. Left to their own devices, districts may be unlikely to embrace innovation and change.[26] New schools have a chance to be innovative in ways that are hard to generate in institutions with established expectations.[27]

Indeed, charter advocates have argued that achieving a critical mass within a particular geography can drive broad improvement. In some districts, charters have substantial market share, and charter advocates argue that having a critical mass of innovative schools can positively impact the entire district[28]—although the Resistance is skeptical of that claim.[29] Some districts have chosen to adopt a "portfolio" approach, in which more flexible governance at the local level is intended to give all schools greater autonomy.[30]

In that same vein, another argument for allowing charter schools is that they provide options for children who would not otherwise have them. As we've seen, wealthy families will often choose their child's school by choosing where to live. Charter school advocates focus on the fact that charter schools empower families who might otherwise have been stuck in an inadequate neighborhood school.[31] Which gets us to the important question of who actually enrolls in charter schools.

Who Charter Schools Serve

The geography of charter schools has evolved to some extent over the years. For one thing, they have become more suburban. While at first charter schools were far more likely to be urban than suburban, during the Obama Administration, the growth of charter schools shifted to include suburban areas.[32]

But charter schools are still located primarily in large city districts, and enrollment in charter schools tends to be similar to the population of the neighborhoods around them.[33] In Fall 2017, 33 percent of children enrolled in charter schools were Hispanic, 32 percent were white, 26 percent were Black, and 4 percent were Asian.[34] Some research has found that charter schools increase segregation within a metropolitan area, even while potentially improving integration between districts.[35]

We have seen that school district boundaries are often a force for segregation, and charter schools aren't immune to that. There are some regional charters that cut across district lines.[36] But a lot of charters simply redistribute populations within existing school district boundaries. A potent critique of charter schools is that they are distraction from what really matters: attacking the structural forces that created segregated district boundaries in the first place.[37]

In conducting redistribution within districts, there are differing views on how important it is that charter schools serve as a force for integration. Some charter schools do seek to emphasize having a diverse student body.[38] Charter schools sometimes locate in diverse neighborhoods specifically to cultivate an integrated student body.[39] Charter schools could become a stronger force for school integration,[40] and during the pandemic, charter school advocates tried to grapple with their role in segregated neighborhoods.[41]

Charter school critics have argued that charter schools have reinforced segregation.[42] But charter school defenders argue that even if the enrollment in charter schools is disproportionately Black and Hispanic, that's not a bad thing—because charter schools are serving those communities well.[43] This is part of why charter schools are popular with some leaders in the Black and Latino communities, who see them as a good alternative to inadequate neighborhood schools.[44]

Charter schools do change the conversation about integration in important ways. Some charters are very intentionally specialized, with a distinct focus that is meant to define them in the marketplace.[45] This includes charters focused on specific ethnic niches.[46] This ability to specialize is one of the potentially significant benefits of chartering.

But as public schools, charters are also expected to be open to all applicants.[47] This can be an awkward fit in a landscape where historically what defined the characteristics of most schools was simply a small geographic area. There is absolutely a public good to having specialized schools that offer distinctive educational experiences—but it does tend to emphasize the nature of education as a positional good.

And one major strand of criticism against charter schools is that they do not help the hardest-to-serve students.[48] In particular, they are seen as excluding children with special needs and children whose home language is not English.[49] It is the case that for some parents of children with special needs, charter schools are an outstanding opportunity, if the particular environment of a given charter school maps well onto what their child needs.[50] But the role of charter schools in serving children with special needs is much debated, and even charter advocates acknowledge that it is complicated.[51]

Adding fuel to the fire of charter critics is the fact that as schools of choice, charter schools by definition are not schools of last resort. To be sure, that has benefits for the charter school itself. Because charter schools are schools of choice, all of the families enrolled there chose to apply.[52] This can be a substantial benefit in setting a culture for a school community.[53]

But when charter schools are having problems with a student they can push that student out and cause a traditional school to have to deal with him or her; neighborhood schools may not have that option.[54] As schools of choice, nobody is enrolled in charter schools automatically.[55] And as a discretionary alternative system, they have been described as operating on a "lifeboat theory of education reform"—getting some kids to a better place, while the majority of children on the main boat sink below the surface.[56]

Charter school efforts to shape the population they enroll and retain are driven in meaningful part by how they are funded. If charter school per-child funding bears no relationship to the characteristics of the children served, then those schools will have a powerful incentive to serve the lowest-expense children they can.[57] That's a policy problem, and one that can be remedied.

Charter advocates' most powerful point is that there are indeed traditional schools serving segregated communities that are struggling, and that creating better options for the children in those communities is a good thing. And charter critics' most powerful point is that whatever good comes to children in charter schools—if those charter schools are in fact better—doesn't help the children left behind, or change the systems that produced the circumstances surrounding the children left behind.

Those points are really two sides of the same coin. Both sides essentially acknowledge that we've walled off certain neighborhoods from the best opportunities. The work we've done to improve the conditions in those neighborhoods may have made incremental impacts, but it hasn't changed the underlying problem.

Charter Schools and Teacher Unions

Just as states use charter schools as a lever for change in districts, so too have some districts embraced charter schools as a lever of change against what they see as one of their primary constraining forces: teacher unions. In many states, charter schools are exempted from the collective bargaining requirements that apply to traditional schools, meaning that charter teachers are far less likely to be unionized.[58] For districts that have embraced charter schools, the leverage provided by that exemption is a key part of the charter school value proposition—and the unions know it.

But while unions have in many instances been vocal critics of charter school expansion, the relationship between teacher unions and charter schools isn't simply one of entrenched opposition. Indeed, one of the early intellectual godfathers of the charter movement was Albert Shanker, a long-time leader of the American Federation of Teachers.[59] His vision of charters is described as one of empowering teachers in a way that would allow them to more creatively serve students.[60] He began publicly discussing the idea in the late 1980s, but by the mid-1990s had turned away from the idea of charters when he saw that it was becoming a vehicle for the "privatization" of public schooling.[61]

Members of the Resistance criticize the current charter school movement for departing from Shanker's original vision.[62] They push for changes in charter laws that will eliminate for-profit providers, return management to the local level, and align salaries across the charter and traditional sectors, among other things.[63] They argue that the current charter movement holds the mistaken notion that the market will do a better job of providing than democracy will, and that it is an error to treat education as a consumer good rather than a public one.[64] In the next chapter, we will take a deeper look at how families experience the market for educational goods.

The Resistance overstates its case when it describes charter schools as a "privatization" movement.[65] Charter schools remain publicly accountable, even if not through the traditional channels. They are in many ways easier to access than the "private public schools" that wall themselves off in the suburbs and allow access only to the wealthy.

It's entirely understandable that unions are resistant to charters when those charters have been set up as a direct threat to union power. It's true that some charter schools are already unionized, with the Green Dot network of charter schools the most famous example.[66] But the fact that the rules of unionization are different for charter schools leads to a situation in which charter schools are far less frequently unionized than traditional schools.[67] This is particularly true in larger charter networks.[68] Charter leaders have been known to fight off unionization[69]—and some charter advocates make it clear they see unions as the enemy.[70]

Some charter networks are recreating the conditions that led to the rise of teachers' unionism decades ago—churning quickly through staff that are treated as easily replaceable. This is one of the reasons that there have been calls for the unionization of charter schools.[71] But it's worth unpacking why charter models so frequently rely on a constant cycling of young teachers. These are hard jobs, and unless charter schools are given extra funding to deal with those needs, it will be hard for them to sustain continuity. As we will see in a little bit, they are not given that extra funding.

Advocates for unionizing charter schools correctly point to the benefits of teacher voice in running a school.[72] And opponents of unionizing charter schools have a legitimate concern that the history of unions as a force for consistency could undermine some of the flexibilities that are meant to represent a key benefit of charters.[73] Reasonable minds can differ on how to strike that balance.

But the whole balancing act takes place within narrow confines. If states and school districts were really committed to supporting schools in the neighborhoods with the greatest need—traditional or charter—it would make it much easier for schools in those neighborhoods to create favorable conditions for teachers, and in turn produce better outcomes for students. Better conditions for teachers is the end to which unionization has been the means; what's most important is not the relationship between teacher unions and charter schools, but the relationship between teachers and students in the neighborhoods served by charter schools.

Are Charter Schools Getting Better Results?

The tension between unions and charter advocates has produced a raft of material claiming that charter schools either do or do not produce better student outcomes.[74] We're not going to try here to sort through all of the available research. But it's probably fair to summarize that research as follows: the incredibly varied charter school sector shows incredibly varied results, using metrics that everybody agrees are imperfect.[75]

It's very much a worthwhile exercise to collect data about the performance of each and use it to support improvement. But we don't have a universal definition of what a "successful school" looks like, and we know that parents want incredibly varied things from their schools. Given that, it seems ill-advised to try to rate two very diverse sectors on whether one is more successful than the other.

That desire for diversity does suggest that the introduction of options is a good thing. Even charter critics will acknowledge as much. But in the fight over limited financial resources, schools are pitted against each other. In many jurisdictions the battle lines are drawn between the traditional and charter sector, which once again may be a distraction from the real funding issue states and districts ought to be confronting.

WHOSE MONEY IS IT ANYWAY?

While charter school funding policies vary across states, student enrollment is generally a key driver of the formula.[76] While these charter formulas may differ from the state's overall approach to funding, the idea of student population as a key driver makes sense. There is an incremental cost to each additional student a school educates, and the funding for that school should reflect that cost.

Historically, the competition for student funds was waged primarily across district lines. The methods states use to distribute funding among districts are also driven in meaningful part by enrollment data.[77] As a general rule, this means that enrollment losses are damaging to school districts, particularly districts that are heavily dependent on the state for funding. The most dependent districts are typically those that serve a lot of children from low-income families—which also tend to be the districts where charter schools are most prevalent.

Urban districts have over time gotten used to competing with suburban districts. As we've seen, they've adopted strategies aimed at keeping a critical mass of wealthy families within city limits. But charter schools have changed the dynamics. Now there's a competition to enroll children from low-income families, who are disproportionately Black and Hispanic. And the combatants may have shifted; it's no longer the entire urban district competing with an array of suburban ones, it's factions within the urban district competing with each other.

In some districts, the charter school operation is essentially a parallel government with its own administrative infrastructure.[78] In other districts, the management is more integrated.[79] But however a district is structured, the entry of charter schools creates a scramble for enrollment that can pit the traditional sector against charters, traditional schools against each other, and charter schools against each other. For a system unused to this kind of competition, that competition can feel very disruptive.

There are a couple of factors that we examined earlier in Part III that exacerbate the stress this competition causes. First, individual schools are not really set up to participate in a competition; many of the key decisions about their attributes are made at a central office.

Second, historically those centralized decisions have led to ongoing instability in the schools serving children from the lowest-income families—the exact children who charter schools are now competing to attract. In some instances, districts have treated low-income neighborhoods as a cash cow, using them to draw down state funds that are then redirected to sustain schools for wealthy white families. It can be hard for districts to adjust when the jig is up.

Another factor that hangs heavily over this calculation is the fact that in the traditional schools sector, district spending is incredibly backloaded (an issue we saw in Part II). Because teacher contracts represent such a significant portion of a district's spending, a loss of enrollment to the charter sector will require the district to shrink its teaching force. When it does so, it will typically have to get rid of the youngest and cheapest teachers first. That leaves it with its most senior and expensive teachers—who, in addition to their salaries, will have health benefits and pension plans that need to be funded.

Districts have set up pay structures where younger teachers have had their income suppressed for the benefit of older teachers; if the younger teachers disappear, the entire model might cave in. This is particularly true given that states and districts have historically underfunded their future obligations—often quite substantially.[80] In effect, the funding model was set up on an assumption of continued growth, and if that growth comes to a halt, the entire structure is threatened with collapse.

So the stakes are very high for the traditional sector.[81] And as we've seen before, it is very hard to give up something that you've gotten used to. You can hear that in the language used to describe the effect of the encroachment of charter schools. Critics talk about money being "siphoned away" or "diverted" from "public schools" to support the charter sector.[82] That language is only accurate if you start with an initial assumption that the money was definitely going to those non-charter public schools.

Charter advocates talk about "money following the child," with the amount of money weighted to reflect the child's needs.[83] Money does, in fact, follow children in basically every single funding distribution formula states use, so this is not a new idea. What's new is that without moving their address, students can now choose to participate in what amounts to a completely different oversight system—which has implications for the system left behind.

Conceptually, the argument of charter advocates makes sense. Parents should have more choices of where their children go to public school, and funding is appropriately allocated based on enrollment. It would not be a compelling argument for a district leader to say, "Decades ago an elite group of white leaders set up a funding approach that pushed most of this district's expenses into the future—and now that future has arrived. So now we have to keep our Black and Hispanic kids in segregated and underfunded schools with no options, because otherwise the model collapses."

Even if you are not a public relations professional, you can see that maybe that strategy is suboptimal. And this reality is why sometimes it's important to have states step in to provide choices, given the pressures some districts face not to do so.

But education—and the work of the traditional education sector—is a public good, paid for not by tuition but by public funds. So it is important to cushion the transition in a way that does not do too much damage to the district left behind; otherwise, the lifeboat criticism becomes a valid one.[84] State law governs how much pressure school districts feel from their sunk costs—so if low-resource districts are struggling under the weight of pension debt, or shrinking districts are burdened by the maintenance costs of excess real estate, state government support could alleviate those burdens through investment or policy change.

Any one-time relief supporting an increase in charter enrollment should be coupled with policy change to make it possible for well-run districts to stay on secure footing in the future; states certainly should not offer relief to high-resource districts that have been financially irresponsible. But as districts evaluate the costs and benefits of allowing charters, states should influence not only their perception of the benefits—they should also look at the costs and how those might be addressed. And it's important not to overdo it; it's bad policy to keep paying school districts for children who have left.[85] Education funding will never be infinite—so the emphasis should be on putting money where the kids actually are, not where they were.[86]

Striking this nuanced balance is hard, and the politics around it are challenging. Right now, there isn't even really agreement about how charter school spending actually works, let alone how it ought to work.

Charter advocates point to research showing that charters get less money per student than traditional public schools do.[87] State law sometimes provides that charter schools will receive less per-pupil funding than traditional schools.[88] Because charter schools are spending less per student, charter advocates argue that charter schools actually increase per-student spending in the traditional district: because they're spending less per child than the original system, they're leaving behind more money to cover proportionately fewer children.[89]

The Resistance isn't having any of it. The Resistance argues that the methodology used to argue that charters get less money is flawed.[90] It says the same about the argument that charter schools are somehow benefiting the traditional system.[91] And it points to instances in which charter schools are spending more per-student that the traditional system while serving fewer children from low-income families, thereby exacerbating intra-district inequality.[92]

All of this should be beside the point. The key distinction in how a school should be funded isn't traditional versus charter; it's whether it serves children from low-income families or high-income families.[93] If it serves children from low-income families, then it should receive state and district funding sufficient to allow it to maintain a talented and stable core of teachers; if it serves children from high-income families, then it should also receive state and district funding sufficient to allow it to maintain a talented and stable core of teachers—with the recognition that such stability should be cheaper to maintain because the job is easier. The charterness or non-charterness shouldn't be the issue.

CHARTER SCHOOLS AND EARLY CHILDHOOD

In some ways the early childhood space ought to be fertile territory for charter schools.[94] In many places there's no established infrastructure to compete with, given that so many children aren't receiving services in the first place. And what infrastructure is there isn't exclusively dominated by school districts. If charters are supposed to provide an opportunity for innovators to be creative in delivering high-quality education, the early childhood space offers far more open territory than K-12.

But that's not how it actually works out. As Sara Mead and Ashley LiBetti Mitchel chronicled in a 2015 report, there are many policy choices states have made that have the effect of excluding charter schools from offering preschool classes.[95] Several of those are driven by how state preschool is funded:

- Charters may be explicitly limited from getting state funds to provide preschool.[96] This is pretty much a deal-killer, because charter schools can't charge tuition or raise property tax revenue. So without state revenue, they can't offer preschool.
- State preschool funds may be distributed through school districts.[97] This isn't automatically a problem if the charter school is authorized by the district or has a good relationship with the district. But if the district and charter school don't have a great relationship, that can reduce the odds the charter school will get the district to include it in preschool funding.
- State preschool funds aren't enough to cover the true cost of service.[98] This is something of an intentional strategy in some states, where the expectation is that school districts will fill in the gaps. That may be overly optimistic on the part of states, as districts have other priorities that may be more important to them.[99] But districts at least have some general revenue options to plug that gap, which charters do not.

These funding barriers are important, but they're not the only barriers. There are additional policies that may discourage charter schools from seeking state preschool funds even when they are available. These include:

- Detailed program quality standards that are seen as limiting autonomy.[100] Many charter schools are trying to create an environment of greater flexibility and attract leadership and staff who want to operate in an environment with less bureaucratic oversight. But early childhood typically has more intrusive requirements than K-12 has.[101] These requirements emerged to ensure child health and safety in an under-resourced field, but may be a bad cultural fit for charter schools.
- Differences in the enrollment process between early learning and charter schools.[102] In states without universal preschool—which is almost all of them—there are often eligibility criteria for state pre-K, or other policies that guide who can and cannot enroll.[103] The enrollment processes for early childhood can end up conflicting with the enrollment policies for charter schools, which are typically done by lottery.[104] This means charter schools can't guarantee that the children they serve in preschool will continue on into their elementary school program; given that many charters are trying to build relationships with families and provide a coherent instructional program, this potential lack of continuity is a significant impediment.

It is entirely appropriate for states to want to ensure quality in the early childhood services they fund. It is also entirely appropriate for states without universal preschool to target funds to the children that need it most. The fact that those policies haven't really been harmonized with state charter school policy reflects a lack of political will more than anything else. These issues haven't been a focus for either early childhood advocates or charter school advocates, so they don't get solved.

It's understandable that state early childhood advocates haven't made this a focus; they're more focused on basic questions of expanding access and improving quality. Moreover, many of those advocates are trying to maintain good relationships with teacher unions and school management groups, who may not actually want to make it easier for charter schools to offer preschool. Or they may be skeptical of the ability of any K-12 schools, traditional or charter, to work effectively in early childhood. Working out complex details on politically fraught terrain—for a comparatively small segment of the market—may not seem to be worth the effort.

It's also understandable that charter schools haven't made a bigger push to do more on early childhood. They too have had bigger political struggles to focus on, and spending political capital on the right to offer one or two additional years of schooling might not be at the top of their list. This may be particularly true given the facilities limitations charter schools often face; if they don't have any extra room, then expanding into preschool might not be a priority.[105]

But inattention to this issue has come in the context of early childhood being undervalued by the K-12 sector generally, and charter schools having contentious relationships with the K-12 establishment. Directionally, policy-makers should be working on changing both of those dynamics. In the short term, it probably isn't essential to resolve these issues, as there are in fact bigger issues that both sectors need to deal with. But as those sectors deal with their bigger issues, they should pay attention to opportunities to resolve these barriers to having charter schools offer preschool classes.

CONCLUSION

When it comes to helping families find the right school for their child, charter schools represent incremental progress. We have seen that district boundaries can be a powerful force for segregation. Charter schools haven't solved that problem and are arguably a distraction from it. But they have created new options for families that didn't have them before—and in some instances, at least, those options are better. That's a good thing and should be continued.

Charter schools have, in many instances, been set up in opposition to district schools, or to teacher unions. They don't inevitably have to be that way. It's valuable to have states or independent authorizers serve as an outside prod to institutions that don't change easily. But if the charter school movement is based on a complete lack of trust in the most powerful institutions on the education landscape, in some ways that makes it harder for those institutions to learn from charter schools and adapt their own behaviors.

Moreover, that lack of trust is based at least in part on accountability data that may not actually be all that useful for measuring the quality of education. Student proficiency is an inadequate way to judge either district or charter schools. If we can do a better job of identifying which schools are doing a good job and which ones aren't—regardless of sector—we have a better chance of helping to support improvement.

Schools will always compete for resources, across districts and within districts. States set the rules of that competition. In doing so, perhaps they should be oriented less toward creating parallel systems that compete with the main one, and more on creating conditions that allow for innovation and choice— and then learning from the experience in ways that inform the evolution of both the traditional and charter sectors.

The goal is to give families good options, so that they can find a school in which their child has the best chance to thrive. Charter schools contribute to the landscape of options, but they also contribute to a sense some families have of being overwhelmed with different choices. Actually choosing from among available schools can be difficult for parents. In the next chapter, we'll take a look at how that process works now, and how it might be improved.

Chapter 11

How Do Families Go
About Choosing?

Having taken an overview of the landscape of school options that parents face, we'll now dig more deeply into how parents navigate that landscape. We know that parents will generally try to maximize what they see as the educational benefits for each of their children, with the recognition that their definition of what those benefits are may vary widely. We also know that some parents have more options than others—but as we will see, having more options doesn't necessarily make the process easier.

We'll start the chapter by looking at some of the methods used to manage the choice process. Then we will take a look at some of the supports that have been put in place to help parents make sense of the process. We'll conclude the chapter by examining the kinds of information parents consider in making decisions about their child's schooling.

METHODS OF PARENT CHOICE

The broad spectrum of attributes parents look for in schools would suggest that the market for schools should be heavily differentiated, with schools emphasizing their distinct features to compete for enrollment.[1] But as we have seen, school choice was historically driven primarily by residential neighborhood.

In a world where school choice is geographically driven, great meaning is invested in school district boundaries and attendance boundaries within school districts. The creation of additional options hasn't rendered those boundaries irrelevant by any means, but it has created new systems for families to exercise the power of choice. There are important values embedded within the design of those systems.

One initial question is whether the system is going to be centralized, or whether individual schools will each run their own enrollment process. For example, charter schools that receive more applications than they have slots may be required to run a lottery in order to select their class.[2] This can be done on a decentralized basis, where each school runs its own lottery, and families apply to each school separately.[3]

But a system where every school has to run its own lottery can be chaotic, for both the families and schools. If each school has its own application process, that can be confusing and difficult for families, particularly those who lack experience with application processes.[4] An unstructured selection process may also mean that families don't learn where their children are going until relatively shortly before school starts in the fall—which can also be a source of stress for the schools themselves.[5]

To bring more structure to the process, an increasing number of jurisdictions are developing centralized enrollment systems. These systems ask families to submit a list of preferences to a centralized authority, which then assigns students to schools based on those preferences.[6] These systems can lead to more equitable access.[7] They are meant to empower parents and make the choice process easier for them to navigate.[8]

But promoting trust in the system is hard regardless of what the system is. In many decentralized systems, there is a perception—often grounded in evidence—that parents with the greatest advantages are able to game the system and make sure that their children get favorable placements.[9]

In centralized systems, the algorithms can be complex and hard to understand for parents—making them hard to trust, and in some cases potentially discriminatory.[10] The algorithms often include factors like geography, sibling preference, or demographic information;[11] these factors are meant to make the system more equitable, but in practice may increase the sense that the preferences of administrators weigh heavily on the selection process.[12]

One of the most well-known examples of centralized enrollment is the OneApp system in New Orleans. After Hurricane Katrina, New Orleans' traditional school system was replaced by a system without neighborhood schools—meaning that all schools were schools of choice.[13] To manage this system, New Orleans instituted a system called OneApp, which allowed for the school application process to be centralized.[14]

One goal of OneApp was to increase the number of students matched to their top choice schools.[15] A study showed that roughly 60 percent of families did get their top choice—but many of the families that did not get their top choice expressed dissatisfaction with the process, including feeling like their child's school was not a good fit.[16]

In early learning, the comparative unimportance of school district boundaries has led to a system where decentralized parent choice is the order of the day. Parents choose among state preschool, Head Start, and child care options; while there are some geographic restrictions on state preschool and eligibility limitations on all three programs, the matching process has been parent-driven with little centralized support.[17]

Efforts have been underway to change that, though, and the issue of coordinated enrollment was prioritized in a 2019 federal grant opportunity for state early childhood systems.[18] Louisiana is one example of a state that has developed a locally administered coordinated enrollment approach.[19]

Early childhood systems will remain different than K-12 systems because they remain voluntary. In a K-12 common enrollment process, families may be essentially obligated to send their child to the assigned school; attendance is compulsory, and they may have no better option. In early childhood, that's not the case—if a parent doesn't like their options, they're not obligated to send their kid anywhere at all. They may desperately want to do so, but the voluntary nature of the exercise changes the dynamic of the matchmaking process.

Another distinction between early childhood and K-12 is that in early childhood the use of community-based non-profits to deliver educational services has been relatively uncontroversial.[20] In K-12, the idea of public funds supporting education in private schools is bitterly contested.[21] This difference in perspective likely comes from the fact that in early childhood, community providers are filling a gap that the schools have never filled—whereas in K-12, private schools have often opened to create direct competition with public schools, sometimes for reasons perceived to be racially motivated.[22]

MANAGING INFORMATION IN THE PROCESS OF PARENT CHOICE

Whether families live in an area where choice is highly structured or a complete free-for-all, support for those families can help them manage the potentially dizzying array of choices they may face. Moreover, they need support because all human beings struggle with decision-making, and decisions about school are particularly important decisions with long-term effects.

Human beings can get overwhelmed when they have too many alternatives.[23] They can have a hard time making sense of available evidence.[24] Given the complexities of the choice it can be tempting to focus on an external definition of "good school," rather than the school that is the best fit for a particular child.[25] Accordingly, giving families more choices doesn't inevitably lead to better outcomes or greater equity.[26] This can be particularly true for low-income families, who may have limited bandwidth that causes them to "tunnel" and not consider all of their available options.[27]

There are all kinds of different challenges families encounter in navigating school options.[28] Families may end up with limited information about their options[29]—or they may have more than they know how to deal with.[30] In some instances information about the available options is factually inaccurate.[31] In other instances information is accurate but incomplete, or presented in a confusing format.[32] Or systems set up to provide parents with information may turn out to not be all that useful.[33] Overall, the choice of schools involves weighing multiple factors—about both the child and the school—in complex ways that can be hard to manage.[34]

These challenges are one reason for the emergence of support organizations created to assist parents with the process of choosing a school.[35] For example:

- EdNavigator was established to help families navigate school choice. The service is paid for by employers as an employee benefit to reduce stress and show support, which can help facilitate retention.[36]
- Families Empowered is a Texas-based organization focused on helping families choose the right school.[37]
- Child Care Aware is a national network of resource and referral agencies, which is available to provide information on early childhood to parents who request it.[38]

These are just some examples of organizations that try to work with families to help them get the right experience for their children.

Of course, while some organizations have as their mission helping the families who need help most, the families with the most substantial resources have their own assistance in navigating school choice systems. Wealthier families often have access to consultants who can help them find the best match for their child.[39]

Families also often rely on word of mouth and the opinions of their friends and neighbors.[40] But the quality of these networks can vary a lot, especially given the complexities of the issues in school choice.[41] Moreover, these networks can have the effect of reinforcing segregation, as parental networks in homogenous neighborhoods will tend to be homogenous.[42]

Schools aren't passive participants in this process. Charter schools—which are dependent on enrollment to survive—may have substantial marketing budgets.[43] Districts whose budgets depend on enrollment may have to market themselves as well.[44] Ironically, the districts that need to do the least marketing are the ones with the most money; districts whose budgets are dependent on property wealth rather than enrollment are arguably better off with fewer kids.

Schools in a competitive market can use various tools to make it clear what kind of students they are hoping to attract—or discourage.[45] This can be done through program design, the availability of transportation (or the lack thereof), active outreach to certain segments of the population, creating cumbersome application processes, and more.[46] When schools and districts market themselves, they may end up creating a stratified market, which can lead to a focus on adding or retaining affluent white families.[47]

In the end, Timothy Daly of EdNavigator sums it up well when he says that students need more than a choice—they need a path.[48] Supports are available to help students find that path. But whatever those supports look like, students and families will need good information to feed the process.[49]

THE KINDS OF INFORMATION PARENTS NEED

Providing useful and relevant information can influence how students choose schools.[50] One proposed approach is to create a market for school appraisals, which would provide information about schools to parents to help them make better choices.[51] In the absence of that kind of comprehensive strategy, we're left with a situation in which family preferences vary, and so different parents will seek out different kinds of information. But there are a few categories of information that we can be confident many parents will seek out, placing a premium on having good information available in those categories.

Community

While it's fair to say that there is a long-standing connection between residential segregation and school segregation in the United States, that doesn't mean that there isn't a value to neighborhood schools. Leaving aside demographics for a moment, convenience is legitimately a major factor in school choice.[52] Many parents understandably want their children to go to school close to home.[53] Transportation is particularly important for low-income families who may not be able to provide it on their own.[54] And it's not just rich families that want to be around each other; regardless of demographics, some children would rather go to school with other children in their community.[55]

It's not unreasonable that parents are interested in the demographics of a school, whether they want diversity or homogeneity.[56] When parents are looking for a diverse school, they may want there to be a critical mass of students from their child's demographic group.[57] Schools may market their diversity, even though in some cases the intended audience may not be all that interested.[58] What's more troubling is how parents use race as a proxy for school quality.[59]

As we've seen, school districts are limited in their ability to force the creation of diverse schools. But they may see benefits in informing parents about

the potential advantages of diverse schools. Leaders in the civil rights movement have argued that integrated schools offer benefits to all involved—that
the experience of being in a diverse setting has its own social benefits.[60] This
is not only true in K-12; in the early childhood years, integrated classrooms
can also have social and developmental benefits.[61] There are some parents
who may seek out schools that are diverse by income, or by race.

Advocates for integration have argued that in schools serving children
from families with low incomes, the academic opportunities are weaker,
both because the content of the classes is less varied and because the student
body's norms are less ambitious.[62] Integrating schools can create substantial
networking opportunities for children from low-income neighborhoods.[63]
Having high-achieving peers is influential on high school students; there are
some students who are successful and motivated when surrounded by other
successful and motivated students, but who are not strong enough on their
own to overcome a harsh academic environment.[64]

There is evidence showing that integrated schools can lead to better academic outcomes for Black students, with no harm to white students.[65] And
white parents may also see benefits to their children of having exposure to
children of different backgrounds.[66] Diverse schools can create cross-racial
friendships and expose children to new ideas.[67]

It is important to emphasize that while many families seek out integrated
schools, many families will not—including families that are neither wealthy
nor white. Dr. Thomas Sowell of the Hoover Institution writes that "white
classmates are neither necessary nor sufficient for non-white students to
achieve educational success."[68] Professor Noliwe Rooks writes, "As W. E. B.
DuBois contended in 1935, 'theoretically the Negro needs neither segregated
schools nor mixed schools. What he needs is education.' " The truth of that
sentiment cannot be overstated."[69]

So regardless of income and racial demographics, families are unlikely
to prioritize schools that have historically been under-resourced and
low-performing. It is not easy to break that cycle, but it won't start with parents choosing those schools in the vague hope that resources will follow. It
will start with an investment in those schools designed to help them succeed,
which will in turn lead parents to choose to send their children there.

In fairness, history shows that sometimes even significant investments in
schools that serve primarily children of color will not be enough to attract
white children to those schools.[70] But if those investments are in the human
capital needed for those schools to provide a strong education, they at least
have a chance to compete—and if nothing else, will serve well the children
who do go there.

Child Experience

While schools are institutions that are embedded in a broader community, they also serve individual children. Parents choosing schools will, to the extent possible, try to find schools that provide the kind of education they want their children to receive. This includes both academic and non-academic factors.

In keeping with the spirit of pluralism, this can include a lot of things, as we've seen:

- If a child has special needs, those special needs will likely be a key driver of the selection process.[71]
- Parents may want their child to have access to career and tech education, or art and music programs.[72]
- Families may want special curricular programs, including language immersion or English Language Learner programs.[73]
- Families might be interested in the unique educational environment offered by magnet schools.[74]
- Or parents may be focused on broader categories like critical thinking skills or civics education.[75]

Information on all of these kinds of offerings will be relevant to parents in the selection process.

Academics are not the only thing parents will focus on, of course. Schools can have widely different approaches to school discipline, as we have seen—and data about that discipline can be difficult to interpret. Schools can have radically different approaches to security and the presence of security guards—and different children can have widely varied reactions to those approaches.[76] Some schools have used controversial seclusion and restraint approaches for dealing with children.[77] All of these factors, too, are potentially relevant to parents' school selection process.

A new wrinkle post-pandemic will be the niche occupied by online schooling. The full impact of the online schooling that was widespread in the pandemic will take years to sort out.[78] For years before the pandemic, online schooling was positioned as an opportunity for school districts to improve efficiency and reach kids in new ways.[79] During the pandemic, online learning was seen by some as a new opportunity, but by many as an unpleasant experience.[80] And a move toward increased digital learning could end up exacerbating equity gaps rather than reducing them.[81] Online learning will surely continue to be important in some form, even if it is hard to predict at this point exactly what form that will be.[82]

Over time, we are learning more about how families choose schools.[83] With greater analytic capacity at the state level, we could learn more still. And over time, what we learn could help to inform the rubrics used in school account-ability. As we noted in Part I, there should be variance in the rubrics to reflect the different kinds of success to which schools might aspire. Accountability and choice systems should work together to generate information that is use-ful not only to state officials but to parents.

Test Scores

Concepts like *community* and *child experience* are complex. Test scores seem simple. And in part because they seem simple, accessible, and standardized, they have been a key element of the information parents have about their schools. This is true even though parents may care more about other aspects of a school's performance.[84] And given the complexity of what schools do, using a single test score as a proxy for school quality is inherently problematic.[85]

Formal definitions of school quality have for years centered around test scores. High test scores based on proficiency can say more about a school's demographics than its practices.[86] But regardless of their role in state account-ability, test scores have been one of the key pieces of information parents have gotten about schools. Improving state accountability systems—as described in Part I—would provide better information and more context for text scores, but probably would not eliminate altogether the parental use of test scores in school selection.

Some of the most commonly available sources of information for parents are websites like GreatSchools, SchoolDigger, or Niche, which historically have focused on proficiency scores.[87] Because of the correlation between demographics and test scores, these websites effectively served as advertise-ments for the whitest and most affluent schools in the system.[88]

GreatSchools, to its credit, has responded by including more data about growth and equity.[89] This additional data on its own won't be enough to change the dynamics of how affluent families choose their schools. But at least it might help to educate parents that proficiency is not the only measure of what makes for a great school.

Compounding the problems of test scores as an informational tool is the fact that much of the test data parents receive is in a form that makes it hard to understand.[90] Parents can use test data to inform how they engage with their child's school, but the form of the data they receive often makes it hard for them to do that.[91] The data parents receive about schools to help them choose among them often isn't any better—and the addition of choice to the con-versation threatens to make the conversation all the harder for lay audiences.

Even in decentralized markets, central authorities can play a role in help-ing to standardize reporting—and can work with parents to figure out what should go into that report to make it accessible.[92] Test scores will continue to matter to parents, and in the interest of transparency, they should continue to be reported.[93] But it will be important to report them in a manner that helps parents make sense of what they mean. Exactly what that looks like should be developed in collaboration with a diverse cross-section of parents, to ensure that it is truly responsive to customer needs.

Early Childhood

The information families want about early childhood programs is in many ways similar to what families want in K-12. Location matters a great deal, particularly given that transportation is less likely to be provided than in K-12.[94] The child's environment is also extremely important, and with young children, families will appropriately focus on how well cared-for they will be outside the home.[95]

Many states have what they call a "mixed delivery system" in which the state funds both schools and private providers to deliver state-funded preschool.[96] In the K-12 world, the concept of mixed delivery is highly contentious, but among early childhood advocates, its benefits are widely understood.[97] The term *mixed delivery system* is actually defined in the Every Student Succeeds Act, which describes it as "a system of early childhood education services that are delivered through a combination of programs, providers, and settings (such as Head Start, licensed family and center-based child care programs, public schools, and community-based organizations); and that is supported with a combination of public funds and private funds."[98] The fact that the funding is public does not mean that the service delivery itself needs to be.[99]

Another major difference between K-12 and early childhood is that in early childhood there is no standardized testing data to inform parents. The replacement, unfortunately, is cost data. While public school is generally free, child care can be very expensive for families.[100] Even when government subsidizes some portion of the care, families may be expected to cover a substantial percentage of the cost.[101] This once again reinforces the idea of early childhood as more of a private and positional good than a public one.

The early childhood system is actually required to provide search tools for parents. The federal child care law requires states to have consumer education websites, and many states include a child care search tool on that website.[102] The consumer education websites are required to include information about certain characteristics of child care providers, focusing on health and safety information.[103] Some states include information about program quality, or a link to a related website providing that information.[104]

CONCLUSION

The fact that parents want many different attributes in their schools is a good thing—and those attributes are in many instances not mutually exclusive.[105] But the complexity of the exercise makes it a difficult one. There are hard trade-offs involved in establishing a choice process; an unstructured process may exacerbate inequity, but a centralized process can be hard for parents to trust.

One criticism of centralized processes is that it's just another version of government picking schools for families.[106] That's accurate only if the algorithm gets too cluttered with government preferences. It is almost surely appropriate to put in sibling preferences for families who want both of their kids to go to the same school; anything else is negotiable and should be subject to significant public scrutiny. That could appropriately include prioritizing children from certain historically underserved area, so long as the preference is made on a legal basis—and is officially adopted through a public engagement process led by the appropriate oversight body (state or local), rather than being slipped into a formula at the staff level.

If the algorithm focuses on parent preferences rather than governmental ones, then it is likely that centralized enrollment is the best way to make sure that most parents get the best outcome. But setting up the enrollment system is not enough. Government also has an important role in making sure that information is shared in a transparent manner.[107]

This too should be a process driven by public engagement. The information families should receive should be based on consumer preference, not policymaker fiat. That information may vary from jurisdiction to jurisdiction, but what should not vary across jurisdictions is a real commitment to soliciting feedback from families about what information would be most helpful to them.

Naturally, any improvements made to a state's accountability system should be reflected here. We know now that current accountability ratings are a poor proxy for the quality of the school. Parents will still use them anyway to some degree—but better accountability ratings would be more useful and could be highlighted by the state in supporting the decision-making process.

Still, regardless of what changes are made to the state accountability system, choice should be driven by what families want for their specific child, not by criteria set by distant experts.[108] For that to happen, some amount of governmental infrastructure is required. But that governmental infrastructure should be designed to support a choice process where families have real options and good information about those options.

The fact that better processes are needed for families to sort among their options doesn't answer the question of what options families should have. As we have seen, those options are currently shaped by geography—and, in some instances, by state charter school laws. In the next chapter, we'll wrap up Part III by examining some policy changes that might create more options for the families who need it most.

Chapter 12

Repositioning School Choice

Education is a public good. Society benefits when all children have the opportunity to get a great education, however, that is defined. That value is consistently acknowledged by advocates across a wide range of viewpoints. We don't always treat education respectfully as a public good, but we at least acknowledge that it is one.

But education is also a private good. The fact that parents want a better education for their child is meaningful and helps reinforce its importance in society. Parents have always chosen schools to the best of their ability and will continue to do so. In an open and pluralistic society that is how it should be.

Any system for managing a good that is both public and private will necessarily entail a host of trade-offs. What we have struggled with is the fact that the trade-offs policymakers have made generally exacerbate inequity in educational opportunity. This is not a partisan political statement; both Republicans and Democrats have at times taken steps to create more equity and diversity, and at times have taken steps to protect the wealthy. But as a positional good, ideally education should create more opportunities for those who have historically been excluded—while not achieving equity by punishing the successful.

Let's start with a premise we've touched on before: if rich people want their children to attend school with other rich children, they're going to find a way. (These rich families will often be white, as there are long-standing racial gaps in income and wealth.)[1] If we really believe that families should be able to choose the best options for their children, that has to apply to the affluent people as well—and let's be real, there's no way to set up a system of choice among publicly funded options in which the affluent people have their choices constrained more than everybody else does. If that happens, the affluent people will just opt out of the system altogether, because they can.

What we don't want, though, is a situation in which only the affluent people have choice. That's where states come in. States should not presume to know what's best for families, but they can make it easier for more families to find what's best for them.

That's a tall order, and not something that will be easily achieved. But perhaps it's possible to at least move in that direction. In this chapter, we'll take a look at what that might entail.

DISTRICT BOUNDARIES

States are responsible for the processes by which districts come into existence—and go out of it. One manner in which districts go out of existence is by consolidating.[2] School district consolidation is a complex issue, and there are many pros and cons of school districts coming together.[3] School district consolidation does not necessarily save money or improve student outcomes.[4] States forcing school districts to consolidate is both politically painful and operationally difficult.[5]

While there is ample evidence that having small and fragmented districts can create educational inequity, there's nothing to suggest that states imposing new district lines on an area is likely to end well—especially because if the new districts created are unfavorable enough to wealthy people, they'll just move.

The bigger concern for states at this point is likely secession. There are instances in which small wealthy enclaves leave larger districts—which gives them more control over attendance boundaries and often spares wealthy parents from having to subsidize the education of lower-income families. State law allows these secessions to occur, and indeed, in some recent instances, special state laws have been passed to facilitate those secessions.[6]

The issue policy can control for is the externalities created by the choices of the affluent people. An externality is the consequence of an activity that is not captured in the cost of that activity.[7] When the wealthy sequester themselves from other families, there is a cost to that. Let's take a look at those costs in the context of secession. From the vantage point of the newly created enclave, there are two major advantages.

- One is that they now have much greater control over who attends their local schools. If the newly formed district is comparatively homogenous demographically, that will be reflected in the school's population. If these students are wealthy, then odds are they will have generally higher test scores, which will help give the district a strong accountability rating—and will help the district look good on school search websites.
- The second is financial. Schools are funded by a mix of property taxes and state funding, with the state funding typically weighted to account

for student characteristics and local property wealth. A wealthy district that secedes will almost certainly lose state funding, because it is serving a more affluent population. But the property wealth in that affluent community will no longer be spread across a larger and economically diverse area, meaning that the new district will likely have more money to spend per pupil—and might be able to increase spending while reducing property taxes. Not having to subsidize the less affluent neighborhoods nearby makes the change a financial win for the smaller community.

From the perspective of the seceding district, these are potentially significant advantages. But for the district left behind, secession can be a big problem. Losing affluent students may well make it harder for the district to meet its performance goals and also may create a serious hole in its budget. These externalities make it much harder for the now-smaller district to be successful. And while this analysis has focused on secession, in many areas the long-standing existence of enclave districts has simply been baked into the system.

District boundaries aren't meant to be set in stone for all eternity, and wealthy districts should be allowed to secede from larger districts if they choose. Ultimately, if the wealthy parents in a community want to avoid sending their kids to school with kids from neighboring communities, they're going to find a way. The key for the state is to ensure that those parents don't save money by doing it—that in fact, secession should lead to breakaway communities subsidizing the neighborhoods around them.

A seceding district is actually taking away options from students from families with low incomes—so if the state is going to allow that to happen, it should demand enough money from that district to make up for the loss of options. It should be more expensive on an ongoing basis for the breakaway district to leave than it would be to stay, and the extra revenue should be used to offset costs for the district left behind. Think of it as a contractual buyout clause: there's some price at which it's worth it for the original district to let go.

REGIONAL ENROLLMENT APPROACHES

Structuring a Regional Approach

If the goal is to create regional approaches that improve opportunities for students from families with low incomes, consolidation is one tool—but historically a difficult one to use effectively. A potentially more promising approach is to create incentives for regional structures that offer better opportunities for students. Those regional approaches would not require dismantling or re-establishing existing district structures, but they would open up more choices for families to enroll in schools across district lines.[8] Through a formal structure of inter-district transfers, they would open the possibility of students in each participating district attending schools in other participating districts.

In thinking about regional approaches, it's important to acknowledge that the concept of "region" is a pretty fluid one. As we saw earlier, school districts in the south already tend to be larger—whereas in the northeast and Midwest, they can be small and fragmented.[9] Most states already provide support for districts through regional structures, although the functions of those structures vary quite a bit.[10] For our purposes, let's use the term "region" to refer to an economically heterogenous area that includes what are now multiple school districts.

Region-wide enrollment options would allow parents to select from a larger universe of schools for their children. As we've seen, inter-district enrollment has historically been a method for school districts that already serve primarily affluent students to attract yet more affluent students, drawing them away from more economically integrated districts. So it would be important to ensure that a region-wide choice option doesn't simply replicate that experience.

Whether that happens or not is likely to be largely a function of how the funding is set up. If regional enrollment plans do not provide adequate funding or transportation—or threaten schools' accountability ratings—they are unlikely to be embraced by affluent communities.[11] But with adequate funding, wealthier districts may be willing to enroll students from families with low incomes.[12]

It would also be important for regional approaches to take into account the implications on accountability. If a school is being judged on proficiency, it will be understandably hesitant to enroll students who are very far behind. If a student who is two or three years behind academically seeks to enroll in a new school, that school can basically assume that this new student will hurt its accountability rating for years to come. That's a disincentive to wanting to take on that student.

But if the school's accountability is based primarily on growth, the implications change. A student who is very far behind entering a strong academic environment may in fact be able to improve their performance when surrounded by talented classmates.[13] Helping that student will likely require targeted supports focused on the impact of the transition and the differences in their new surroundings.[14]

There have already been some successful attempts to develop regional magnet schools, which can potentially provide specialized options within a larger regional context.[15] We'll talk in a moment about how charter schools might fit into this picture. But the bottom line is that both affluent and non-affluent parents might appreciate having the broader set of choices that a regional framework provides—especially if the finances are favorable.

Paying for a Regional Approach

If states want inter-district transfers to help create more options for students from families with low incomes, there's a simple way to do it: pay for it. If states make it an attractive option for higher-resource districts to take on new students—and states invest in the systems needed to make an inter-district transfer system effective—at some point districts will find it worth their while. In the past, attempts to force integration and diversity have sparked substantial resistance; attempts to buy it will surely do the same, but at least create an incentive for politically responsive bodies to take desired action. State investment and action are a potentially important catalyst to inter-district cooperation.

It is possible to put together regional approaches through the collaborative efforts of individual districts.[16] But so far, those efforts haven't had a lot of impact.[17] Affluent communities may be reluctant to give up what they see as their competitive advantage. Less affluent communities may feel like hyper-localism at least gives them control of their own resources, which they may not want to surrender.[18] The potential disadvantages are real for all concerned, and in many metropolitan areas, those potential disadvantages will carry the day.

One of the most well-known examples of inter-district transfer is from Missouri, where the Normandy district lost its accreditation in 2013.[19] Under state law this meant that Normandy students could transfer to other districts, and Normandy had to pay for it.[20] Normandy was a largely Black district, and most of the districts where its students ended up were largely white—creating significant racial tension in the reassignment.[21] But in describing Normandy's travails, Professor Noliwe Rooks notes that in the 1980s white districts willingly took in Black students, because the finances made sense for them.[22]

Part of why the Normandy district lost its accreditation is that low levels of wealth within the district made it hard to stay financially viable.[23] We've talked earlier about the need for greater equity across districts. But even if states make progress in that direction, it's unlikely they're going to completely solve the problem any time soon.

That's why the key to successful inter-district approaches is the state's willingness to subsidize students from families with low incomes. If a wealthy district is considering taking on a low-income student and the state is offering it $3,000, chances are it won't take the deal. If the state is offering $30,000 per student, a lot of districts would take the deal.[24]

The exact numbers will change over time, but the principle will remain the same: there's some amount of money that would be tempting enough to get school districts to want to take on new students from lower-income families. In keeping with the discussion from Part II, this additional funding would also help to attract and support talented teachers.

Providing subsidies for inter-district transfers is similar in principle to the arguments for funding equity in state education formulas. In school funding advocacy and litigation, advocates have argued that students from families with low incomes should receive more support from the state. Historically most of that advocacy has focused on supporting those students in their current district, but the idea is the same if the student is going to a nearby school across what is now a political boundary.

While the mechanics could vary from state to state, the basic approach a state could take would be to offer incentives for high-resource districts to take on students from families with low incomes. To create a truly balanced market, the state might also have to offer incentives that encourage students from high-resource districts to choose alternative schools in other districts.

The exact amount of money would have to vary from region to region, and would likely need to change over time. And states could shift the incentives to respond to market conditions; states could start with lower incentives and raise them steadily until uptake approaches desired levels. But incentives can drive behavior in a more open-choice market,[25] and states should be strategic in how they set up those incentives.

The incentives will also need to be calibrated to support what are now lower-resource communities, who may see students leaving for other districts. These districts will only enter inter-district agreements if their needs are also met, which means that the resource levels they receive must continue to be commensurate with their population. The incentives could be packaged with the reforms needed to incentivize putting the best teachers with the students who need them most, as described in Part II; the gravitational pull of those two efforts should be aligned.

As discussed earlier, the ideal would be for these districts to receive the resources needed for teachers and students to compete effectively and offer higher-quality schools. Even if that's not the case, it will be important for the financial incentives to align so that these districts can be successful even with potentially reduced populations—but without creating expensive hold harmless funding that forces states to pay for students that aren't there. This, too, will require ongoing balancing.

Importantly, this approach would still leave the final decisions about participation to individual districts and parents. Districts could choose to participate or not in an incentive program, which would create an ongoing negotiation between the state and districts. Parents could survey the existing landscape and choose the option best for their child, which might well be the school closest to their home. The state would change the incentives, but the choices would remain as close to the ground as possible.

Part of the package states would have to fund to make a regional approach appealing is the core infrastructure needed to actually run the ongoing operation. If a regional inter-district transfer agreement is going to be successful, it will need ongoing capacity to manage the choice process, as well as to provide transportation. While individual districts might reasonably be expected to contribute to those costs, state subsidies would surely go a long way toward encouraging local participation.

In effect, this amounts to states trying to buy economic integration. But arguably that's a better approach than trying to force it, which generally hasn't worked. And it's a recognition that right now the governmentally designed market has aligned multiple incentives to favor schools serving the more affluent families.

Right now, there are wealthy parents who would be willing to send their children to a more economically diverse school—but not if it means moving, or paying higher taxes, or sending their kid to a school that seems really under-resourced and/or academically insufficient, or sending their kid to a school with no critical mass of demographically similar children. If the government shifted its role in regulating the market to create different incentives, parents—of all incomes—might start making different choices. In some communities there is latent demand for something different, and a new incentive structure favoring regional collaboration might unleash that latent demand.

Offering incentives for inter-district collaboration would also likely have a meaningful effect on local school board elections. In metropolitan areas with lots of small districts, new incentives for inter-district partnership would confront districts with new kinds of choices—and it's likely that candidates for school board seats would offer different visions of how to resolve those choices. That's a good thing, as participation in inter-district agreements is exactly the kind of issue that ought to be contested through the democratic process.[26]

Indeed, in some metropolitan areas there would likely be a bit of a sorting, as some districts choose to participate and others do not. Those district-level choices would impact real estate markets, as some families choose housing based in part on the available school options in a particular district. And this dynamic market would shift over time with residential patterns and electoral results, which would in turn require ongoing responses from the state.

It is of course reasonable to ask why a state should provide these incentives and pay for all of this infrastructure to support inter-district transfers. There are a few reasons why it might.

- For progressives, this approach supports equity. It's a tangible action that can support improved options and outcomes for low-income families, and in many contexts families of color. In the long term it could also create conditions in which diversity in schools is normalized, which could help increase the demand for diverse and integrated schools. That can give it political appeal on the left.
- For conservatives, it offers more choices for families. The conservative Heritage Foundation has argued that attendance zone boundaries should be eliminated, with more choice made available across districts;[27] the Foundation for Excellence in Education—founded by Jeb Bush, a Republican and the former governor of Florida—has advocated for open enrollment across district lines.[28] Those proposals are directionally similar to the one here. Conservatives often articulate increased choice as a key value in education, and a plan like this creates more options in a broader market. That's particularly true if a state also includes charter school reforms as part of the package; we'll get to that in a minute.
- For the wealthy—well, the wealthy probably aren't going to get out and lobby for a proposal like this. But they might not oppose it too vehemently, because districts that want to sit out the process will still have the right to do so. Indeed, they might see this as a useful compromise that helps to stave off the likelihood of more forcible interventions.

A voluntary regional approach like this should be much more politically viable than mandated consolidation or other state-imposed mandates.

There's no question that a central challenge of this approach is that states may struggle to effectively balance competing interests over time. There are a lot of forces at play in an inter-district approach like this one: a broad spectrum of district interests, and an even broader spectrum of parental interests.

It is reasonable to be skeptical of the ability of states to calibrate incentives to keep those interests in equilibrium. This will be particularly true in states where districts are highly fragmented, which are also the states where regional approaches would be most impactful.[29] Some states may have regional governance structures that could in theory be helpful,[30] although that can't be assumed.

But even if states struggle to do this well, it will still likely be an improvement over the status quo. The fact that families have limited choices now is a function of state policies that make it easy for districts to exclude low-income families from outside their borders, and even give them incentives to do so.

So even if these new agreements are implemented imperfectly, districts will have better incentives to consider different approaches—and families will have more choices than they do now. The choices will still be with districts and families, but the factors they take into consideration in making those choices could be very different.

It would undoubtedly take a few years for states to figure out how to support these partnerships most effectively and to maximize the leverage of their investment in greater equity. That process will not be costless, nor is it guaranteed to go well. But that is a process worth going through and a capacity worth building.

INCLUDING CHARTERS

One of the key ideas of a regional approach to school choice is to give families more options, so it makes sense to include charter schools in such an approach. State law governs whether or not charter schools can enroll students from multiple districts, and in some cases, this practice is already permitted.[31] The inclusion of charter schools in regional choice plans should be done in a manner consistent with the overall goals of the enterprise.

The most important animating principle of the proposal here is to improve the outcomes for children from low-income families. For that to work, the per-student funding attached to children from low-income families would have to be sufficient to cover the real cost of their education—whether that student is in a school serving primarily children from low-income families, or in a more economically heterogenous school. That per-student weighted funding should extend to charters. This would allow those schools to pay teachers more, offer additional student services, or take whatever other steps they see as most necessary to serve their community effectively.

Even in a broader choice environment where families have more options among existing schools, the potential of charter schools is to create something different and new—and fresh starts can be important to educational innovation.[32] This is not to say that charters are inevitably better than traditional schools; they aren't.[33] But in a complex market with varying parent preferences, including charter schools increases the potential for parents to find the right match for their children.

Moreover, when charter schools are forced to focus only on individual districts, then in a geographic area with multiple small districts there may be no logical place for a charter school—even if that charter school could add substantial value in the overall region. Placing charter schools in a regional context makes them less threatening to each individual school district. Charter schools can at times fill a valuable niche that traditional neighborhood schools don't fill, and in the context of a regional approach to enrollment, states should require that charter options be considered.[34]

In considering those charter options, there's a balance to be struck between the right of authorizers to open charters where they see fit and the desire of collaborating school districts to manage enrollment options. It's reasonable to consider the impact of charters on surrounding schools.[35] School districts collectively managing a regional enrollment approach should have some ability to influence the entry of charter schools into their region, but not the ability to keep them out altogether. State law will have to set a framework for this interaction, preserving some rights and flexibility for authorizers while requiring their engagement with regional collaboratives in filling niches.

Choice enthusiasts sometimes argue that the key to success goes beyond the design of individual charter schools and must encompass the management systems used to oversee charter schools.[36] There is surely truth in that.

But what's interesting is that the most important example of a completely fresh start, New Orleans, actually kept in place one of the most important limitations on school options. As noted previously, after Hurricane Katrina, New Orleans essentially shut down its entire school system and replaced it with a charter-driven approach.[37] As Professor Terry Moe points out, post-hurricane, the structures that frequently stand in the way of reform—school administrations and teacher unions—were too weakened to stop the dramatic changes sought by reformers.[38]

In New Orleans, though, there wasn't a regional approach—the entirely new school system was built essentially on the geographic footprint of the old one. Moe talks about the vested interests that obstruct change, but without much focus on perhaps the most important one: the largely white suburbs surrounding a largely Black central city that were not included in the reform effort.[39] When all other institutions had been wiped out, school district boundaries still held firm.

Regional approaches aren't a magical cure-all, and neither are charter schools. But some of the core principles underlying them are the same: families should have multiple options for schooling, and family choice should drive student placement. These are sound values, and should be harmonized to the extent possible in developing systems to help students from families with low incomes. But as we've seen, really helping those students from families with low incomes cannot be the sole province of the K-12 system.

THE FEDERAL ROLE IN HELPING STATES
TO CREATE MORE OPTIONS

There are undoubtedly some number of state leaders who would like very much to implement a system of incentives like the ones described earlier. But change is hard. Even if there is a political majority that agrees with the principles underlying Part III, there may be reasonable skepticism about the likelihood the state will implement the changes successfully. Moreover, as we've seen, the history of state efforts to build and sustain capacity is not a great one.

This is where the federal government can come in. If states are willing to take efforts to support greater income-based equity at the local level—including building capacity to sustain ongoing efforts—the federal government should provide resources to support those state efforts. The federal government provides a very small percentage of the nation's overall education funding, but it exercises substantial leverage over state behavior. If the federal government committed to supporting state efforts to build more equitably financed systems of school choice, the odds that states would do so go up substantially.[40]

Just as states should create financial incentives that are voluntary for districts, so too should the federal government create incentives that are voluntary for states. One way to approach the distribution of funds would be to borrow the model used for State Advisory Council startup grants described in chapter 3. To briefly refresh, money was allocated to each state, based largely on population. States had a lot of discretion as to how they wanted to use the funds; they had to prepare applications describing how they planned to use their allocation, and the applications were approved as long as they fell within the statute's permitted uses.

Here that funding approach could once again make sense. The federal government could define parameters that states would have to meet to support the creation of an improved ecosystem for family choice—which could include support for regional collaborations, new approaches to funding and secession, infrastructure to support the choice process, or other ideas that states generate. States would get an annual allocation of funds to implement those plans, and would be held accountable to for following those plans.

Over time, the accountability for the program should be consistent with the goals of the program. States should be able to show that students from families with low incomes have multiple options, and that more of them are ultimately attending well-resourced schools. These results should be tracked against accountability results to see if those schools are actually providing a better experience. Especially if states have built analytic capacity, the education community will learn more about what it takes to sustain schools that provide a strong education to diverse student bodies; state plans should be allowed to evolve so as to implement those lessons. States also will learn from each other.[41]

STARTING EARLY

Early childhood doesn't have the same local governance structure as school districts—which would have implications for any attempt to develop regional governance. But if regional structures are being developed to improve educational outcomes, those structures should include a focus on the early years, given their importance to long-term child outcomes. As we've seen, the early years are the best opportunity to catch up students who have fallen behind. If more children are proficient by third grade, that's good for the kids—and it also increases the odds that a regional collaboration will be successful.

One major challenge to early success is student mobility, which can be high in the early years when families have less wealth. A 2009 analysis found that only 55 percent of children enter third grade in the same school where they attended kindergarten.[42] If anything, this emphasizes the value of a regional approach with younger children, given that they may be moving through multiple residences in the same metropolitan area.

Some states have already established regional early childhood advisory councils, with varying responsibilities.[43] If states are seeking to create new regional structures to support K-12 education, they will have to figure out how these early childhood structures fit in. But given that many of these structures are advisory or narrowly focused, it is likely that the design of the K-12 inter-district collaboration will be the primary driver—and that early childhood will be fit into that structure.

One of the historical arguments against inter-district transfers came from schools with high proficiency rates, arguing that taking on low-performing kids would hurt their accountability scores. That argument was, unfortunately, valid, as taking on kids who were behind could in fact have adverse consequences for a district's rating.

As noted earlier (and discussed in more depth in chapter 3), shifting the focus to growth reduces the potency of that argument. And another way to mitigate the issue is to have a higher percentage of children in the eligible pool who are already proficient. Schools are more likely to willingly accept children who are already at grade level, and better early childhood services could contribute to that proficiency.

We have seen that the parents of academically successful children want their kids to go to school with other academically successful children.

However much they say they value diversity, history shows that many afflu-ent families value diversity less than they value surrounding their kids with other successful kids. So now we connect another dot: improved outcomes in the early years may be an important strategy to increasing diversity in schools, because having more students proficient by third grade—and kinder-garten—is likely to help the cause of voluntary integration.

The exact role of regional structures in supporting early childhood will vary from region to region and from state to state, depending on existing conditions. But including early childhood in regional strategies should be a key part of the approach. Having more children on track academically is good for children, and should also reduce adult resistance to regional enroll-ment approaches. That could open up options for more children to find the school setting that best fits their interests and personalities—with all of those school settings more likely to have a critical mass of children who are already proficient.

CONCLUSION

The underlying principle of Part III is that all choices are contextual. The decisions made by parents, school districts, and states that have led to our cur-rent inequities were all driven by factors that will remain present in the future. It's not possible to legislate those factors out of existence. But it is possible to use resources to change the decision-making context, and rebalance the scales in favor of communities that have historically been underserved.

The school choice environment for low-income families is heavily influ-enced by state policy. To maximize the number of good options those families have, states need to align their financial incentives to ensure that:

- Districts are motivated to work with each other to create regional part-nerships that offer new options for low-income families;
- Inter-district partnerships—and larger individual districts—have the capacity to advocate thoughtfully designed supports for parents exercis-ing choice, and the resources to overcome practical obstacles (including transportation);
- Wealthy enclaves that want to secede from large and diverse districts can only do so if they subsidize the district they leave behind;
- Neighborhood schools have the chance to be successful financially even if they serve substantial numbers of students from families with low incomes; and

- Charter schools have the opportunity to be a part of choice processes at the regional and district level, offering useful alternatives to neighborhood schools.

In establishing these incentives, states should still leave important choices to the local level; having a thumb on the scale is different than forcing districts to act in particular ways. If the incentives don't work, the state should consider whether stronger incentives might be appropriate. And while states should be responsible for managing choice ecosystems, the federal government will be an important backstop of support. Federal mandates on states and districts have led to pushback even when their aims are noble; federal support for the process of locally driven change will likely be a more effective and sustainable approach.

Conclusion

Applying for federal grants can be a stressful experience for state education leaders. Ideally, it's an opportunity for multiple stakeholders to come together to try to find common solutions to shared problems. But it isn't always that way.

So picture a conference room filled with more than a dozen stakeholders—mostly mid-level managers in state agencies—discussing a grant application that has them tied in knots. The agencies involved have different visions for how to use the money, and the outside advocates are deeply skeptical of state government. The application deadline is closing in, and a desperate last-ditch attempt is being made to reach some agreement.

As the facilitator's efforts flounder, one of the senior agency leaders rises to command the floor. Her exact words are lost to history, but the general gist was something like this:

> This grant is an incredible opportunity for our state to make some really important changes. We can change our systems to better meet the needs of families. We can try new approaches that can lead to better child outcomes. Or at least the rest of you can, because our agency is all good and we're going to keep doing what we've always done.

The state ended up not applying for the grant.

Change is hard. It is easy for tour guides to point out changes that ought to get made.[1] It is much harder for the people actually doing the work to change their behaviors, potentially at some risk to their careers.

Policy is all about tradeoffs. And when we talk about the tradeoffs involved in a particular policy direction, many of us like to tell ourselves that we're a reasonable arbiter trying to provide a realistic view of what's actually possible. And sometimes we are. But sometimes, we're proposing a completely unrealistic approach that could never actually happen in real life.

This book was written as if there is some realistic hope that stakeholders would actually take the deals it proposes. That might be true in some places. But it's also possible that everybody reading will just stand up, say they're doing fine, and keep doing what they're doing.

The issues raised here are far from the only important ones when it comes to improving education. And the education system as a whole can only do so much to improve child experiences.[2] But these issues are important, and a great deal of energy has already been spent on them. Perhaps there are ways in which that energy could be channeled more effectively, especially at a time when the fiery debates of the pandemic have taken so much out of people.

No Child Left Behind (NCLB) represented a moment when the federal government decided to expend some energy on improving education. Federal legislators recognized that there was a tradeoff between consistent excellence on the one hand and local control on the other. In NCLB, they decided to start emphasizing the former at the expense of the latter.

Ultimately, they were right to do that, even if they got the mechanics wrong. The Every Student Succeeds Act attempted to shift that balance somewhat back toward local control while improving slightly on the mechanics. That might also have been correct, but it didn't represent a fundamental change in approach to accountability.

In fact, there are two fundamental shifts that are needed in accountability. One is a shift from thinking about measurement to thinking about capacity-building. The federal and state governments have the power to put pressure on school districts to improve, without actually offering them the tools they need to get better; for years, they have been using that power.

That's an easy political tradeoff for federal and state leaders: they get to claim they're doing something to improve education, without having to do the hard work of paying for the capacity needed to make things better. Given how politics works, it's unlikely that federal and state leaders will ever change their approach as fully as district and school leaders might hope, but it's important to keep pushing them in that direction.

The second fundamental shift is to stop pretending that accountability for results in third grade and up is a viable strategy for getting kids ready to succeed at the end of high school. The earlier years are so important developmentally, and so under-resourced compared to the later ones. Those years are our best chance to actually produce the results we want, and under-investing in them is a strategy that's bound to fail.

There are good reasons that shift has proven difficult. For one thing, it's expensive. For another thing, the current early childhood system is fragmented and complicated, which can make it hard for policymakers to have confidence that their investments in it will have the intended impact. And, what's more, much of the payoff it offers is long term; while there are immediate benefits to the families it serves, the systemic benefits unfold over the course of many years.

These obstacles are real, but they're not insurmountable. The popularity of early childhood services—and the research base demonstrating their importance—has led to continued investment over the years. That's promising, but the pace hasn't been fast enough. Solving the problems of K-12 will require solving the problems of early childhood, and K-12 advocates who ignore those years are consigning themselves to a cycle of disappointment with which the field is all too familiar.

So let's say that policymakers are able to shift these tradeoffs to invest a little bit more in supportive capacity and more still in early childhood, while taking an approach to quality measurement that is more respectful of local prerogatives. Now they've started to make teaching a more appealing job. The adult work will be better, because teachers will have better resources to work with—and the children will be further along thanks to their early childhood experiences. That's a better value proposition.

But the hard tradeoff here will be the work needed to get the best teachers into classrooms with more students from families with low incomes. Part of that will come from changing how teachers are assigned. Right now we pay teachers based on their characteristics; instead, we need to pay them based on roles. And the roles that we need to value are the ones that are hardest to fill, including the ones focused on working with students from lower-income families. Limited resources should be spent on the things that matter most, and good teachers for students from families with low incomes matter a great deal.

In making this shift, policymakers need to be respectful of the work teachers do and the value they add. It's not the fault of the teachers in the system today that there's such a misalignment between need and capacity. Shifting the system to prioritize the right things will come at some cost to current teachers, and that cost should be accounted for—especially in the context of an effort to create greater trust between policymakers and teachers. It's better to pay the cost of a respectful transition than to sustain a misaligned system in perpetuity, or to try to create a new system in a firestorm of justified frustration.

Part of the work of getting teachers into the classrooms where they're most needed is rethinking how school choice is organized and managed. The existing system of school districts is deeply grounded in our nation's history and has a democratic legitimacy that should not be ignored. But it also has led to significant inequities and constrained the choices of families with limited means. We need to make that tradeoff differently, and create new opportunities for those families to find the right school for their kids.

In doing so, structures of support will matter. Families need more options, but they also need support for the process of navigating those options. In developing support systems, we should leverage existing infrastructure, while acknowledging the new infrastructure we need to build to make it work. We have underinvested in the infrastructure of choice, and because of that, wealthy people are able to navigate the system much more effectively than people who are not.

What's proposed here requires spending money, including to build capacity that doesn't currently exist. That's not an accident. As the old saying goes, every system is perfectly set up to get the results it's currently getting. If we're going to set up a system to do something different, we need to set up a different system, and that's not free.

In that vein, it's worth acknowledging that even if policymakers fully embrace the goals articulated here, transition is hard. That's been flagged at a few points along the way, but almost surely the difficulties of transition have been understated.

In fact, you'll see in all of these proposals an attempt to provide some balance between what is and what could be. There are plenty of policy proposals that are thrilling in their ambition but utterly implausible to execute. There are also plenty of policy proposals that are thoroughly banal and unlikely to have any meaningful impact.[3] This book has attempted to steer between those outcomes; it surely has missed in both directions along the way, but that's been the goal.

One of the consistent themes in this book is that on key policy issues, we've had the wrong primary driver. All three parts of this book, Parts I–III, propose replacing what is currently the primary driver with something new. To summarize those proposed changes:

Table D.1 Summary of Policy Drivers

Policy Area	Current Primary Driver	Proposed Primary Driver
Accountability	*Test scores*. School ratings are determined primarily by how students perform on standardized tests.	*Success in the early years*. School ratings should be designed to help schools focus on strengthening their work in the years before third grade.
Teacher Hiring in Schools Serving Children from Low-Income Families	*Characteristics*. Senior teachers can choose where they work, and are paid the same even if they work primarily with students who are affluent and successful.	*Role*. The roles in the district most likely to help children from low-income backgrounds should be paid in a manner that demonstrates the district's commitment to the success of those roles.
Parent Choice for Low-Income Families	*Political boundaries*. Lines among districts – and drawn within districts – are the primary determinant of which families can enroll in which schools.	*Parent interest*. The primary driver of school choice should be parent interest, with financial incentives for schools that choose to welcome students from low-income families.

Even if policymakers don't come close to doing everything proposed in this book, making the directional shifts described here would represent an incremental improvement for the children who need the most help. And for policymakers, it's important to think in terms of directional shifts; policymakers cannot possibly get all the details right and often shouldn't even try. What they can do is create conditions where districts, schools, teachers, and parents are more likely to be successful in what they're trying to accomplish. These directional shifts are all proposed in that spirit.

But think about what it might mean for children if we do accomplish all of these changes. The early years of education—which are so critical to long-term outcomes—will receive more focus from educational leaders. The children who need the most help from great teachers will be more likely to receive it. And it will be easier for families to enroll their children in the schools that best meet their needs. Add it up, and it makes for a very different experience of the public education system than many children have today.

The history of education reform suggests that these changes won't happen quickly—if they happen at all, which may not actually be all that likely. But all of the approaches proposed here are meant to be within the realm of the possible. Leaders willing to take fresh angles at long-standing problems may be able to build unexpected alliances and make meaningful headway toward a better system in the coming years.

And in taking fresh approaches, it will be important for everybody involved to have more empathy. We've seen repeatedly that distrust is built into the system, and that's a necessary feature of large government systems. That distrust could be channeled more constructively, but it will always be there.

So while we can't get rid of distrust, we can moderate it with empathy. Empathy for the parents who are trying to support their child's education. Empathy for the teachers who are doing their best to educate children under difficult conditions. Empathy for the administrators who are trying to manage a complex system with myriad competing demands.[4] Empathy for the policymakers who are trying to use the limited tools at their disposal to better serve their constituents. And even empathy for the advocates who argue passionately for diametrically opposed outcomes, many of whom have deep and authentic reasons for their beliefs.

None of these categories of people are villains, and attempting to characterize them as such doesn't advance the debate.[5] We have much to learn from each other when we listen with empathy, including—or maybe even particularly—to people we disagree with. At the very least, we probably all agree that kids should go to schools with toilet paper in the bathrooms; perhaps in time consensus can be forged on the other issues we've toured along the way.

We can do better. Hopefully, we even will. Good luck to all of us in the pursuit.

Notes

PREFACE

1. Conor Williams, "Reform Era Is Ending and American Schools Need a New Paradigm for Tackling Ingrained Inequity," *The 74 Million*, last modified July 22, 2020, https://www.the74million.org/article/williams-the-education-reform-era-is-ending -and-american-schools-need-a-new-paradigm-for-tackling-ingrained-inequity/.

2. Yuval A. Levin, *Time to Build: From Family and Community to Congress and the Campus, How Recommitting to Our Institutions Can Revive the American Dream* (New York: Basic Books, 2020), 54. ("Our political culture is particularly bad at finding durable compromises now. It is even bad at pursuing them—at forcing political actors to face the reality that people with whom they disagree aren't going away, to confront the unavoidable need for trade-offs, and to recognize that politics in our democracy is more of a tug of war than a fight to the death.")

3. Andy Smarick, *The Urban School System of the Future: Applying the Principles and Lessons of Chartering* (Lanham, MD: Rowman & Littlefield, 2012); Frederick M. Hess, *The Same Thing Over and Over: How School Reformers Get Stuck in Yesterday's Ideas* (Cambridge, MA: Harvard University Press, 2010); Charles M. Payne, *So Much Reform, So Little Change: The Persistence of Failure in Urban Schools* (Cambridge, MA: Harvard Education Press, 2008).

4. Frederick M. Hess, "How to Help K-12 Policymakers Help You," *Education Week*, last modified April 2, 2015, https://www.edweek.org/teaching-learning/opinion -how-to-help-k-12-policymakers-help-you/2015/04.

CHAPTER 1

1. Frederick M. Hess and Michael Q. McShane (eds.), *Bush-Obama School Reform: Lessons Learned* (Cambridge, MA: Harvard Education Press, 2018).

2. Kathryn A. McDermott, *High-Stakes Reform: The Politics of Educational Accountability* (Washington, DC: Georgetown University Press, 2011), 72.

3. Deven Carlson, "Testing and Accountability: What Have We Learned and Where Do We Go?"; and Patrick McGuinn, "Incentives and Inducements: The Feds Fight Federalism," in *Bush-Obama School Reform: Lessons Learned*, eds. Hess and McShane (Cambridge, MA: Harvard Education Press, 2018), 17, 52–53.

4. Daniel Koretz, *The Testing Charade: Pretending to Make Schools Better* (Chicago, IL: University of Chicago Press, 2017), 205.

5. U.S. Bureau of Labor Statistics, "Median Weekly Earnings $606 for High School Dropouts, $1,559 for Advanced Degree Holders," last modified October 21, 2019, https://www.bls.gov/opub/ted/2019/median-weekly-earnings-606-for-high-school -dropouts-1559-for-advanced-degree-holders.htm; Alliance for Excellent Education, "The High Cost of High School Dropouts: The Economic Case for Reducing the High School Dropout Rate," accessed July 1, 2021, https://all4ed.org/take-action/action -academy/the-economic-case-for-reducing-the-high-school-dropout-rate/.

6. Arne Duncan, *How Schools Work: An Inside Account of Failure and Success from One of the Nation's Longest-Serving Secretaries of Education* (New York: Simon & Schuster, 2018), 12, 21.

7. David C. Berliner, "The Scandalous History of Schools That Receive Public Financing, But Do Not Accept the Public's Right of Oversight," in *Public Education: Defending a Cornerstone of American Democracy*, eds. David C. Berliner and Carl Hermanns (New York: Teachers College Press, 2021), 273–74; Jason P. Nance, "The Justifications for a Stronger Federal Response to Address Educational Inequities," in *A Federal Right to Education: Fundamental Questions for Our Democracy*, ed. Kimberly Jenkins Robinson (New York: New York University Press, 2019), 52.

8. Koretz, *Testing Charade*, 47.

9. "In some instances under No Child Left Behind well-intentioned federal law led to well-intended state policies that pushed well-intended local educators into educational malpractice." Elliot Regenstein, Maia Connors, and Rio Romero-Jurado, "Valuing the Early Years in State Accountability Systems under the Every Student Succeeds Act," 2, *Start Early*, last modified February 16, 2016, https://startearly.org/app/ uploads/2020/09/PUBLICATION_-Valuing-the-Early-Years-in-State-Accountability -Systems-Under-the-Every-Student-Succeeds-Act.pdf.

10. Carlson, "Testing and Accountability: What Have We Learned and Where Do We Go?," in *Bush-Obama School Reform*, eds. Hess and McShane, (Cambridge, MA: Harvard Education Press, 2018), 18.

11. Andrew Karch and Shanna Rose, *Responsive States: Federalism and American Public Policy* (New York: Cambridge University Press, 2019), 162–85.

12. Every Student Succeeds Act, 20 U.S.C. §6311(c)(4), accessed July 10, 2021, https://www.congress.gov/114/plaws/publ95/PLAW-114publ95.pdf.

13. Elizabeth A. City, Richard F. Elmore, and Doug Lynch, "Redefining Education: The Future of Learning Is Not the Future of Schooling," in *The Futures of School Reform*, eds. Jal Mehta, Robert B. Schwartz, and Frederick M. Hess (Cambridge, MA: Harvard Education Press, 2012), 166; E. D. Hirsch Jr., *How to Educate a Citizen: The Power of Shared Knowledge to Unify a Nation* (New York: Harper, 2020); Thomas Sowell, *Charter Schools and Their Enemies* (New York: Basic Books, 2020),

78; Natalie Wexler, *The Knowledge Gap: The Hidden Cause of America's Broken Education System—and How to Fix It* (New York: Avery, 2019), 29–30.

14. 20 U.S.C. §6311 (c)(4)(B)(i)(II), 20 U.S.C. §6311(c)(4)(B)(ii)(I).

15. For example, David Osborne, *Reinventing America's Schools: Creating a 21st Century Education System* (Berryville, VA: Bloomsbury, 2017), 260–61; Chad Aldeman, "The Case against ESSA: A Very Limited Law," in *The Every Student Succeeds Act: What It Means for Schools, Systems, and States*, eds. Frederick M. Hess and Max Eden (Cambridge, MA: Harvard Education Press, 2017), 95; Bonnie O'Keefe, "From Pandemic to Progress: Eight Education Pathways from COVID-19 Recovery: Redesigning Accountability," *Bellwether Education Partners*, 3–4, last modified February 8, 2021, https://bellwethereducation.org/sites/default/files/Bellwether_PandemictoProgress_RedesignAccountability_Final.pdf; Michael J. Petrilli, "The Problem with Proficiency," *Thomas B. Fordham Institute*, last modified August 14, 2013, https://fordhaminstitute.org/national/commentary/problem-proficiency.

16. Linda Darling-Hammond, *The Flat World and Education: How America's Commitment to Equity Will Determine Our Future* (New York: Teachers College Press, 2010), 118; The Wing Institute, "How Does Reading Proficiency Correlate with a Student's Socio-economic Status?," accessed July 14, 2021, https://www.winginstitute.org/how-does-reading-proficiency; The Wing Institute, "How Does Math Proficiency Correlate with a Student's Socio-economic Status?."

17. Aldeman, "The Case Against ESSA," in *The Every Student Succeeds Act: What It Means for Schools, Systems, and States*, eds. Hess and Eden (Cambridge, MA: Harvard Education Press, 2017), 95.

18. 20 U.S.C. §6311(c)(4)(B)(iii).

19. Charles Barone, "What ESSA Says: Continuities and Departures," in *The Every Student Succeeds Act: What It Means for Schools, Systems, and States*, eds. Hess and Eden(Cambridge, MA: Harvard Education Press, 2017), 65–66; Students Can't Wait, "Setting New Accountability for English-Learner Outcomes in ESSA Plans," last modified 2017, https://studentscantwait.edtrust.org/resource/setting-new-accountability-english-learner-outcomes-essa-plans/.

20. Leslie Villegas and Delia Pompa, "The Patchy Landscape of State English Learner Policies under ESSA," *Migration Policy Institute*, last modified February 2020, https://www.migrationpolicy.org/research/state-english-learner-policies-essa; Corey Mitchell, "In Some States, ESSA Goals for English-Learners Are 'Purely Symbolic,' Report Finds," *EducationWeek*, last modified February 14, 2020, https://www.edweek.org/policy-politics/in-some-states-essa-goals-for-english-learners-are-purely-symbolic-report-finds/2020/02.

21. 20 U.S.C. §6311(c)(4)(B)(v).

22. 20 U.S.C. §6311(c)(4)(B)(v)(I).

23. 20 U.S.C. §6311 (c)(4)(B)(v)(II).

24. Barone, "What ESSA Says," in *The Every Student Succeeds Act: What It Means for Schools, Systems, and States*, eds. Hess and Eden (Cambridge, MA: Harvard Education Press, 2017), 67–68.

25. Jennifer O'Day and Marshall S. Smith, *Opportunity for All: A Framework for Quality and Equality in Education* (Cambridge, MA: Harvard Education Press, 2019), 38.

26. 20 U.S.C. §6311(c)(4)(C).

27. National Institute for Early Education Research, "State(s) of Head Start," *Rutgers Graduate School of Education*, 8, last modified December 2016, https://nieer.org/wp-content/uploads/2016/12/HS_Full_Reduced.pdf.

28. National Head Start Association, "2022 National Head Start & Early Head Start Profile," accessed May 10, 2022, https://nhsa.org/wp-content/uploads/2022/01/National.pdf.

29. National Head Start Association, "Early Head Start Facts and Figures," accessed May 10, 2022, https://nhsa.org/wp-content/uploads/2021/12/Early-Head-Start-Facts-and-Figures_21-22-1.pdf.

30. Head Start Early Childhood Learning & Knowledge Center, "Head Start Approach to School Readiness—Overview," accessed July 14, 2021, https://eclkc.ohs.acf.hhs.gov/school-readiness/article/head-start-approach-school-readiness-overview.

31. Head Start Early Childhood Learning & Knowledge Center, "Designation Renewal System," accessed July 14, 2021, https://eclkc.ohs.acf.hhs.gov/designation-renewal-system.

32. Head Start Early Childhood Learning & Knowledge Center. "Designation Renewal System Overview."

33. Head Start Early Childhood Learning & Knowledge Center. "Designation Renewal System Overview."

34. Head Start Early Childhood Learning & Knowledge Center, "Use of Classroom Assessment Scoring System (CLASS®) in Head Start," accessed July 14, 2021, https://eclkc.ohs.acf.hhs.gov/designation-renewal-system/article/use-classroom-assessment-scoring-system-class-head-start.

35. For example, Douglas B. Downey, *How Schools* Really *Matter: Why Our Assumption about Schools and Inequality Is Mostly Wrong* (Chicago, IL: University of Chicago Press, 2020); Derrick Darby and John L. Rury, *The Color of Mind: Why the Origins of the Achievement Gap Matter for Justice* (Chicago, IL: The University of Chicago Press, 2018), 10; Jeffrey Henig, Helen Janc Malone, and Paul Reville, "Addressing the Disadvantages of Poverty: Why Ignore the Most Important Challenge of the Post-Standards Era?" in *The Futures of School Reform*, eds. Mehta, Schwartz, and Hess, 120, 15–18; Diane Ravitch, *Reign of Error: The Hoax of the Privatization Movement and the Danger to America's Public Schools* (New York: Vintage Books, 2013), 59, 230; National Center for Education Statistics, "Achievement Gaps," *Institute of Education Sciences*, accessed July 14, 2021, https://nces.ed.gov/nationsreportcard/studies/gaps/.

36. McDermott, *High-Stakes Reform*, 77, 169.

37. Cynthia G. Brown, "From ESEA to ESSA: Progress or Regress?" in *The Every Student Succeeds Act: What It Means for Schools, Systems, and States*, eds. Hess and Eden (Cambridge, MA: Harvard Education Press, 2017), 160.

38. Alliance for Excellent Education, "When Equity Is Optional: Results from Early ESSA Implementation," accessed July 14, 2021, https://all4ed.org/When

-Equity-Is-Optional/; Keven Mahnken, "Five Years On, ESSA's Hallmark Flexibility May Be Undermining Equity, Report Finds," *The 74 Million*, last modified December 10, 2020, https://www.the74million.org/five-years-on-essas-hallmark-flexibility-may-be-undermining-equity-report-finds/.

39. Chester E. Finn Jr., "Testing: Education's Indispensable GPS," *Hoover Institution*, last modified May 2021, https://www.hoover.org/research/testing-educations-indispensable-gps; Chester E. Finn Jr., "Results-Based Accountability for Schools: Education's Heaviest Lift," *Hoover Institution*, last modified May 2021, https://www.hoover.org/research/results-based-accountability-schools-educations-heaviest-lift.

40. National Urban League, League of United Latin American Citizens (LULAC), National Action Network (NAN), National Indian Education Association (NIEA), Southeast Asia Resource Action Center (SEARAC), UnidosUS, Council of Parent Attorneys and Advocates (COPAA), National Center for Learning Disabilities, National Center for Special Education in Charter Schools, The Education Trust, Education Reform Now, and Alliance for Excellent Education, "Letter to U.S. Department of Education Deputy Assistant Secretary Ryder," last modified November 20, 2020, http://www.eduwonk.com/wp-content/uploads/2020/11/Civil-Rts-Letter-to-DoED-.pdf.

41. Conor P. Williams, "On Testing, Meritocracy and Educational Equity: How Exams Forced Alexandria Ocasio-Cortez's School to See beyond Stereotypes," *The 74 Million*, last modified March 2019, https://www.the74million.org/article/williams-on-testing-meritocracy-and-educational-equity-how-exams-forced-alexandria-ocasio-cortezs-school-to-see-beyond-stereotypes/; Sharif El-Mekki, "No, You Should Not Be Teaching Black Children If You Reject Anti-Racism," *Education Post*, last modified May 5, 2021, https://educationpost.org/no-you-should-not-be-teaching-black-children-if-you-reject-anti-racism/.

42. Jack Schneider, *Beyond Test Scores: A Better Way to Measure School Quality* (Cambridge, MA: Harvard University Press, 2017), 33.

43. Anya Kamenetz, *The Test: Why Our Schools Are Obsessed with Standardized Testing—But You Don't Have to Be* (Philadelphia, PA: Public Affairs, 2015), 63.

44. Noliwe Rooks, *Cutting School: The Segrenomics of American Education* (New York: The New Press, 2017), 187; Schneider, *Beyond Test Scores*, 19; Jesse Hagopian, "The Testocracy versus the Education Spring," in *More than a Score: The New Uprising against High-Stakes Testing*, ed. Jesse Hagopian, (Chicago, IL: Haymarket Books, 2014), 15.

45. Brian Jones, "Standardized Testing and Students of Color," in *More than a Score*, ed. Hagopian, 72.

46. Koretz, *Testing Charade*; see also Ravitch, *Reign of Error*, 266–70; Deborah Meier, *In Schools We Trust: Creating Communities of Learning in an Era of Testing and Standardization* (Boston, MA: Beacon Press, 2002), 97.

47. Wayne Camara, Michelle Croft, and Alina von Davier, "Data Access, Ethics, and Use in Learning and Navigation Organizations," in *The Ethical Use of Data in Education: Promoting Responsible Policies and Practices*, eds. Ellen B. Mandinach and Edith S. Gummer (New York: Teacher's College Press, 2021), 176, 180, 181; Meier, *In Schools We Trust*, 97; Michael T. Kane, "Validating the Interpretations and

Uses of Test Scores," *Wiley Online Library*, last modified March 14, 2013, https://onlinelibrary.wiley.com/doi/abs/10.1111/jedm.12000.

48. Koretz, *Testing Charade*, 8, 159; Hagopian, "The Testocracy versus the Education Spring," in, *More than a Score*, ed. Hagopian, 16; John Kuhn, *Fear and Learning in America: Bad Data, Good Teachers, and the Attack on Public Education* (New York: Teachers College Press, 2014), 48.

49. Koretz, *Testing Charade*, 121; Kuhn, *Fear and Learning in America*, 54; Richard Rothstein, Rebecca Jacobsen, and Tamara Wilder, *Grading Education: Getting Accountability Right* (Washington, DC and New York: Economic Policy Institute and Teachers College Press, 2008), 60–66.

50. Koretz, *Testing Charade*, 124; Kamenetz, *The Test*, 90; Kuhn, "The Word that Made Me an Activist," in *More than a Score*, ed. Hagopian, 246.

51. Andrew Dean Ho, "The Problem with 'Proficiency': Limitations of Statistics and Policy Under No Child Left Behind," *Educational Researcher*, Vol. 37, No. 6, Aug.–Sep. 2008, pp. 351–60, https://www.jstor.org/stable/25209011.

52. Rothstein, Jacobsen, and Wilder, *Grading Education*, 65–66; Kevin Carey, "The Pangloss Index: How States Game the No Child Left Behind Act," *Education Sector*, last modified November 2007, https://www.issuelab.org/resources/1074/1074.pdf.

53. Schneider, *Beyond Test Scores*, 15.

54. Downey, *How Schools Really Matter*, 13.

55. Darling-Hammond, *The Flat World and Education*, 118; Sam Redding, "Poverty's Impact on Learning," in *Opportunity and Performance: Equity for Children from Poverty: From State Policy to Classroom Practice*, ed. Sam Redding (Charlotte, NC: Information Age Publishing and Academic Development Institute, 2021), 73–74.

56. Richard Rothstein, *Class and Schools: Using Social, Economic, and Educational Reform to Close the Black-White Achievement Gap* (Washington, DC and New York: Economic Policy Institute and Teacher's College Press, 2004), 46–47; Kevin Mahnken, "Research Shows Changing Schools Can Make or Break a Student, But the Wave of Post-COVID Mobility May Challenge the Systems in Ways We've Never Seen," *The 74 Million*, last modified December 15, 2020, https://www.the74million.org/changing-schools-can-make-or-break-a-student-but-the-wave-of-post-covid-mobility-may-challenge-the-systems-in-ways-weve-never-seen/; Russell W. Rumberger, "Student Mobility: Causes, Consequences, and Solutions," *National Education Policy Center*, last modified June 1, 2015, https://nepc.colorado.edu/publication/student-mobility; Sarah D. Sparks, "Student Mobility: How It Affects Learning," *EducationWeek*, last modified August 11, 2016, https://www.edweek.org/leadership/student-mobility-how-it-affects-learning/2016/08.

57. Elliot Regenstein, "Building a Coherent P-12 Education System in California," *Foresight Law + Policy*, last modified February 2021, https://www.flpadvisors.com/uploads/4/2/4/2/42429949/flp_buildingcoherent_tp-12_edsysteminca_020921.pdf; Petrilli, "The Problem with Proficiency."

58. For one of many other examples of this kind of argument, see Petrilli, "The Problem with Proficiency."

59. Damian W. Betebenner, "Norm-and Criterion-Referenced Student Growth," National Center for the Improvement of Educational Assessment, last modified March 2008, https://www.nciea.org/publications/normative_criterion_growth_DB08 .pdf.

60. Matt Barnum and Garbrielle LaMarr LeMee, "Looking for a Home? You've Seen GreatSchools Ratings. Here's How They Nudge Families toward Schools with Fewer Black and Hispanic Students," *Chalkbeat*, last modified December 5, 2019, https://www.chalkbeat.org/2019/12/5/21121858/looking-for-a-home-you-ve-seen -greatschools-ratings-here-s-how-they-nudge-families-toward-schools-wi. Also, as we'll see, these are often white parents who want their children going to school with other white children. Jack Dougherty, Diane Zannoni, Maham Chowhan, Courteney Coyne, Benjamin Dawson, Tehani Guruge, and Begaeta Nukic, "School Information, Parental Decisions, and the Digital Divide: The SmartChoices Project in Hartford, Connecticut," in *Educational Delusions? Why Choice Can Deepen Inequality and How to Make Schools Fair*, eds. Gary Orfield and Erica Frankenberg and Associates (Berkeley: University of California Press, 2013), 228.

61. Jack Schneider and Jennifer Berkshire, *A Wolf at the Schoolhouse Door: The Dismantling of Public Education and the Future of School* (New York: The New Press, 2020), 145.

62. Koretz, *Testing Charade*, 38. Other critiques that address Campbell's law include Sharon L. Nichols, "Educational Policy Contexts and the (Un)ethical Use of Data," in *The Ethical Use of Data in Education*, eds. Mandinach and Gummer (New York: Teacher's College Press, 2021), 85; Diane Ravitch, *Slaying Goliath: The Passionate Resistance to Privatization and the Fight to Save America's Public Schools* (New York: Alfred A. Knopf, 2020), 127; Robert Pondiscio, *How the Other Half Learns: Equality, Excellence, and the Battle over School Choice* (New York: Avery, 2019), 202; Osborne, *Reinventing America's Schools*, 256; Kamenetz, *The Test*, 5; and Rothstein, Jacobsen, and Wilder, *Grading Education*, 77.

63. Ashley Jochim, "The Limits of Policy for School Turnaround," in *Bush-Obama School Reform*, eds. Hess and McShane (Cambridge, MA: Harvard Education Press), 37–38.

64. Jochim, "The Limits of Policy for School Turnaround," 36.

65. Jochim, "The Limits of Policy for School Turnaround," 37–38; Paul Manna, *Collision Course: Federal Education Policy Meets State and Local Realities* (Washington, DC: CQ Press, 2011), 67–96.

66. Jochim, "The Limits of Policy for School Turnaround," 38–43; Manna, *Collision Course*, 67–96.

67. Jochim, "The Limits of Policy for School Turnaround," 43; Chester E. Finn Jr., "School Accountability—Past, Present, and Future," *Hoover Institution*, 21, last modified November 2020, https://www.hoover.org/sites/default/files/research/docs/ finn_webready.pdf; Paul Manna and Arnold Shober, "Answering the Call? Explaining How States Have (or Have Not) Taken Up the ESSA Accountability Challenge," *Hoover Institution*, 2–3, last modified in 2020, https://www.hoover.org/sites/default/ files/research/docs/mannashober_hesi_webreadypdf.pdf.

68. Sowell, *Charter Schools and Their Enemies*, 78.

69. Edward B. Fiske and Helen F. Ladd, "Values and Education Policy," in *Public Education: Defending a Cornerstone of American Democracy*, eds. Berliner and Hermanns, 40; Jack Jennings, *Fatigued by School Reform* (Lanham, MD: Rowman & Littlefield, 2021), 63; Wexler, *The Knowledge Gap*, 8; William Damon, "Restoring Purpose and Patriotism," in *How to Educate an American: The Conservative Vision for Tomorrow's Schools*, eds. Michael J. Petrilli and Chester E. Finn (West Conshohocken, PA: Templeton Press, 2020), 78; Pondiscio, *How the Other Half Learns*, 202–3; Koretz, *Testing Charade*, 194–95; Schneider, *Beyond Test Scores*, 9; Kamenetz, *The Test*, 14–15; Dana Goldstein, *The Teacher Wars: A History of America's Most Embattled Profession* (New York: Anchor Books, 2014), 187; Monty Neill, "Building the Movement against High-Stakes Testing," and "What Could Be," Interview with Phyllis Tashlik, in *More than a Score*, ed. Hagopian, 255 and 285; Rothstein, *Class and Schools*, 117; Frederick M. Hess, *Education Unbound: The Promise and Practice of Greenfield Schooling* (Alexandria, VA: ASCD, 2010), 73; Darling-Hammond, *The Flat World and Education*, 71; Manna, *Collision Course*, 115–18; Deven Carlson, "Holding Accountability Accountable: Taking Stock of the Past 20 Years," *American Enterprise Institute*, 5, last modified May 2020, https://www.aei.org/wp-content/uploads/2021/05/Holding-Accountability-Accountable.pdf?x91208.

70. Koretz, *Testing Charade*, 97.

71. Koretz, *Testing Charade*, 93.

72. Nichols, "Educational Policy Contexts," 87; Pondiscio, *How the Other Half Learns*, 205; Koretz, *Testing Charade*, 93–117.

73. Koretz, *Testing Charade*, 73–92.

74. Ellen B. Mandinach and Edith S. Gummer, "The Landscape of Data Ethics in Education: What Counts as Responsible Data Use," in *The Ethical Use of Data in Education*, eds. Mandinach and Gummer (New York: Teacher's College Press, 2021), 36–37; Nichols, "Educational Policy Contexts," 88–90; Koretz, *Testing Charade*, 91–92.

75. Ellen B. Mandinach and Jo Beth Jimerson, "The Role of Classroom, School, and District to Ensure the Ethical Use of Data: It's More than Just FERPA," in, *The Ethical Use of Data in Education*, ed. Mandinach and Gummer, 110–11; Carlson, "Testing and Accountability: What Have We Learned and Where Do We Go?," in *Bush-Obama School Reform*, eds. Hess and McShane, 25; Koretz, *Testing Charade*, 69; Harry Brighouse, Helen F. Ladd, Susanna Loeb, and Adam Swift, *Educational Goods: Values, Evidence, and Decision-Making* (Chicago, IL: University of Chicago Press, 2018), 122; Rothstein, Jacobsen, and Wilder, *Grading Education*, 67; David L. Kirp, *Improbable Scholars: The Rebirth of a Great American School System and a Strategy for America's Schools* (New York: Oxford University Press, 2013), 172.

76. Koretz, *Testing Charade*, 155.

77. Education Commission of the States, "50-State Comparison: States' School Accountability Systems," last modified May 31, 2018, https://www.ecs.org/50-state-comparison-states-school-accountability-systems/.

78. Meier, *In Schools We Trust*.

79. Jennifer A. O'Day and Marshall S. Smith, *Opportunity for All*, 91; Michael Fullan and Joanne Quinn, *Coherence: The Right Drivers in Action for Schools,*

Districts, and Systems (Thousand Oaks, CA: Corwin, 2016), 3; W. Patrick Dolan, *Restructuring Our Schools: A Primer on Systemic Change* (Naperville, IL: Westport Group, 1994), 23.

80. Fullan and Quinn, *Coherence*, 109; see also O'Day and Smith, *Opportunity for All*, 90–91; Jal Mehta, *The Allure of Order: High Hopes, Dashed Expectations, and the Troubled Quest to Remake American Schooling* (New York: Oxford University Press, 2013), 260–61.

81. Larry Cuban, *Chasing Success and Confronting Failure in American Public Schools* (Cambridge, MA: Harvard Education Press, 2020), 82–87; Mehta, *Allure of Order*, 30–31.

82. Katherine Schultz, *Distrust and Educational Change: Overcoming Barriers to Just and Lasting Reform* (Cambridge, MA: Harvard Education Press, 2019), 109; Finn Jr., "School Accountability," 14.

83. Nichols, "Educational Policy Contexts," 85; Fullan and Quinn, *Coherence*, 3–4; Richard F. Elmore, *School Reform from the Inside Out: Policy, Practice, and Performance* (Cambridge, MA: Harvard Education Press, 2004), 221.

84. Daarel Burnette II, "Face It, School Governance Is a Mess," *EducationWeek*, last modified January 7, 2020, https://www.edweek.org/leadership/face-it-school -governance-is-a-mess/2020/01; see also David Tyack and Larry Cuban, *Tinkering toward Utopia: A Century of Public School Reform* (Cambridge, MA: Harvard University Press, 1995), 60–61.

85. Erica O. Turner, *Suddenly Diverse: How School Districts Manage Race & Inequality* (Chicago, IL: The University of Chicago Press, 2020), 86; Claudierre McKay, Aaron Regunberg, and Tim Shea, "Testing Assumptions: Zombies, Flunkies, and the Providence Student Union," in ed. J. Hagopian, *More than a Score*, 136; Kuhn, *Fear and Learning in America*, 12–14; Dolan, *Restructuring Our Schools*, 25.

86. Downey, *How Schools Really Matter*; Koretz, *Testing Charade*, 126, 130; Elliot Regenstein, Ben Boer, and Paul Zavitkovsky, "Establishing Achievable Goals," *Advance Illinois, Foresight Law + Policy, and Center for Urban Education Leadership*, last modified December 2018, https://www.advanceillinois.org/publications/ establishing-achievable-goals/.

87. Dolan, *Restructuring Our Schools*, 25.

88. Turner, *Suddenly Diverse*, 26, 86.

89. Schultz, *Distrust and Educational Change*; Katherine Schultz, "There Is Rampant Distrust in Education. Here's How to Fix That," *EducationWeek*, last modified June 19, 2019, https://www.edweek.org/leadership/opinion-there-is-rampant-distrust -in-education-heres-how-to-fix-that/2019/06.

CHAPTER 2

1. "Education and Lifetime Earnings," *Social Security Administration*, last modified November 2015, https://www.ssa.gov/policy/docs/research-summaries/education -earnings.html.

2. NCLB-focused research: Kevin Mahnken, "'Probably the Best News for Federal Accountability Policy, Ever': New Study Shows No Child Left Behind's Tough Oversight Led to Big Boost in High School Graduation Rates," *The 74 Million*, last modified March 11, 2020, https://www.the74million.org/probably-the-best-news-for -federal-accountability-policy-ever-new-study-shows-no-child-left-behinds-tough -oversight-led-to-big-boost-in-high-school-graduation-rates/; and Douglas N. Harris, Lihan Liu, Nathan Barrett, and Ruoxi Li, "Is the Rise in High School Graduation Rates Real? High-Stakes School Accountability and Strategic Behavior," *Brown Center on Education Policy at Brookings Institution*, last modified March 2020, https://www.brookings.edu/wp-content/uploads/2020/02/Is-the-Rise-in-High-School -Graduation-Rates-Real-FINAL.pdf.

3. "Table 1. Public High School 4-Year Adjusted Cohort Graduation Rate (ACGR), by Race/Ethnicity and Selected Demographic Characteristics for the United States, the 50 States, the District of Columbia, and Puerto Rico: School Year 2017–18," *National Center for Education Statistics*.

4. "Public High School Graduation Rates," *National Center for Education Statistics*, last modified May 2021, https://nces.ed.gov/programs/coe/indicator_coi.asp; "Table 1. Public High School 4-Year Adjusted Cohort Graduation Rate (ACGR)," National Center for Education Statistics, https://nces.ed.gov/ccd/tables/ACGR_RE_ and_characteristics_2017-18.asp.

5. McDermott, *High Stakes Reform* 121; Brandon L. Wright, "Has the High School Diploma Lost All Meaning?," *Thomas B. Fordham Institute*, last modified December 4, 2017, https://fordhaminstitute.org/national/commentary/has-high-school-diploma -lost-all-meaning; Sarah Butrymowicz, "Most Colleges Enroll Many Students Who Aren't Prepared for Higher Education," *The Hechinger Report*, last modified January 30, 2017, https://hechingerreport.org/colleges-enroll-students-arent-prepared-higher -education/.

6. Dan Goldhaber, Macolm Wolff, and Timothy Daly, "Assessing the Accuracy of Elementary School Test Scores as Predictors of Students' High School Outcomes," *American Institutes for Research*, last modified May 2020, https://files.eric.ed.gov /fulltext/ED605735.pdf; see also Jeffrey T. Dennings, Richard Murphy, and Felix Weinhardt, "Class Rank and Long-Run Outcomes," *Annenberg Institute at Brown University*, last modified March 2021, https://www.edworkingpapers.com/sites/ default/files/TexasRank_Restat_2ndRound_final_03312021.pdf. See also Michael J. Petrilli, "The college gender gap begins in kindergarten," *Thomas B. Fordham Institute*, last updated October 7, 2021, https://fordhaminstitute.org/national/commentary/ college-gender-gap-begins-kindergarten.

7. Analysis conducted by Paul Zavitkovsky, based on the SEDA national percentiles reported in *The New York Times*; Emily Badger and Kevin Quealy, "How Effective Is Your School District? A New Measure Shows Where Students Learn the Most," *The New York Times*, last modified December 5, 2017, https://www.nytimes .com/interactive/2017/12/05/upshot/a-better-way-to-compare-public-schools.html . This chart first appeared in Regenstein, "Building a Coherent P-12 Education System in California," 9, n.15.

8. Regenstein, "Building a Coherent P-12 Education System in California," 10–11.

9. Regenstein, "Building a Coherent P-12 Education System in California," 12–14.

10. For another thoughtful discussion of this issue that relies on some of the same data, see Downey, *How Schools Really Matter*, 16–27.

11. "National Assessment of Educational Progress," *National Center for Education Statistics*, accessed July 14, 2021, https://nces.ed.gov/nationsreportcard/.

12. "Scale Scores and NAEP Achievement," National Assessment of Educational Progress. *National Center for Education Statistics*, accessed July 14, 2021, https://nces.ed.gov/nationsreportcard/guides/scores_achv.aspx.

13. "NAEP Report Card: Mathematics," *The Nation's Report Card*, accessed on July 14, 2021, https://www.nationsreportcard.gov/mathematics/nation/achievement/?grade=4.

14. "NAEP Report Card: Reading: National Achievement-Level Results," *The Nation's Report Card*, accessed July 14, 2021, https://www.nationsreportcard.gov/reading/nation/achievement/?grade=4.

15. "Understanding Student Learning: Insights from Fall 2021," *Curriculum Associates*, 15, 19, accessed November 8, 2021, https://www.curriculumassociates.com/-/media/mainsite/files/i-ready/iready-understanding-student-learning-paper-fall-results-2021.pdf; see also Marianna McMurdock, "The Pandemic Exposed the Severity of Academic Divide along Race and Class: New 2021 Data on Math and Reading Progress Reveal It's Only Gotten Worse," *The 74 Million*, last modified November 8, 2021, https://www.the74million.org/the-pandemic-exposed-the-severity-of-the-academic-divide-along-race-class-new-test-data-show-its-only-gotten-worse/.

16. "Early Learning Standards and Guidelines," *Department of Health and Human Services Administration for Children & Families Office of Child Care*, accessed July 14, 2021, https://childcareta.acf.hhs.gov/sites/default/files/public/state_elgs_web_final_2.pdf.

17. "Early Learning Standards and Guidelines," *Department of Health and Human Services Administration for Children & Families Office of Child Care.*

18. "The State of Preschool 2020," *The National Institute for Early Education Research*, 9, last modified April 2021, https://nieer.org/wp-content/uploads/2021/04/YB2020_Full_Report.pdf.

19. "The State of Preschool 2020," *The National Institute for Early Education Research*, 18. Retrieved from: https://nieer.org/wp-content/uploads/2021/04/YB2020_Full_Report.pdf.

20. "The State of Preschool 2020," *The National Institute for Early Education Research*, 12–23; Lynn A. Karoly, Jill S. Cannon, Celia J. Gomez, and Anamarie A. Whitaker, "Understanding the Cost to Deliver High-Quality Publicly Funded Pre-Kindergarten Programs," *RAND Corporation*, last modified 2021, https://www.rand.org/pubs/research_reports/RRA252-1.html.

21. "The State of Preschool 2020," *The National Institute for Early Education Research*, 19.

22. "The State of Preschool 2020," *The National Institute for Early Education Research*, 18.

23. "Joyful Learning in Kindergarten," *NAEYC: Young Children*, Vol. 73, No. 1, last modified March 2018, https://www.naeyc.org/resources/pubs/yc/mar2018.

24. Elliot Regenstein, Bryce Marable, and Jelene Britten, "Starting at Five Is Too Late: Early Childhood Education and Upward Mobility," in *Education for Upward Mobility*, ed. Michael J. Petrilli (Lanham, MD: Rowman and Littlefield, 2016), 161.

25. Elliot Regenstein, "How Early Childhood Education Uses Social Emotional Learning," *American Enterprise Institute*, last modified December 2019, https://www.aei.org/research-products/report/how-early-childhood-education-uses-social-and-emotional-learning/.

26. Regenstein, Marable, and Britten, "Starting at Five Is Too Late," 162–63.

27. Regenstein, Marable, and Britten, "Starting at Five Is Too Late," 166; "What Does a High-Quality Preschool Program Look Like?," *NAEYC*, accessed July 14, 2021, https://www.naeyc.org/our-work/families/what-does-high-quality-program-for-preschool-look-like.

28. James J. Heckman, "Invest in Early Childhood Development: Reduce Deficits, Strengthen the Economy," *The Heckman Equation*, last modified December 7, 2012, https://heckmanequation.org/www/assets/2013/07/F_HeckmanDeficitPieceCUSTOM-Generic_052714-3-1.pdf.

29. Center on the Developing Child, "Brain Architecture," *Harvard University*, accessed July 14, 2021, https://developingchild.harvard.edu/science/key-concepts/brain-architecture/; Jin Zhou, Alison Baulos, James J. Heckman, and Bei Liu, "The Economics of Investing in Early Childhood: Importance of Understanding the Science of Scaling," in *The Scale-Up Effect in Early Childhood and Public Policy: Why Interventions Lose Impact at Scale and What We Can Do about It*, eds. John A. List, Dana Suskind, and Lauren H. Supplee (New York: Routledge, 2021), 78–80.

30. National Institute for Early Education Research, "State(s) of Head Start.."

31. Hirokazu Yoshikawa, Christina Weiland, Jeanne Brooks-Gunn, Margaret R. Burchinal, Linda M. Espinosa, Williams T. Gormley, Jens Ludwig, Katherine A. Magnuson, Deborah Phillips, and Martha J. Zaslow, "Investing in Our Future: The Evidence Base on Preschool Education," *Society for Research in Child Development and Foundation for Child Development*, last modified October 2013, https://www.fcd-us.org/assets/2013/10/Evidence20Base20on20Preschool20Education20FINAL.pdf.

32. Bryan Kelley, Matt Weyer, Meghan McCann, Shanique Broom, and Tom Keily, "50-State Comparison: State K-3 Policies," *Education Commission of the States*, last updated September 28, 2020, https://www.ecs.org/kindergarten-policies/.

33. Elliot Regenstein, "Why the K-12 World Hasn't Embraced Early Learning," *Foresight Law + Policy*, 20, last modified February 2021, https://www.flpadvisors.com/uploads/4/2/4/2/42429949/why_the_k12_world_hasnt_embraced_early_learning.pdf_final.pdf.

34. Jason A. Grissom, Demetra Kalogrides, and Susanna Loeb, "Strategic Staffing: How Accountability Pressure Affect the Distribution of Teachers within Schools and Resulting Students Achievement," *University of Arkansas College of Education and Health Professions*, last modified November 2014, http://www.uaedreform.org/downloads/2014/11/strategic-staffing-how-accountability-pressures-affect-the-distribution-of-teachers-within-schools-and-resulting-student-achievement.pdf; Sarah C. Fuller and Helen F. Ladd, "School Based Accountability and the Distribution of Teacher Quality among Grades in Elementary Schools," *National Center for*

Analysis of Longitudinal Data in Education Research, last modified April 2012, https://files.eric.ed.gov/fulltext/ED532767.pdf.

35. 50-State Comparison, "State K-3 Policies," *Education Commission of the States*, accessed July 14, 2021, https://internal-search.ecs.org/comparisons/state-k-3-policies-05.

36. 50-State Comparison, "State K-3 Policies."

37. "2019–2020 Kindergarten Readiness Assessment Report," *Maryland State Department of Education and Ready at Five*, last modified July 14, 2021, https://earlychildhood.marylandpublicschools.org/system/files/filedepot/4/200178_ready5_book_web.pdf; Illinois State Board of Education, "2019–2020 Illinois Kindergarten Individual Survey (KIDS) Report: A Look at Kindergarten Readiness," accessed July 14, 2021, https://www.isbe.net/Documents/Fall-2019-KIDS-Report.pdf.

38. Michelle Croft, "State Adoption and Implementation of K-2 Assessments," *ACT*, last modified 2014, https://www.act.org/content/dam/act/unsecured/documents/5738_Issue_Brief_State_Adoption_of_K-2_Assess_WEB_secure.pdf.

39. Croft, "State Adoption and Implementation of K-2 Assessments."

40. Walter Herrin, Luke C. Miller, Daphna Bassok, James H. Wyckoff, and Anita McGinty, "Racial and Socioeconomic Disparities in the Relationship between Children's Early Literacy Skills and Third-Grade Outcomes: Lessons from a Kindergarten Readiness Assessment," *Annenberg Institute for School Reform at Brown University*, accessed June 2021, https://www.edworkingpapers.com/sites/default/files/ai21-429.pdf.

41. Andrew Karch, Early Start: Preschool Politics in the United States (Ann Arbor: University of Michigan Press, 2014); Bruce Fuller, *Standardized Childhood: The Political and Cultural Struggle over Early Education* (Stanford, CA: Stanford University Press, 2007).

42. "Key Statistics from the National Survey of Family Growth—B Listing," *Centers for Disease Control and Prevention*, accessed July 14, 2021, https://www.cdc.gov/nchs/nsfg/key_statistics/b.htm#agefb.

43. Economic News Release, "Table 3. Median Usual Weekly Earnings of Full-Time Wage and Salary Workers by Age, Race, Hispanic or Latino Ethnicity, and Sex, Second Quarter 2021 Averages, Not Seasonally Adjusted," *U.S. Bureau of Labor Statistics*, last modified July 16, 2021, https://www.bls.gov/news.release/wkyeng.t03.htm; Deloitte Consulting, "Are We Headed for a Poorer United States? Growing Wealth Inequality by Age Puts Younger Households Behind," last modified March 12, 2018, https://www2.deloitte.com/us/en/insights/economy/issues-by-the-numbers/march-2018/us-average-wealth-inequality-by-age.html.

44. Child Care Aware of America, "The US and the High Price of Child Care: An Examination of a Broken System" (Full Report), 24, last modified 2019, https://info.childcareaware.org/hubfs/2019%20Price%20of%20Care%20State%20Sheets/Final-TheUSandtheHighPriceofChildCare-AnExaminationofaBrokenSystem.pdf; and Center for the Study of Child Care Employment, "Why Do Parents Pay So Much for Child Care When Early Educators Earn So Little?," last modified April 6, 2020, https://cscce.berkeley.edu/why-do-parents-pay-so-much-for-child-care-when-early-educators-earn-so-little/.

45. One of the most prominent critics of publicly funded preschool has been Russ Whitehurst, the founding director of the federal Institute of Education Sciences. "Russ Whitehurst," *Urban Institute*, accessed July 14, 2021, https://www.urban.org/author/ russ-whitehurst-0; Russ Whitehurst, "Does State Pre-K Improve Children's Achievement?," *Brookings Institution*, last modified July 12, 2018, https://www.brookings .edu/research/does-state-pre-k-improve-childrens-achievement/; Response: National Institute for Early Education Research, "Why Preschool Critics Are Wrong," last modified February 28, 2014, https://nieer.org/2014/02/28/why-preschool-critics-are -wrong; Hirokazu Yoshikawa, Christina Weiland, Jeanne Brooks-Gunn, Margaret R. Burchinal, Linda M. Espinosa, William T. Gormley, Jens Ludwig, Katherine A. Magnuson, Deborah Phillips, Martha J. Zaslow, "Investing in Our Future: The Evidence Base on Preschool Education," *Society for Research in Child Development and Foundation for Child Development*, last modified October 2013, https://www.fcd-us .org/assets/2013/10/Evidence20Base20on20Preschool20Education20FINAL.pdf.

46. Lindsey M. Burke and Rachel Sheffield, "The Preschool Mirage," *The Heritage Foundation*, last modified December 15, 2014, https://www.heritage.org/education /commentary/the-preschool-mirage; Rachel Greszler and Lindsey Burke, "Rethinking Early Childhood Education and Childcare in the COVID-19 Era," *The Heritage Foundation*, last modified September 30, 2020, https://www.heritage.org/education/ report/rethinking-early-childhood-education-and-childcare-the-covid-19-era.

47. Elliot Regenstein and Chris Strausz-Clark, "Improving Parent Choice in Early Learning," *American Enterprise Institute*, last modified January 25, 2021, https: //www.aei.org/research-products/report/improving-parent-choice-in-early-learning/.

48. Elliot Regenstein, "An Unofficial Guide to the Why and How of State Early Childhood Data Systems," *Start Early (formerly known as the Ounce of Prevention) Policy Conversations*, 5, last modified August 22, 2017, https://startearly.org/app/ uploads/pdf/PolicyPaper_UnofficialGuide.pdf. For an example of what change might look like, see Ajay Chaudray, Taryn Morrissey, Christina Weiland, and Hirokazu Yoshikawa, *Cradle to Kindergarten: A New Plan to Combat Inequality* (New York: Russell Sage Foundation, 2017).

49. Regenstein, Connors, and Romero-Jurado, "Valuing the Early Years in State Accountability Systems under the Every Student Succeeds Act."

50. In Illinois there was a persistent advocate—specifically, me—who pressed hard within the state's Early Learning Council to see this addressed, and then continued to make the case to the State Board of Education. Regenstein. *Why the K-12 World Hasn't Embraced Early Learning*, 9.

51. "ESSA P-2 Indicator Working Group Report," *Illinois State Board of Education*, last modified December 31, 2017, https://www.isbe.net/Documents/17-3249_P -2_Indicator_Working_Group_Report.pdf.

52. The narrative in the next two paragraphs is drawn in part from my experience working on the issue directly in Illinois and conversations with leaders in other states. Those conversations include a meeting hosted by the Council of Chief State School Officers with state early childhood staff in June 2018, where this issue was discussed.

53. Michelle Horowitz, "Stakeholder Engagement in State ESSA Plans: ARE Early Childhood Stakeholders Involved and in What Ways?," *Center on Enhancing Early*

Learning Outcomes, last modified September 2016, http://ceelo.org/wp-content/uploads/2016/09/2ESSAStateScanSept2016update.pdf.

54. Regenstein, Connors, and Romero-Jurado, "Valuing the Early Years in State Accountability Systems under the Every Student Succeeds Act"; "ESSA P-2 Indicator Working Group Report," *Illinois State Board of Education*. Dale Chu has argued that accountability should include growth on assessments in the K-2 years. Dale Chu, "The Case for K-2 Testing," *Thomas B. Fordham Institute*, last modified October 28, 2021, https://fordhaminstitute.org/national/commentary/case-k-2-testing. One important argument against implementing this practice quickly is that current K-2 assessments were not designed for accountability purposes, and that it is bad practice to use formative assessments for school accountability. Accountability tests could theoretically be developed for the K-2 years, but given the current politics of K-12 assessment that seems unlikely. Regardless of their propriety for accountability formulas K-2 assessments can yield valuable information about how children in a school are progressing and might appropriately be used as part of a school's improvement strategy.

55. Regenstein, "Why the K-12 World Hasn't Embraced Early Learning," 9–10.

CHAPTER 3

1. Those adults should include families and community members. Ken Zeichner, "Tensions between Teacher Professionalism and Authentic Community Voice in Public Schools Serving Nondominant Communities," in *Public Education: Defending a Cornerstone of American Democracy*, eds. Berliner and Hermanns (New York: Teachers College Press, 2021), 179.

2. Beth Salamon, "Rutgers Study Finds Students Are Taking More Time to Graduate from High School," *Rutgers*, last modified May 9, 2014, https://www.rutgers.edu/news/rutgers-study-finds-students-are-taking-more-time-graduate-high-school.

3. Regenstein, "Why the K-12 World Hasn't Embraced Early Learning," 9.

4. Finn, Jr., *School Accountability—Past, Present, and Future*, 29.

5. Finn, Jr., *School Accountability—Past, Present, and Future*, 13–14.

6. Education Commission of the States, "50 State Comparison: States' School Accountability Systems," last modified May 31, 2018, https://www.ecs.org/50-state-comparison-states-school-accountability-systems/; Education Commission of the States, "Accountability and Reporting: ESSA Plans," last modified May 9, 2014, http://ecs.force.com/mbdata/mbQuest5E?rep=SA172.

7. Education Commission of the States, "50 State Comparison: States' School Accountability Systems."

8. California Department of Education, "California School Dashboard and System of Support," last modified July 14, 2021, https://www.cde.ca.gov/ta/ac/cm/; Education Commission of the States, "Accountability and Reporting: ESSA Plans."

9. Bellwether Education Partners, "An Independent Review of ESSA State Plan," last modified December 2017, https://bellwethereducation.org/sites/default/files/Bellwether_ESSAReview_ExecSumm_1217_Final.pdf; Brandon L. Wright and Michael J. Petrilli, "Rating the Ratings: An Analysis of the 51 ESSA Accountability

Plans," *Thomas B. Fordham Institute*, last modified November 14, 2017, https://fordhaminstitute.org/national/research/rating-ratings-analysis-51-essa-accountability-plans.

10. A conceptually similar chart appears in W. L. Sanders and J. C. Rivers, "Choosing a Value-Added Model," in *A Grand Bargain for Education Reform: New Rewards and Supports for New Accountability*, eds. Theodore Hershberg and Claire Roberston-Kraft (Cambridge, MA: Harvard Education Press, 2009), 45.

11. Downey, *How Schools Really Matter*, 51; see also Rothstein, *Class and Schools*, 56–59.

12. Regenstein, Connors, and Romero-Jurado, "Valuing the Early Years in State Accountability Systems under the Every Student Succeeds Act," 13.

13. Rothstein, Jacobsen, and Wilder, *Grading Education*, 119–39, 154–55; see also Anthony Bryk, Penny Bender Sebring, David Kerbow, Sharon Rollow, and John Q. Easton, *Charting Chicago School Reform: Democratic Localism as a Lever for Change* (Boulder, CO: Westview Press, 1998), 300–302.

14. Rothstein, Jacobsen, and Wilder, *Grading Education*, 131–32.

15. Rothstein, Jacobsen, and Wilder, *Grading Education*, 135; see also Fiske and Ladd, "Values and Education Policy," 41.

16. Rothstein, Jacobsen, and Wilder, *Grading Education*, 155–56; Brighouse, Ladd, Loeb, and Swift, *Educational Goods*, 127–28.

17. David Osborne argues for a similar approach to the one proposed in Part I: a balance between student test scores and "Quality School Reviews." David Osborne, "States Still Reply Too Heavily on Test Scores to Hold Schools Accountable. Here's a Better Way for Them to Break It All Down," *The 74 Million*, last modified February 9. 2021, https://www.the74million.org/article/osborne-states-still-rely-too-heavily-on-test-scores-to-hold-schools-accountable-heres-a-better-way-for-them-to-break-it-all-down/.

18. Head Start Early Childhood Learning & Knowledge Center, "Designation Renewal System Overview," accessed July 14, 2021, https://eclkc.ohs.acf.hhs.gov/designation-renewal-system/article/designation-renewal-system-overview.

19. Head Start Early Childhood Learning & Knowledge Center, "Use of Classroom Assessment Scoring System (CLASS®) in Head Start," accessed July 14, 2021, https://eclkc.ohs.acf.hhs.gov/designation-renewal-system/article/use-classroom-assessment-scoring-system-class-head-start.

20. Rothstein, Jacobsen, and Wilder, *Grading Education*, 154–56; Darling-Hammond, *The Flat World and Education*, 303; Finn Jr., *School Accountability—Past, Present, and Future*, 38–48. Iftikhar Hussain, "The School Inspector Calls," *Education Next* (Summer 2013), last modified May 2013, https://www.educationnext.org/the-school-inspector-calls/; Elliot Regenstein and Rio Romero-Jurado, "A Framework for Rethinking State Education Accountability and Support from Birth through High School," *Start Early*, last modified June 3, 2014, https://startearly.org/app/uploads/pdf/Policy-Convo-03-Accountability.pdf. States have used audit teams to evaluate low-performing districts. Kirp, *Improbable Scholars*, 52–54, 97–98. And some districts have already chosen to use inspectorates for their own internal accountability systems. Heather Zavadsky, *School Turnarounds: The Essential Role*

of Districts (Cambridge, MA: Harvard Education Press, 2012), 71; Jonathan Gyurko and Jeffrey Henig, "Strong Vision, Learning by Doing, or the Politics of Muddling Through?" in *Between Public and Private: Politics, Governance, and the New Portfolio Models for Urban School Reform*, eds. Katrina E. Bulkley, Jeffrey R. Henig, and Henry M. Levin (Cambridge, MA: Harvard Education Press, 2010), 104–5.

21. 20 U.S.C. §6311(c)(4)(B)(v).

22. 34 C.F.R. §200.3(b)(5); 34 C.F.R. §200.26(a)(1), accessed July 14, 2021, https://ecfr.federalregister.gov/current/title-34/subtitle-B/chapter-II/part-200.

23. 20 U.S.C. §6311(c)(V)(I)(aa).

24. Penny Bender Sebring, Elaine Allensworth, Anthony S. Bryk, John Q. Easton, and Stuart Luppescu, "The Essential Supports for School Improvement," *Consortium on Chicago School Research at the University of Chicago*, last modified September 2006, https://consortium.uchicago.edu/sites/default/files/2018-10/EssentialSupports.pdf. At the time the organization was known as the Consortium on Chicago School Research at the University of Chicago; see also Regenstein and Romero-Jurado, "A Framework for Rethinking State Education Accountability and Support from Birth through High School," 5.

25. J. M. Beach, *Can We Measure What Matters Most? Why Educational Accountability Metrics Lower Student Learning and Demoralize Teachers* (Landham, MD: Rowman & Littlefield, 2021), 133; Schneider, *Beyond Test Scores*, 227.

26. Beach, *Can We Measure What Matters Most?*, 133; Mehta, *Allure of Order*, 266.

27. David Osborne makes an analogous argument, pushing for the use of particularized performance goals that recognize that schools focused on different outcomes and approaches should not all be held to the exact same standard. Osborne, *Reinventing America's Schools*, 251.

28. In any accountability system, ongoing midcourse corrections are critical. O'Day and Smith, *Opportunity for All*, 90–91; Schneider, *Beyond Test Scores*, 220; Koretz, *The Testing Charade*, 239–40.

29. For example, Mehta, *Allure of Order*, 163.

30. Sara E. Dahill-Brown, "Challenging, Building, and Changing Capacity in State Education Agencies," in *Bush-Obama School Reform*, eds. Hess and McShane 150, 15455; Patrick Murphy and Lydia Rainey, "Modernizing the State Education Agency: Different Paths toward Performance Management," *Center on Reinventing Public Education*, 12, last modified September 2012, https://www.crpe.org/sites/default/files/pub_states_ModernizingSEAs_sept12.pdf.

31. Frederick M. Hess and Michael Q. McShane (eds.), *Educational Entrepreneurship Today* (Cambridge, MA: Harvard Education Press, 2016); Larry Berger and David Stevenson, "K-12 Entrepreneurship: Slow Entry, Distant Exit," *American Enterprise Institute Conference*, last modified October 25, 2007, https://d3btwko586hcvj.cloudfront.net/uploads/pdf/file/15/K12_Entrepreneurship_-1523562447.pdf.

32. Sara E. Dahill-Brown, "Challenging, Building, and Changing Capacity in State Education Agencies," in *Bush-Obama School Reform*, eds. Hess and McShane, 152, 156–57; Joanne Weiss and Patrick McGuinn, "The Evolving Role of the State Education Agency in the Era of ESSA and Trump: Past, Present, and Uncertain Future," *Consortium for Policy Research in Education,* 11, last modified September 13, 2017,

https://files.eric.ed.gov/fulltext/ED586782.pdf; Sara E. Dahill-Brown, *Education, Equity, and the States: How Variations in State Governance Make or Break Reforms* (Cambridge, MA: Harvard Education Press, 2019), 39–41.

33. Dahill-Brown, "Challenging, Building, and Changing Capacity in State Education Agencies," in *Bush-Obama School Reform*, eds. Hess and McShane, 162; Andy Smarick and Juliet Squire, "The State Education Agency: At the Helm, Not the Oar," *Thomas B. Fordham Institute*, 18–19, 26–27, last modified April 2014, https://edex .s3-us-west-2.amazonaws.com/publication/pdfs/State-Education-Agency-Helm-Not -Oar-FINAL.pdf.

34. Dahill-Brown, "Challenging, Building, and Changing Capacity in State Education Agencies," in *Bush-Obama School Reform*, eds. Hess and McShane, 162.

35. Rothstein, Jacobsen, and Wilder, *Grading Education*, 119–39; see also Christopher H. Tienken, *The School Reform Landscape Reloaded: More Fraud, Myths, and Lies* (Lanham, MD: Rowman & Littlefield, 2021), 172–73.

36. Rothstein, Jacobsen, and Wilder, *Grading Education*, 131.

37. David Osborne, "Test Scores Give Only a Partial Picture of How a School Is Doing. School Quality Reviews Can Help Fill the Gap," *The 74 Million*, last modified March 10, 2021, https://www.the74million.org/article/osborne-test-scores-give-only -a-partial-picture-of-how-a-school-is-doing-school-quality-reviews-can-help-fill-the -gap/; Helen F. Ladd and Edward Fiske, "Equity-Oriented Accountability for Charter Schools: Lessons from Massachusetts," *Annenberg Institute for School Reform at Brown University*, last modified January 2021, https://www.edworkingpapers.com/ sites/default/files/ai21-353.pdf.

38. Brighouse, Ladd, Loeb, and Swift, *Educational Goods*, 126–27.

39. Brighouse, Ladd, Loeb, and Swift, *Educational Goods*, 127.

40. Brighouse, Ladd, Loeb, and Swift, *Educational Goods*, 127.

41. Smarick and Squire, *The State Education Agency: At the Helm, Not the Oar*.

42. Rothstein, Jacobsen, and Wilder, *Grading Education*, 156.

43. 42 U.S.C. 9837B(b)(2), accessed July 14, 2021, https://eclkc.ohs.acf.hhs.gov/ sites/default/files/pdf/hs-act-pl-110-134.pdf.

44. Office of Early Childhood Development, "State Advisory Councils Fact Sheet," *Department of Health and Human Services*, accessed July 14, 2021, https://www.acf .hhs.gov/ecd/state-advisory-councils.

45. Office of Early Childhood Development, "State Advisory Councils Fact Sheet." I worked with several states on their applications, including California and Georgia. As a brief aside, the Georgia team would get into the office at 7 am Eastern time and immediately get to work; leaders of the California team, meanwhile, mostly seemed to want to talk things over while driving home at the end of the day, around 6 pm Pacific time. The good news was that I didn't have a lot of scheduling conflicts between the two; the bad news was that it made for some long days.

46. Brighouse, Ladd, Loeb, and Swift, *Educational Goods*, 81 ("Even the best evidence requires careful interpretation.").

47. Amanda Datnow, Marie Lockton, and Hayley Weddle, "When Data Use Raises Equity and Ethical Dilemmas in Schools," in *The Ethical Use of Data in Education*, eds. Mandinach and Gummer, 220; Frederick M. Hess, *Cage-Busing Leadership*

(Cambridge, MA: Harvard Education Press, 2013), 72–79; Emily Krone Philips, *The Make-or-Break Year* (New York: Two Rivers Distribution, 2019), 78–80, 307.

48. Hess, *The Same Thing Over and Over*, 105.

49. Brennan McMahon Parton and Taryn A. Hochleitner, "Policies that Promote Student Data Privacy and Teacher Data Literacy Are Essential for Ethical Data Use," in *The Ethical Use of Data in Education*, eds. Mandinach and Gummer, 77; Tim Harford, *The Data Detective: Ten Easy Rules to Make Sense of Statistics* (New York: Riverhead Books, 2021), 64; Michael Barber, Nick Rodriguez, and Ellyn Artis, *Deliverology in Practice: How Education Leaders Are Improving Student Outcomes* (Thousand Oaks, CA: Corwin, 2016), 93.

50. Barber, Rodriguez, and Artis, *Deliverology in Practice*, 191–232; Michael Barber with Andy Moffit and Paul Kihn, *Deliverology 101: A Field Guide for Educational Leaders* (Thousand Oaks, CA: Corwin, 2011), 134–36.

51. Jal Mehta, Louis M. Gomez, and Anthony S. Bryk, "Building on Practical Knowledge: The Key to a Stronger Profession Is Learning from the Field," in *The Futures of School Reform*, eds. Mehta, Schwartz, and Hess, 38; see also Mehta, *Allure of Order*, 272–73.

52. Chester E. Finn Jr., "The Sorry History of 'What Works' in School," *Thomas B. Fordham Institute*, last modified April 1, 2021, https://fordhaminstitute.org/national/commentary/sorry-history-what-works-school.

53. Mehta, *Allure of Order*, 272–73; Eric Kalenze, "What It Will Take to Improve Evidence-Informed Decision-Making in Schools," *American Enterprise Institute*, last modified June 2020, https://www.aei.org/wp-content/uploads/2020/06/What-it-will-take-to-improve-evidence-informed-decision-making-in-schools.pdf.

54. Lorraine M. McDonnell and M. Stephen Weatherford, *Evidence, Politics, and Education Policy* (Cambridge, MA: Harvard Education Press, 2020); Mehta, Gomez, and Bryk, "Building on Practical Knowledge," in *The Futures of School Reform*, eds. Mehta, Schwartz, and Hess, 35–64. Jennifer A. Rippner, *The American Education Policy Landscape* (New York: Routledge, 2016), 153–70; Kalenze, *What It Will Take to Improve Evidence-Informed Decision-Making in Schools*.

55. For example, Turner, *Suddenly Diverse*, 107–8.

56. Michael Lewis, *The Undoing Project* (New York: W. W. Norton & Co., 2017), 21–51.

57. Ellen B. Mandinach and Edith S. Gummer, "Data Ethics: An Introduction," in *The Ethical Use of Data in Education*, eds. Mandinach and Gummer, 3; Mandinach and Gummer, "The Landscape of Data Ethics in Education: What Counts as Responsible Data Use," in *The Ethical Use of Data in Education*, eds. Mandinach and Gummer, 37–42.

58. For example, Turner, *Suddenly Diverse*, 108; James C. Scott, *Seeing Like a State: How Certain Schemes to Improve the Human Condition Have Failed* (New Haven, CT: Yale University Press, 1998).

59. Dan Heath, *Upstream: The Quest to Solve Problems before They Happen* (New York: Avid Reader Press, 2020).

60. Koretz, *The Testing Charade*, 54–57; Duncan, *How Schools Work*, 54–58; Jeffrey R. Henig, *The End of Exceptionalism in American Education: The Changing Politics of School Reform* (Cambridge, MA: Harvard Education Press, 2013), 176.

61. Arnold F. Shober, "ESSA and State Capacity: Can States Take Accountability Seriously?" in *The Every Student Succeeds Act: What It Means for Schools, Systems, and States*, eds. Hess and Eden, 115–16.

62. Heath, *Upstream*, 180.

63. Heath, *Upstream*, 182–83.

64. Heath, *Upstream*, 88.

65. O'Day and Smith, *Opportunity for All*, 90–91.

66. For a broad discussion of how policy travels among states, see Andrew Karch, *Democratic Laboratories: Policy Diffusion among the American States* (Ann Arbor, MI: University of Michigan Press, 2007).

67. Although it is fair to question who actually is an expert in any given enterprise. Lewis, *The Undoing Project*, 37; Frederick M. Hess, *Letters to a Young Education Reformer* (Cambridge, MA: Harvard Education Press, 2017), 31–36.

68. Elliot Regenstein, "Early Childhood Governance: Getting There from Here," *Foresight Law + Policy*, 46, last modified June 2020, https://www.flpadvisors.com/uploads/4/2/4/2/42429949/flp_gettingtherefromhere_061120.pdf; Smarick and Squire, *The State Education Agency: At the Helm, Not the Oar*.

69. This story was told to me as part of research for an analysis of state education agency capacity that was never formally published.

70. Mehta, Gomez, and Bryk, "Building on Practical Knowledge," in *The Futures of School Reform*, eds. Mehta, Schwartz, and Hess, 41–44.

71. Smarick and Squire, *The State Education Agency: At the Helm, Not the Oar*, 8–9, 15, 26–27.

72. Results for America, "2021 Moneyball for Education Policy Recommendations," 17, last modified March 2021, https://results4america.org/wp-content/uploads/2021/03/2021-Moneyball-for-Education-Policy-Recommendations-FINAL.pdf.

73. Hess, *Letters to a Young Education Reformer*, 63–69.

74. Results for America, *2021 Moneyball for Education Policy Recommendations*, 15–20; Kumar Garg, "Research Is One Area of Education the Federal Government Does Best. It's Time for Congress to Boost Funding for Education R&D," *The 74 Million*, last modified September 11, 2019, https://www.the74million.org/article/garg-research-is-one-area-of-education-the-federal-government-does-best-its-time-for-congress-to-boost-funding-for-education-rd/.

75. Results for America, "2021 Moneyball for Education Policy Recommendations," 16; O'Day and Smith, *Opportunity for All*, 150–51; Mehta, *Allure of Order*, 272–76; Mehta, Gomez, and Bryk, "Building on Practical Knowledge," in *The Futures of School Reform*, eds. Mehta, Schwartz, and Hess, 41–44; Daniel T. Willingham and David B. Daniel, "Making Education Research Relevant," *Education Next*, last modified Summer 2021, https://www.educationnext.org/making-education-research-relevant-how-researchers-can-give-teachers-more-choices/.

76. Robert Pianta and Tara Hofkens, "The Bush-Obama Agenda for Education Research and Innovation," in *Bush-Obama School Reform*, eds. Hess and McShane,

87–105; see also O'Day and Smith, *Opportunity for All*, 150–51; Deven Carlson, "Holding Accountability Accountable: Taking Stock of the Past 20 Years," *American Enterprise Institute*, 3–4, last modified May 2021, https://www.aei.org/research-products/report/holding-accountability-accountable-taking-stock-of-the-past-20-years/; For a conservative argument in favor of the federal government supporting transparency and research, see Frederick M. Hess and Andrew P. Kelly, "A Federal Education Agenda," *American Enterprise Institute National Affairs*, last modified Fall 2012, https://www.nationalaffairs.com/publications/detail/a-federal-education-agenda.

77. Statewide Longitudinal Data Systems Grant Program, "About the SLDS Grant Program," *National Center for Education Statistics*, accessed July 14, 2021, https://nces.ed.gov/programs/slds/about_SLDS.asp.

78. Statewide Longitudinal Data Systems Grant Program, "History of the SLDS Grant Program: Expanding States' Capacity for Data-Driven Decisionmaking," *Institute of Education Sciences*, last modified April 2020, https://nces.ed.gov/programs/slds/pdf/History_of_the_SLDS_Grant_Program_Apr2020.pdf.

79. "State Progress," *Data Quality Campaign*, accessed July 14, 2021, https://dataqualitycampaign.org/why-education-data/state-progress/.

80. "The Next Step: Using Longitudinal Data Systems to Improve Student Success," *Data Quality Campaign*, last modified March 2016, https://dataqualitycampaign.org/wp-content/uploads/2016/03/384_NextStep.pdf.

81. Allison Crean Davis, "Creating an Institute for Education Improvement," *Bellwether Education Partners*, last modified February 2021, https://bellwethereducation.org/sites/default/files/Bellwether_PandemictoProgress_CreateInstitute_Final.pdf.

82. Pianta and Hofkens, "The Bush-Obama Agenda for Education Research and Innovation," in *Bush-Obama School Reform*, eds. Hess and McShane, 103.

83. Karch and Rose, *Responsive States*, 166–67; Paul Manna, *School's In: Federalism and the National Education Agenda* (Washington, DC: Georgetown University Press, 2006), 141–48; Weiss and McGuinn, "The Evolving Role of the State Education Agency in the Era of ESSA and Trump," 170.

84. Harford, *The Data Detective*, 197–212.

85. Downey, *How Schools Really Matter*.

86. Rothstein, *Class and Schools*.

87. Darby and Rury, *The Color of Mind*, 11; Eden, "Reflections on the Futures of K-12 Assessment and Accountability," 2.

88. Finn Jr., "School Accountability—Past, Present, and Future," 31–32.

89. Michael Fullan, "Choosing the Wrong Drivers for Whole System Reform," *Center for Strategic Education*, 8–9. Last modified April 2011, https://edsource.org/wp-content/uploads/old/Fullan-Wrong-Drivers11.pdf.

90. Osborne, "Test Scores Give Only a Partial Picture of How a School Is Doing."

91. Finn Jr., "School Accountability—Past, Present, and Future," 37–38.

92. This does not happen automatically; indeed, bad inspection practice can end up reinforcing bad teaching practice. Koretz, *The Testing Charade*, 230.

93. Berger and Stevenson, K-12 Entrepreneurship: Slow Entry, Distant Exit, 10–12; See also Harford, *The Data Detective*, 197–212.

CHAPTER 4

1. "Fast Facts: Teacher Qualifications," *National Center for Education Statistics*, accessed July 14, 2021, https://nces.ed.gov/fastfacts/display.asp?id=58#:~:text=Some%2055%20percent%20of%20elementary,postbaccalaureate%20degree%20in%201999%E2%80%932000.

2. "Occupational Outlook Handbooks: Preschool Teachers," *U.S. Bureau of Labor Statistics*, accessed November 22, 2021, https://www.bls.gov/ooh/education-training-and-library/preschool-teachers.htm. Not all of the preschool teachers in the sample have bachelor's degrees.

3. "Employment Status of the Civilian Population by Sex and Age," *Bureau of Labor Statistics*, accessed December 5, 2021, https://www.bls.gov/news.release/empsit.t01.htm.

4. The BLS treats high school, elementary/K, and preschool as different categories, which is why they are not on the top 10 list. "Occupational Employment and Wage Statistics," *U.S. Bureau of Labor Statistics*, last modified May 2020, https://www.bls.gov/oes/current/area_emp_chart/area_emp_chart_data.htm#United_States. But if you add them up they would make it.

5. "Characteristics of Public School Teachers," *National Center for Education Statistics*, accessed November 22, 2021, https://nces.ed.gov/programs/coe/indicator_clr.asp.

6. "Characteristics of Public School Teachers," *National Center for Education Statistics*.

7. "Household Data Annual Averages: Employed Persons by Detailed Occupation, Sex, Race, and Hispanic or Latino ethnicity," *U.S. Bureau of Labor Statistics*, accessed July 14, 2021, https://www.bls.gov/cps/cpsaat11.pdf.

8. "Fast Facts: Teacher Qualifications" *National Center for Education Statistics*.

9. "The State of Preschool 2020," *National Institute for Early Education Research*, 31.

10. Emma García and Elaine Weiss, "Examining the Factors That Play a Role in the Teacher Shortage Crisis," *Economic Policy Institute*, last modified October 15, 2020, https://www.epi.org/publication/key-findings-from-the-perfect-storm-in-the-teacher-labor-market-series/.

11. Douglas N. Harris, *Charter School City: What the End of Traditional Public Schools in New Orleans Means for American Education* (Chicago, IL: The University of Chicago Press, 2020), 103; Pondiscio, *How the Other Half Learns*, 112; Zachary W. Oberfield, *Are Charters Different? Public Education, Teachers, and the Charter School Debate* (Cambridge, MA: Harvard Education Press, 2017), 47, 50–51; Baris Gumus-Dawes, Thomas Luce, and Myron Orfield, "The State of Public Schools in Post-Katrina New Orleans: The Challenge of Creating Equal Opportunity," in *Educational Delusions?*, eds. Orfield and Frankenberg, 166.

12. García and Weiss, "Examining the Factors That Play a Role in the Teacher Shortage Crisis."

13. Madeline Will, "Enrollment in Teacher-Preparation Programs Is Declining Fast. Here's What the Data Show," *Education Week*, last modified December 3, 2019, https:

//www.edweek.org/teaching-learning/enrollment-in-teacher-preparation-programs-is
-declining-fast-heres-what-the-data-show/2019/12; Lisette Partelow, "What to Make
of Declining Enrollment in Teachers Preparation Programs," *Center for American
Progress*, last modified December 3, 2019, https://www.americanprogress.org/issues
/education-k-12/reports/2019/12/03/477311/make-declining-enrollment-teacher
-preparation-programs/.

14. García and Weiss, "Examining the Factors That Play a Role in the Teacher
Shortage Crisis"; Emma García and Elaine Weiss, "U.S. Schools Struggle to Hire
and Retain Teachers," *Economic Policy Institute*, last modified April 16, 2019, https://
www.epi.org/publication/u-s-schools-struggle-to-hire-and-retain-teachers-the-second
-report-in-the-perfect-storm-in-the-teacher-labor-market-series/.

15. García and Weiss, "Examining the Factors That Play a Role in the Teacher
Shortage Crisis"; García and Weiss, "Low Relative Pay and High Incidence of Moonlighting Play a Role in the Teacher Shortage, Particularly in High-Poverty Schools."

16. Emma García and Elaine Weiss, "Challenging Working Environment ('School
Climates'), Especially in High-Poverty Schools, Play a Role in the Teacher Shortage," *Economic Policy Institute*, last modified May 30, 2019, https://www.epi
.org/publication/school-climate-challenges-affect-teachers-morale-more-so-in-high
-poverty-schools-the-fourth-report-in-the-perfect-storm-in-the-teacher-labor-market
-series/.

17. Sadly, he passed away not long after completing his service on the State
Board of Education. Kaitlin Cordes, "Craig Lindvahl Remembered for Impact on
Community," *Effingham Daily News*, last modified January 2, 2020, https://www
.effinghamdailynews.com/news/local_news/craig-lindvahl-remembered-for-impact
-on-community/article_e275358a-2dc9-11ea-bd4c-4b396a25b17e.html.

18. This anecdote is drawn from a conversation I had with Mr. Lindvahl while giving him a tour of Educare Chicago, an outstanding early childhood center operated
by my then-employer.

19. Elmore, *School Reform from the Inside Out*; Seymour B. Sarason, *The Predictable Failure of Educational Reform: Can We Change Course before It's Too Late?*
(San Francisco: Jossey-Bass, 1990), 101; *School Reform from the Inside Out.*

20. Elmore, *School Reform from the Inside Out*, 54; Sarason, *The Predictable Failure of Educational Reform*, 123.

21. Goldstein, *The Teacher Wars*, 247.

22. Goldstein, *The Teacher Wars*, 261.

23. Mehta, *Allure of Order*, 17; Ravitch, *Reign of Error*, 274; Jonathan Kozol, *The
Shame of the Nation: The Restoration of Apartheid Schooling in America* (New York:
Three Rivers Press, 2005), 299.

24. Jal Mehta, "How Social and Emotional Learning Can Succeed," *American Enterprise Institute*, last modified May 2020, https://www.aei.org/wp-content
/uploads/2020/05/How-social-and-emotional-learning-can-succeed.pdf; citing last
David K. Cohen and Jal D. Mehta, "Why Reform Sometimes Succeeds: Understanding the Conditional That Produce Reforms That Last," *Sage Journals*, first published
April 11, 2017, https://journals.sagepub.com/doi/abs/10.3102/0002831217700078.

25. Sarason, *The Predictable Failure of Educational Reform*, 64; see also Krone Philips, *The Make-or-Break Year*, 122–23.

26. Manna, *Collision Course*, 66; Goldstein, *The Teacher Wars*, 247; Hess, *The Same Thing Over and Over*, 199–201; Payne, *So Much Reform*, 154, 179; Frederick M. Hess, *Spinning Wheels: The Politics of Urban School Reform* (Washington, DC: Brookings Institution Press, 1999), 153–73; Tyack and Cuban, *Tinkering toward Utopia*, 54–55.

27. Payne, *So Much Reform*, 64–65.

28. Karch and Rose, *Responsive States*, 64; Dahill-Brown, "Challenging, Building, and Changing Capacity in State Education Agencies," in *Bush-Obama School Reform*, eds. Hess and McShane, 159. Chester E. Finn and Michael J. Petrilli, "The Failures of U.S. Education Governance Today," in *Education Governance for the 21st Century: Overcoming the Structural Barriers to School Reform*, eds. Paul Manna and Patrick McGuinn (Washington, DC: Brookings Institution Press, 2013), 29. John E. Chubb and Terry M. Moe, *Politics, Markets, and America's Schools* (Washington, DC: Brookings Institution Press, 1990), 38–41.

29. Schultz, *Distrust and Educational Change*, 121–26.

30. Payne, *So Much Reform*, 182; Larry Cuban, "A Critique of Contemporary Edu-Giving," in *The New Education Philanthropy: Politics, Policy, and Reform*, eds. Frederick M. Hess and Jeffrey R. Henig (Cambridge, MA: Harvard Education Press, 2015), 155–58; Megan E. Tompkins-Stange, *Policy Patrons: Philanthropy, Education Reform, and the Politics of Influence* (Cambridge, MA: Harvard Education Press, 2016), 121.

31. Cuban, "A Critique of Contemporary Edu-Giving," 155–58.

32. Leo Casey, *The Teacher Insurgency: A Strategic and Organizing Perspective* (Cambridge, MA: Harvard Education Press, 2020), 56.

33. The author is keenly aware that this book is not likely to be exempted from this rule.

34. Nathan Levenson, *Six Shifts to Improve Special Education and Other Interventions: A Commonsense Approach for School Leaders* (Cambridge, MA: Harvard Education Press, 2020), 119; Oberfield, *Are Charters Different?*, 58; Barry A. Farber, *Crisis in Education: Stress and Burnout in the American Teacher* (San Francisco: Jossey-Bass, 1991), 108; Liana Loewus, "Why Teachers Leave—or Don't: A Look at the Numbers," *Education Week*, last modified May 4, 2021, https://www.edweek.org/teaching-learning/why-teachers-leave-or-dont-a-look-at-the-numbers/2021/05; Yongmei Ni and Andrea K. Rorrer, "Why Do Teachers Choose Teaching and Remain Teaching: Initial Results from the Educator Career and Pathway Survey (ECAPS) for Teachers," *Utah Education Policy Center*, last modified 2018, https://daqy2hvnfszx3.cloudfront.net/wp-content/uploads/sites/2/2018/04/19110358/ECAPS_for_Teachers_report_Feb2018_Final.pdf.

35. Anthony Birat, Pierre Bourdier, Enzo Piponnier, Anthony J. Blazevich, Hugo Maciejewski, Pascale Duché, and Sébastien Ratel, "Metabolic and Fatigue Profiles Are Comparable between Prepubertal Children and Well-Trained Adult Endurance Athletes," *Frontiers in Physiology*, last modified April 24, 2018, https://www.frontiersin.org/articles/10.3389/fphys.2018.00387/full.

36. David F. Labaree, *Someone Has to Fail: The Zero-Sum Game of Public Schooling* (Cambridge, MA: Harvard University Press, 2010), 138; James Q. Wilson, *Bureaucracy* (New York: Basic Books, 1989), 21; David B. Tyack, *The One Best System: A History of American Urban Education* (Cambridge, MA: Harvard University Press, 1974), 28, 43.

37. Goldstein, *The Teacher Wars*, 77–78.

38. Pondiscio, *How the Other Half Learns*, 54.

39. Farber, *Crisis in Education*, 52–53.

40. Carla Shedd, *Unequal City: Race, Schools, and Perceptions of Injustice* (New York: Russell Sage Foundation, 2015), 90.

41. Darby and Rury, *The Color of Mind*, 2.

42. Sowell, *Charter Schools and Their Enemies*, 110; David Griffith and Adam Tyner, "Discipline Reform through the Eyes of Teachers," The Thomas B. Fordham Institute, last modified July 2019, http://teachersondiscipline.com/.

43. Petrilli and Finn (eds.), *How to Educate an American*, 93.

44. Farber, *Crisis in Education*, 52–53.

45. O'Day and Smith, *Opportunity for All*, 105 (citing the Consortium for Chicago School Research).

46. Julia A. McWilliams, *Compete or Close: Traditional Neighborhood Schools under Pressure* (Cambridge, MA: Harvard Education Press, 2019), 145; Farber, *Crisis in Education*, 213.

47. McWilliams, *Compete or Close*, 142, 177.

48. Mandinach and Gummer, "The Landscape of Data Ethics in Education: What Counts as Responsible Data Use," in *The Ethical Use of Data in Education*, eds. Mandinach and Gummer, 41 (discussing Erin D. Atwood, Jo Beth Jimerson, and Brianna Holt, "Equity-Oriented Data Use: Identifying and Addressing Food Insecurity at Copper Springs Middle School," *Journal of Cases in Educational Leadership*, first published June 28, 2019, https://journals.sagepub.com/doi/abs/10.1177/1555458919859932); David Osher, Pamela Cantor, Juliette berg, Lily Steyer, and Todd Rose, "Drivers of Human Development: How Relationships and Context Shape Learning and Development," *Applied Developmental Science*, Volume 24, 2020, Issue 1, last modified January 24, 2018, https://www.tandfonline.com/doi/full/10.1080/10888691.2017.1398650; Pamela Cantor, David Osher, Juliette Berg, Lily Steyer, and Todd Rose, "Malleability, Plasticity, and Individuality: How Children Learn and Develop in Context," *Applied Developmental Science*, Vol. 23, No. 4, 2019, last modified January 24, 2018, https://www.tandfonline.com/doi/full/10.1080/10888691.2017.1398649.

49. J. Stuart Abion, "School Discipline Is Trauma-Insensitive and Trauma-Uninformed," *Psychology Today*, last modified January 9, 2020, https://www.psychologytoday.com/us/blog/changeable/202001/school-discipline-is-trauma-insensitive-and-trauma-uninformed; Linda Darling-Hammond, Lisa Flook, Channa Cook-Harvey, Brigid Barron, and David Osher, "Implications for Educational Practice of the Science of Learning and Development," *Applied Developmental Science*, Volume 24, 2020, Issue 2, last modified February 7, 2019, https://www.tandfonline.com/doi/full/10.1080/10888691.2018.1537791.

50. Griffith and Tyner, *Discipline Reform through the Eyes of Teachers.*

51. Griffith and Tyner, *Discipline Reform through the Eyes of Teachers.*

52. Anne Gregory, Kysa Nygreen, and Dana Michiko Moran, "The Discipline Gap and the Normalization of Failure," in *Unfinished Business: Closing the Racial Achievement Gap in Our Schools*, eds. Pedro Noguera and Jean Yonemura Wing (San Francisco: Jossey-Bass, 2006), 125, 145.

53. Kalman Hettleman, "Most Students in Special Education Don't Need to Be There. It's Time to End the Broken Promises and Reinvent the Process," *The 74 Million*, last modified August 20, 2020, https://www.the74million.org/article/hettleman-most-students-in-special-education-dont-need-to-be-there-its-time-to-end-the-broken-promises-and-reinvent-the-process/.

54. McWilliams, *Compete or Close*, 156–58, 176–77.

55. McWilliams, *Compete or Close*, 176–80.

56. Gregory, Nygreen, and Moran, "The Discipline Gap and the Normalization of Failure," in *Unfinished Business*, eds. Noguera and Wing, 125.

57. Farber, *Crisis in Education*, 65; Labaree, *Someone Has to Fail*, 149.

58. Griffith and Tyner, *Discipline Reform through the Eyes of Teachers*; Farber, *Crisis in Education*, 55, 219–20.

59. Andrew C. Johnston, "Preferences, Selection, and the Structure of Teacher Compensation," *Annenberg Institute for School Reform at Brown University*, 4, last modified February 18, 2021, https://www.edworkingpapers.com/sites/default/files/Teacher%20Utility%20and%20Compensation%20Structure%20vJPE%20v3_0.pdf.

60. Melissa Gutwein, "What Will Draw More Teachers to Low-Performing Schools?," *Thomas B. Fordham Institute*, last modified March 18, 2021, https://fordhaminstitute.org/national/commentary/what-will-draw-more-teachers-low-performing-schools; Samantha Viano, Lam D. Pham, Gary T. Henry, Adam Kho, and Ron Zimmer, "What Teachers Want: School Factors Predicting Teachers' Decisions to Work in Low-Performing Schools," *American Educational Research Journal*, first published June 11, 2020, https://journals.sagepub.com/doi/abs/10.3102/0002831220930199?journalCode=aera.

61. Sowell, *Charter Schools and Their Enemies*, 111.

62. Pondiscio, *How the Other Half Learns*, 40, 54, 303.

63. Wagma Mommandi and Kevin Welner, *School's Choice: How Charter Schools Control Access and Shape Enrollment* (New York: Teacher's College Press, 2021), 94–96. McWilliams, *Compete or Close*, 36.

64. McWilliams, *Compete or Close*, 170.

65. Sowell, *Charter Schools and Their Enemies*, 111; Pondiscio, *How the Other Half Learns*, 303.

66. Richard M. Ingersoll, Philip Sirinides, and Patrick Dougherty, "Leadership Matters: Teachers' Roles in School Decision Making and School Performance," *American Educator*, 17, last modified Spring 2018, https://files.eric.ed.gov/fulltext/EJ1173452.pdf.

67. Frederick M. Hess and Pedro A. Noguera, *A Search for Common Ground: Conversations about the Toughest Questions in K-12 Education* (New York: Teachers

College Press, 2021), 64; see also Levenson, *Six Shifts to Improve Special Education and Other Interventions*, 110–15.

68. McWilliams, *Compete or Close*, 90–91.

69. Farber, *Crisis in Education*, 116.

70. Arianna Prothero, "How to Manage Discord over Student Discipline," *Education Week*, last modified October 15, 2019, https://www.edweek.org/leadership/how-to-manage-discord-over-student-discipline/2019/10.

71. Many states prohibit corporal punishment in schools, and it is most prevalent in the southeastern part of the country. Elizabeth T. Gershoff and Sarah A. Font, "Corporal Punishment in U.S. Public Schools: Prevalence, Disparities in Use, and Status in State and Federal Policy," *U.S. National Library of Medicine National Institutes of Health*, last modified 2016, https://www.ncbi.nlm.nih.gov/pmc/articles/PMC5766273/; see also Mark Keierleber, "Kids Keep Getting Hit at School, Even Where Corporal Punishment Is Banned," *The 74 Million*, last modified May 19, 2021, https://www.the74million.org/article/kids-keep-getting-hit-at-school-even-where-corporal-punishment-is-banned/.

72. Andre M. Perry, *Know Your Price: Valuing Black Lives and Property in America's Black Cities* (Washington, DC: Brookings Institution Press, 2020), 147; Daniel J. Losen and Paul Martinez, "Lost Opportunities: How Disparate School Discipline Continues to Drive Differences in the Opportunity to Learn," *Civil Rights Project*, last modified October 2020, https://www.civilrightsproject.ucla.edu/research/k-12-education/school-discipline/lost-opportunities-how-disparate-school-discipline-continues-to-drive-differences-in-the-opportunity-to-learn/Lost-Opportunities-REPORT-v17.pdf.

73. Darby and Rury, *The Color of Mind*, 137; Amanda E. Lewis and John B. Diamond, *Despite the Best Intentions: How Racial Inequality Thrives in Good Schools* (New York: Oxford University Press, 2015), 46; Jean Yonemura Wing, "Integration across Campus, Segregation across Classrooms: A Close-up Look at Privilege," in *Unfinished Business*, eds. Noguera and Wing, 103.

74. Lewis and Diamond, *Despite the Best Intentions*, 46, 49.

75. Lewis and Diamond, *Despite the Best Intentions*, 51.

76. McWilliams, *Compete or Close*, 82.

77. Lewis and Diamond, *Despite the Best Intentions*, 54–60, 62, 75, 91.

78. Lewis and Diamond, *Despite the Best Intentions*, 52–54, 91–93.

79. Lewis and Diamond, *Despite the Best Intentions*, 65.

80. Sarah Carr, "Why Are Black Students Facing Corporal Punishment in Public Schools?," *The Nation*, last modified April 8, 2014, https://www.thenation.com/article/archive/why-are-black-students-facing-corporal-punishment-public-schools/.

81. Michael Petrilli, "For the New Year, Districts Should Make a Fresh Start on School Discipline Reform," *The 74 Million*, last modified January 2, 2019, https://www.the74million.org/article/petrilli-for-the-new-year-districts-should-make-a-fresh-start-on-school-discipline-reform/.

82. Daniel J. Losen and Paul Martinez, "Lost Opportunities: How Disparate School Discipline Continues to Drive Differences in the Opportunity to Learn," *The Center for Civil Rights Remedies and the Learning Policy Institute*, 8–16, last updated

February 17, 2021, https://www.civilrightsproject.ucla.edu/research/k-12-education/school-discipline/lost-opportunities-how-disparate-school-discipline-continues-to-drive-differences-in-the-opportunity-to-learn/Lost-Opportunities-REPORT-v14.pdf.

83. Michael Petrilli, "For the New Year, Districts Should Make a Fresh Start on School Discipline Reform"; Colleen Brooks and Benjamin Erwin, "School Discipline," *National Conference of State Legislatures*, last modified June 24, 2019, https://www.ncsl.org/research/education/school-discipline.aspx; Max Eden, "The Bitter Debate over School Discipline," *Quillette*, last modified May 31, 2019, https://quillette.com/2019/05/31/the-bitter-debate-over-school-discipline/.

84. Jordan G. Starck, Travis Riddle, Stacey Sinclair, and Natasha Warikoo, "Teachers Are People Too: Racial Bias among American Educators," *Brookings Institution*, last modified July 13, 2020, https://www.brookings.edu/blog/brown-center-chalkboard/2020/07/13/teachers-are-people-too-racial-bias-among-american-educators/.

85. Turner, *Suddenly Diverse*, 98.

86. Turner, *Suddenly Diverse*, 114.

87. Turner, *Suddenly Diverse*, 97.

88. Asher Lehrer-Small, "A Test Case in Providence: Can Majority-White Teachers Unions Be Anti-Racist?," *The 74 Million*, last modified December 1, 2020, https://www.the74million.org/article/a-test-case-in-providence-can-majority-white-teachers-unions-be-anti-racist/.

89. "From Zero to SB100: Teachers' Views on Implementation of School Discipline Reform," *Teach Plus*, last modified 2018, https://teachplus.org/sites/default/files/publication/pdf/from_zero_to_sb100-_teachers_views_on_implementation_of_school_discipline_reform_final.pdf.

90. National Center on Early Childhood Health and Wellness, "Understanding and Eliminating Expulsion in Early Childhood Programs," accessed September 28, 2021, https://eclkc.ohs.acf.hhs.gov/sites/default/files/pdf/understanding-eliminating-expulsion-early-childhood-factsheet.pdf; Dolores A. Stegelin, "Preschool Suspension and Expulsion: Defining the Issues," *Institute for Child Success*, last modified December 2018, https://www.instituteforchildsuccess.org/wp-content/uploads/2018/12/ICS-2018-PreschoolSuspensionBrief-WEB.pdf; Walter S. Gilliam and Golan Shahar, "Preschool and Child Care Expulsion and Suspension: Rates and Predictors in One State," *Infants & Young Children*, Vol. 19, No. 3, last modified 2006, https://medicine.yale.edu/childstudy/zigler/publications/Gilliam%20and%20Shahar%20-%202006%20Preschool%20and%20Child%20Care%20Expulsion%20and%20Suspension-%20Rates%20and%20Predictors%20in%20One%20State_251491_5379_v3.pdf; Walter S. Gilliam, "Prekindergarteners Left Behind: Expulsion Rates in State Prekindergarten Systems," *Foundation for Child Development*, last modified May 4, 2005, https://www.fcd-us.org/assets/2016/04/ExpulsionCompleteReport.pdf.

91. National Center on Early Childhood Health and Wellness, "Understanding and Eliminating Expulsion in Early Childhood Programs."

92. Stegelin, "Preschool Suspension and Expulsion: Defining the Issues."

93. Adrienne Fischer and Matt Weyer, "School Discipline in Preschool through Grade 3," *National Conference of State Legislatures*, last modified March 29, 2019,

https://www.ncsl.org/research/education/school-discipline-in-preschool-through
-grade-3.aspx; Stegelin, "Preschool Suspension and Expulsion: Defining the Issues."

94. National Center on Early Childhood Health and Wellness, "Understanding and
Eliminating Expulsion in Early Childhood Programs"; Walter S. Gilliam, Angela
N. Maupin, Chin R. Reyes, Maria Accavitti, and Frederick Shic, "Do Early Educa-
tors' Implicit Biases Regarding Sex and Race Relate to Behavior Expectations and
Recommendations of Preschool Expulsions and Suspensions?," *Yale Child Study
Center*, last modified September 28, 2016, https://medicine.yale.edu/childstudy/
zigler/publications/Preschool%20Implicit%20Bias%20Policy%20Brief_final_9_26
_276766_5379_v1.pdf.

95. Tyack, *The One Best System*, 10.

96. Bryk, Sebring, Kerbow, Rollow, and Easton, *Charting Chicago School Reform*.

97. Zavadsky, *School Turnarounds*, 25; Ingersoll, Sirinides, and Dougherty,
Leadership Matters; Sebring, Allensworth, Bryk, Easton, and Luppescu, "The Essential Supports for School Improvement"; Partnership for the Future of Learning,
"Building a Strong and Diverse Teaching Profession," 87–102, accessed September 28, 2021, https://static1.squarespace.com/static/5f4048bbd7dba74d40ec9c46/t
/608edfd555f6f13a4cecb5e9/1619976159553/Teaching+Profession+Playbook+-+Par
tnership+for+the+Future+of+Learning+-+050121.pdf.

98. Ingersoll, Sirinides, and Dougherty, Leadership Matters; Jason A. Grissom, Anna J. Egalite, and Constance A. Lindsay, "How Principals Affect Students and Schools," *The Wallace Foundation*, last modified February 2021, https:
//www.wallacefoundation.org/knowledge-center/Documents/How-Principals-Affect
-Students-and-Schools.pdf.

99. Grissom, Egalite, and Lindsay, "How Principals Affect Students and Schools,"
54–72; see also "The School Principal as Leader: Guiding Schools to Better Teaching and Learning," *The Wallace Foundation*, last modified January 2013, https://
www.wallacefoundation.org/knowledge-center/pages/the-school-principal-as-leader
-guiding-schools-to-better-teaching-and-learning.aspx.

100. In addition to teacher leadership, principals should be able to draw on assistant principals—although the roles of assistant principals are varied and not always
well defined. Ellen Goldring, Mollie Rubin, and Mariesa Herrmann, "The Role of
Assistant Principals: Evidence and Insights for Advancing School Leadership," *The
Wallace Foundation*, last modified April 2021, https://www.wallacefoundation.org
/knowledge-center/Documents/The-Role-of-Assistant-Principals-Evidence-Insights
-for-Advancing-School-Leadership.pdf; Denisa R. Superville, "Is the Assistance
Principal the Most Overlooked, Undervalued Person at School?," *Education Week*,
last modified April 15, 2021, https://www.edweek.org/leadership/is-the-assistant
-principal-the-most-overlooked-undervalued-person-at-school/2021/04.

101. Ingersoll, Sirinides, and Dougherty, Leadership Matters; Sebring, Allensworth,
Bryk, Easton, and Luppescu, "The Essential Supports for School Improvement."

102. Mark Teoh, Lena Rothfarb, Anthony Castro, Melody Coryell, Aja Currey,
Darlene Fortier, John Gensic, Jamita Horton, Jennifer Smith, Tory Tripp, and James
Jack, "Barriers to Bridges: Teacher Perspectives on Accelerating Learning, Leader-
ship, and Innovation in the Pandemic," *Teach Plus*, accessed September 28, 2021,

https://teachplus.org/sites/default/files/downloads/Documents/teach_plus_barriers
_to_bridges.pdf; Advance Illinois, "Transforming Teacher Work," 8–9, last modified November 2011, https://media.advanceillinois.org/wp-content/uploads/2014/11
/04001242/FINAL-Transforming-Teacher-Work.pdf.

103. Deborah Meier, "Rethinking Trust," in *I Used to Think . . . And Now I Think
. . . Twenty Leading Educators Reflect on the Work of School Reform* (Cambridge,
MA: Harvard Education Press, 2011), 115–16.

104. Chubb and Moe, *Politics, Markets, and America's Schools*, 52.

105. Oberfield, *Are Charters Different?*, 78.

106. Sarason, *The Predictable Failure of Educational Reform*, 61.

107. Terry M. Moe, *Special Interest: Teachers Unions and America's Public
Schools* (Washington, DC: Brookings Institution Press, 2011), 190; Osborne, *Rein-
venting America's Schools*, 239–41; Paul T. Hill, "The Costs of Collective Bargaining
Agreements and Related District Policies," in *Collective Bargaining in Education:
Negotiating Change in Today's Schools*, eds. Jane Hannaway and Andrew J. Rother-
ham (Cambridge, MA: Harvard Education Press, 2006), 98–99; Chubb and Moe,
Politics, Markets, and America's Schools, 48–49.

108. Mehta, *Allure of Order*, 278–79.

109. Bryk, Sebring, Kerbow, Rollow, and Easton, *Charting Chicago School
Reform*, 252–53.

110. Goldstein, *The Teacher Wars*, 121.

111. Ravitch, *Reign of Error*, 107.

112. Seth Gershenson, Michael Hansen, and Constance A. Lindsay, *Teacher
Diversity and Student Success: Why Racial Representation Matters in the Classroom*
(Cambridge, MA: Harvard Education Press, 2021).

113. Fullan and Quinn, *Coherence*.

114. Mehta, *Allure of Order*, 260; Elmore, *School Reform from the Inside Out*, 114.

115. Darling-Hammond, *The Flat World and Education*, 321; Denisa R. Superville,
"Principals and Teachers Don't Always See Eye to Eye. Can Getting in Sync Reduce
Turnover?," *Education Week*, last modified May 4, 2021, https://www.edweek.org
/leadership/principals-and-teachers-dont-always-see-eye-to-eye-can-getting-in-sync
-reduce-turnover/2021/05.

116. Karin Chenoweth, *Districts That Succeed: Breaking the Correlation between
Race, Poverty, and Achievement* (Cambridge, MA: Harvard Education Press, 2021),
21; Perry, *Know Your Price*, 142; O'Day and Smith, *Opportunity for All*, 18–20;
García and Weiss, "Examining the Factors That Play a Role in the Teacher Shortage
Crisis"; García and Weiss, "U.S. Schools Struggle to Hire and Retain Teachers"; Gar-
cía and Weiss, "Low Relative Pay and High Incidence of Moonlighting Play a Role
in the Teacher Shortage, Particularly in High-Poverty Schools"; García and Weiss,
"Challenging Working Environment ('School Climates'), Especially in High-Poverty
Schools, Play a Role in the Teacher Shortage."

117. Gershenson, Hansen, and Lindsay, *Teacher Diversity and Student Success*,
92–98; O'Day and Smith, *Opportunity for All*, 18–20; Payne, *So Much Reform*,
72–73.

118. Darling-Hammond, *The Flat World and Education*, 43.

119. O'Day and Smith, *Opportunity for All*, 18–20; Payne, *So Much Reform*, 72–81.

120. Susan DeJarnatt and Barbara Ferman, "Preserving Education as a Collective Good," in Barbara Ferman (ed.), *The Fight for America's Schools: Grassroots Organizing in Education* (Cambridge, MA: Harvard Education Press, 2017), 134.

121. Oberfield, *Are Charters Different?*, 167.

122. Dale Russakoff, *The Prize: Who's in Charge of America's Schools?* (New York: Mariner Books, 2015), 193.

123. McWilliams, *Compete or Close*, 139.

124. Jeffrey R. Henig, Richard C. Hula, Marion Orr, and Desiree S. Pedescleaux, *The Color of School Reform: Race, Politics, and the Challenge of Urban Education* (Princeton, NJ: Princeton University Press, 1999), 44.

125. Henig, Hula, Orr, and Pedescleaux, *The Color of School Reform*, 44.

126. Gershenson, Hansen, and Lindsay, *Teacher Diversity and Student Success*, 71–72; Ansley T. Erickson, *Making the Unequal Metropolis: School Desegregation and Its Limits* (Chicago, IL: The University of Chicago Press, 2016), 220.

127. Erickson, *Making the Unequal Metropolis*, 218.

128. Goldstein, *The Teacher Wars*, 118–19; Farah Z. Ahmad and Ulrich Boser, "America's Leaky Pipeline for Teachers of Color," *Center for American Progress*, last modified May 2014, https://cdn.americanprogress.org/wp-content/uploads/2014/05/TeachersOfColor-report.pdf.

129. Gershenson, Hansen, and Lindsay, *Teacher Diversity and Student Success*, 44–53; Turner, *Suddenly Diverse*, 94; Russakoff, *The Prize*, 41; Goldstein, *The Teacher Wars*, 120; Jennifer Jellison Holme, Anjalé Welton, and Sarah Diem, "Pursuing 'Separate but Equal' in Suburban San Antonio: A Case Study of Southern Independent School District," in *The Resegregation of Suburban Schools: A Hidden Crisis in American Education*, eds. Erica Frankenberg and Gary Orfield (Cambridge, MA: Harvard Education Press, 2012), 63; Darling-Hammond, *The Flat World and Education*, 208; Madeleine Will, "Teachers' Low Expectations for Students of Color Found to Affect Students' Success," *Education Week*, last modified May 18, 2017, https://www.edweek.org/leadership/teachers-low-expectations-for-students-of-color-found-to-affect-students-success/2017/05.

130. Goldstein, *The Teacher Wars*, 137; Payne, *So Much Reform*, 74–81.

131. H. Richard Milner IV, "Public Education for the Public Good: Black Teachers and Teaching," in *Public Education: Defending a Cornerstone of American Democracy*, eds. Berliner and Hermanns, 130; Perry, *Know Your Price*, 140; "Program Diversity," *National Council on Teacher Quality*, last modified 2021, https://www.nctq.org/review/standard/Program-Diversity#researchRationale; Seth Gershenson, Cassandra M. D. Hart, Constance A. Lindsay, and Nicholas W. Papageorge, "The Long-Run Impacts of Same-Race Teachers," *IZA Institute of Labor Economics*, last modified March 2017, http://ftp.iza.org/dp10630.pdf; see also Ethan Scherer, Christopher Cleveland, and Rebecca Ivester, "The Effects of Teacher–Student Demographic Matching on Social-Emotional Learning," *Annenberg Institute for School Reform at Brown University*, last modified May 2021, https://www.edworkingpapers.com/sites

/default/files/ai21-399.pdf; Gershenson, Hansen, and Lindsay, *Teacher Diversity and Student Success*, 41–60.

132. Sarah Schwartz, "Teachers of Color More Likely than White Peers to Tackle 'Controversial' Civics Topics," *EducationWeek*, last modified January 5, 2021, https://www.edweek.org/teaching-learning/teachers-of-color-more-likely-than-white-peers-to-tackle-controversial-civics-topics/2021/01.

133. Payne, *So Much Reform*, 78–79.

134. Milner, "Public Education for the Public Good: Black Teachers and Teaching," in *Public Education: Defending a Cornerstone of American Democracy*, eds. Berliner and Hermanns, 130; Perry, *Know Your Price*, 143.

135. Kozol, *The Shame of the Nation*, 198–200.

136. Gershenson, Hansen, and Lindsay, *Teacher Diversity and Student Success*, 95–98; James Paterson, "When Educators of Color Are Asked to Be 'Everything' for Students of Color," *National Education Association*, last modified October 9, 2019, https://www.nea.org/advocating-for-change/new-from-nea/when-educators-color-are-asked-be-everything-students-color; John King, "The Invisible Tax on Teachers of Color," *The Washington Post*, last modified May 15, 2016, https://www.washingtonpost.com/opinions/the-invisible-tax-on-black-teachers/2016/05/15/6b7bea06-16f7-11e6-aa55-670cabef46e0_story.html.

137. Gershenson, Hansen, and Lindsay, *Teacher Diversity and Student Success*, 95–98; Jaclyn Borowski and Madeline Will, "What Black Men Need from Schools to Stay in the Teaching Profession," *Education Week*, last modified May 4, 2021, https://www.edweek.org/leadership/what-black-men-need-from-schools-to-stay-in-the-teaching-profession/2021/05; Youki Terada, "Why Black Teachers Walk Away," *Edutopia*, last modified March 26, 2021, https://www.edutopia.org/article/why-black-teachers-walk-away; Toya Jones Frank, Marvin G. Powell, Jenice L. View, Christina Lee, Jay A. Bradley, and Asia Williams, "Exploring Racialized Factors to Understand Why Black Mathematics Teachers Consider Leaving the Profession," *Sage Journals*, first published February 22, 2021, https://journals.sagepub.com/doi/10.3102/0013189X21994498; https://www.edweek.org/leadership/what-black-men-need-from-schools-to-stay-in-the-teaching-profession/2021/05.

138. Turner, *Suddenly Diverse*, 77; see also Partnership for the Future of Learning, "Building a Strong and Diverse Teaching Profession," 63–67.

139. "Detailed Languages Spoken at Home and Ability to Speak English for the Population 5 Years and Over: 2009–2013," *United States Census Bureau*, accessed September 28, 2021, https://www.census.gov/data/tables/2013/demo/2009-2013-lang-tables.html.

140. Kevin Mahnken, "Why the Race to Find Bilingual Teachers? Because in Some States, 1 in 5 Students Is an English Language Learner," *The 74 Million*, last modified September 25, 2017, https://www.the74million.org/why-the-race-to-find-bilingual-teachers-because-in-some-states-1-in-5-students-are-english-language-learners/; Corey Mitchell, "Schools Are Falling Short for Many English-Learners," *EducationWeek*, last modified March 7, 2017, https://www.edweek.org/policy-politics/schools-are-falling-short-for-many-english-learners/2017/03; "Promoting the Educational Success of Children and Youth Learning English," *The National*

Academies of Sciences, Engineering, and Medicine, last modified February 28, 2017, https://www.nationalacademies.org/news/2017/02/promoting-the-educational-success-of-children-and-youth-learning-english-new-report.

141. Corey Mitchell, "The Invisible Burden Some Bilingual Teachers Face," *Education Week*, last modified February 7, 2020, https://www.edweek.org/teaching-learning/the-invisible-burden-some-bilingual-teachers-face/2020/02; Cathy Amanti, "The (Invisible) Work of Dual Language Bilingual Education Teachers," *The Journal of the National Association for Bilingual Education*, Volume 31, 2019,—Issue 4, published online December 2, 2019, https://www.tandfonline.com/doi/abs/10.1080/15235882.2019.1687111.

142. Dolan, *Restructuring Our Schools*, 22–23.

143. Farber, *Crisis in Education*, 55.

144. Farber, *Crisis in Education*, 220, 255.

145. Dolan, *Restructuring Our Schools*, 26.

146. Dolan, *Restructuring Our Schools*, 25; see also Beach, *Can We Measure What Matters Most?*, 141–42.

147. Doris A. Santoro, "Teacher Demoralization Isn't the Same as Teacher Burnout," *EducationWeek*, last modified November 11, 2020, https://www.edweek.org/teaching-learning/opinion-teacher-demoralization-isnt-the-same-as-teacher-burnout/2020/11.

148. Sarason, *The Predictable Failure of Educational Reform*, 59.

149. Bruce Fuller, *Organizing Locally: How the New Decentralists Improve Education, Health Care, and Trade* (Chicago, IL: University of Chicago Press, 2015), 135, 142.

150. Dolan, *Restructuring Our Schools*, 120–24; Jose Vilson, "Less Is More: The Value of a Teacher's Time," *Edutopia*, last modified January 29, 2015, https://www.edutopia.org/blog/value-of-a-teachers-time-jose-vilson; Advance Illinois, "Transforming Teacher Work," 4–6.

151. Dolan, *Restructuring Our Schools*, 108.

152. Elmore, *School Reform from the Inside Out*, 133–99; Dolan, *Restructuring Our Schools*, 34–36.

153. Farber, *Crisis in Education*, 22–24.

154. Farber, *Crisis in Education*, 85.

155. Farber, *Crisis in Education*, 63.

156. Tyack, *The One Best System*, 139–40.

157. Tyack, *The One Best System*, 140.

158. Elmore, *School Reform from the Inside Out*, 27; Casey, *The Teacher Insurgency*, 166.

159. Wexler, *The Knowledge Gap*, 113.

160. O'Day and Smith, *Opportunity for All*, 75–78.

161. Beach, *Can We Measure What Matters Most?*, 113–14; Morgan Polikoff, *Beyond Standards: The Fragmentation of Education Governance and the Promise of Curriculum Reform* (Cambridge, MA: Harvard Education Press, 2021), 35; Casey, *The Teacher Insurgency*, 164–65; Wexler, *The Knowledge Gap*, 112; O'Day and Smith, *Opportunity for All*, 71; Susan Moore Johnson and Morgaen L. Donaldson,

"The Effects of Collective Bargaining on Teacher Quality," in *Collective Bargaining in Education*, eds. Hannaway and Rotherham, 135; Hess, *Cage-Busting Leadership*, 160–61; Jane L. David and Larry Cuban, *Cutting through the Hype: The Essential Guide to School Reform* (Cambridge, MA: Harvard Education Press, 2010), 145; Robert Pondiscio, "High-Quality Curriculum Doesn't Teach Itself," The Thomas B. Fordham Institute, last modified April 8, 2021, https://fordhaminstitute.org/national /commentary/high-quality-curriculum-doesnt-teach-itself; "The Mirage: Confronting the Hard Truth about Our Quest for Teachers Development," *The New Teacher Project*, last modified 2015, https://tntp.org/assets/documents/TNTP-Mirage_2015.pdf.

162. Casey, *The Teacher Insurgency*, 164–65; Darling-Hammond, *The Flat World and Education*, 204.

163. Pondiscio, "High-Quality Curriculum Doesn't Teach Itself."

164. Polikoff, *Beyond Standards*, 91–93; Darling-Hammond, *The Flat World and Education*, 266; "The Mirage," *The New Teacher Project*.

165. Elmore, *School Reform from the Inside Out*, 125–32.

CHAPTER 5

1. Tyack, *The One Best System*, 16–17.
2. Tyack, *The One Best System*, 66.
3. Tyack, *The One Best System*, 58.
4. Tyack, *The One Best System*, 60.
5. Goldstein, *The Teacher Wars*, 20.
6. Goldstein, *The Teacher Wars*, 40; see also Tyack, *The One Best System*.
7. "19th Amendment to the U. S. Constitution: Women's Right to Vote (1920)," accessed September 29, 2021, https://www.ourdocuments.gov/doc.php?flash=false &doc=63.
8. Tyack, *The One Best System*, 61.
9. Tyack, *The One Best System*, 62.
10. Tyack, *The One Best System*, 45.
11. Goldstein, *The Teacher Wars*, 22, 26.
12. Tyack, *The One Best System*.
13. Tyack, *The One Best System*, 78–104.
14. Tyack, *The One Best System*, 100.
15. Tyack, *The One Best System*, 175.
16. Tyack, *The One Best System*, 267.
17. Tyack, *The One Best System*, 257.
18. Goldstein, *The Teacher Wars*, 69; Moe, *Special Interest: Teachers Unions and America's Public Schools*, 44.
19. Tyack, *The One Best System*, 255–68.
20. Goldstein, *The Teacher Wars*, 69–74.
21. Goldstein, *The Teacher Wars*, 69–74.
22. Richard Kahlenberg, "The History of Collective Bargaining among Teachers," in *Collective Bargaining in Education*, eds. Hannaway and Rotherham, 8.

23. Kahlenberg, "The History of Collective Bargaining among Teachers," 9.

24. Kahlenberg, "The History of Collective Bargaining among Teachers," 10.

25. Moe, *Special Interest*, 46–47. The 1962 strike built on a one-day walkout in 1960.

26. Kahlenberg, "The History of Collective Bargaining among Teachers," 9.

27. Kahlenberg, "The History of Collective Bargaining among Teachers," 9–11.

28. Kahlenberg, "The History of Collective Bargaining among Teachers," 11.

29. Kahlenberg, "The History of Collective Bargaining among Teachers," 11.

30. Kahlenberg, "The History of Collective Bargaining among Teachers," 15–16.

31. Moe, *Special Interest*, 38.

32. Moe, *Special Interest*, 41–44.

33. *Janus v. American Federation of State, County, and Municipal Employees, Council 31, et al.*, 585 U.S. ___, 138 S. Ct. 2448 (2017), https://www.supremecourt.gov/opinions/17pdf/16-1466_2b3j.pdf.

34. Moe, *Special Interest*, 179, Johnson and Donaldson, "The Effects of Collective Bargaining on Teacher Quality," in *Collective Bargaining in Education*, eds. Hannaway and Rotherham, 116–19.

35. Hess, *The Same Thing Over and Over*, 150; Susan Moore Johnson and John P. Papay, *Redesigning Teacher Pay: A System for the Next Generation of Educators* (Washington, DC: Economic Policy Institute, 2009), 11.

36. Goldstein, *The Teacher Wars*, 178.

37. Moe, *Special Interest*, 193.

38. Moe, *Special Interest*, 165–67; Chad Aldeman, "How to Address the Rising Cost of Employee Benefits," in *Getting the Most Bang for the Education Buck*, eds. Frederick M. Hess and Brandon L. Wright (New York: Teacher's College Press, 2020), 21–25.

39. Goldstein, *Teacher Wars*, 264; *Someone Has to Fail*, 128.

40. Moe, *Special Interest*, 188; Hill, "The Costs of Collective Bargaining Agreements and Related District Policies," in *Collective Bargaining in Education*, eds. Hannaway and Rotherham, 99.

41. Ravitch, *Reign of Error*, 131.

42. Madeline Will, "How COVID-19 Is Hurting Teacher Diversity," *EducationWeek*, last modified September 14, 2020, https://www.edweek.org/teaching-learning/how-covid-19-is-hurting-teacher-diversity/2020/09.

43. Michael Hansen and Diana Quintero, "Scrutinizing Equal Pay for Equal Work among Teachers," *The Brookings Institution*, last modified September 7, 2017, https://www.brookings.edu/research/scrutinizing-equal-pay-for-equal-work-among-teachers/.

44. Hansen and Quintero, "Scrutinizing Equal Pay for Equal Work among Teachers."

45. Bruce D. Baker, *Educational Inequality and School Finance: Why Money Matters for America's Students* (Cambridge, MA: Harvard Education Press, 2018), 96.

46. Moe, *Special Interest*; 165.

47. Bryan Hassel and Emily Ayscue Hassel, "Rethinking School Staffing," in *Getting the Most Bang for the Education Buck*, eds. Frederick M. Hess and Brandon L. Wright (New York: Teacher's College Press, 2020), 95.

48. Matthew D. Henricks, "Towards an Optimal Teacher Salary Schedule: Designing Base Salary to Attract and Retain Effective Teachers," *Economics of Education Review*, last modified 2015, https://ideas.repec.org/a/eee/ecoedu/v47y2015icp143-167.html.

49. Hannaway and Rotherham (eds.), *Collective Bargaining in Education*, 147.

50. Goldstein, *The Teacher Wars*, 220.

51. Moe, *Special Interest*, 180.

52. Derek A. Neal, *Information, Incentives, and Education Policy* (Cambridge, MA: Harvard University Press, 2018), 42–44; Moe, *Special Interest*, 180; Kency Nittler, "You Don't Get What You Pay for: Paying Teachers More for Master's Degrees," *National Council on Teacher Quality*, last modified September 26, 2019, https://www.nctq.org/blog/You-dont-get-what-you-pay-for:-paying-teachers-more-for-masters-degrees.

53. Moe, *Special Interest*; Nittler, "You Don't Get What You Pay for: Paying Teachers More for Master's Degrees"; citing Marguerite Roza and Raegen Miler, "Separation of Degrees: State-by-State Analysis of Teacher Compensation for Master's Degrees," *Center for American Progress*, last modified July 2009, https://cdn.americanprogress.org/wp-content/uploads/issues/2009/07/pdf/masters_degrees.pdf.

54. Kahneman, *Thinking, Fast and Slow*, 343–46.

55. Wilson, *Bureaucracy*, 144.

56. Ravitch, *Reign of Error*, 116.

57. Tyack and Cuban, *Tinkering toward Utopia*, 130; David and Cuban, *Cutting through the Hype*, 48–49.

58. Even proponents of performance pay have acknowledged as much. Dale Chu, "Merit Pay Melts Away," *Thomas B. Fordham Institute*, last modified August 29, 2019, https://fordhaminstitute.org/national/commentary/merit-pay-melts-away; Rick Hess, "Missing the POINT: Tomorrow's Big Merit Pay Study Will Tell Us . . . Nothing," *EducationWeek*, last modified September 20, 2010, https://www.edweek.org/teaching-learning/opinion-missing-the-point-tomorrows-big-merit-pay-study-will-tell-us-nothing/2010/09. See also Deborah Stone, *Counting: How We Use Numbers to Decide What Matters* (New York: Liveright, 2020), 125–33; Matthew Di Carlo, "Test-Based Teacher Evaluation," in *Failure Up Close: What Happens, Why It Happens, and What We Can Learn from It*, eds. Jay P. Greene and Michael Q. McShane (Lanham, MD: Rowman & Littlefield, 2018), 71–87.

59. Johnson and Papay, *Redesigning Teacher Pay*, 45.

60. Johnson and Papay, *Redesigning Teacher Pay*, 50.

61. Tyack and Cuban, *Tinkering toward Utopia*, 126–31.

62. Hess, *Education Unbound*, 149.

63. Martin West, "If Many More Private Schools Close, All Schools Will Suffer," *Education Next*, Vol. 20, No. 4, last modified Fall 2020, https://www.educationnext.org/if-many-more-private-schools-close-all-schools-will-suffer/; Chad Aldeman, "Why Aren't College Grads Becoming Teachers? The Answer Seems to Be

Economic—and the Labor Market May be Starting to Improve," *The 74 Million*, last modified April 1, 2019, https://www.the74million.org/article/aldeman-why-arent -college-grads-becoming-teachers-the-answer-seems-to-be-economic-and-the-labor -market-may-be-starting-to-improve/.

64. Josh Barro, "3 Big Economic Trends of the 2010s," *Intelligencer*, last modified December 30, 2019, https://nymag.com/intelligencer/2019/12/3-big-economic-trends -of-the-2010s.html.

65. Will, "Enrollment in Teacher-Preparation Programs Is Declining Fast. Here's What the Data Show"; Partelow, "What to Make of Declining Enrollment in Teachers Preparation Programs."

66. Derek W. Black, *School House Burning: Public Education and the Assault on American Democracy* (New York: Public Affairs, 2020), 46–47; Garcia and Weiss, "Low Relative Pay and High Incidence of Moonlighting Play a Role in the Teacher Shortage, Particularly in High-Poverty Schools."

67. Sandi Jacobs, "In Demand: The Real Teacher Shortages and How to Solve Them," *FutureEd and EducationCounsel*, last modified October 2021, https://ib5uamau5i20f0e91hn3ue14-wpengine.netdna-ssl.com/wp-content/uploads /2021/10/FutureEd_EdCounsel_Teacher-Shortages_Report.pdf; Andrew G. Biggs and Jason Richwine, "The Truth about Teacher Pay," *National Affairs, Inc and the American Enterprise Institute*, last modified Fall 2019, https://www.nationalaffairs .com/publications/detail/the-truth-about-teacher-pay; Kaitlin Pennington McVey and Justin Trinidad, "Nuance in the Noise: The Complex Reality of Teacher Shortages," *Bellwether Education Partners*, 14, last modified January 2019, https://bellwethereducation.org/sites/default/files/Nuance%20In%20The%20Noise _Bellwether.pdf; Dan Goldhaber, "Analysis: COVID-19 Raised Fears of Teacher Shortages. But the Situation Varies from State to State, School to School & Subject to Subject," *The 74 Million*, last modified May 18, 2021, https://www.the74million.org /article/analysis-covid-19-raised-fears-of-teacher-shortages-but-the-situation-varies -from-state-to-state-school-to-school-subject-to-subject/.

68. Samuel Stebbins, "College Coaches Dominate List of Highest-Paid Public Employees with Seven-Digit Salaries," *USA Today*, last modified September 23, 2020, https://www.usatoday.com/story/money/2020/09/23/these-are-the-highest-paid -public-employees-in-every-state/114091534/. This is not to argue that college foot- ball coaches *should* be the highest paid public employees. It's just to observe that the competitive market for football coaches is clearly the reason that they actually are so highly paid.

69. McVey and Trinidad, "Nuance in the Noise," 14.

70. Jacobs, "In Demand," 3–4; McVey and Trinidad, "Nuance in the Noise," 25; see also Levenson, *Six Shifts to Improve Special Education*, 79; Marie Fazio, "Solv- ing Illinois' Teachers Shortage Is Complicated. These Five Charts Explain Why," *Chalkbeat*, last modified May 14, 2020, https://chicago.chalkbeat.org/2020/5/14 /21257678/solving-illinois-teacher-shortage-is-complicated-here-are-five-charts-that -explain-why.

71. Admittedly, my views here are shaped by my experiences as a lawyer. While I was working on this book, I had a conversation with a lawyer from a corporate firm

who told me that his billing rate was over $1000 an hour—which is not uncommon at major corporate firms. Samantha Stokes, "Associate Hourly Billing Rates Surge Past $1k as Firms Snap Up Bankruptcy Work," *The American Lawyer*, last modified May 22, 2020, https://www.law.com/americanlawyer/2020/05/22/associate-billing-rates -surpass-1k-as-firms-snap-up-bankruptcy-work/; Needless to say, lawyers specializing in education policy are paid substantially less.

72. The Hechinger Report, "Is the Teaching Profession Not Pink Enough?," *U.S. News & World Report*, last modified March 9, 2015, https://www.usnews.com/news/ articles/2015/03/09/is-the-teaching-profession-not-pink-enough.

73. Kahlenberg, "The History of Collective Bargaining among Teachers," in *Collective Bargaining in Education*, eds. Hannaway and Rotherham, 10.

74. Neal Morton, "Rural Schools Have a Teacher Shortage. Why Don't People Who Live There, Teach There?," *The Hechinger Report*, last modified April 13, 2021, https://hechingerreport.org/rural-schools-have-a-teacher-shortage-why-dont-people -who-live-there-teach-there/.

75. Jacobs, "In Demand," 4–5; Morton, "Rural Schools Have a Teacher Shortage"; Kelly Latterman and Sarah Steffes, "Tackling Teacher and Principal Shortages in Rural Areas," *National Conference of State Legislatures*, Vol. 25, No. 40, last modified October 2017, https://www.ncsl.org/research/education/tackling-teacher-and -principal-shortages-in-rural-areas.aspx; see also Elaine Weiss and S. Paul Reville, *Broader, Bolder, Better: How Schools and Communities Help Students Overcome the Disadvantages of Poverty* (Cambridge, MA: Harvard Education Press, 2019), 73–89.

76. Hess, *Education Unbound*, 78.

77. Hess, *Education Unbound*, 78.

78. Michael Q. McShane, "Schools and Systems That Are Getting More Bang for Their Buck," and Hassel and Hassel, "Rethinking School Staffing," in *Getting the Most Bang for the Education Buck*, eds. Hess and Wright, 55–59, 89–109.

CHAPTER 6

1. Tim Keller, "Myth: Private School Choice Is Unconstitutional," in *School Choice Myths: Setting the Record Straight on Education Freedom*, eds. Corey A. DeAngelis and Neal P. McCluskey (Washington, DC: Cato Institute, 2020), 77.

2. Desiree Carver-Thomas and Linda Darling-Hammond, "Teacher Turnover: Why It Matters and What We Can Do about It," *Learning Policy Institute*, 24, last modified August 2017, https://learningpolicyinstitute.org/sites/default/files/product-files /Teacher_Turnover_REPORT.pdf; Eric A. Hanushek, John F. Kain, and Steven G. Rivkin, "Why Public Schools Lose Teachers," *The Journal of Human Resources*, last modified Spring 2004, http://hanushek.stanford.edu/sites/default/files/publications /Hanushek%2BKain%2BRivkin%202004%20JHumRes%2039%282%29.pdf; see also Farber, *Crisis in Education*, 59.

3. Griffith and Tyner, *Discipline Reform through the Eyes of Teachers*.

4. Matthew P. Steinberg and Lauren Sartain, "What Explains the Race Gap in Teacher Performance Ratings? Evidence from Chicago Public Schools," *Sage*

Journals, last modified December 9, 2020, https://journals.sagepub.com/doi/full/10 .3102/0162373720970204; Madeline Will, "Teachers in High-Poverty Schools Penalized Unfairly on Observations, Study Says," *Education Week*, last modified December 14, 2020, https://www.edweek.org/teaching-learning/teachers-in-high-poverty -schools-penalized-unfairly-on-observations-study-says/2020/12.

5. Linda Darling-Hammond, *Getting Teacher Evaluation Right: What Really Matters for Effectiveness and Improvement* (New York: Teachers College Press, 2013), 12–14; Payne, *So Much Reform*, 67–92.

6. Hill, "The Costs of Collective Bargaining Agreements and Related District Policies," in *Collective Bargaining in Education*, eds. Hannaway and Rotherham,101–2; "Beneath the Surface: Ensuring LA Schools Have Equitable Access to Educators," *Partnership for Los Angeles Schools*, last modified February 2019, https:// partnershipla.org/wp-content/uploads/2019/02/BeneathTheSurface-EquitableStaffing .pdf.

7. García and Weiss, "U.S. Schools Struggle to Hire and Retain Teachers"; McVey and Trinidad, "Nuance in the Noise," 14–16.

8. Hill, "The Costs of Collective Bargaining Agreements and Related District Policies," 97; Charles Clotfelter, Helen F. Ladd, Jacob Vigdor, and Justin Wheeler, "High-Poverty Schools and the Distribution of Teachers and Principals," *North Carolina Law Review*, Vol. 85, last modified 2007, https://scholarship.law.duke.edu/cgi/ viewcontent.cgi?article=2558&context=faculty_scholarship.

9. O'Day and Smith, *Opportunity for All*, 70.

10. Hill, "The Costs of Collective Bargaining Agreements and Related District Policies," 108.

11. Paul T. Hill and Ashley E. Jochim, *A Democratic Constitution for Public Education* (Chicago, IL: University of Chicago Press, 2015), 79.

12. Hill, "The Costs of Collective Bargaining Agreements and Related District Policies," 103.

13. Hill, "The Costs of Collective Bargaining Agreements and Related District Policies," 104.

14. David C. Berliner, Gene V. Glass, and Associates, *50 Myths & Lies That Threaten America's Public Schools: The Real Crisis in Education* (New York: Teacher's College Press, 2014), 64–67.

15. Moe, *Special Interest*, 179.

16. Kahlenberg, "The History of Collective Bargaining among Teachers," in *Collective Bargaining in Education*, eds. Hannaway and Rotherham, 10.

17. Marc J. Wallace Jr., "Compensation," in *A Grand Bargain for Education Reform*, eds. Theodore Hershberg and Claire Roberston-Kraft (Cambridge, MA: Harvard Education Press, 2009), 92.

18. This "carrots" approach should be handled very differently than a "stick" approach of forcing highly rated teachers into low-performing schools, which has very little chance of working. Hess, *The Same Thing Over and Over*, 199–200.

19. Hill and Jochim, *A Democratic Constitution for Public Education*, 31; Marguerite Roza, "Allocation Anatomy: District Resource Distribution Practices & Reform Strategies," *School Finance Redesign Project, Center on Reinventing Public*

Education, last modified May 2008, https://www.crpe.org/sites/default/files/brief _sfrp_aa_may08_0.pdf.

20. Baker, *Educational Inequality*, 94.

21. Johnson and Papay, *Redesigning Teacher Pay*, 67.

22. College and Career Readiness State Legislation, "Per-Pupil Expenditure Reporting Requirement," *National Conference of State Legislatures*, accessed July 14, 2021, https://www.ccrslegislation.info/essa/reporting-expenditures/; "Funding Transparency under ESSA," *Education Commission of the States*, last modified February 2018, https://www.ecs.org/wp-content/uploads/Funding_Transparency_Under _ESSA.pdf.

23. Reetchel Presume and Ivy Smith Morgan, "Going Beyond ESSA Compliance: A 50-State Scan of School Spending Reports," *The Education Trust*, accessed September 29, 2021, https://edtrust.org/school-spending-beyond-compliance/.

24. John Fullerton, "Bridging the Gaps in Education Data," *American Enterprise Institute*, 4, last modified October 2021, https://www.aei.org/wp-content/uploads /2021/11/Bridging-the-gaps-in-education-data.pdf.

25. Patricia Saenz-Armstrong, "Smart Money 2.0," *National Council on Teacher Quality*, last modified July 2021, https://www.nctq.org/publications/Smart-Money -2.0; Patricia Saenz-Armstrong, "Upping the Ante: The Current State of Teacher Pay in the Nation's Large Schools Districts," *National Council on Teacher Quality*, last modified February 11, 2021, https://www.nctq.org/blog/Upping-the-ante:-The -current-state-of-teacher-pay-in-the-nations-large-school-districts.

26. Zavadsky, *School Turnarounds*, 59–61.

27. Darling-Hammond, *Getting Teacher Evaluation Right*, 95.

28. "Recognition and Rewards for Teaching Performance," *Texas Teacher Incentive Allotment*, accessed September 29, 2021, https://tiatexas.org/; Bekah McNeel, "A Big Raise for Texas Teachers; New Plan Will Give Top Educators $100,000 to Fight COVID Learning Loss at State's Poorest Schools," *The 74 Million*, last modified May 17, 2021, https://www.the74million.org/article/a-big-raise-for-texas-teachers-new -plan-will-give-top-educators-100000-to-fight-covid-learning-loss-at-states-poorest -schools/.

29. Saenz-Armstrong, "Upping the Ante"; "Voices from the Classroom: A Survey of America's Educators," *Educators for Excellence*, 12, last modified 2018, https:// e4e.org/sites/default/files/2018_voices_from_the_classroom_teacher_survey.pdf.

30. Melissa Gutwein, "What Will Draw More Teachers to Low-Performing Schools ?"; Viano, Pham, Henry, Kho, and Zimmer, "What Teachers Want."

31. Patricia Saenz-Armstrong, "Do State Collective Bargaining Rules Influence District Teacher Policies?," *National Council on Teacher Quality*, last modified November 11, 2021. https://www.nctq.org/blog/Do-state-collective-bargaining-rules -influence-district-teacher-policies.

32. McDermott, *High-Stakes Reform*, 49.

33. Justin Trinidad, "Analysis: How Bad Are the Nation's Teacher Shortages? With All the Conflicting and Unreliable Data Out There, We Don't Really Know," *The 74 Million*, last modified January 30, 2019, https://www.the74million.org/article/trinidad

-how-bad-are-the-nations-teacher-shortages-with-all-the-conflicting-and-unreliable
-data-out-there-we-dont-really-know/.

34. Saenz-Armstrong. *Upping the Ante.*

35. Lisette Partelow, "What to Make of Declining Enrollment in Teacher Preparation Programs," *Center for American Progress*, last modified December 3, 2019, https://www.americanprogress.org/issues/education-k-12/reports/2019/12/03/477311/make-declining-enrollment-teacher-preparation-programs/.

36. Thomas S. Dee and Dan Goldhaber, "Understanding and Addressing Teacher Shortages in the United States," *The Hamilton Project*, 12, last modified April 2017, https://www.brookings.edu/wp-content/uploads/2017/04/es_20170426_understanding_and_addressing_teacher_shortages_in_us_pp_dee_goldhaber.pdf.

37. Regenstein, "Why the K-12 World Hasn't Embraced Early Learning"; Regenstein, "Building a Coherent P-12 Education System in California."

38. Daniel Kahneman, *Thinking, Fast and Slow* (New York: Farrar, Straus and Giroux, 2011), 289–99.

39. Goldstein, *The Teacher Wars*, 121.

40. Saenz-Armstrong, "Do State Collective Bargaining Rules Influence District Teacher Policies?"

41. Saenz-Armstrong, "Do State Collective Bargaining Rules Influence District Teacher Policies?"

42. "Is Your State Prioritizing Teacher Diversity & Equity?," *The Education Trust*, accessed September 29, 2021, https://edtrust.org/educator-diversity/; Elizabeth Heubeck, "How School Districts Are Keeping Diverse Teacher Recruitment at the Top of Their Agenda," *Education Week*, last modified February 17, 2021, https://www.edweek.org/leadership/how-school-districts-are-keeping-diverse-teacher-recruitment-at-the-top-of-their-agenda/2021/02; Wayne D'Orio, "46 Years after Divisive Court Order, Boston Schools Still Struggle to Hire Black Teachers," *The 74 Million*, last modified September 8, 2020, https://www.the74million.org/article/46-years-after-divisive-court-order-boston-schools-still-struggle-to-hire-black-teachers/.

43. Leo Casey, "The Educational Value of Democratic Voice: A Defense of Collective Bargaining in American Education," in *Collective Bargaining in Education*, eds. Hannaway and Rotherham, 181.

44. *Janus,* 585 U.S. ___, 138 S. Ct. 2448.

45. Daniel DiSalvo and Michael Hartney, "Teacher Unions in the Post-Janus World," *Education Next*, Vol. 20, No. 4, last modified Fall 2020, https://www.educationnext.org/teachers-unions-post-janus-world-defying-predictions-still-hold-major-clout/.

46. Moe, *Special Interest*, 70, 77–79, 110.

47. Moe, *Special Interest*, 66–79.

48. Ravitch, *Reign of Error*, 130.

49. Casey, "The Educational Value of Democratic Voice: A Defense of Collective Bargaining in American Education," in *Collective Bargaining in Education*, eds. Hannaway and Rotherham, 197.

50. Sendhil Mullainathan and Eldar Shafir, *Scarcity: The New Science of Having Less and How It Defines Our Lives* (New York: Picador, 2013).

51. Kahneman, *Thinking, Fast and Slow*, 300–309.

52. Mehta, Gomez, and Bryk, "Building on Practical Knowledge," in *The Futures of School Reform*, eds. Mehta, Schwartz, and Hess, 39; Brad Jupp, "Rethinking Unions' Role in Education Reform," in *I Used to Think . . .* , ed. Elmore, 89–99.

53. Kirp, *Improbable Scholars*, 206–207; Jennifer Dubin, "In Connecticut, a Road Map for Union–District Relations," *American Educator*, published Winter 2013–2014, https://www.aft.org/periodical/american-educator/winter-2013-2014/moving-meriden; Indira Dammu, "Diversifying the Teacher Workforce," *Bellwether Education*, last modified February 2021, https://bellwethereducation.org/sites/default/files/Bellwether_PandemictoProgress_DiversifyingWorkforce_Final.pdf.

54. Julia E. Koppich, "The As-Yet-Unfulfilled Promise of Reform Bargaining: Forging a Better Match between the Labor Relations System We Have and the Education System We Want," in *Collective Bargaining in Education*, eds. Hannaway and Rotherham, 213.

55. Koppich, "The As-Yet-Unfulfilled Promise of Reform Bargaining," in *Collective Bargaining in Education*, eds. Hannaway and Rotherham, 212.

56. Moe, *Special Interest*, 272.

57. Dolan, *Restructuring Our Schools*, 79–81.

58. Mehta, *Allure of Order*, 151.

59. Linda Darling-Hammond, "Assuring Essential Educational Resources through a Federal Right to Education," in *A Federal Right to Education*, ed. Robinson, 241–45.

60. One benefit of seniority is that it is completely predictable. A salary schedule based on roles, however, will require some ongoing management. The roles that are most valuable—based on student demographics, subject matter, or other factors—will vary over time. Districts will need to have some capacity to manage that ongoing process of change.

CHAPTER 7

1. Michael Griffith, "State Teacher Salary Schedules," *Education Commission of the States*, last modified March 2016, https://www.ecs.org/wp-content/uploads/State-Teacher-Salary-Schedules-1.pdf.

2. Hansen and Quintero, "Scrutinizing Equal Pay for Equal Work among Teachers."

3. Hansen and Quintero. "Scrutinizing Equal Pay for Equal Work among Teachers"; see also Barone, "What ESSA Says," in *The Every Student Succeeds Act: What It Means for Schools, Systems, and States*, eds. Hess and Eden, 64; Partnership for the Future of Learning, "Building a Strong and Diverse Teaching Profession," 107; Berliner, Glass, and associates, *50 Myths & Lies That Threaten America's Public Schools*, 177.

4. Rooks, *Cutting School*, 45; Darling-Hammond, *The Flat World and Education*, 40, 312.

5. Diane Rado, "Tax Proposal Shifts Pain," *Chicago Tribune*, last modified May 18, 2005, https://www.chicagotribune.com/nation-world/chi-0505180257may18 -story.html.

6. In Chicago, under then-mayor Richard M. Daley, being an alderman was a much bigger deal than being a state legislator. Chicago state legislators were routinely ignored and disrespected by the Mayor's Office—but everybody knew that if the mayor needed their vote, they had no choice but to give it (which they resented). Because the education bill was widely understood to be dead, the meeting CEO Duncan and Board President Scott had with legislators ended up being a venting session where the legislators yelled at the CPS team about how badly CPS staff had treated them over the years. CEO Duncan, to his credit, picked up on the negative vibe and tried to make peace; Scott remained confrontational throughout. I remember thinking at the time that legislators generally hated Governor Rod Blagojevich so much that it was unusual to be in a meeting with him and legislators where the legislators were directing their fury toward somebody other than him.

7. Rick Pearson and Monique Garcia, "Rauner Win on Schools Bill Comes at a Price," *Chicago Tribune*, last modified August 31, 2017, https://www.chicagotribune .com/politics/ct-bruce-rauner-school-funding-met-0901-20170831-story.html. It helped that the 2017 bill was supported by an advocacy organization that hadn't yet been founded when the 2005 bill ran aground. Jose Garcia, "Advance Illinois Receives Game Changer of the Year Award at Industry Summit," *Advance Illinois*, last modified October 27, 2017, https://www.advanceillinois.org/news-media/archive /2017/10/press-release-advance-illinois-receives-game-changer-year-award-industry -summit.

8. Amy Gutmann, *Democratic Education* (Princeton, NJ: Princeton University Press, 1987), 142.

9. Baker, *Educational Inequality*, 145.

10. "Public School Revenue Sources," *National Center for Education Statistics*, last updated May 2021, https://nces.ed.gov/programs/coe/indicator_cma.asp.

11. Isaac William Martin, *The Permanent Tax Revolt: How the Property Tax Transformed American Politics* (Stanford, CA: Stanford University Press, 2008), 79.

12. "Property Taxes," *Urban Institute*, accessed September 29, 2021, https://www .urban.org/policy-centers/cross-center-initiatives/state-and-local-finance-initiative/ projects/state-and-local-backgrounders/property-taxes.

13. Martin, *The Permanent Tax Revolt.*

14. Gloria Ladson-Billings, "Is There Still a Public for Public Education?," in *Public Education: Defending a Cornerstone of American Democracy*, eds. Berliner and Hermanns, 229; Jennifer Jellison Holme and Kara S. Finnigan, *Striving in Common: A Regional Equity Framework for Urban Schools* (Cambridge, MA: Harvard Education Press, 2018), 8–9; Ivy Morgan and Ary Amerikaner, "Funding Gaps 2018: An Analysis of School Funding Equity across the U.S. and within Each State," *The Education Trust*, last modified February 2018, https://edtrust.org/resource/funding -gaps-2018/.

15. Daarel Burnette II, "As Districts Seek Revenue due to Pandemic, Black Homeowners May Feel the Biggest Hit," *EducationWeek*, last modified July 23, 2020,

https://www.edweek.org/leadership/as-districts-seek-revenue-due-to-pandemic-black
-homeowners-may-feel-the-biggest-hit/2020/07.

16. Rothstein, *The Color of Law*, 169–72; Carlos Avenancio-Leon and Troup Howard, "The Assessment Gap: Racial Inequalities in Property Taxation," *Washington Post*, last modified June 2020, https://context-cdn.washingtonpost.com/notes/prod/default/documents/19fd7c55-911a-448f-a089-d299c773b5fb/note/84507c99-e0be-42bc-8c01-bd105496bebb.#page=1; Burnette II, "As Districts Seek Revenue due to Pandemic, Black Homeowners May Feel the Biggest Hit"; Carlos Fernando Avenancio-Leon and Troup Howard, "Misvaluations in Local Property Tax Assessments Cause the Tax Burden to Fall More Heavily on Black, Latinx Homeowners," *Washington Center for Equitable Growth*, last modified June 10, 2020, https://equitablegrowth.org/misvaluations-in-local-property-tax-assessments-cause-the-tax-burden-to-fall-more-heavily-on-black-latinx-homeowners/; Carlos Fernando Avenancio-Leon and Troup Howard, "The Assessment Gap: Racial Inequities in Property Taxation," *Washington Center for Equitable Growth*, last modified June 10, 2020, https://equitablegrowth.org/working-papers/the-assessment-gap-racial-inequalities-in-property-taxation/.

17. John E. Coons, William H. Clune III, and Stephen D. Sugarman, *Private Wealth and Public Education* (Cambridge, MA: Harvard University Press, 1970), 65, 86.

18. Baker, *Educational Inequality*, 24; Brighouse, Ladd, Loeb, and Swift, *Educational Goods*, 34–35; Sterling C. Lloyd and Alex Harwin, "Nation Earns a 'C' on School Finance, Reflecting Inconsistency in K-12 Funding and Equity," *EducationWeek*, last modified June 1, 2021, https://www.edweek.org/policy-politics/nation-earns-a-c-on-school-finance-reflecting-inconsistency-in-k-12-funding-and-equity/2021/06.

19. Baker, *Educational Inequality*, 103–29; Lloyd and Harwin, "Nation Earns a 'C' on School Finance, Reflecting Inconsistency in K-12 Funding and Equity"; Urban Institute, "School Funding: Do Poor Kids Get Their Fair Share?," accessed December 5, 2021, https://apps.urban.org/features/school-funding-do-poor-kids-get-fair-share/.

20. Baker, *Educational Inequality*, 109–117; Coons, Clune, and Sugarman, *Private Wealth and Public Education*, 98–99; Lloyd and Harwin, "Nation Earns a 'C' on School Finance, Reflecting Inconsistency in K-12 Funding and Equity."

21. Baker, *Educational Inequality*, 124–29.

22. Baker, *Educational Inequality*, 147.

23. Danielle Farrie and David G. Sciarra, "Making the Grade 2021: How Fair Is School Funding In Your State?," *Education Law Center*, 11–13, last modified October 2021, https://edlawcenter.org/assets/MTG%202021/2021_ELC_MakingTheGrade_Report.pdf; Jennifer O'Neal Schiess, "Prioritizing Equity in School Funding," *Bellwether Education Partners*, last modified February 2021, https://bellwethereducation.org/sites/default/files/Bellwether_PandemictoProgress_SchoolFunding_Final.pdf; Andre Perry, "Black Families Don't Need 'Fixing.' They Need Better School Financing," *EducationWeek*, last modified August 26, 2020, https://www.edweek.org/policy-politics/opinion-black-families-dont-need-fixing-they-need-better-school-financing/2020/08; Linda Darling-Hammond, "Investing for Student Success: Lessons from State School Finance Reforms," *Learning Policy Institute*, last modified April 2019, https://learningpolicyinstitute.org/sites/default/files/product-files/Investing_Student

_Success_REPORT.pdf; Jeff Raikes and Linda Darling-Hammond, "Why Our Education Funding Systems Are Derailing the American Dream," *Learning Policy Institute*, last updated February 18, 2019, https://learningpolicyinstitute.org/blog/why-our-education-funding-systems-are-derailing-american-dream; Ivy Morgan and Ary Amerikaner," An Analysis of School Funding Equity across the U.S. and within Each State," *The Education Trust*, last modified February 27, 2018, https://edtrust.org/resource/funding-gaps-2018/; "5 Things to Advance Equity in State Funding Systems," *The Education Trust*, last modified December 8, 2019, https://edtrust.org/resource/5-things-to-advance-equity-in-state-funding-systems/. For a more optimistic view of current school funding, see Adam Tyner, "In Almost Every State, Funding Gaps between Rich and Poor Schools Have Been Closed," *Thomas B. Fordham Institute*, last modified November 18, 2021, https://fordhaminstitute.org/national/commentary/almost-every-state-funding-gaps-between-rich-and-poor-schools-have-been-closed (discussing Kenneth A. Shores, Hojung Lee, and Elinor Williams, "The Distribution of School Resources in The United States: A Comparative Analysis across Levels of Governance, Student Sub-groups, and Educational Resources," *Annenberg Institute for School Reform at Brown University*, last modified July 2021, https://www.edworkingpapers.com/sites/default/files/ai21-443.pdf).

24. Mark Keierleber, "Exit Interview: EdBuild's Rebecca Sibilia on America's 'Jacked Up' School Funding System, Her Organization's Successes and Failures & the Coming 'Tsunami' in Ed Finance," *The 74 Million*, last modified May 28, 2020, https://www.the74million.org/article/edbuild-exit-interview-rebecca-sibilia/; Mark Keierleber, "EdBuild Report: As Pandemic Threatens School Budgets, Researchers Urge Neighboring Districts to Pool Resources," *The 74 Million*, last modified May 27, 2020, https://www.the74million.org/edbuild-report-as-pandemic-threatens-school-budgets-researchers-urge-neighboring-districts-to-pool-resources/; Mark Keierleber, "Next Door but Worlds Apart: School District Borders Segregate Millions of Kids Based on Race and Revenue, Report Finds," *The 74 Million*, last modified July 25, 2019, https://www.the74million.org/next-door-but-worlds-apart-school-district-borders-segregate-millions-of-kids-based-on-race-and-revenue-report-finds/.

25. Baker, *Educational Inequality*, 198–99; Schneider and Berkshire, *A Wolf at the Schoolhouse Door*, 133; "5 Things to Advance Equity in State Funding Systems," *The Education Trust*.

26. O'Day and Smith, *Opportunity for All*, 156–57.

27. Baker, *Educational Inequality*, 138.

28. Marguerite Roza and Hannah Jarmolowski, "When It Comes to School Funds, Hold-Harmless Provisions Aren't 'Harmless,' " *Education Next*, Vol. 21, No. 4, last modified Fall 2021, https://www.educationnext.org/when-it-comes-to-school-funds-hold-harmless-provisions-arent-harmless/.

29. Hannah Jarmolowski and Marguerite Roza, "Proceed with Caution: With Enrollment Drops, States Are Looking to Hold District Budgets Harmless," *Edunomics*, February 2021, https://edunomicslab.org/wp-content/uploads/2021/02/Proceed-with-caution.pdf; Beth Hawkins, "Phantom Students, Very Real Red Ink: Why Efforts to Keep Student Disenrollment from Busting School Budgets Can Backfire," *The 74 Million*, last modified December 16, 2020, https://www.the74million.org/article/

phantom-students-very-real-red-ink-why-efforts-to-keep-student-disenrollment-from
-busting-school-budgets-can-backfire/; Roza and Jarmolowski, "When It Comes to
School Funds, Hold-Harmless Provisions Aren't 'Harmless'; Julien Lafortune and
Radhika Mehlotra, "Enrollment Changes May Create Winner and Loser in K-123
Budget Deal," *Public Policy Institute of California*, last modified July 14, 2020,
https://www.ppic.org/blog/enrollment-changes-may-create-winners-and-losers-in-k
-12-budget-deal/ .

30. Kenneth A Shores, Christopher A. Candelaria, and Sarah E. Kabourek, "Spending More on the Poor? A Comprehensive Summary of State-Specific Responses to School Finance Reforms from 1990–2014," *Annenberg Institute for School Reform at Brown University*, last modified May 2020, https://www.edworkingpapers.com/sites/default/files/ai19-52_v2.pdf; Amber M. Northern, "How States Have Responded to School Finance Reforms," *Thomas B. Fordham Institute*, last modified July 22, 2020, https://fordhaminstitute.org/national/commentary/how-states-have-responded-school-finance-reforms.

31. Northern, "How States Have Responded to School Finance Reforms"; Shores, Candelaria, and Kabourek, "Spending More on the Poor?"

32. Northern, "How States Have Responded to School Finance Reforms."

33. National Center for Education Statistics, "Inequalities in Public School District Revenues: Chapter II Categorical versus General Revenues," accessed September 29, 2021, https://nces.ed.gov/pubs98/inequalities/chapter2.asp.

34. National Center for Education Statistics, "Inequalities in Public School District Revenues."

35. M. Roza, "How Current Education Governance Distorts Financial Decision-making," in *Education Governance for the 21st Century*, eds. Manna and McGuinn, 38–39.

36. Osborne, *Reinventing America's Schools*, 281; Sara E. Dahill-Brown, *Education, Equity, and the States: How Variations in State Governance Make or Break Reforms* (Cambridge, MA: Harvard Education Press, 2019), 191–92; Brighouse, Ladd, Loeb, and Swift, *Educational Goods*, 102–103.

37. Karch and Rose, *Responsive States*, 129; Marshall S. Smith, "Musings," in ed. Elmore, *I Used to Think . . .* , 161.

38. This was a conversation I had frequently as a governor's office staffer, particularly with regard to the FY 2006 and FY 2007 Illinois budgets. As the person responsible for maintaining good relationships with various education groups I loved categoricals; they generated a lot of goodwill. Moreover, we knew that the unions and superintendents would complain about the primary formula even if we added a lot of money to it (which in historical terms we did); as long as we weren't increasing taxes, we would always fall short of their expectations. My Office of Management and Budget colleague Ginger Ostro was constantly arguing that we should hold categoricals flat and put more money into the formula. From a policy standpoint she was right, but the fact that I ended up largely winning those arguments shows why this is hard.

39. Lewis and Diamond, *Despite the Best Intentions*, 28–35, 46–58.

40. Emily Parker, "50-State Comparison: K-12 Special Education Funding," *Education Commission of the States*, last modified March 20, 2019, https://www.ecs.org/50-state-comparison-k-12-special-education-funding/.

41. Emily Parker, "Five Ways That States Limit Special Education Spending," *EdNote by Education Commission of the States*, last modified March 27, 2019, https://ednote.ecs.org/five-ways-that-states-limit-special-education-spending/.

42. National Center for Education Statistics, "Inequalities in Public School District Revenues: Chapter II Categorical versus General Revenues."

43. Bryk, Sebring, Kerbow, Rollow, and Easton, *Charting Chicago School Reform*, 277–78.

44. *California Department of Education*, "Local Control Funding Formula," last modified September 10, 2021, https://www.cde.ca.gov/fg/aa/lc/index.asp. The California reforms did not address special education. Jason Willis Sara Menlove Doutre, Kelsey Krausen, Tyson Barrett, Tye Pipma, and Ruthie Caparas, "California Special Education Funding System Study," *WestEd*, last modified October 2020, https://www.wested.org/wp-content/uploads/2020/10/WestEd_SpecialEdFundingReport_Final_508.pdf; That issue was addressed in 2020. Carolyn Jones, "Why Special Education Funding Will Be More Equitable under New State Law," *EdSource*, last modified August 7, 2020, https://edsource.org/2020/why-special-education-funding-will-be-more-equitable-under-new-state-law/637864.

45. Julien Lafortune, "School Resources and the Local Control Funding Formula: Is Increased Spending Reaching High-Need Students?," *Public Policy Institute of California*, last modified August 2019, https://www.ppic.org/publication/school-resources-and-the-local-control-funding-formula-is-increased-spending-reaching-high-need-students/.

46. Rucker C. Johnson and Sean Tanner, "Money and Freedom: The Impact of California's School Finance Reform on Academic achievement and the Composition of District Spending," last modified March 2018, https://gsppi.berkeley.edu/~ruckerj/Johnson_Tanner_LCFFpaper.pdf; Rucker Johnson and Sean Tanner, "Money and Freedom: The Impact of California's School Finance Reform," *Learning Policy Institute*, last modified February 2, 2018, https://learningpolicyinstitute.org/product/ca-school-finance-reform-brief.

47. Julien Lafortune, "School Resources and the Local Control Funding Formula: Is Increased Spending Reaching High-Need Students?"; John Fensterwald, "California School Funding Formula Has a Spending Loophole; Is a Recession the Time to Fix It?," *EdSource*, last modified May 7, 2020, https://edsource.org/2020/california-school-funding-formula-has-a-spending-loophole-is-a-recession-the-time-to-fix-it/631012.

48. *Data Lab*, "Federal Deficit Trends over Time," accessed September 29, 2021, https://datalab.usaspending.gov/americas-finance-guide/deficit/trends.

49. National Association of State Budget Officers, "Budget Processes in the States," 52, last modified Spring 2015, https://higherlogicdownload.s3.amazonaws.com/NASBO/9d2d2db1-c943-4f1b-b750-0fca152d64c2/UploadedImages/Budget%20Processess/2015_Budget_Processes_-_S.pdf.

50. Richard H. Thaler, *Misbehaving: The Making of Behavioral Economics* (New York: W. W. Norton & Co., 2016), 89–90.

51. Aldeman, "How to Address the Rising Cost of Employee Benefits," in *Getting the Most Bang for the Education Buck*, eds. Hess and Wright, 19.

52. Aldeman, "How to Address the Rising Cost of Employee Benefits," 20.

53. U.S. Department of Labor, "Types of Retirement Plans," accessed September 29, 2021, https://www.dol.gov/general/topic/retirement/typesofplans.

54. U.S. Department of Labor, "Types of Retirement Plans."

55. Aldeman, "How to Address the Rising Cost of Employee Benefits," 20.

56. Aldeman, "How to Address the Rising Cost of Employee Benefits," 20.

57. Aldeman, "How to Address the Rising Cost of Employee Benefits," 21.

58. Aldeman, "How to Address the Rising Cost of Employee Benefits," 21; Cory Koedel, Shawn Ni, and Michael Podgursky, "The School Administrator Payoff from Teacher Pensions," *Education Next*, Vol. 21, No. 4, last modified Fall 2021, https://www.educationnext.org/the-school-administrator-payoff-from-teacher-pensions/.

59. Chad Aldeman, "In Mississippi, There's a Path to Better Retirement Plan Options for K-12 Teachers," *Teacherpensions.org*, last modified June 14, 2021, https://www.teacherpensions.org/blog/californias-hidden-pension-gap-state-spending-teacher-pensions-exacerbates-school-district; Max Marchitello, "In Maryland, Teacher Pension Spending Compounds School Finance Inequities," *TeachersPensions.org*, last modified October 24, 2019, https://www.teacherpensions.org/blog/maryland-teacher-pension-spending-compounds-school-finance-inequities; Max Marchitello, "Illinois' Teacher Pension Plans Deepen School Funding Inequities," *Bellwether Education Partners and TeachPensions.org*, last modified August 2017, https://bellwethereducation.org/sites/default/files/Bellwether_TP_IL_PlanInequity_Final-082317.pdf; Ted Dabrowski and John Klingner, "Illinois Regressive Pension Funding Scheme: Wealthiest School Districts Benefit Most," *Wirepoints*, last modified March 9, 2016, https://wirepoints.org/illinois-regressive-pension-funding-scheme-wealthiest-school-districts-benefit-most-wirepoints-special-report/; James V. Shuls, Collin Hitt, and Robert M. Costrell, "How State Pension Subsidies Undermine Equity," *Phi Delta Kappan*, last modified April 29, 2019, https://kappanonline.org/state-teacher-pension-subsidies-equity-shuls-hitt-costrell/.

60. Koedel, Ni, and Podgursky, "The School Administrator Payoff from Teacher Pensions."

61. Kevin Mahnken, "New Report Gives Low Grades to Most Teacher Retirement Programs," *The 74 Million*, last modified September 29, 2021, https://www.the74million.org/new-report-gives-low-grades-to-most-teacher-retirement-systems/; Max Marchitello, Andrew J. Rotherham, and Juliet Squire, "Teacher Retirement Systems: A Ranking of the States," *Bellwether Education Partners*, last modified August 31, 2021, https://bellwethereducation.org/sites/default/files/Teacher%20Retirement%20Systems%20-%20A%20Ranking%20of%20the%20States%20-%20Bellwether%20Education%20Partners%20-%20FINAL.pdf;

62. Aldeman, "How to Address the Rising Cost of Employee Benefits," 24–25.

63. Aldeman, "How to Address the Rising Cost of Employee Benefits," 27–28.

64. For a discussion of the harm caused by complexity in public policy, see Steven M. Teles, "Kludgeocracy in America," *National Affairs*, Fall 2013, https://www.nationalaffairs.com/publications/detail/kludgeocracy-in-america.

65. Michael Griffith, "An Unparallel Investment in U.S. Public Education: Analysis of the American Rescue Plan Act of 2021," *The Learning Policy Institute*, last modified March 11, 2021, https://learningpolicyinstitute.org/blog/covid-analysis-american-rescue-plan-act-2021; Andrew Ujifusa, "See What the Huge COVID-19 Aid Deal Biden Has Signed Means for Education, in Two Charts," *Education eek*, last modified March 11, 2021, https://www.edweek.org/policy-politics/see-what-the-huge-covid-19-aid-deal-biden-has-signed-means-for-education-in-two-charts/2021/03.

66. Andrew Ujifusa, "COVID-19 Aid Package Protects Funding for Students in Poverty, But Could Challenge Schools," *EducationWeek*, last modified March 18, 2021, https://www.edweek.org/policy-politics/covid-19-aid-package-protects-funding-for-students-in-poverty-but-could-challenge-schools/2021/03.

67. David K. Cohen and Susan L. Moffitt, *The Ordeal of Equality: Did Federal Regulation Fix the Schools?* (Cambridge, MA: Harvard Education Press, 2009), 2.

68. National Center for Education Statistics, "Fast Facts: Title I," accessed September 29, 2021, https://nces.ed.gov/fastfacts/display.asp?id=158.

69. Cohen and Moffitt, *The Ordeal of Equality*, 113.

70. Baker, *Educational Inequality*, 219–22; see also Coons, Clune, and Sugarman, *Private Wealth and Public Education*, 254–56, 465–68.

71. Baker, *Educational Inequality*, 219–22; see also Farrie and Sciarra, "Making the Grade 2021," 14–16.

72. Kimberly Jenkins Robinson, "An American Dream Deferred: A Federal Right to Education," in *A Federal Right to Education*, ed. Robinson, 330–31.

73. Farrie and Sciarra, "Making the Grade 2021," 17–18; Kalman R. Hettleman, "The Renewal of a Bipartisan National Bargain on Education Reform," *Thomas B. Fordham Institute*, last modified August 28, 2020, https://fordhaminstitute.org/national/commentary/renewal-bipartisan-national-bargain-education-reform.

74. Evie Blad, "Why the Feds Still Fall Short on Special Education Funding," *EducationWeek*, last modified January 10, 2020, https://www.edweek.org/teaching-learning/why-the-feds-still-fall-short-on-special-education-funding/2020/01.

75. "The State of Preschool 2020," *The National Institute for Early Education Research*, 18; "FY 2021 Head Start Funding Increase ACF-PI-HS-21–01," *Head Start Early Childhood Learning & Knowledge Center*, accessed September 29, 2021, https://eclkc.ohs.acf.hhs.gov/policy/pi/acf-pi-hs-21-01.

76. "The State of Preschool 2020," *The National Institute for Early Education Research*, 18.

77. Sarah D. Sparks, "Title I Explained: 5 Things Educators Need to Understand about Federal Money for Students in Poverty," *EducationWeek*, last modified May 9, 2019, https://www.edweek.org/leadership/title-i-explained-5-things-educators-need-to-understand-about-federal-money-for-students-in-poverty/2019/05; Ulrich Boser and Catherine Brown, "5 Key Principles to Guide Consideration of Any ESEA Title I Formula Change," *Center for American Progress*, last modified July 7, 2015, https:/

/www.americanprogress.org/issues/education-k-12/reports/2015/07/07/116696/5-key
-principles-to-guide-consideration-of-any-esea-title-i-formula-change/.

78. Cohen and Moffitt, *The Ordeal of Equality*, 150–51.

79. For a different proposal based on similar principles, see Scott Sargrad, Lisette Partelow, Jessica Yin, and Khalilah M. Harris, "Public Education Opportunity Grants," *Center for American Progress*, last modified October 8, 2020, https://www.americanprogress.org/issues/education-k-12/reports/2020/10/08/491255/public
-education-opportunity-grants/.

80. For a proposal that is spiritually similar if subtly different in the particulars, see *Learning Policy Institute*, "The Federal Role in Advancing Education Equity and Excellence," 6–7, last modified August 2020, https://learningpolicyinstitute.org/sites/
default/files/product-files/LPI_Ed2020_BRIEF.pdf.

81. "President Obama, U.S. Secretary of Education Duncan Announce National Competition to Advance School Reform," *U.S. Department of Education*, last modified July 24, 2009, https://www2.ed.gov/news/pressreleases/2009/07/07242009.html.

82. "History of the ESSA Title I-A Formulas," *EveryCRSReport.com*, last modified July 17, 2017, https://www.everycrsreport.com/reports/R44898.html#
_Toc488412041.

83. Karch and Rose, *Responsive States*, 14–25. See also O'Day and Smith, *Opportunity for All*, 147–50.

84. *EducationWeek*'s analysis of state-level funding equity shows that there is an imperfect correlation between a state's political orientation and whether its education funding is equitable. "How Each State Performed on School Spending and Equity (Map and Rankings)," *EducationWeek*, last modified June 4, 2019, https://www.edweek.org/policy-politics/how-each-state-performed-on-school-spending-and
-equity-map-and-rankings/2019/06.

85. "The State of Preschool 2020," *2020 The National Institute for Early Education Research*.

86. Nance, "The Justifications for a Stronger Federal Response to Address Educational Inequalities," in *A Federal Right to Education*, ed. Robinson, 46–50; Aldeman, "The Case Against ESSA," in *The Every Student Succeeds Act: What It Means for Schools, Systems, and States*, eds. Hess and Eden, 102; "History of the ESSA Title I-A Formulas," *EveryCRSReport.com*; Ulrich Boser and Catherine Brown, "5 Key Principles to Guide Consideration of any ESEA Title I Formula Change"; see also Mark Lieberman, "Some School Districts Are Feeling COVID-19 Stimulus Envy," *EducationWeek*, last modified July 13, 2021, https://www.edweek.org/leadership/
some-school-districts-are-feeling-covid-19-stimulus-envy/2021/07.

87. Melissa Junge and Sheara Krvaric, "How Confusion over Federal Rules Can Get in the Way of Smart School Spending," in *Rethinking K-12 Education Procurement: Why Promising Programs, Practices, and Products Seem to Rarely Get Adopted, Implemented, or Used*, ed. Frederick M. Hess (Washington, DC: American Enterprise Institute, 2021), 55–58.

88. Andrew Ujifusa, "Trump seeks to Slash Education Budget, Combine 29 Programs into Block Grant," *EducationWeek*, last modified February 10, 2020, https://

www.edweek.org/policy-politics/trump-seeks-to-slash-education-budget-combine-29
-programs-into-block-grant/2020/02.

89. Marshall S. Smith, "Musings," in *I Used to Think . . .* , ed. Elmore, 161.

90. Gutmann, *Democratic Education*, 159.

91. For example, "Commission Report of Fundings and Recommendations," *Illinois Commission on Equitable Early Childhood Education and Care Funding*, 18–26, last modified Spring 2021, https://www2.illinois.gov/sites/OECD/Documents/Early %20Childhood%20Funding%20Commission%20Full%20Report.pdf.

92. Regenstein, *Building a Coherent P-12 Education System in California*, 22.

93. Goldstein, *The Teacher Wars*, 92.

94. Daniel Weisberg, Susan Sexton, Jennifer Mulhern, and David Keeling, "The Widget Effect: Our National Failure to Acknowledge and Act on Differences in Teacher Effectiveness," *The New Teacher Project*, last modified June 8, 2009, https:/ /tntp.org/publications/view/the-widget-effect-failure-to-act-on-differences-in-teacher -effectiveness.

95. Matthew A. Kraft, "What Have We Learned from the Gates-Funded Teacher Evaluation Reforms?," *Education Next*, Vol. 4, No. 21, last modified Fall 2021, https: //www.educationnext.org/learned-gates-funded-teacher-evaluation-reforms/.

96. For example, Madeline Will, "Efforts to Toughen Teacher Evaluations Show No Positive Impact on Students," *EducationWeek*, last modified November 29, 2021, https://www.edweek.org/teaching-learning/efforts-to-toughen-teacher-evaluations -show-no-positive-impact-on-students/2021/11; Madeline Will, "Teachers of Color Get Lower Evaluation Scores than Their White Peers, Study Finds," *EducationWeek*, last modified May 22, 2019, https://www.edweek.org/teaching-learning/teachers -of-color-get-lower-evaluation-scores-than-their-white-peers-study-finds/2019/05; Monica Disare, "97 percent of New York City teachers earn high marks on latest evaluations, union president says," *Chalkbeat New York*, last modified October 10, 2017, https://ny.chalkbeat.org/2017/10/10/21103518/97-percent-of-new-york-city -teachers-earn-high-marks-on-latest-evaluations-union-president-says.

97. O'Day and Smith, *Opportunity for All*, 71–72; Johnson and Donaldson, "The Effects of Collective Bargaining on Teacher Quality," in *Collective Bargaining in Education*, eds. Hannaway and Rotherham, 128; Noonshin Yazhari-Minutes, "3 Reasons Why Companies Make Bad Hired," *Fast Company*, last modified February 10, 2020, https://www.fastcompany.com/90461913/3-reasons-why-companies -make-bad-hires; Allan R. Odden, & Phi Delta Kappan, "Manage 'Human Capital' Strategically," *EducationWeek*, last modified April 1, 2011, https://www.edweek.org/ leadership/opinion-manage-human-capital-strategically/2011/04.

98. Human Resources, "The Cost of a Bad Hire," *Northwestern*, last modified February 2019, https://www.northwestern.edu/hr/about/news/february-2019/the-cost -of-a-bad-hire.html; Aaron Lowenberg, "The Pre-K Funding Debate: Formulas or Grants?," *New America*, last modified January 17, 2019, https://www.newamerica.org /education-policy/edcentral/pre-k-funding-debate-formulas-or-grants/; Jaime Potter and Gunnar Schrah, "3 Reasons Why Organizations Make Bad Hiring Decisions," *McKinsey & Company*, last modified December 17, 2018, https://www.mckinsey

.com/business-functions/organization/our-insights/the-organization-blog/3-reasons
-why-organizations-make-bad-hiring-decisions.

99. Emily Parker, "How States Fund Pre-K: A Primer for Policymakers," *Educa-tion Commission of the States*, last modified February 2018, https://www.ecs.org/wp
-content/uploads/How-States-Fund-Pre-K_A-Primer-for-Policymakers.pdf; see also
Ellen Boylan and Shad White, "Formula for Success: Adding High-Quality Pre-k to
State School Funding Formulas," *The PEW Center on the States*, last modified May
2010, https://www.pewtrusts.org/-/media/legacy/uploadedfiles/pcs_assets/2010/pewp
knschoolfundingformulamay2010pdf.pdf.

100. Regenstein. *Why the K-12 World Hasn't Embraced Early Learning*, 14.

101. Cassie Walker Burke, "Two Jobs, No Benefits: Can Illinois Rescue Its
Early Childhood Workforce?," *Chalkbeat Chicago*, last modified June 21, 2021,
https://chicago.chalkbeat.org/2021/6/21/22543976/child-care-workers-illinois-early
-childhood-workforce-efforts-to-boost-pay-stem-turnover; Lea J. E. Austin, Bethany
Edwards, Raúl Chávez, and Marcy Whitebook, "Racial Wage Gaps in Early Educa-tion Employment," *Center for the Study of Child Care Employment*, last modified
December 19, 2019, https://cscce.berkeley.edu/racial-wage-gaps-in-early-education
-employment/.

102. "The State of Preschool 2020," *The National Institute for Early Education
Research*, 18. These percentages include special education preschool.

103. *National Center for Education Statistics*, "Enrollment Rates of Young Chil-dren," last modified May 2021, https://nces.ed.gov/programs/coe/indicator_cfa.asp.

104. Caitlin McLean, Lea J. E. Austin, Marcy Whitebook, and Krista L. Olson,
"Early Childhood Workforce Index 2020," *Center for the Study of Child Care
Employment*, 42, last modified 2021, https://cscce.berkeley.edu/workforce-index
-2020/wp-content/uploads/sites/2/2021/02/Early-Childhood-Workforce-Index-2020
.pdf.

105. "The State of Preschool 2020," *The National Institute for Early Education
Research*, 31.

106. Head Start Early Childhood Learning & Knowledge Center, "Head Start Pro-gram Fact: Fiscal Year 2019," last modified April 20, 2021, https://eclkc.ohs.acf.hhs
.gov/about-us/article/head-start-program-facts-fiscal-year-2019.

107. *National Center on Early Childhood Quality Assistance*, "Early Learning and
Development Guidelines," last modified July 2019, https://childcareta.acf.hhs.gov/
sites/default/files/public/075_1907_state_eldgs_web_final508.pdf.

108. Office of Child Care, "OCC Fact Sheet," last modified June 23, 2021, https:/
/www.acf.hhs.gov/occ/fact-sheet.

109. McLean, Austin, Whitebook, and Olson, "Early Childhood Workforce Index
2020," 42.

110. "Transforming the Workforce for Children Birth through Age 8: A Unifying
Foundation," 6–8, 434–39, The National Academies of Science, Engineering, and
Medicine, last modified July 23, 2015, https://www.nap.edu/download/19401.

111. "Unifying Framework for the Early Childhood Education Profession," *Power
to the Profession*, 13–14, last modified March 2020, http://powertotheprofession.org
/wp-content/uploads/2020/03/Power-to-Profession-Framework-03312020-web.pdf.

112. Kate Stringer, "Do Pre-K Teachers Need and Bachelor's Degree? National Initiative Seeks Consensus on Decades-Old Debate," *The 74 Million*, last modified April 27, 2018, https://www.the74million.org/article/do-pre-k-teachers-need-a-bachelors-degree-national-initiative-seeks-consensus-on-decades-old-debate/.

113. "Transforming the Workforce for Children Birth through Age 8," 7, 434–39.

114. "Transforming the Workforce for Children Birth through Age 8," 7, 434–39.

115. "Transforming the Workforce for Children Birth through Age 8," 437; see also Regenstein, "Building a Coherent P-12 Education System in California," 25.

116. "A National Overview of Grantee CLASS® Scores in 2019," *Head Start Early Childhood Learning & Knowledge Center*, last modified August 14, 2020, https://eclkc.ohs.acf.hhs.gov/data-ongoing-monitoring/article/national-overview-grantee-class-scores-2019.

117. "Transforming the Workforce for Children Birth through Age 8," 515; see also Debra Pacchiano, Maia Connors, Rebecca Klein, and Kelly Woodlock, "Embedding Workforce Development into Scaled Innovations to Prevent Declines in Administration Quality," in *The Scale-Up Effect in Early Childhood and Public Policy*, eds. List, Suskind, and Supplee, 352.

118. "Transforming the Workforce for Children Birth through Age 8," 380–81.

119. Graham Vyse, "Is D.C. 'Insanely Stupid' for Requiring Child-Care Workers to Have College Degrees?," *The New Republic*, last modified March 31, 2017, https://newrepublic.com/article/141782/dc-insanely-stupid-requiring-child-care-workers-college-degrees.

120. "Transforming the Workforce for Children Birth through Age 8," 515–17; Linda Smith, "Moving beyond the Degree Debate," *Bipartisan Policy Center*, last modified April 30, 2018, https://bipartisanpolicy.org/blog/moving-beyond-the-degree-debate/.

121. Cody Komack and Ashley LiBetti, "Broader, Deeper, Fairer: Five Strategies to Radically Expand the Talen Pool in Early Education," *National Head Start Association, The Headstarter Network, and Bellwether Education Partners*, 5, last modified January 2021, https://www.nhsa.org/knowledge-center/center-for-policy-data-and-research/reports-and-recommendations/broader-deeper-fairer/.

122. Austin, Edwards, Chávez, and Whitebook, "Racial Wage Gaps in Early Education Employment."

123. Kirsten Cole, Jean-Yves Plaisir, Mindi Reich-Shapiro, and Antonio Freitas, "Building a Gender-Balanced Workforce: Supporting Male Teachers," *National Association for the Education of Young Children*, Vol. 74, No. 4, last modified September 2019, https://www.naeyc.org/resources/pubs/yc/sept2019/building-gender-balanced-workforce-supporting-male-teachers.

124. In 2016–2017 employee salaries and benefits accounted for 80 percent of district expenditures. National Center for Education Statistics, "Public School Expenditures," *Institute of Education Sciences*, last modified April 2020, https://nces.edu.gov/programs/coe/indicator_cmb.asp; Teachers represent 65 percent of school system employees. TED: The Economics Daily, "A Look at Elementary and Secondary School Employment," *U.S. Bureau of Labor Statistics*, last modified September 2018,

https://www.bls.gov/opub/ted/2018/a-look-at-elementary-and-secondary-school
-employment.htm.

125. Rooks, *Cutting School*, 45.

126. For example, Hess and Wright (eds.), *Getting the Most Bang for the Education Buck*; Frederick M. Hess and Eric Osberg (eds.), *Stretching the School Dollar: How Schools and Districts Can Save Money while Serving Students Best* (Cambridge, MA: Harvard Education Press, 2011).

CHAPTER 8

1. Eve L. Ewing, *Ghosts in the Schoolyard: Racism and School Closings on Chicago's South Side* (Chicago, IL: The University of Chicago Press, 2018).

2. Lawrence Blum and Zoë Burkholder, *Integrations: The Struggle for Racial Equality and Civic Renewal in Public Education* (Chicago, IL: University of Chicago Press, 2021), 148; Turner, *Suddenly Diverse*, 134; Rucker C. Johnson with Alexander Nazaryan, *Children of the Dream: Why School Integration Works* (New York: Basic Books, 2019); Darby and Rury, *The Color of Mind*, 77, 107–109; Genevieve Siegel -Hawley, *When the Fences Come Down: Twenty-First-Century Lessons from Metropolitan School Desegregation* (Chapel Hill: The University of North Carolina Press, 2016), 16–17; Linn Posey-Maddox, *When Middle-Class Parents Choose Urban Schools: Class, Race & The Challenge of Equity in Public Education* (Chicago, IL: The University of Chicago Press, 2014), 79–80; Goldstein, *The Teacher Wars*, 181; Richard D. Kahlenberg and Halley Potter, *A Smarter Charter: Finding What Works for Charter Schools and Public Education* (New York: Teachers College Press, 2014), 45–67; Erica Frankenberg and Gary Orfield, "Why Racial Change in the Suburbs Matters," in *The Resegregation of Suburban Schools*, eds. Frankenberg and Orfield, 19; Kozol, *The Shame of the Nation*, 316; Dara Zeehandelaar Shaw and Amber M. Northern, "What Parents Want: Education Preferences and Trade-Offs: A National Survey of K-12 Parents," *The Thomas B. Fordham Institute*, 35, last modified August 26, 2013, https://fordhaminstitute.org/national/research/what-parents-want-education -preferences-and-trade-offs; "Integrated Schools: Families Choosing Integration," accessed September 29, 2021, https://integratedschools.org/.

3. Sigal R. Ben-Porath and Michael Johanek, *Making Up Our Mind: What School Choice Is Really About* (Chicago, IL: University of Chicago Press, 2019), 108; see also Courtney E. Martin, *Learning in Public: Lessons for a Racially Divided America from My Daughter's School* (New York: Hachette, 2021), 191–93. While there are arguably benign versions of this, it's obviously a historically fraught idea given the history of segregated schools in this country. Darby and Rury, *The Color of Mind*, 87; Kevin Mahnken, "Power Is Knowledge: New Study Finds that Wealthy, Educated Families Are Using School Ratings to Self-Segregate," *The 74 Million,* last modified February 5, 2019, https://www.the74million.org/power-is-knowledge-new-study -finds-that-wealthy-educated-families-are-using-school-ratings-to-self-segregate/.

4. Peter Greene, "Our Schools and Our Towns Belong to Each Other," in *Public Education: Defending a Cornerstone of American Democracy*, eds. Berliner and

Hermanns, 61–65; Ewing, *Ghosts in the Schoolyard*, 134; Jessica Trounstine, *Segregation by Design: Local Politics and Inequality in American Cities* (Cambridge, UK: Cambridge University Press, 2018); DeJarnatt and Ferman, "Preserving Education as a Collective Good," *The Fight for America's Schools*, ed. in Ferman, 137; Siegel-Hawley, *When the Fences Come Down*, 41; Shedd, *Unequal City*, 40; Posey-Maddox, *When Middle-Class Parents Choose Urban Schools*; Barbara Shircliffe and Jennifer Morley, "Valuing Diversity and Hoping for the Best: Choice in Metro Tampa," in *Educational Delusions?*, eds. Orfield and Frankenberg, and Associates, 97.

5. Elliot Regenstein and Chris Strausz-Clark, "Improving Parent Choice in Early Learning," *American Enterprise Institute*, last modified January 25, 2021, https://www.aei.org/research-products/report/improving-parent-choice-in-early-learning/; Regenstein and Strausz-Clark, "Improving Parent Choice in Early Learning."

6. Genevieve Siegel-Hawley and Erica Frankenberg, "Designing Choice: Magnet School Structures and Racial Diversity," in *Educational Delusions?*, eds. Orfield and Frankenberg.

7. Shaw and Northern, *What Parents Want*, 37.

8. Shaw and Northern, *What Parents Want*, 30; Patricia Saenz-Armstrong, "Is the One-Track Mind of the Ed Reform Movement Doing More Harm Than Good?," *The Thomas B. Fordham Institute*, September 29, 2020, https://fordhaminstitute.org/national/commentary/one-track-mind-ed-reform-movement-doing-more-harm-good.

9. Shaw and Northern, *What Parents Want*, 32.

10. Hirsch, *How to Educate a Citizen: The Power of Shared Knowledge to Unify a Nation*; Wexler, *The Knowledge Gap*.

11. Hess, *Cage-Busting Leadership*, 149.

12. Paul Reville, "Beyond the Coronavirus Shutdown, an Opportunity for a Whole-Child Paradigm Shift," *The 74 Million*, last modified April 8, 2020, https://www.the74million.org/article/reville-beyond-the-coronavirus-shutdown-an-opportunity-for-a-whole-child-paradigm-shift/.

13. Pondiscio, *How the Other Half Learns*, 40, 54.

14. Cuban *Chasing Success and Confronting Failure*, 34–38; "Personalized Learning," *Education Week*, accessed September 29, 2021, https://www.edweek.org/technology/personalized-learning.

15. Cuban, *Chasing Success and Confronting Failure*.

16. Shaw and Northern, *What Parents Want*.

17. Lindsey M. Burke and Jason Bedrick, "Myth: School Choice Needs Regulation to Ensure Access and Quality," in *School Choice Myths*, eds. DeAngelis and McCluskey, 140; Ewing, *Ghosts in the Schoolyard*, 104–105; Shaw and Northern. *What Parents Want*, 7; Robert Pondiscio, "It's School Culture, Stupid," *The Thomas B. Fordham Institute*, last modified September 2, 2020, https://fordhaminstitute.org/national/commentary/its-school-culture-stupid.

18. Schneider, *Beyond Test Scores*, 230.

19. Osborne, *Reinventing America's Schools*, 234.

20. Petrilli and Finn (eds.), *How to Educate an American*, 237; Chester E. Finn Jr., Bruno V. Manno, and Brandon L. Wright, *Charter Schools at the Crossroads:*

Predicaments, Paradoxes, Possibilities (Cambridge, MA: Harvard Education Press, 2016), 27.

21. Ben-Porath and Johanek, *Making Up Our Mind*, 11.

22. Ben-Porath and Johanek, *Making Up Our Mind*, 11–12; Henry M. Levin, "A Framework for Designing Governance in Choice and Portfolio Districts," in *Between Public and Private*, eds. Bulkley, Henig, and Levin, 221–22.

23. *U.S. Bureau of Labor Statistics*, "Learn More, Earn More: Education Leads to Higher Wages, Lower Unemployment," last modified May 2020, https://www.bls.gov /careeroutlook/2020/data-on-display/education-pays.htm.

24. Labaree, *Someone Has to Fail*, 194, 224, 236.

25. Ben-Porath and Johanek, *Making Up Our Mind*, 11–12; see also Fiske and Ladd, "Values and Education Policy," in *Public Education: Defending a Cornerstone of American Democracy*, eds. Berliner and Hermanns, 34; David F. Labaree, "Public Schooling as Social Welfare," in *Public Education: Defending a Cornerstone of American Democracy*, eds. Berliner and Hermanns, 46; Blum and Burkholder, *Integrations*, 146–47, 163; Black, *School House Burning*, 173; Cuban, *Chasing Success and Confronting Failure*, 49; Harris, *Charter School City*, 25; Ravitch, *Slaying Goliath*, 11; O'Day and Smith, *Opportunity for All*, 193; DeJarnatt and Ferman, "Preserving Education as a Collective Good," in *The Fight for America's Schools*, ed. Ferman, 134, 137, 142; William J. Congdon, Jeffrey R. Kling, and Sendhil Mullainathan, *Policy and Choice: Public Finance through the Lens of Behavioral Economics* (Washington, DC: Brookings Institution Press, 2011), 136–39; Levin, "A Framework for Designing Governance in Choice and Portfolio Districts," in *Between Public and Private*, eds. Bulkley, Henig, and Levin, 222.

26. Congdon, Kling, and Mullainathan, *Policy and Choice*, 136.

27. O'Day and Smith, *Opportunity for All*, 193; Black, *School House Burning*, 173, Cuban, *Chasing Success and Confronting Failure*, 49.

28. Congdon, Kling, and Mullainathan, *Policy and Choice*, 136; see also Nance, "The Justifications for a Stronger Federal Response to Address Educational Inequalities," in *A Federal Right to Education*, ed. Robinson, 43–44. Patrick Wolf argues that education is not a public good because schools exclude children based on geography. Patrick Wolf, "Myth: Public Schools Are Necessary for a Stable Democracy," in *School Choice Myths*, eds. DeAngelis and McCluskey, 42. But the fact that certain schools are exclusive does not mean that education as a broader category is not a public good, a point acknowledged by Cory DeAngelis in the same volume. DeAngelis, "Myth: Children Are Not Widgets, So Education Must Not Be Left to the Market," in *School Choice Myths*, eds. DeAngelis and McCluskey, 72–73.

29. Ben-Porath and Johanek, *Making Up Our Mind*, 11; see also Cuban, *Chasing Success and Confronting Failure*, 186; Darby and Ruby, *The Color of Mind*, 128–41; Joshua E. Weishart, "Protecting a Federal Right to Educational Equality and Adequacy," in *A Federal Right to Education*, ed. Robinson, 312; Brighouse, Ladd, Loeb, and Swift, *Educational Goods*, 33; Shedd, *Unequal City*, 18.

30. Baker, *Educational Inequality*, 23.

31. Trounstine, *Segregation by Design*, 15.

32. Jeremy Bauer-Wolf, "California Vote Signals Affirmative Action Remains Divisive," *Higher Ed Dive*, last modified November 3, 2020, https://www.highereddive.com/news/california-vote-signals-affirmative-action-remains-divisive/588433/; see also Matthew Ladner, "No Excuses Charter Schools: The Good, the Bad, and the Overprescribed?" in *Failure Up Close: What Happens, Why It Happens, and What We Can Learn from It*, eds. Greene and McShane, 117–18.

33. Maia Bloomfield Cucchiara, *Marketing Schools, Marketing Cities: Who Wins and Who Loses When Schools Become Urban Amenities* (Chicago, IL: University of Chicago Press, 2013), 206; see also Martin, *Learning in Public*, 27.

34. This is similar to the argument Professor David Labaree makes that education policy has been a contest between reformers and consumers, with the consumers ultimately winning. Labaree, *Someone Has to Fail*, 6, 194, 224, 236.

35. Henig, Hula, Orr, and Pedescleaux, *The Color of School Reform*, 201.

36. Gutmann, *Democratic Education*, 66–67; Ravitch, *Reign of Error*, 203.

37. Darby and Rury, *The Color of Mind*, 106; see also Julia Sass Rubin, "Organizing Goes Statewide: The Case of Save Our Schools NJ," in *The Fight for America's Schools*, ed. Ferman,104; Rooks, *Cutting School*, 12.

38. Jeanne Allen, *An Unfinished Journey: Education and the American Dream* (Bloomington, IN: Xlibris, 2020), 66–67; Ben-Porath and Johanek, *Making Up Our Mind*, 84.

39. Frederick M. Hess, *Breaking the Mold: Charter Schools Contract Schools, and Voucher Plans*, in *American Educational Governance on Trial: Change and Challenges*, eds. William Lowe Boyd and Debra Miretzky (Chicago, IL: The University of Chicago Press, 2003), 114; see also Labaree, *Someone Has to Fail*, 6, 194, 224, 236.

40. Petrilli and Finn (eds.), *How to Educate an American*, 137.

41. Hess and Noguera, *A Search for Common Ground*, 21.

42. Ben-Porath and Johanek, *Making Up Our Mind*, 12–13.

43. "From Best Practices to Breakthrough Impacts: A Science-Based Approach to Building a More Promising Future for Young Children and Families," *Center on the Developing Child at Harvard University*, last modified May 2016, 12–14, https://46y5eh11fhgw3ve3ytpwxt9r-wpengine.netdna-ssl.com/wp-content/uploads/2016/05/From_Best_Practices_to_Breakthrough_Impacts-4.pdf.

44. "From Best Practices to Breakthrough Impacts," *Center on the Developing Child at Harvard University*, 7–9.

45. "From Best Practices to Breakthrough Impacts," *Center on the Developing Child at Harvard University*, 9–10.

46. Cassidy Francies and Zeke Perez Jr., "50-State Comparison: Free and Compulsory School Age Requirements," Education Commission of the States, last modified August 19, 2020, https://www.ecs.org/50-state-comparison-free-and-compulsory-school-age-requirements/.

47. Elana Lyn Gross, "Inside the Insanely Competitive World of Elite New York City Preschools," *Insider*, last modified June 14, 2018, https://www.businessinsider.com/preschools-in-new-york-city-2018-6; Anna Bahr, "When the College Admissions Battle Starts at Age Three," *The New York Times*, last modified July 29, 2014

https://www.nytimes.com/2014/07/30/upshot/when-the-college-admissions-battle
-starts-at-age-3.html.

48. National Center for Education Statistics, "The Condition of Education: Preschool and Kindergarten Enrollment," last modified April 2020, https://nces.ed.gov/
programs/coe/indicator_cfa.asp#f1.

49. "The State of Preschool 2020," *The National Institute for Early Education
Research*, 18.

50. "The State of Preschool 2020," *The National Institute for Early Education
Research*, 18.

51. "The State of Preschool 2020," *The National Institute for Early Education
Research*, 18. Enrollment figure includes state-funded Head Start.

52. James J. Heckman, "Early Childhood Education: Quality and Access Pay Off,"
The Heckman Equation, accessed September 29, 2021, https://heckmanequation.org
/www/assets/2017/01/F_Heckman_Moffitt_093016.pdf; Sneha Elango, Jorge Luis
Garcia, James J. Heckman, and Andres Hojman, "Early Childhood Education," *University of Chicago*, last modified August 29, 2016, 44–56, https://cehd.uchicago.edu/
wp-content/uploads/2016/12/Moffitt-ECE-Paper_2016-08-29a_jld.pdf.

53. "The State of Preschool 2020," *The National Institute for Early Education
Research*, 9.

54. "The State of Preschool 2020," *The National Institute for Early Education
Research*, 18.

55. "The State of Preschool 2020," *The National Institute for Early Education
Research*, 19.

56. "The State of Preschool 2020," *The National Institute for Early Education
Research*, 19–20, 28.

57. "The State of Preschool 2020," *The National Institute for Early Education
Research*, 28.

58. "The State of Preschool 2020," *The National Institute for Early Education
Research*, 28.

59. "The State of Preschool 2020," *The National Institute for Early Education
Research*, 28.

60. Regenstein, "Why the K-12 World Hasn't Embraced Early Learning," 21.

61. Regenstein, "Why the K-12 World Hasn't Embraced Early Learning," 21.

62. Regenstein, "Why the K-12 World Hasn't Embraced Early Learning," 21.

63. Regenstein, "Building a Coherent P-12 Education System in California," 20.

64. Denisa R. Superville, "How Long Do Big-City Superintendents Actually
Last?," *Education Week*, last modified May 15, 2018, https://www.edweek.org/
leadership/how-long-do-big-city-superintendents-actually-last/2018/05.

65. Which does not always work out. Hess, *Spinning Wheels*.

66. Kirp, *Improbable Scholars*, 59; Regenstein, "Why the K-12 World Hasn't
Embraced Early Learning," 9–10.

67. Regenstein, "Building a Coherent P-12 Education System in California," 20;
David T. Burkam, Valerie E. Lee, and Julie Dwyer, "School Mobility in the Early
Elementary Grades: Frequency and Impact from Nationally-Representative Data,"
Foundation for Child Development, last modified June 1, 2010, https://www.fcd

-us.org/school-mobility-in-the-early-elementary-grades-frequency-and-impact-from
-nationally-representative-data/.

68. "The State of Preschool 2020," *The National Institute for Early Education Research*, 18; see also pages 12–16.

69. Regenstein and Strausz-Clark, "Improving Parent Choice in Early Learning," 3–4; Regenstein, "Why the K-12 World Hasn't Embraced Early Learning," 22–23.

70. Regenstein and Strausz-Clark, "Improving Parent Choice in Early Learning," 3–4; "The US and the High Price of Child Care: An Examination of a Broken System" (Interactive Map). *Child Care Aware of America*, 24, last modified 2019, https://info .childcareaware.org/hubfs/2019%20Price%20of%20Care%20State%20Sheets/Final -TheUSandtheHighPriceofChildCare-AnExaminationofaBrokenSystem.pdf.

71. Regenstein and Strausz-Clark, "Improving Parent Choice in Early Learning," 3–4; Gerry Cobb, "The Investment Our Youngest Learners Need," *Governing*, last modified April 24, 2019, https://www.governing.com/gov-institute/voices/col -investment-infants-toddlers-early-childhood-education.html.

72. CityHealth, "High-Quality, Accessible Pre-K: Policy Breakdown," accessed December 7, 2021, https://www.cityhealth.org/wp-content/uploads/2021/07/CH_PRE -K_2019_B-1.pdf; The National Institute for Early Education Research, "New Report on Pre-K in Cities Shows 33 of Nation's Largest Cities Now Have Public Pre-K Program," last modified December 8, 2020, https://nieer.org/press-release/new-report-on -pre-k-in-cities-shows-33-of-nations-largest-cities-now-have-public-pre-k-program; Regenstein, "Why the K-12 World Hasn't Embraced Early Learning," 23, 25; see also Chenoweth, *Districts That Succeed*, 71 (discussing Steubenville, Ohio, a highly successful district that invested discretionary funds in preschool).

73. *First Five Years Fund*, "2021 National Poll: Full Results Deck," last modified January 29, 2021, https://www.ffyf.org/2021-national-poll-full-results-deck/.

74. Elizabeth Shapiro, "De Blasio's Win on pre-K Is Making an Easy Campaign Even Easier," *Politico*, last modified October 17, 2017, https://www.politico.com/ states/new-york/albany/story/2017/10/16/de-blasios-win-on-pre-k-is-making-an-easy -campaign-even-easier-115084.

75. National Center for Educational Statistics, "Rural Education in America: Number and Percentage Distribution of Public Elementary and Secondary Students, by Race/Ethnicity and School Urban-Center 12-Category Locale: Fall 2013," accessed September 29, 2021, https://nces.ed.gov/surveys/ruraled/tables/B.1.b.-1.asp. Note that the data is old.

76. Frederick M. Hess, "Schooling Choice," *The American Mind*, last modified May 8, 2019, https://americanmind.org/features/post-trump-politics/schooling -choice/; Frederick M. Hess and Andy Smarick, "In Defense of Local Schools," *National Review*, last modified March 1, 2018, https://www.nationalreview.com/ magazine/2018/03/19/education-reform-local-schools-key/; see also Redding, "Poverty's Impact on Learning," in *Opportunity and Performance*, ed. Redding, 69–70 (discussing the challenges of rural schools).

77. Erickson, *Making the Unequal Metropolis*.

78. Levin, "A Framework for Designing Governance in Choice and Portfolio Districts," in *Between Public and Private*, eds. Bulkley, Henig, and Levin, 217–18.

79. Jon N. Hale, *The Choice We Face: How Segregation, Race, and Power Have Shaped America's Most Controversial Education Reform Movement* (Boston, MA: Beacon Press, 2021), 119–23; Siegel-Hawley, *When the Fences Come Down*, 118–24. Siegel-Hawley and Frankenberg, "Designing Choice: Magnet School Structures and Racial Diversity," in *Educational Delusions?*, eds. Orfield and Frankenberg, 107–25; Ben-Porath and Johanek, *Making Up Our Minds*, 59.

80. Halley Potter, "Charter without Borders: Using Inter-District Charter Schools as a Tool for Regional School Integration," *The Century Foundation*, last modified September 16, 2015, https://tcf.org/content/report/charters-without-borders/?agreed =1.

81. Matt Ladner, "Myth: School Choice Harms Children Left Behind in Public Schools," in *School Choice Myths*, eds. DeAngelis and McCluskey, 103–8.

82. McWilliams, *Compete or Close*, 192–96.

83. Payne, *So Much Reform*, 62.

84. McWilliams, *Compete or Close*, 13.

85. Harris, *Charter School City*, 125.

86. Ewing, *Ghosts in the Schoolyard*, 100–101.

87. McWilliams, *Compete or Close*, 28–30; Ewing, *Ghosts in the Schoolyard*, 47, 123.

88. Perry, *Know Your Price*, 112; Ewing, *Ghosts in the Schoolyard*, 8.

89. Perry, *Know Your Price*, 112.

90. For example, Schultz, *Distrust and Educational Change*, 4–11; Ewing, *Ghosts in the Schoolyard*, 138–53.

91. Ewing, *Ghosts in the Schoolyard*, 123; Duncan, *How Schools Work*, 59–65.

92. Ewing, *Ghosts in the Schoolyard*, 74–89.

93. Ewing, *Ghosts in the Schoolyard,* 115, 134.

94. Turner, *Suddenly Diverse*, 73, 125, 147.

CHAPTER 9

1. National Center for Education Statistics, "Number of Public School Districts and Public and Private Elementary and Secondary Schools: Selected Years, 1869–70 through 2017–18," accessed September 29, 2021, https://nces.ed.gov/programs/digest /d19/tables/dt19_214.10.asp.

2. Harris, *Charter School City*, 12.

3. Ben-Porath and Johanek, *Making Up Our Mind*, 105; Albert A. Cheng, "School Choice Only Helps the Rich Get Richer," in *School Choice Myths*, eds. DeAngelis and McCluskey, 116.

4. Amy Stuart Wells, Miya Warner, and Courtney Grzesikowski, "The Story of Meaningful School Choice: Lessons from Interdistrict Transfer Plans," in *Educational Delusions?*, eds. Orfield and Frankenberg, 187–218; Jellison Holme and Finnigan, *Striving in Common*, 43, 53; Turner, *Suddenly Diverse*, 53–54.

5. Matthew F. Delmont, *Why Busing Failed: Race, Media, and the National Resistance to School Desegregation* (Berkeley: University of California Press, 2016), 86.

6. Turner, *Suddenly Diverse*, 54; Jellison Holme and Finnigan, *Striving in Common*, 35; Annie Waldman, "Held Back: Inside a Lost School Year," *ProPublica*, last modified June 28, 2021, https://www.propublica.org/article/held-back-inside-a-lost-school-year.

7. Henig, *The End of Exceptionalism in American Education*, 135.

8. Finn, Manno, and Wright, *Charter Schools at the Crossroads*, 18.

9. Finn, Manno, and Wright, *Charter Schools at the Crossroads*, 28, 89–93.

10. Ben-Porath and Johanek, *Making Up Our Minds*, 5–7; Neal, *Information, Incentives, and Education Policy*, 149–74; Ben Erwin, Emily Brixey, and Eric Syverson, "50-State Comparison: Private School Choice," *Education Commission of the States*, last modified March 24, 2021,
https://www.ecs.org/50-state-comparison-private-school-choice/.

11. Schneider and Berkshire, *A Wolf at the Schoolhouse Door*, 69.

12. Petrilli and Finn (eds.), *How to Educate an American*, 237; Finn, Manno, and Wright, *Charter Schools at the Crossroads*, 27; Hess, "Schooling Choice."

13. Center for sustainable Systems, "U.S. Cities Factsheet," last modified 2021, http://css.umich.edu/factsheets/us-cities-factsheet; United States Census Bureau, "Urban Areas Facts," accessed September 29, 2021, https://www.census.gov/programs-surveys/geography/guidance/geo-areas/urban-rural/ua-facts.html.

14. Tim DeRoche, *A Fine Line: How Most American Kids Are Kept Out of the Best Public Schools* (Los Angeles: Redtail Press, 2020); see also Henig, Hula, Orr, and Pedescleaux, *The Color of School Reform*, 198.

15. Cheng, "Myth: School Choice Only Helps the Rich Get Richer," in *School Choice Myths*, eds. DeAngelis and McCluskey, 116.

16. Michael J. Petrilli and Janie Scull, "America's Private Public Schools," *Thomas B. Fordham Institute*, last modified October 21, 2011, https://fordhaminstitute.org/national/research/americas-private-public-schools.

17. Turner, *Suddenly Diverse*, 147; see also Rod Paige, *Focusing on Student Effort*, in *How to Educate an American*, eds. Petrilli and Finn, 111.

18. Cucchiara, *Marketing Schools, Marketing Cities*.

19. Turner, *Suddenly Diverse*, 69; Alvin Chang, "We Can Draw School Zones to Make Classrooms Less Segregated. This Is How Well Your District Does," *Vox*, last modified August 27, 2018, https://www.vox.com/2018/1/8/16822374/school-segregation-gerrymander-map.

20. Johnson, *Children of the Dream*, 164, 235; Rooks, *Cutting School*, 113; Richard Rothstein, *The Color of Law: A Forgotten History of How Our Government Segregated America* (New York: Liveright Publishing, 2017), 93–99; Siegel-Hawley, *When the Fences Come Down*, 106; Delmont, *Why Busing Failed*, 52; Charles T. Clotfelter, *After Brown: The Rise and Retreat of School Desegregation* (Princeton, NJ: Princeton University Press, 2004); Henig, Hula, Orr, and Pedescleaux, *The Color of School Reform*, 53; Benjamin Herold, "How the Fight for America's Suburbs Started in Public Schools," *Education Week*, last modified October 26, 2020, https://www.edweek.org/leadership/how-the-fight-for-americas-suburbs-started-in-public-schools/2020/10; Daniel C. Vock, Mike Maciag, and J. Brian Charles, "Still Separate after All

These Years: How Schools Fuel White Flight," *Governing*, last modified January 16, 2019, https://www.governing.com/archive/gov-segregation-schools.html.

21. Neal P. McCluskey, "Myth: School Choice Balkanizes," in *School Choice Myths*, eds. DeAngelis and McCluskey, 13.

22. Frankenberg and Orfield, "Why Racial Change in the Suburbs Matters," in *The Resegregation of Suburban Schools*, eds. Frankenberg and Orfield, 17; Siegel -Hawley, *When the Fences Come Down*, 20.

23. Justin McCarthy, "Most Americans Say Segregation in Schools a Serious Problem," *Gallup*, last modified September 17, 2019, https://news.gallup.com/poll/266756/americans-say-segregation-schools-serious-problem.aspx.

24. DeRoche, *A Fine Line*, 39.

25. Darby and Rury, *The Color of Mind*, 32–33.

26. Fabaree, *Someone Has to Fail*, 27–31.

27. Blum and Burkholder, *Integrations*, 56–57; Shedd, *Unequal City*, 10.

28. DeRoche, *A Fine Line*, 64; see also Tomas Monarrez and Carina Chien, "Dividing Lines: Racially Unequal School Boundaries in US Public School Systems," *Urban Institute*, last updated September 2021, https://www.urban.org/sites/default/files/publication/104736/dividing-lines-racially-unequal-school-boundaries-in-us-public-school-systems.pdf; Asher Lehrer-Small, "New Study: 5 Ways Racist 1930s Housing Policies Still Haunt Schools," *The 74 Million*, last modified March 22, 2021, https://www.the74million.org/new-study-5-ways-racist-1930s-housing-policies-still-haunt-schools/; Dylan Lukes and Christopher Cleveland, "The Lingering Legacy of Redlining on School Funding, Diversity, and Performance," *Annenberg Institute at Brown University*, EdWorkingPapers, 21–363, last modified March 2021, https://www.edworkingpapers.com/ai21-363; Lindsey Burke and Jude Schwalbach, "Housing Redlining and Its Lingering Effects on Education Opportunity," *The Heritage Foundation*, March 11, 2021, https://www.heritage.org/education/report/housing-redlining-and-its-lingering-effects-education-opportunity.

29. Siegel-Hawley, *When the Fences Come Down*, 37.

30. Ewing, *Ghosts in the Schoolyard*, 60–68.

31. Rothstein, *The Color of Law*, 30–37.

32. Ewing, *Ghosts in the Schoolyard*, 68–84.

33. Ewing, *Ghosts in the Schoolyard*, 84–89.

34. Trounstine, *Segregation by Design*, 73–97; Rothstein, *The Color of Law*, 43–54.

35. Trounstine, *Segregation by Design*, 23.

36. Rothstein, *The Color of Law*, 77–91, 106–9.

37. Rothstein, *The Color of Law*, 133, 180; Burke and Schwalbach, "Housing Redlining and Its Lingering Effects on Education Opportunity."

38. National Center for Education Statistics, "How Old Are America's Public Schools?," *U.S. Department of Education Office of Educational Research and Improvement*, last modified January 1999, https://nces.ed.gov/pubs99/1999048.pdf.

39. Shedd, *Unequal City*, 25.

40. Shedd, *Unequal City*, 28–32; Chang, "We Can Draw School Zones to Make Classrooms Less Segregated. This Is How Well Your District Does."

41. DeRoche, *A Fine Line*, 44; Henig, Hula, Orr, and Pedescleaux, *The Color of School Reform*, 198.

42. Shedd, *Unequal City*, 44. Decoupling geography from school attendance has been controversial, as communities worry that creating schools of choice will skim the best students into those optional schools—making it harder for neighborhood schools to succeed. Patrick Wall, "A Vast Divide: Newark's Magnet Schools Excel while Traditional High Schools Struggle," *Chalkbeat Newark*, last modified November 24, 2020, https://newark.chalkbeat.org/2020/11/24/21683672/newark-magnet -comprehensive-high-schools.

43. Andrew Campanella, *The School Choice Roadmap: 7 Steps to Finding the Right School for Your Child* (New York: Beaufort Books, 2020), 38–40.

44. Shedd, *Unequal City*, 3–38, 159.

45. Ewing, *Ghosts in the Schoolyard*, 118–21.

46. DeRoche, *A Fine Line*, 61.

47. Delmont, *Why Busing Failed*.

48. Delmont, *Why Busing Failed*, 3.

49. Delmont, *Why Busing Failed*, 8.

50. Delmont, *Why Busing Failed*, 73.

51. Delmont, *Why Busing Failed*, 40.

52. *Parents Involved in Community Schools v. Seattle School Dist. No. 1*, 551 U.S. 701 (2007), accessed September 29, 2021, https://www.supremecourt.gov/opinions/ boundvolumes/551bv.pdf.

53. *Parents Involved*, 551 U.S. at 748 (Roberts, C. J., plurality opinion).

54. *Parents Involved*, 551 U.S. at 782–98 (Kennedy, J., concurring).

55. Erwin Chemerinsky, "Making Schools More Separate and Unequal: Parents Involved in Community Schools v. Seattle School District No. 1," *Michigan State Law Review*, UC Irvine School of Law Research Paper No. 2014–59, last modified November 20, 2014, https://ssrn.com/abstract=2528809.

56. Johnson, *Children of the Dream*, 212–23.

57. Alexander Russo, "Pulling Back the Curtain on Desegregation in Louisville," *The Grade*, last modified March 3, 2021, https://kappanonline.org/pulling-back-the -curtain-on-desegregation-efforts-in-louisville-russo/; Olivia Krauth and Mandy McLaren, "The Last Stop: Louisville's Troubled Busing Legacy May Be Nearing Its End," *Courier Journal*, March 22, 2021, https://www.courier-journal.com/ story/news/education/2021/02/01/courier-journal-series-explores-jcps-desegregation -legacy/4177102001/.

58. Daarel Burnette II, "We Now Know How Much Districts Spend on Almost Every School in America," *Education Week*, July 24, 2020, https://www.edweek .org/education/we-now-know-how-much-districts-spend-on-almost-every-school-in -america/2020/07; Lucy Hadley, Elizabeth Ross, and Marguerite Roza, "A Moment of (Early) Truth: Taking Stock of School-by-School Spending Data," *Edunomics Lab*, last modified July 2020, https://edunomicslab.org/wp-content/uploads/2020/07/ School-Level-Data-Brief_R5.pdf.

59. Burnette II, "We Now Know How Much Districts Spend on Almost Every School in America"; Hadley, Ross, and Roza, "A Moment of (Early) Truth."

60. Linda Jacobson, "New Requirement to Publish Per-Pupil Spending Data Could Help Schools Direct Funding to the Neediest Students. But Even in the Face of Budget Cuts, State Implementation Lags," *The 74 Million*, last modified November 29, 2020, https://www.the74million.org/article/new-requirement-to-publish-per-pupil -spending-data-could-help-schools-direct-funding-to-neediest-students-but-even-in -the-face-of-budget-cuts-state-implementation-lags/.

61. Hadley, Ross, and Roza. "A Moment of (Early) Truth"; Regenstein, "Building a Coherent P-12 Education System in California," 16; California Department of Educa- tion, "Local Control Funding Formula," accessed September 29, 2021, https://www .cde.ca.gov/fg/aa/lc/index.asp.

62. Katie Silberstein and Marguerite Roza, "Analysis: California Gives Districts Extra Money for Highest-Need Students. But It Doesn't Always Get to the Highest -Needs Schools," *The 74 Million*, last modified November 11, 2020, https://www .the74million.org/article/analysis-california-gives-districts-extra-money-for-highest -needs-students-but-it-doesnt-always-get-to-the-highest-needs-schools/.

63. Posey-Maddox, *When Middle-Class Parents Choose Urban Schools*; Yana Kunichoff, "In Chicago, Parent Fundraising Eases Reopening at Some Schools—and Leaves Others Out," *Chalkbeat Chicago*, last modified April 5, 2021, https://chicago .chalkbeat.org/2021/4/5/22363000/in-chicago-parent-fundraising-eases-reopening-at -some-schools-and-leaves-others-out.

64. Chenoweth, *Districts That Succeed*, 102; Kevin Mahnken, "Integrating Schools by Income, Not Race: Why Cities Are Embracing 'an Idea Whose Time Has Come,'" *The 74 Million*, last modified October 12, 2021, https://www.the74million .org/article/integrating-schools-by-income-not-race-why-more-cities-are-embracing -an-idea-whose-time-has-come/; Beth Hawkins, "Texas, 78207: American's Most Radical School Integration Experiment," *The 74 Million*, last modified October 17, 2018, https://www.the74million.org/article/texas-78207-americas-most-radical -school-integration-experiment/.

65. Conor Williams, "As D.C. Feels Gentrification Pressures, New Study Finds Its Pre-K Lottery Provides Equal—But Not Necessary Equitable—Access," *The 74 Million*, last modified September 8, 2020, https://www.the74million.org/article/as-dc -feels-gentrification-pressures-new-study-finds-its-pre-k-lottery-provides-equal-but -not-necessary-equitable-access/.

66. Manna, *Collision Course*, 11.

67. Of course, the same is true in reverse, and when states lack trust in community -level leaders, they will often take steps to ensure that they are stripped of deci- sion-making power. Domingo Morel, *Takeover: Race, Education, and American Democracy* (New York: Oxford University Press, 2018); see also Frank J. Thompson, Kenneth K. Wong, and Barry G. Rabe, *Trump, the Administrative Presidency, and Federalism* (Washington, DC: Brookings Institution Press, 2020), 158 (noting that the Trump Administration devolved power to the states only when doing so was seen as serving its larger policy goals). This phenomenon is not limited to education. For example, Liz Crampton, " 'Rogue City Leaders': How Republicans Are Taking Power away from Mayors," *Politico*, last modified June 23, 2021, https://www.politico.com/ news/2021/06/23/republicans-are-taking-power-away-from-mayors-495564.

68. Johnson, *Children of the Dream*, 144; Dahill-Brown, *Education, Equity, and the States*, 197.

69. Morel, *Takeover*, 138.

70. Ben-Porath and Johanek, *Making Up Our Mind*, 51–53.

71. Ben-Porath and Johanek, *Making Up Our Mind*, 52; Rothstein, *The Color of Law*, 52–54, Clotfelter, *After Brown*, 78–96.

72. Ben-Porath and Johanek, *Making Up Our Mind*, 53; Trounstine, *Segregation by Design*, 25–38; Clotfelter, *After Brown*, 14–22.

73. Rothstein, *The Color of Law*, 66–75.

74. Rothstein, *The Color of Law*, 5.

75. Trounstine, *Segregation by Design*, 67.

76. Trounstine, *Segregation by Design*, 67.

77. Turner, *Suddenly Diverse*, 126; Ben-Porath and Johanek, *Making Up Our Mind*, 78; Gary Orfield, "Choice Theories and the Schools," in Orfield and Frankenberg, *Educational Delusions*, 53; Erickson, *Making the Unequal Metropolis*; Holme and Finnigan, *Striving in Common*, 21.

78. Trounstine, *Segregation by Design*, 27; Siegel-Hawley, *When the Fences Come Down*, 21; William Voegeli, "The Truth about White Flight," *City Journal*, last modified Autumn 2020, https://www.city-journal.org/truth-about-white-flight-from-cities.

79. Clotfelter, *After Brown*, 9, 78–96; Siegel-Hawley, *When the Fences Come Down*, 41.

80.Erickson, *Making the Unequal Metropolis*, 143; Rothstein, *The Color of Law*, 77–91.

81. Rothstein, *The Color of Law*, 12, 95–96.

82. Clotfelter, *After Brown*, 26–27.

83. Johnson, *Children of the Dream*, 43; Clotfelter, *After Brown*, 26–27.

84. *Milliken v. Bradley*, 418 U.S. 717 (1974), accessed September 29, 2021, https://www.law.cornell.edu/supremecourt/text/418/717.

85. Delmont, *Why Busing Failed*, 118, 140–41, 210; *Milliken*, 418 U.S. 717.

86. Elissa Nadworny and Cory Turner, "This Supreme Court Case Made School District Lines a Tool for Segregation," *NPR*. last modified July 25, 2019, https://www.npr.org/2019/07/25/739493839/this-supreme-court-case-made-school-district-lines-a-tool-for-segregation; Kalyn Belsha and Koby Levin, "45 Years Later, This Case Is Still Shaping School Segregation in Detroit—and America," *Chalkbeat*, last modified July 25, 2019, https://www.chalkbeat.org/2019/7/25/21121021/45-years-later-this-case-is-still-shaping-school-segregation-in-detroit-and-america.

87. Keierleber, "Next Door but Worlds Apart"; Susie An, "Hundreds of School Districts Nationally Deeply Divided Based on Race and Funding," *NPR*, last modified July 25, 2019, https://www.npr.org/local/309/2019/07/25/745201598/hundreds-of-school-districts-nationally-deeply-divided-based-on-race-and-funding.

88. Alex Spurrier, Sara Hodges, and Jennifer O'Neal Schiess, "Priced Out of Public Schools: District Lines, Housing Access, and Inequitable Educational Options," *Bellwether Education Partners*, last modified October 2021, https://bellwethereducation.org/sites/default/files/Bellwether_PricedOutofPublicSchools-EDB_1021_Final.pdf; Monarrez and Chien, "Dividing Lines."

89. Mark Keierleber, "Haves and Have-Nots: The Borders between School Districts often Mark Extreme Economic Segregation. A New Report Outlines America's 50 Worst Cases," *The 74 Million*, last modified January 22, 2020, https://www.the74million.org/haves-and-have-nots-the-borders-between-school-districts-often-mark-extreme-segregation-a-new-study-outlines-americas-50-worst-cases/.

90. Siegel-Hawley, *When the Fences Come Down*, 3; Clotfelter, *After Brown*, 184.

91. Mark Keierleber, "America's $23 Billion School Funding Gap: Despite Court Rulings on Equity, New Report Finds Startling Racial Imbalance," *The 74 Million*, last modified February 26, 2019, https://www.the74million.org/americas-23-billion-school-funding-gap-despite-court-rulings-on-equity-new-report-finds-startling-racial-imbalance/; Kathy Wise, "A New Study Shows Why White School Districts Have More Money," *Frontburner*, last modified March 7, 2019, https://www.dmagazine.com/frontburner/2019/03/a-new-study-shows-why-white-school-districts-have-more-money/.

92. Keierleber, *Next Door but Worlds Apart*.

93. Frankenberg and Orfield, "Why Racial Change in the Suburbs Matters," and Erica Frankenberg, "Understanding Suburban School District Transformation: A Typology of Suburban Districts," in *The Resegregation of Suburban Schools*, eds. Frankenberg and Orfield, 42; Corey Mitchell, "Suburban Schools Have Changed Drastically. Our Understanding of Them Has Not," *EducationWeek*, last modified January 26, 2021, https://www.edweek.org/leadership/suburban-schools-have-changed-drastically-our-understanding-of-them-has-not/2021/01; Geoffrey Skelley, Elena Megia, Amelia Thomson-DeVeaux, and Laura Bronner, "Thy the Suburbs Have Shifted Blue," *FiveThirtyEight*, last modified December 16, 2020, https://fivethirtyeight.com/features/why-the-suburbs-have-shifted-blue/; Benjamin Herold, "Suburban Public Schools Are Now Majority-Nonwhite. The Backlash Has Already Begun," *Education Week*, last modified March 17, 2021, https://www.edweek.org/leadership/suburban-public-schools-are-now-majority-nonwhite-the-backlash-has-already-begun/2021/03.

94. Richard Florida, "The Changing Demographics of America's Suburbs," *City Lab*, last modified November 7, 2019, https://www.bloomberg.com/news/articles/2019-11-07/the-changing-demographics-of-america-s-suburbs.

95. Richard Fry, "Prior to COVID-19, Urban Core Counties in the U.S. Were Gaining Vitality on Key Measures," *Pew Research Center*, last modified July 29, 2020, https://www.pewresearch.org/social-trends/2020/07/29/prior-to-covid-19-urban-core-counties-in-the-u-s-were-gaining-vitality-on-key-measures/.

96. Frankenberg, "Understanding Suburban School District Transformation," in *The Resegregation of Suburban Schools*, eds. Frankenberg and Orfield, 42–43; see also Kozol, *The Shame of the Nation*, 157–60.

97. Gary Orfield, "Conclusion: Going Forward," in *The Resegregation of Suburban Schools*, eds. Frankenberg and Orfield, 221; Herold, *Suburban Public Schools Are Now Majority-Nonwhite.*

98. Rooks, *Cutting School*, 161–75.

99. Rooks, *Cutting School*, 161–75, DeRoche, *A Fine Line*, 100–104.

100. DeRoche, *A Fine Line*, 75, 101.

101. Rooks, *Cutting School*, 161–75.

102. Kevin Carey, "No More School Districts!," *Democracy Journal*, Winter No. 55, accessed September 29, 2021, https://democracyjournal.org/magazine/55/no -more-school-districts/.

103. Ted Dabrowski and John Klinger, "Too Many Districts: Illinois School District Consolidation Provides Path to Increased Efficiency, Lower Taxpayer Burdens," *Illinois Policy*, 7, last modified Spring 2016, https://files.illinoispolicy.org/wp-content /uploads/2016/04/School-District-Consolidation-and-Executive-summary.pdf.

104. Dabrowski and Klinger, "Too Many Districts," 7. Some of the single-building districts actually have enrollments in the thousands, particularly among suburban Chicago high schools.

105. Frankenberg, "Understanding Suburban School District Transformation," in *The Resegregation of Suburban Schools*, eds. Frankenberg and Orfield, 43; see also Dahill-Brown, *Education, Equity, and the States*, 115.

106. National Center for Education Statistics, "Number of Public School Districts and Public and Private Elementary and Secondary Schools: Selected Years 1869–70 through 2015–16," *Institute of Education Sciences*, accessed September 29, 2021, https://nces.ed.gov/programs/digest/d17/tables/dt17_214.10.asp.

107. National Center for Education Statistics, "Number of Public School Districts and Public and Private Elementary and Secondary Schools."

108. Dahill-Brown, *Education, Equity, and the States*, 134.

109. Siegel-Hawley, *When the Fences Come Down*, 20.

110. Carey, *No More School Districts!*

111. Mark Keierleber, "Report: School District Secessions Are Accelerating, Furthering 'State Sanctioned' Segregation," *The 74 Million*, last modified April 16, 2019, https://www.the74million.org/report-school-district-secessions-are-accelerating -furthering-state-sanctioned-segregation/; Sarah D. Sparks, "The Splintering of Wealthy Areas from School Districts Is Speeding Up," *Education Week*, last modified April 16, 2019, https://www.edweek.org/leadership/the-splintering-of-wealthy-areas -from-school-districts-is-speeding-up/2019/04.

112. Keierleber, "Report: School District Secessions Are Accelerating, Furthering 'State Sanctioned' Segregation."

113. Johnson, *Children of the Dream*, 200–204.

114. Black, *School House Burning*, 230–31; Johnson, *Children of the Dream*, 189.

115. Siegel-Hawley, *When the Fences Come Down*, 11–12; Dahill-Brown, *Education, Equity, and the States*, 134–37.

116. Hale, *The Choice We Face*, 167–68; Kevin Mehnken, "Secessions Have Heightened the Racial Divide between Southern School Districts, New Research Shows," *The 74 Million*, last modified September 4, 2019, https://www.the74million .org/secessions-have-heightened-the-racial-divide-between-southern-school-districts -new-research-shows/.

117. Sparks, "The Splintering of Wealthy Areas from School Districts Is Speeding Up"; Dahill-Brown, *Education, Equity, and the States*, 219.

118. Sparks, "The Splintering of Wealthy Areas from School Districts Is Speeding Up."

119. Siegel-Hawley, *When the Fences Come Down*, 139–46; Wells, Warner, and Grzesikowski, "The Story of Meaningful School Choice," in *Educational Delusions?*, eds. Orfield and Frankenberg, 189; Campanella, *School Choice Roadmap*, 38–40.

120. Wells, Warner, and Grzesikowski, "The Story of Meaningful School Choice," in Orfield and Frankenberg, *Educational Delusions?*, 192; Kozol, *The Shame of the Nation*, 226–36; Kara S. Finnigan and Jennifer Jellison Holme, "Regional Educational Equity Policies: Learning from Inter-district Integration Programs," *The National Coalition on School Diversity*, Brief No. 9, last modified September 2015, https://school-diversity.org/pdf/DiversityResearchBriefNo9.pdf.

121. Matthew Ladner, "A Bright Future for Open Enrollment," *The Thomas B. Fordham Institute*, last modified August 27, 2021, https://fordhaminstitute.org/national/commentary/bright-future-open-enrollment.

122. Wells, Warner, and Grzesikowski, "The Story of Meaningful School Choice," in *Educational Delusions?*, eds. Orfield and Frankenberg, 192–94, 197–99; Finnigan and Holme, *Regional Educational Equity Policies*; John Brittain, Larkin Willis, and Peter W. Cookson Jr., "Sharing the Wealth: How Regional Finance and Desegregation Plans Can Enhance Educational Equity," *Learning Policy Institute*, last modified February 2019, https://learningpolicyinstitute.org/sites/default/files/product-files/Sharing_The_Wealth_BRIEF.pdf.

123. DeRoche, *A Fine Line*, 74–77; Holme and Finnigan, *Striving in Common*, 61; Burke and Schwalbach, "Housing Redlining and Its Lingering Effects on Education Opportunity."

124. Holme and Finnigan, *Striving in Common*, 61–62.

125. DeRoche, *A Fine Line*, 74–77; Holme and Finnigan, *Striving in Common*, 61.

126. Aaron Churchill, "Public Schools Should Be Open to All," *The Thomas B. Fordham Institute*, last modified February 11, 2021, https://fordhaminstitute.org/ohio/commentary/public-schools-should-be-open-all; Kevin Mahnken, "Falling Birth Rates Spur Clash over Race and School Choice in Michigan," *The 74 Million*, last modified June 24, 2021, https://www.the74million.org/article/falling-birth-rates-spur-clash-over-race-and-school-choice-in-michigan/.

127. Turner, *Suddenly Diverse*, 53–55, 116; Holme and Finnigan, *Striving in Common*, 35.

128. Trounstine, *Segregation by Design*, 31, 171; Rooks, *Cutting School*, 83, 147.

129. Emma García, "Schools Are Still Segregated, and Black Children Are Paying a Price," *Economic Policy Institute*, last modified February 12, 2020, https://www.epi.org/publication/schools-are-still-segregated-and-black-children-are-paying-a-price/.

CHAPTER 10

1. Anna Jacob Egalite, "Federal Support for Charter Schooling," in *Bush-Obama School Reform*, eds. Hess and McShane, 127.

2. National Center for Education Statistics, "Public Charter School Enrollment," last modified May 2021, https://nces.ed.gov/programs/coe/indicator_cgb.asp.

3. Finn, Manno, and Wright, *Charter Schools at the Crossroads*, 18; Alyssa Rafa, Ben Erwin, Bryan Kelley, and Micah Ann Wixom, "50-State Comparison: Charter School Policies," *Education Commission of the States*, last modified January 28, 2020, https://www.ecs.org/charter-school-policies/.

4. Campanella, *School Choice Roadmap*, 44; Finn, Manno, and Wright, *Charter Schools at the Crossroads*, 28–29; "Charter Schools: What Organizations May Authorize Charter Schools, and Is There a Statewide Authorizing Body?," *Education Commission of the States*, last modified January 2020, http://ecs.force.com/mbdata/MBQuestNB2C?rep=CS2010.

5. Finn, Manno, and Wright, *Charter Schools at the Crossroads*, 89–94; "Charter Schools: What Organizations May Authorize Charter Schools, and Is There a Statewide Authorizing Body?" *Education Commission of the States.*

6. Finn, Manno, and Wright, *Charter Schools at the Crossroads*, 89–94.

7. Finn, Manno, and Wright, *Charter Schools at the Crossroads*, 92–93.

8. Finn, Manno, and Wright, *Charter Schools at the Crossroads*, 89–93.

9. Jamison White and Jessica Snydman, "Who Authorizes Charter Schools?," *National Alliance for Public Charter Schools*, last modified July 19, 2021, https://data.publiccharters.org/digest/charter-school-data-digest/who-authorizes-charter-schools/.

10. Finn, Manno, and Wright, *Charter Schools at the Crossroads*, 28–29.

11. Finn, Manno, and Wright, *Charter Schools at the Crossroads*, 28–29.

12. "NACSA's National Policy Index." *National Association of Charter School Authorizers*, accessed September 29, 2021, https://policyindex.qualitycharters.org/.

13. Finn, Manno, and Wright, *Charter Schools at the Crossroads*, 90.

14. Rebecca David, "National Charter School Management Overview," *National Alliance for Public Charter Schools*, 2, last modified June 2019, https://www.publiccharters.org/sites/default/files/documents/2019-06/napcs_management_report_web_06172019.pdf.

15. Finn, Manno, and Wright, *Charter Schools at the Crossroads*, 72.

16. Ben-Porath and Johanek, *Making Up Our Mind*, 100.

17. Oberfield, *Are Charters Different?*, 28, 66.

18. Schneider and Berkshire, *A Wolf at the Schoolhouse Door*, 127; O'Day and Smith, *Opportunity for All*, 30; Dahill-Brown, *Education, Equity, and the States*, 34.

19. Katrina E. Bulkley, Julie A. Marsh, Katharine O. Strunk, Douglas N. Harris, and Ayesha K. Hashim, *Challenging the One Best System: The Portfolio Management Model and Urban School Governance* (Cambridge, MA: Harvard Education Press, 2020), 144–46; Schneider and Berkshire, *A Wolf at the Schoolhouse Door*, 127–29; Hess, *Education Unbound*, 47–49.

20. Finn, Manno, and Wright, *Charter Schools at the Crossroads*, 90.

21. Schneider and Berkshire, *A Wolf at the Schoolhouse Door*, 93–95.

22. Henig, *The End of Exceptionalism in American Education*, 131–39.

23. "Charter Schools: Does the State Have a Charter School Law?," *Education Commission of the States*, last updated January 2020, http://ecs.force.com/mbdata/MBQuestNB2C?rep=CS2001.

24. Ravitch, *Reign of Error*, 162; Dahill-Brown, *Education, Equity, and the States*, 48.

25. Terry M. Moe, *The Politics of Institutional Reform: Katrina, Education, and the Second Face of Power* (New York: Cambridge University Press, 2019).

26. Moe, *The Politics of Institutional Reform*, 149; Allen, *An Unfinished Journey*, 79–80.

27. Smarick, *The Urban School System of the Future*, 83–87; Hess, *Education Unbound*.

28. David Griffith, "Rising Tide: Charter School Market Share and Student Achievement," *Thomas B. Fordham Institute*, last modified September 2019, https://fordhaminstitute.org/national/research/rising-tide-charter-market-share.

29. Yongmei Ni, "NEPC Review: Rising Tide: Charter School Market Share and Student Achievement," *National Education Policy Center*, last modified November 2019, https://nepc.colorado.edu/thinktank/rising-tide.

30. Bulkley, Marsh, Strunk, Harris, and Hashim, *Challenging the One Best System*; see also Hill and Jochim, *A Democratic Constitution for Public Education*.

31. Allen, *An Unfinished Journey*, 66–67; Finn, Manno, and Wright, *Charter Schools at the Crossroads*, 208.

32. Oberfield, *Are Charters Different?*, 37–39.

33. Finn, Manno, and Wright, *Charter Schools at the Crossroads*, 64.

34. *National Center for Education Statistics*, "Public Charter School Enrollment."

35. Tomas Monarrez, Biran Kisida, and Matthew Chingos, "The Effect of Charter Schools on School Segregation," *Annenberg Institute for School Reform at Brown University*, last modified October 2020, https://www.edworkingpapers.com/sites/default/files/ai20-308.pdf; Tomas Monarrez, Biran Kisida, and Matthew Chingos, "Charter School Effects on School Segregation," *Urban Institute*, last modified July 2019, https://www.urban.org/sites/default/files/publication/100689/charter_school_effects_on_school_segregation_0.pdf.

36. Siegel-Hawley, *When the Fences Come Down*, 125.

37. Lois Weiner, "The Liberal Education Reform Revolt," *Jacobin*, last modified July 31, 2013, https://www.jacobinmag.com/2013/07/the-liberal-education-reform-revolt/.

38. Siegel-Hawley, *When the Fences Come Down*, 125.

39. Kahlenberg and Potter, *A Smarter Charter*, 128–30.

40. Kahlenberg and Potter, *A Smarter Charter*, 54–67.

41. Robert Pondiscio, "Urban Charter Schools Offer Unprecedented Educational Opportunity for Historically Underserved Kids. How, They're under Attack from Within. Who'll Stand Up for Them?," *The 74 Million*, last modified November 15, 2020, https://www.the74million.org/article/pondiscio-urban-charter-schools-offer-unprecedented-educational-opportunity-for-historically-underserved-kids-now-theyre-under-attack-from-within-wholl-stand-up-for-them/.

42. Julian Vasquez Heilig, "Scrutinizing the School Choice Equity Ethos for Black Parents," in *Public Education: Defending a Cornerstone of American Democracy*, eds. Berliner and Hermanns, 261; Fiske and Ladd, "Values and Education Policy," in *Public Education: Defending a Cornerstone of American Democracy*, eds. Berliner

and Hermanns, 44; Tienken, *The School Reform Landscape Reloaded*, 145; Rooks, *Cutting School*, 40; Erica Frankenberg and Genevieve Siegel-Hawley, "A Segregating Choice? An Overview of Charter School Policy, Enrollment Trends, and Segregation," in *Educational Delusions?*, eds. Orfield and Frankenberg, 131; Kari Dalane and Dave E. Marcotte, "Charter Schools and the Segregation of Students by Income," *Annenberg Institute for School Reform at Brown University*, last modified April 2021, https://www.edworkingpapers.com/ai21-378.

43. Sowell, *Charter Schools and Their Enemies*, 95.

44. Barbara Ferman, "Lessons from the Grass Roots," in *The Fight for America's Schools*, ed. Ferman, 122; Lauren Camera, "Charter School Advocates Punch Back at Democratic Candidates," *U.S. News & World Report*, last modified June 28, 2019, https://www.usnews.com/news/education-news/articles/2019-06-28/charter-school -advocates-punch-back-at-democratic-presidential-candidates.

45. Osborne, *Reinventing America's Schools*, 88; Finn, Manno, and Wright, *Charter Schools at the Crossroads*, 121–24.

46. Kahlenberg and Potter, *A Smarter Charter*, 18–21; Myron Orfield, Baris Gurus -Dawes, and Thomas Luce, "Failed Promises: Assessing Charter Schools in the Twin Cities," in Orfield and Frankenberg, *Educational Delusions*, 151.

47. Finn, Manno, and Wright, *Charter Schools at the Crossroads*, 121–24; see also Tienken, *The School Reform Landscape Reloaded*, 146–47.

48. Vasquez Heilig, "Scrutinizing the School Choice Equity Ethos for Black Parents," in *Public Education: Defending a Cornerstone of American Democracy*, eds. Berliner and Hermanns, 257; Fiske and Ladd, "Values and Education Policy," in *Public Education: Defending a Cornerstone of American Democracy*, eds. Berliner and Hermanns, 44; Mommandi and Welner, *School's Choice*; Tienken, *The School Reform Landscape Reloaded*, 145; Jennings, *Fatigued by School Reform*, 81; Hess and Noguera, *A Search for Common Ground*, 32; McWilliams, *Compete or Close*, 10; Ben-Porath and Johanek, *Making Up Our Mind*, 111; Russakoff, *The Prize*, 46; Ben -Porath and Johanek, *Making Up Our Mind*, 111.

49. Berliner, "The Scandalous History of Schools That Receive Public Financing, but Do Not Accept the Public's Right of Oversight," in *Public Education: Defending a Cornerstone of American Democracy*, eds. Berliner and Hermanns, 270; Mommandi and Welner, *School's Choice*, 82–85; McWilliams, *Compete or Close*, 10, 41.

50. Inez Feltscher Stepman, "Myth: Students with Special Needs Lose with School Choice," in *School Choice Myths*, eds. DeAngelis and McCluskey, 163–76; Finn, Manno, and Wright, *Charter Schools at the Crossroads*, 125.

51. Ben-Porath and Johanek, *Making Up Our Mind*, 113; Finn, Manno, and Wright, *Charter Schools at the Crossroads*, 125–30; Bulkley, Marsh, Strunk, Harris, and Hashim, *Challenging the One Best System*, 86.

52. Pondiscio, *How the Other Half Learns*, 278.

53. Pondiscio, *How the Other Half Learns*, 278.

54. McWilliams, *Compete or Close*, 10, 43, 170; Adam Kho, Ron Zimmer, and Andrew McEachin, "A Descriptive Analysis of Cream Skimming and Pushout in Choice versus Traditional Public Schools," *Annenberg Institute for School Reform at*

Brown University, last modified December 2020, https://www.edworkingpapers.com
/sites/default/files/ai20-332.pdf.

55. Campanella, *School Choice Roadmap*, 45; Oberfield, *Are Charters* Different?,
12. Mommandi and Welner point out that charter schools may also use marketing
efforts and enrollment requirements to limit the applicant pool, discouraging enrollment from families that they do not want to serve. Mommandi and Welner, *School's
Choice*, 37–77.

56. Russakoff, *The Prize*, 118.

57. Mommandi and Welner, *School's Choice*, 16, 138–41, 159–60.

58. Arianna Prothero, "Why, and Where, Charter School Teachers Unionize," *EducationWeek,* last modified March 22, 2019, https://www.edweek.org/policy-politics/
why-and-where-charter-school-teachers-unionize/2019/03; see also National Alliance
for Public Charter Schools, "Automatic Collective Bargaining Exemption," https://
www.publiccharters.org/our-work/charter-law-database/components/14.

59. Ravitch, *Reign of Error*, 156–57, 250.

60. Ravitch, *Reign of Error*, 250.

61. Ravitch, *Reign of Error*, 157–58.

62. Casey, *The Teacher Insurgency*, 35–37; Ravitch, *Reign of Error*, 156–79.

63. Ravitch, *Reign of Error*, 250–51.

64. Black, *School House Burning*, 233–34.

65. Ravitch, *Slaying Goliath*, 52; Ravitch, *Reign of Error*, 6.

66. Kahlenberg and Potter, *A Smarter Charter*, 87–99.

67. Oberfield, *Are Charters Different?*, 52; Moe, *Special Interest*, 325–40.

68. Oberfield, *Are Charters Different?*, 60.

69. Kahlenberg and Potter, *A Smarter Charter*, 25–29.

70. Jeanne Allen, "Charter Schools Don't Need Blood Money," *Real Clear Education*, last modified July 15, 2020, https://www.realcleareducation.com/articles/2020
/07/15/charter_schools_dont_need_blood_money_110442.html.

71. Kahlenberg and Potter, *A Smarter Charter*, 87–99.

72. Kahlenberg and Potter, *A Smarter Charter*, 87–99.

73. Osborne, *Reinventing America's Schools*, 13.

74. For example, Tienken, *The School Reform Landscape Reloaded*, 138–42; Smarick, *Urban School System of the Future*, 27–38, 69–81; Sowell, *Charter Schools and
Their Enemies*, 1–50; Black, *School House Burning*, 233; David Griffith and Michael
J. Petrilli, "The Case for Urban Charter Schools," *Thomas B. Fordham Institute*, last
modified October 14, 2020, https://fordhaminstitute.org/national/commentary/case
-urban-charter-schools; *Network for Public Education*, "Do Charter Schools Get Better Academic Results than Public Schools?," accessed September 29, 2021, https://
networkforpubliceducation.org/wp-content/uploads/2019/01/Do-charter-schools-get
-better-academic-results-than-public-schools%C6%92.pdf.

75. Egalite, "Federal Support for Charter Schooling," in *Bush-Obama School
Reform*, eds. Hess and McShane, 142–43; Finn, Manno, and Wright, *Charter Schools
at the Crossroads*, 62; Ravitch, *Reign of Error*, 174–75; Smarick, *The Urban School
System of the Future*, 27–38.

76. *Education Commission of the States*, "Charter Schools: How Is the Funding for a Charter School Determined?," last modified January 2018, http://ecs.force.com /mbdata/mbquestNB2C?rep=CS1716.

77. Baker, *Educational Inequality*, 106–8; Karole Dachelet, "50-State Comparison: K-12 Funding, *Education Commission of the States*, last modified August 5, 2019, https://www.ecs.org/50-state-comparison-k-12-funding.

78. Russakoff, *The Prize*, 118; Bulkley, Marsh, Strunk, Harris, and Hashim, *Challenging the One Best System*, 53, 159; DeJarnatt and Ferman, "Preserving Education as a Collective Good," in *The Fight for America's Schools*, ed. Ferman, 135.

79. Bulkley, Marsh, Strunk, Harris, and Hashim, *Challenging the One Best System*.

80. Aldeman, "How to Address the Rising Cost of Employee Benefits," in *Getting the Most Bang for the Education Buck*, eds. Hess and Wright, 19–33; Moe, *Special Interest*, 161–62.

81. Moe, *The Politics of Institutional Reform*, 22; Labaree, *Someone Has to Fail*, 186.

82. Diane Ravitch, "A Brief History of Public Education," in *Public Education: Defending a Cornerstone of American Democracy*, eds. Berliner and Hermanns, 27; Fiske and Ladd, "Values and Education Policy," in *Public Education: Defending a Cornerstone of American Democracy*, eds. Berliner and Hermanns, 44; Tienken, *The School Reform Landscape Reloaded*, 69; Hale, *The Choice We Face*, 11, 173; Matt Barnum, "Critics of Charter Schools Say They're Hurting School Districts. Are They Right?," *Chalkbeat*, last modified June 11, 2019, https://www.chalkbeat.org/2019/6 /11/21108318/critics-of-charter-schools-say-they-re-hurting-school-districts-are-they -right.

83. Terry M. Moe and Paul T. Hill, "Moving to a Mixed Model: Without an Appropriate Role for the Market, the Education Sector Will Stagnate," in *The Futures of School Reform*, eds. Mehta, Schwartz, and Hess, 69–70.

84. Baker, *Educational Inequality*, 29–30.

85. Roza and Jarmolowski, "When It Comes to School Funds, Hold-Harmless Provisions Aren't 'Harmless.' "

86. Christian Barnard, "Stop Tring to Claim Charter Schools 'Steal' Money from Traditional Public Schools," *Reason Foundation*, last modified November 26, 2018, https://reason.org/commentary/stop-trying-to-claim-charter-schools-steal-money -from-traditional-public-schools/.

87. Victoria McDougald, "Mind the Gap: Persistent and Growing Inequities in Charter School Funding," *The Thomas B. Fordham Institute*, last modified December 17, 2020, https://fordhaminstitute.org/national/commentary/mind-gap-persistent-and -growing-inequities-charter-school-funding; Patrick J. Wolf, Corey A. Deangelis, Larry D. Maloney, and Jay F. May, "The Shortchanging of Public Charter School Students: Why Do They Get So Much Less per Pupil than Students at Traditional Schools?," *The 74 Million*, last modified January 8, 2019, https://www.the74million .org/article/the-shortchanging-of-public-charter-school-students-why-do-they-get -so-much-less-per-pupil-than-students-at-traditional-schools/; Corey A. DeAngelis, Patrick J. Wolf, Larry D. Maloney, and Jay F. May, "Charter School Funding: (More) Inequity in the City," *School Choice Demonstration Project, University of*

Arkansas Department of Education Reform, last modified November 2018, http://www.uaedreform.org/downloads/2018/11/charter-school-funding-more-inequity-in-the-city.pdf.

88. Hess, *Education Unbound*, 47.

89. Mark Weber, "Robbers or Victims? Charter Schools and District Finances," *The Thomas B. Fordham Institute*, last modified February 9, 2021, https://fordhaminstitute.org/national/research/robbers-or-victims-charter-schools-and-district-finances; Patrick Wolf, "Charter School Growth Increases Resources in District-Run Schools," *The Thomas B. Fordham Institute*, last modified February 25, 2021, https://fordhaminstitute.org/national/commentary/charter-school-growth-increases-resources-district-run-schools.

90. Valerie Strauss and Carol Corbett Burriss, "Answer Sheet: A Look at Whether Charter Schools Are Fiscal Threats to Local School Districts," *National Education Policy Center*, last modified April 7, 2021, https://nepc.colorado.edu/blog/look-charters; Carol Corbett Burris, "The Fordham Institute Misleads the Public with False Claims about New Report," *Network for Public Education*, last modified March 1, 2021, https://networkforpubliceducation.org/fordham-institute-attempts-to-mislead-the-public-regarding-the-impact-of-charter-schools-on-public-school-districts/; Bruce D. Baker, "Review of Charter Funding: Inequity Expands," *National Education Policy Center*, last modified May 2014, https://nepc.colorado.edu/sites/default/files/ttr-uark-charterfunding.pdf.

91. Burris, "The Fordham Institute Misleads the Public with False Claims about New Report."

92. Baker, *Educational Inequality*, 155–57.

93. Mommandi and Welner, *School's Choice*, 16, 138–41, 159–60.

94. Sara Mead, "Why Should Charter Schools Offer Pre-K?," *The Thomas B. Fordham Institute*, last modified July 20, 2015, https://fordhaminstitute.org/national/commentary/why-should-charter-schools-offer-pre-k.

95. Sara Mead and Ashley LiBetti Mitchel, "Pre-K and Charter Schools: Where State Policies Create Barriers to Collaboration," *Bellwether Education Partners*, last modified July 2015, http://edex.s3-us-west-2.amazonaws.com/publication/pdfs/fordham-prek_and_charters-complete_rev1_0.pdf.

96. Mead and LiBetti Mitchel, "Pre-K and Charter Schools," 20–21.

97. Mead and LiBetti Mitchel, "Pre-K and Charter Schools," 21–22.

98. Mead and LiBetti Mitchel, "Pre-K and Charter Schools," 22–23.

99. E.g., Regenstein, "Building a Coherent P-12 Education System in California," 20; Tara Ryan and GG Weisenfeld, "A Survey of ECE Visibility and Alignment in California School Districts," *Center for District Innovation and Leadership in Early Education*, 14, last modified January 2021, https://drive.google.com/file/d/12dk_x-OWLyEJZQRJmOHtO0YPc9vGg0z8/view.

100. Mead and LiBetti Mitchel, "Pre-K and Charter Schools."

101. Mead and LiBetti Mitchel, "Pre-K and Charter Schools," 23–24.

102. Mead and LiBetti Mitchel, "Pre-K and Charter Schools," 24–25.

103. Mead and LiBetti Mitchel, "Pre-K and Charter Schools," 24–25.

104. Mead and LiBetti Mitchel, "Pre-K and Charter Schools," 6, 24–25.

105. Sowell, *Charter Schools and Their Enemies*, 58–67; Finn, Manno, and Wright, *Charter Schools at the Crossroads*, 105–7.

CHAPTER 11

1. Kim Smith and Julie Peterson, "Creating Responsive Supply in Public Education," in *Customized Schooling: Beyond Whole-School Reform*, eds. Frederick M. Hess and Bruno V. Manno (Cambridge, MA: Harvard Education Press, 2011), 14–19; Katrina E. Bulkley, "Introduction—Portfolio Management Models in Urban School Reform," in *Between Public and Private*, eds. Bulkley, Henig, and Levin, 17–19.

2. Bulkley, Marsh, Strunk, Harris, and Hashim, *Challenging the One Best System*, 95; Adam Gerstenfeld, "What Is a Charter School Lottery?," *National Alliance for Public Charter Schools*, last modified February 7, 2019, https://www.publiccharters.org/latest-news/2019/02/07/what-charter-school-lottery.

3. Bulkley, Marsh, Strunk, Harris, and Hashim, *Challenging the One Best System*, 95.

4. Bulkley, Marsh, Strunk, Harris, and Hashim, *Challenging the One Best System*, 95.

5. Bulkley, Marsh, Strunk, Harris, and Hashim, *Challenging the One Best* System, 95–96.

6. Bulkley, Marsh, Strunk, Harris, and Hashim, *Challenging the One Best System*, 96.

7. Bulkley, Marsh, Strunk, Harris, and Hashim, *Challenging the One Best System*, 96.

8. Harris, *Charter School City*, 145; Thomas Toch, "School Choice Is Here to Stay. But How to Make It Fair and Equitable for All Families? High-Tech Common-Enrollment System Can Help," *The 74 Million*, last modified February 12, 2020, https://www.the74million.org/article/toch-school-choice-is-here-to-stay-but-how-to-make-it-fair-and-equitable-for-all-families-high-tech-common-enrollment-system-can-help/.

9. Bulkley, Marsh, Strunk, Harris, and Hashim, *Challenging the One Best System*, 106–107; Ben-Porath and Johanek, *Making Up Our Mind*, 14–15; Ewing, *Ghosts in the Schoolyard*, 23; Richard H. Thaler and Cass R. Sunstein, *Nudge: Improving Decisions about Health, Wealth, and Happiness* (New York: Penguin, 2009), 203–205.

10. Harford, *The Data Detective*, 154, 180–83; Bulkley, Marsh, Strunk, Harris, and Hashim, *Challenging the One Best System*, 96, 113; DeRoche, *A Fine Line*, 110; Stephen Danley and Julia Sass Rubin, "A Tale of Two Cities: Community Resistance in Newark and Camden," in *The Fight for America's Schools*, ed. Ferman, 39; Colin Lecher and Maddy Varner "NYC's School Algorithms Cement Segregation. This Data Shows How," *The Markup*, 25–28, last modified May 26, 2021, https://themarkup.org/investigations/2021/05/26/nycs-school-algorithms-cement-segregation-this-data-shows-how; *Actionable Intelligence for Social Policy, University of Pennsylvania*, "A Toolkit for Centering Racial Equity Throughout Data Integration," accessed September 29, 2021, https://www.aisp.upenn.edu/wp-content/uploads/2020/08/AISP-Toolkit_5.27.20.pdf.

11. Bulkley, Marsh, Strunk, Harris, and Hashim, *Challenging the One Best System*, 96.

12. Mike McShane, "How Unified Enrollment Systems Solve Some Problems and Cause Other Ones," *Forbes*, last modified September 19, 2018, https://www.forbes.com/sites/mikemcshane/2018/09/19/how-unified-enrollment-systems-solve-some-problems-and-cause-other-ones/?sh=3b89757c71c6.

13. The radical change to schooling in New Orleans has been the subject of heated debate between Reformers—who see it as a harbinger of the possible—and the Resistance, which sees it as an example of replacing a Black-dominated school infrastructure with one that privileged young white reformers. Harris, *Charter School City*; Bulkley, Marsh, Strunk, Harris, and Hashim, *Challenging the One Best System*; Perry, *Know Your Price*, 126–57; Ravitch, *Slaying Goliath*, 218–19; Moe, *The Politics of Institutional Reform*; Osborne, *Reinventing America's Schools*, 21–79; Baris Gumus-Dawes, Thomas Luce, and Myron Orfield, "The State of Public Schools in Post-Katrina New Orleans: The Challenge of Creating Equal Opportunity," in Orfield and Frankenberg, *Educational Delusions?*, 159–84.

14. Harris, *Charter School City*, 144–46.

15. Harris, *Charter School City*, 145.

16. Harris, *Charter School City*, 146–48.

17. Regenstein and Strausz-Clark, "Improving Parent Choice in Early Learning."

18. "FOA Renewal Grant HHS-2019-ACF-OCC-TP-1567_1," *Office of Elementary & Secondary Education*, 58, last modified April 29, 2021, https://oese.ed.gov/offices/office-of-discretionary-grants-support-services/innovation-early-learning/preschool-development-grants/applicant-information/foa-renewal-grant-hhs-2019-acf-occ-tp-1567_1/; "Ideas on How to Approach the Preschool Development Grant 2019 Bonus—Coordinated Application, Eligibility, Enrollment," *Build Initiative*, accessed September 29, 2021, https://buildinitiative.org/wp-content/uploads/2021/06/PDG-B5-2019-Bonus-on-Coordinated-Application-Eligibility-Enrollment-1.pdf.

19. "Coordinated Enrollment and Funding," *Louisiana Department of Education*, accessed September 29. 2021, https://www.louisianabelieves.com/early-childhood/coordinated-enrollment-and-funding.

20. Sara Mead, "Question for the Democratic Presidential Hopefuls—Why Are Government-Funding Nonprofits Fine for Pre-K but Not for K-12?," *The 74 Million*, last modified March 17, 2020, https://www.the74million.org/article/mead-question-for-the-democratic-presidential-hopefuls-why-are-government-funded-nonprofits-fine-for-pre-k-but-not-for-k-12/.

21. For example, DeAngelis and McCluskey, "Introduction," in *School Choice Myths*, eds. DeAngelis and McCluskey, 1–6; Schneider and Berkshire, *A Wolf at the Schoolhouse Door*, 14–26; Ashley Rogers Berner, *No One Way to School: Pluralism and American Public Education* (New York: Palgrave Macmillan, 2017); Jay P. Greene and James D. Paul, "Does School Choice Need Bipartisan Support? An Empirical Analysis of the Legislative Record," *American Enterprise Institute*, last modified September 2021, https://www.aei.org/wp-content/uploads/2021/09/Does-School-Choice-Need-Bipartisan-Support.pdf.

22. Ben-Porath and Johanek, *Making Up Our Mind*, 55; Rooks, *Cutting School*, 79–107; Clotfelter, *After Brown*, 100–123.

23. Congdon, Kling, and Mullainathan, *Policy and Choice*, 21; Arianna Prothero, "Why Don't Parents Always Choose the Best Schools?," *Education Week*, last modified January 7, 2020, https://www.edweek.org/leadership/why-dont-parents-always -choose-the-best-schools/2020/01.

24. Congdon, Kling, and Mullainathan, *Policy and Choice*, 21–24.

25. Schneider, *Beyond Test Scores*, 79.

26. Ben-Porath and Johanek, *Making Up Our Mind*, 121–22.

27. Mullainathan and Shafir, *Scarcity*.

28. Harris, *Charter School City*, 39–41; see also Martin, *Learning in Public*, 1–89.

29. Ben-Porath and Johanek, *Making Up Our Mind*, 95; DeJarnatt and Ferman, "Preserving Education as a Collective Good," in *The Fight for America's Schools*, ed. Ferman, 133; "Lost in the Crowd: The Fragility of High Performance among Low-Income Students," *EdNavigator*, 12–13, last modified April 2018, https://www .ednavigator.com/downloads/Lost-in-the-Crowd-041618.pdf.

30. Dougherty, Zannoni, Chowhan, Coyne, Dawson, Guruge, and Nukic, "School Information, Parental Decisions, and the Digital Divide," in *Educational Delusions?*, eds. Orfield and Frankenberg, 219.

31. Duncan, *How Schools Work*, 33.

32. Finn, Manno, and Wright, *Charter Schools at the Crossroads*, 83; Thaler and Sunstein, *Nudge*, 203–4.

33. Regenstein and Strausz-Clark, "Improving Parent Choice in Early Learning," 6.

34. Hale, *The Choice We Face*, 177–78; Schneider and Berkshire, *A Wolf at the Schoolhouse Door*, 146–48; Ben-Porath and Johanek, *Making Up Our Mind*, 94.

35. Campanella, *School Choice Roadmap*, 209–10; Travis Pillow and Paul Hill, "Funding a Nimble System," *Center for Reinventing Public Education*, 4–5, last modified November 2018, https://www.crpe.org/sites/default/files/crpe-thinking-forward -funding-nimble-system.pdf.

36. EdNavigator, "World-Class Education Support for Companies that Care," accessed September 29, 2021, https://www.ednavigator.com/how-we-help/employers.

37. Families Empowered, "Find the Right School for Your Kids," accessed September 29, 2021, https://familiesempowered.org/; Mike McShane, "How Do Families Find the Best School for Their Child?," *Forbes*, last modified January 24, 2019, https://www.forbes.com/sites/mikemcshane/2019/01/24/how-do-families-find-the -best-school-for-their-child/.

38. Child Care Aware of America, accessed September 29, 2021, https://www .childcareaware.org/.

39. DeRoche, *A Fine Line*, 93–100.

40. Mommandi and Welner, *School's Choice*, 39–40; Schneider, *Beyond Test Scores*, 69–70.

41. Schneider, *Beyond Test Scores*, 69–70.

42. For example, Conor Williams, "White Parents Horrified by George Floyd Video Still Go to Great Lengths to Keep Their Children in Segregated Schools," *The 74 Million*, last modified April 20, 2021, https://www.the74million.org/article/

white-parents-horrified-by-george-floyd-video-still-go-to-great-lengths-to-keep-their
-children-in-segregated-schools/; Vanessa Williamson, Jackson Gode, and Hao Sun,
"We All Want What's Best for Our Kids: Discussions of D.C. Public School Options
in an Online Forum," *Governance Studies at Brookings Institution*, accessed September 29, 2021, https://www.brookings.edu/wp-content/uploads/2021/03/Discussions
_DC_public_school_options_online_forum_Brookings-Report.pdf.

43. Mommandi and Welner, *School's Choice*, 37–44; Schneider and Berkshire, *A Wolf at the Schoolhouse Door*, 159–65.

44. Schneider and Berkshire, *A Wolf at the Schoolhouse Door*, 168–69.

45. Mommandi and Welner, *School's Choice*; Harris, *Charter School City*, 125–29;
Bulkley, Marsh, Strunk, Harris, and Hashim, *Challenging the One Best System*, 94;
Cucchiara, *Marketing Schools, Marketing Cities*.

46. Mommandi and Welner, *School's Choice*; Harris, *Charter School City*, 125–29.

47. Mommandi and Welner, *School's Choice*, 37–44; Turner, *Suddenly Diverse*,
125, 147; Harris, *Charter School City*, 45; Cucchiara, *Marketing Schools, Marketing Cities*.

48. Timothy Daly, "Having a Path Is Better than Having a Choice," *EdNavigator*,
last modified May 22, 2017, https://mailchi.mp/ednavigator/having-a-path-is-better
-than-having-a-choice.

49. Thaler and Sunstein, *Nudge*, 208.

50. Schneider, *Beyond Test Scores*; Dougherty, Zannoni, Chowhan, Coyne, Dawson, Guruge, and Nukic, "School Information, Parental Decisions, and the Digital
Divide," in *Educational Delusions?*, eds. Orfield and Frankenberg, 219–37; Chester
E. Finn and Eric Osberg, "Reframing the Choice Agenda for Education Reform," and
Thomas Stewart and Patrick J. Wolf, "The Evolution of Parental School Choice," and
Curtis Johnson and Ted Kolderie, "Will Policy Let Demand Drive Change?," in *Customized Schooling*, eds. Hess and Manno, 40–41, 92, 198–99; Jon Valant and Lindsay
Weixler, "Informing School-Choosing Families about Their Options: A Field Experiment from New Orleans," *Annenberg Institute for School Reform at Brown University*, last modified November 2020, https://www.edworkingpapers.com/ai20-325.

51. Lindsey M. Burke, "An Appraisal Market for K-12 Education," *American
Enterprise Institute*, last modified June 2020, https://www.aei.org/wp-content/
uploads/2020/06/An-Appraisal-Market-for-K%E2%80%9312-Education.pdf.

52. Schneider, *Beyond Test Scores*, 69.

53. Dougherty, Zannoni, Chowhan, Coyne, Dawson, Guruge, and Nukic, "School
Information, Parental Decisions, and the Digital Divide," in *Educational Delusions?*,
eds. Orfield and Frankenberg, 234.

54. Mommandi and Welner, *School's Choice*, 154–55; Wells, Warner, and Grzesikowski, "The Story of Meaningful School Choice: Lessons from Interdistrict Transfer Plans," in *Educational Delusions?*, eds. Orfield and Frankenberg, 210; Bulkley,
Marsh, Strunk, Harris, and Hashim, *Challenging the One Best System*, 114; Levin, "A
Framework for Designing Governance in Choice and Portfolio Districts," in *Between
Public and Private*, eds. Bulkley, Henig, and Levin, 241–42.

55. Shedd, *Unequal City*, 40.

56. Dougherty, Zannoni, Chowhan, Coyne, Dawson, Guruge, and Nukic, "School Information, Parental Decisions, and the Digital Divide," in *Educational Delusions?*, eds. Orfield and Frankenberg, 233; Shaw and Northern, *What Parents Want*, 35.

57. Blum and Burkholder, *Integrations*, 175–76; Posey-Maddox, *When Middle -Class Parents Choose Urban Schools*, 52; Darby and Rury, *The Color of Mind*, 133, 150; Lewis and Diamond, *Despite the Best Intentions*, 106; Labaree, *Someone Has to Fail*, 180–81. The concept of critical mass was discussed by the Supreme Court in *Grutter v. Bollinger*, a case upholding the diversity goals used by the admissions office at the University of Michigan Law School. *Grutter v. Bollinger*, 539 U.S. 306, 329–30 (2003).

58. Turner, *Suddenly Diverse*, 134.

59. Schneider, *Beyond Test Scores*, 3, 72–76; Jay Mathews, *An Optimist's Guide to American Public Education*, Santa Anita Publishing, 2021, 23–24.

60. Kozol, *The Shame of the Nation*, 312–17 (discussing the views of the late Member of Congress John Lewis).

61. Jeanne L. Reid and Sharon Lynn Kagan with Michael Hilton and Hailey Potter. "A Better Start: Why Classroom Diversity Matters in Early Education," *The Century Foundation*, last modified April 2015, https://www.prrac.org/pdf/A_Better_Start.pdf.

62. Ravitch, *Reign of Error*, 295.

63. Orfield, G. *Choice Theories and the Schools*, in *Educational Delusions?*, eds. Orfield and Frankenberg, 59.

64. Kahlenberg and Potter, *A Smarter Charter*, 59; Ravitch, *Reign of Error*, 295.

65. Johnson, *Children of the Dream*, 41–66.

66. Susan Eaton "Help Wanted: The Challenges and Opportunities of Immigration and Cultural Change in a Working-Class Boston Suburb," in *The Resegregation of Suburban Schools*, eds. Frankenberg and Orfield, 98; Posey-Maddox, *When Middle -Class Parents Choose Urban Schools*, 80; G. Orfield and E. Frankenberg, *Experiencing Integration in Louisville: Attitudes on Choice and Diversity in a Changing Legal Environment*, in *Educational Delusions?*, eds. Orfield and Frankenberg, 243–44; Clotfelter, *After Brown*, 4.

67. Frankenberg and Orfield, "Why Racial Change in the Suburbs Matters," in *The Resegregation of Suburban Schools*, eds. Frankenberg and Orfield, 19; see also Siegel -Hawley, *When the Fences Come Down*, 99.

68. Sowell, *Charter Schools and Their Enemies*, 95.

69. Rooks, *Cutting School*, 104.

70. Sowell, *Charter Schools and Their Enemies*, 83.

71. Stepman, "Myth: Students with Special Needs Lose with School Choice," in *School Choice Myths*, eds. DeAngelis and McCluskey, 163–76.

72. Shaw and Northern, *What Parents Want*.

73. Harris, *Charter School City*, 155; Turner, *Suddenly Diverse*, 133; McWilliams, *Compete or Close*, 66.

74. Siegel-Hawley and Frankenberg, "Designing Choice: Magnet School Structures and Racial Diversity," in *Educational Delusions?*, eds. Orfield and Frankenberg, 110–12.

75. Schneider, *Beyond Test Scores*, 133; Shaw and Northern, *What Parents Want*.

76. Shedd, *Unequal City*, 34, 93–99.

77. Jennifer Smith Richards, Jodi S. Cohen, and Lakeidra Chavis, "The Quiet Rooms: Children Locked Away in Illinois Schools," *ProPublica*, last modified November 19, 2019, https://www.propublica.org/series/illinois-school-seclusions-timeouts-restraints.

78. For some early attempts: Emma García and Elaine Weiss, "COVID-19 and Student Performance, Equity, and U.S. Education Policy," *Economic Policy Institute*, last modified September 10, 2020, https://www.epi.org/publication/the-consequences-of-the-covid-19-pandemic-for-education-performance-and-equity-in-the-united-states-what-can-we-learn-from-pre-pandemic-research-to-inform-relief-recovery-and-rebuilding/.

79. John E. Chubb, "More Productive Schools Through Online Learning," in *Stretching the School Dollar*, eds. Hess and Osberg (Cambridge, MA: Harvard Education Press), 155–78.

80. Michael B. Horn, "Schools Squandered Virtual Learning: A Timid Response, with Lessons for the Future," *Education Next*, Vol. 21, No. 4, last modified Fall 2021, https://www.educationnext.org/schools-squandered-virtual-learning-timid-response-lessons-for-future/; Catherine Gewertz, "Remote Learning Isn't Going Away. Will It Create Separate—and Unequal—School Systems?," *Education Week*, last modified May 4, 2021, https://www.edweek.org/leadership/remote-learning-isnt-going-away-will-it-create-separate-and-unequal-school-systems/2021/05.

81. Justin Reich, *Failure to Disrupt: Why Technology Alone Can't Transform Education* (Cambridge, MA: Harvard University Press, 2020), 148–60.

82. Donna St. George, Valerie Strauss, Laura Meckler, Joe Heim, and Hannah Natanson, "How the Pandemic Is Reshaping Education," *Washington Post*, last modified March 15, 2021, https://www.washingtonpost.com/education/2021/03/15/pandemic-school-year-changes/.

83. For example, Nicholas D. E. Mark, Sean Cocoran, and Jennifer Jennings, "Choosing Alone? Peer Similarity in High School Choices," *Annenberg Institute for School Reform at Brown University*, last modified May 2021, https://www.edworkingpapers.com/sites/default/files/ai21-396.pdf.

84. Ben-Porath and Johanek, *Making Up Our Mind*, 95–96; Schneider, *Beyond Test Scores*; Virginia Walton Ford, "Myth: Only Rich Parents Can Make Good Choices," in *School Choice Myths*, eds. DeAngelis and McCluskey, 179; see also Shaw and Northern, *What Parents Want*, 33–35 (discussing parents for whom test scores are in fact the top priority in choosing a school).

85. Burke and Bedrick, "Myth: School Choice Needs Regulation to Ensure Access and Quality," in *School Choice Myths*, eds. DeAngelis and McCluskey, 140.

86. Harris, *Charter School City*, 137; Schneider, *Beyond Test Scores*, 21.

87. Schneider, *Beyond Test Scores*, 62–68; Schneider and Berkshire, *A Wolf at the Schoolhouse Door*, 144–46.

88. Barnum and LaMarr LeMee, "Looking for a Home? You've seen GreatSchools Ratings"; Sharique Hasan and Anuj Kumar, "Digitization and Divergence: Online School Ratings and Segregation in America," *SSRN*, last modified July 23, 2019, https://papers.ssrn.com/sol3/papers.cfm?abstract_id=3265316; Mahnken, "Power Is

Knowledge: New Study Finds That Wealthy, Educated Families Are Using School Ratings to Self-Segregate."

89.Christina A. Samuels, "GreatSchools' Ratings Revamp Credits Schools for Boosting Academic Growth," *Education Week*, last modified September 24, 2020, https://www.edweek.org/policy-politics/greatschools-ratings-revamp-credits-schools -for-boosting-academic-growth/2020/09; Matt Barnum, "Great Schools Overhauls Ratings in Bid to Reduce Link with Race and Poverty," *Chalkbeat*, last modified September 24, 2020, https://www.chalkbeat.org/2020/9/24/21453357/greatschools -overhauls-ratings-reduce-link-race-poverty; Jon Deane, "To Help Parents Better Understand Their Children's Schools, Student Growth Is Now Key in Our Great-Schools Ratings," *The 74 Million*, last modified September 23, 2020, https://www .the74million.org/article/deane-to-help-parents-better-understand-their-childrens -schools-student-growth-is-now-key-in-our-greatschools-ratings/.

90. Finn, Manno, and Wright, *Charter Schools at the Crossroads*, 83; Cindi Williams, "More than Ever, Parents Need Data about Their Kids in a Form They Can Understand. Test Makers Are Starting to Get on Board," *The 74 Million*, last modified December 14, 2020, https://www.the74million.org/article/analysis-more-than -ever-parents-need-data-about-their-kids-in-a-form-they-can-understand-test-makers -are-starting-to-get-on-board/; *Data Quality Campaign*, "Show Me the Data 2020," accessed September 29. 2021, https://dataqualitycampaign.org/showmethedata-2020 /.

91. Max Eden, "Reflections on the Futures of K-12 Assessment and Accountability," *American Enterprise Institute and Conservative Education Reform Network*, last modified July 2021, https://www.aei.org/wp-content/uploads/2021/07/Reflections -on-the-future-of-K%E2%80%9312-assessment-and-accountability.pdf; Williams, "More Than Ever, Parents Need Data about Their Kids in a Form They Can Understand"; EdNavigator, "Muddled: How Confusing Information from Schools Is Failing American Families," last modified December 12, 2018, https://www.ednavigator .com/ideas/muddled-how-confusing-information-from-schools-is-failing-american -families; *Learning Heroes*, "Parents 2018: Going beyond Good Grades," last modified December 2018, https://r50gh2ss1ic2mww8s3uvjvq1-wpengine.netdna-ssl.com/ wp-content/uploads/2018/12/2018_Research_Report-final_WEB.pdf.

92. For example, "Award-Winning 2014 School Report Card Offers New Metrics to Better Capture Schools' Performance and Learning Environments," *Illinois State Board of Education*, last modified October 15, 2014, https://www.isbe.net/Lists/News /NewsDisplay.aspx?ID=148.

93. Max Eden, "Reflections on the Futures of K-12 Assessment and Accountability," 3.

94. Regenstein and Strausz-Clark, "Improving Parent Choice in Early Learning," 6.

95. "What Does a High-Quality Program for Infants Look Like," *National Association for the Education of Young Children*, accessed September 29, 2021, https://www .naeyc.org/our-work/families/high-quality-program-for-infant; "What Does a High -Quality Program for Toddlers Look Like?," *National Association for the Education of Young Children*, accessed September 29, 2021, https://www.naeyc.org/our-work /families/what-does-high-quality-program-for-toddler-look-like; "A High-Quality

Program for your Preschools," *National Association for the Education of Young Children*, accessed September 29, 2021, https://www.naeyc.org/our-work/families/high-quality-program-for-preschooler.

96. "The State of Preschool 2020," *The National Institute for Early Education Research*, 9.

97. For example, Suzann Morris and Linda Smith, "Examples of Mixed-Delivery Early Care and Education Systems," *Bipartisan Policy Center*, last modified June 17, 2021, https://bipartisanpolicy.org/blog/examples-of-mixed-delivery-early-care-and-education-systems/; Meghan McCormick and Shira Mattera, "To Build High-Quality Universal Pre-K, Invest in Community-Based Providers," *New America*, last modified June 2, 2021, https://www.newamerica.org/education-policy/edcentral/universal-prek-community-based-providers/. But this is not to say that mixed delivery systems don't come with a host of challenges. For example, Karch, *Early Start*, 183–88; Fuller, *Standardized Childhood*, 268; Carly Sitrin, "Biden's Model Pre-K System Becomes 'a Crisis' in New Jersey," *Politico*, last modified July 30, 2021, https://www.politico.com/states/new-jersey/story/2021/07/27/this-is-a-crisis-private-pre-k-providers-in-new-jersey-say-program-is-rife-with-improprieties-1388796; Regenstein and Strausz-Clark, "Improving Parent Choice in Early Learning."

98. 42 U.S.C. 9831(b)(5), accessed September 29, 2021, https://www.congress.gov/114/plaws/publ95/PLAW-114publ95.pdf.

99. Moe and Hill, "Moving to a Mixed Model," in *The Futures of School Reform*, eds. Mehta, Schwartz, and Hess, 65–93; Chester E. Finn Jr. "Preschool Support, Sure. Biden's Plan, No," *Thomas B. Fordham Institute*, https://fordhaminstitute.org/national/commentary/preschool-support-sure-bidens-plan-no.

100. *Center for the Study of Child Care Employment*, "Why Do Parents Spend So Much on Child Care, Yet Early Childhood Educators Earn So Little?," last modified July 11, 2018, https://cscce.berkeley.edu/why-do-parents-spend-so-much-on-child-care-yet-early-childhood-educators-earn-so-little/; *Child Care Aware of America*, "The US and the High Price of Child Care: An Examination of a Broken System," accessed September 29, 2021, https://www.childcareaware.org/our-issues/research/the-us-and-the-high-price-of-child-care-2019/.

101. Louise Stoney, "Rate Setting in Reality: Moving beyond the Myth of Market-Based Pricing," *Opportunities Exchange*, last modified September 2020, https://static1.squarespace.com/static/5f4d7a7ef6c82325c5ec80c0/t/602555ebdeab0977a18848bb/1613059565324/OppEx_2020_RateSetting_IssueBrf.pdf.

102. Patti Banghart, Zoelene Hill, Gabriella Guerra, Denise Covington, and Kathryn Tout, "Supporting Families' Access to Child Care and Early Education: A Descriptive Profile of States' Consumer Education Websites," *Office of Planning, Research, and Evaluation, Administration for Children and Families, U.S. Department of Health and Human Services*, 10–12, last modified November 2021, https://www.acf.hhs.gov/sites/default/files/documents/opre/cceepra-consumer-education-report.pdf.

103. Banghart, Hill, Guerra, Covington, and Tout, "Supporting Families' Access to Child Care and Early Education," *Office of Planning, Research, and Evaluation, Administration for Children and Families, U.S. Department of Health and Human Services*, 3.

104. Banghart, Hill, Guerra, Covington, and Tout, "Supporting Families' Access to Child Care and Early Education," *Office of Planning, Research, and Evaluation, Administration for Children and Families, U.S. Department of Health and Human Services*, 10–12.

105. Schneider, *Beyond Test Scores*, 230.

106. DeRoche, *A Fine Line*, 110; McShane, "How Unified Enrollment Systems Solve Some Problems and Cause Other Ones."

107. Harris, *Charter School City*, 224; Levin, "A Framework for Designing Governance in Choice and Portfolio Districts," in *Between Public and Private*, eds. Bulkley, Henig, and Levin, 238–39.

108. Campanella, *School Choice Roadmap*, xv, 5.

CHAPTER 12

1. Neil Bhutta, Andrew C. Chang, Lisa J. Dettling, and Joanna W. Hsu, "Disparities in Wealth by Race and Ethnicity in the 2019 Survey of Consumer Finances," *Board of Governors of the Federal Reserve System*, last modified September 28, 2020, https://www.federalreserve.gov/econres/notes/feds-notes/disparities-in-wealth-by-race-and-ethnicity-in-the-2019-survey-of-consumer-finances-20200928.htm; Valerie Wilson, "Racial Disparities in Income and Poverty Remain Largely Unchanged amid Strong Income Growth in 2019," *Economic Policy Institute*, last modified September 16, 2020, https://www.epi.org/blog/racial-disparities-in-income-and-poverty-remain-largely-unchanged-amid-strong-income-growth-in-2019/; Kriston McIntosh, Emily Moss, Ryan Nunn, and Jay Shambaugh, "Examining the Black-White Wealth Gap," *The Brookings Institution*, last modified February 27, 2020, https://www.brookings.edu/blog/up-front/2020/02/27/examining-the-black-white-wealth-gap/.

2. Orfield, "Conclusion: Going Forward," in *The Resegregation of Suburban Schools: A Hidden Crisis in American Education*, eds. Frankenberg and Orfield, 232.

3. William D. Duncombe and John M. Yinger, "School District Consolidation: The Benefits and Costs," *The School Superintendents Association*, accessed September 29, 2021, https://www.aasa.org/SchoolAdministratorArticle.aspx?id=13218.

4. Josh B. McGee, Jonathan Mills, Jessica Goldstein, "The Effect of School District Consolidation on Student Achievement: Evidence from Arkansas," *Annenberg Institute for School Reform at Brown University*, last modified January 2021, https://www.edworkingpapers.com/ai21-347.

5. Scott Shepard, "A Scalpel, Not a Sledge Hammer: Studies Show Statewide, Forced Consolidation Bad for Students, Budgets," *Yankee Institute*, last modified February 4, 2019, https://yankeeinstitute.org/2019/02/04/a-scalpel-not-a-sledge-hammer-studies-show-statewide-forced-consolidation-bad-for-students-budgets/. In 2005 I worked on a bill that reframed how school district consolidation works in Illinois. Diane Rado, "State Urges District Mergers," *Chicago Tribune*, last modified December 2, 2005, https://www.chicagotribune.com/news/ct-xpm-2005-12-22-0512220271-story.html. Very few districts took advantage of the new framework. The next governor then proposed more school district consolidation: "Little Support

for Gov. Pat Quinn's School Consolidation Plan," *Illinois Public Media*, accessed September 29, 2021, https://will.illinois.edu/news/story/little-support-for-gov.-pat -quinns-school-consolidation-plan. That didn't go much of anywhere either. As of 2021, Illinois still had 852 school districts, down from 875 when the bill I worked on passed in 2006. *Illinois State Board of Education*, "School District Reorganizations 1983–84–2021–22," accessed September 29, 2021, https://www.isbe.net/Documents /reorg_history.pdf; Danish Murtaza, "Too Many School Districts in Illinois? What You Should Know about School Consolidation," *Better Government Association*, last modified January 17, 2018, https://www.bettergov.org/news/too-many-school -districts-in-illinois-what-you-should-know-about-school-consolidation/.

6. Black, *School House Burning*, 230–31; Johnson, *Children of the Dream*, 189.

7. Congdon, Kling, and Mullainathan, *Policy and Choice*, 5.

8. Brighouse, Ladd, Loeb, and Swift, *Educational Goods*, 133.

9. Siegel-Hawley, *When the Fences Come Down*, 20.

10. Dahill-Brown, *Education, Equity, and the States*, 111.

11. Siegel-Hawley, *When the Fences Come Down*, 16–117.

12. Siegel-Hawley, *When the Fences Come Down*, 129. While data is still limited, there is at least some data indicating that urban students might benefit from being able to enroll in suburban schools. Aaron Churchill, "Suburban School Districts Can Help Urban Students Succeed," *Thomas B. Fordham Institute*, last updated September 20, 2021, https://fordhaminstitute.org/ohio/commentary/suburban-school-districts-can -help-urban-students-succeed.

13. Wells, Warner, and Grzesikowski, "The Story of Meaningful School Choice," in Orfield and Frankenberg, *Educational Delusions?*, 192–94.

14. Siegel-Hawley, *When the Fences Come Down*, 130; Wells, Warner, and Grzesikowski, "The Story of Meaningful School Choice," in Orfield and Frankenberg, *Educational Delusions?*, 211–15.

15. Siegel-Hawley, *When the Fences Come Down*, 119–22; Orfield, "Conclusion: Going Forward," in *The Resegregation of Suburban Schools*, eds. Frankenberg and Orfield, 231.

16. Holme and Finnigan, *Striving in Common*, 43.

17. Holme and Finnigan, *Striving in Common*, 44.

18. Holme and Finnigan, *Striving in Common*, 15.

19. Holme and Finnigan, *Striving in Common*, 1–3; Rooks, *Cutting School*, 106; Denisa R. Superville, "Missouri's Normandy District Sheds Its Unaccredited Status," *Education Week*, last modified December 1, 2017, https://www.edweek.org/ leadership/missouris-normandy-district-sheds-its-unaccredited-status/2017/12.

20. Holme and Finnigan, *Striving in Common*, 1–3; Rooks, *Cutting School*, 106–7.

21. Holme and Finnigan, *Striving in Common*, 4–9; Rooks, *Cutting School*, 106–7.

22. Rooks, *Cutting School*, 107.

23. Holme and Finnigan, *Striving in Common*, 4–9.

24. For comparison, on a per-pupil basis, the highest-spending state in the country is New York, where schools spend $24,020 per student. *United States Census Bureau*, "Spending per Pupil Increased for Sixth Consecutive Year," last modified May 11, 2020, https://www.census.gov/newsroom/press-releases/2020/school-system

-finances.html. Thus, $30,000 per student would be an above-average per-student expenditure in any state in the country. And to be clear, I am not advocating that the going rate should be $30,000—only that the going rate should be sufficient to make it worthwhile for receiving districts.

25. Ladner, "A Bright Future for Open Enrollment."

26. It is important to acknowledge that school board elections typically have low turnout. Dahill-Brown, *Education, Equity, and the States*, 150–51; Jeffrey R. Henig, Rebecca Jacobsen, and Sarah Reckhow, *Outside Money in School Board Elections: The Nationalization of Education Politics* (Cambridge, MA: Harvard Education Press, 2019), 35–36. That may mean that local priorities may shift based on who actually shows up to vote in a given election. But the broader point is that the issue of how school choice is exercised is one to which local school boards should give thoughtful consideration. Aaron Churchill, "Reform-Minded School Board Members Should Push for Choice, Science of Reading," *The Thomas B. Fordham Institute*, last modified November 23, 2021, https://fordhaminstitute.org/ohio/commentary/reform -minded-school-board-members-should-push-choice-science-reading; Neal McCluskey, "Yes, We Should Focus on Peace in Education," *Cato at Liberty*, last modified August 12, 2021, https://www.cato.org/blog/yes-we-should-focus-peace-education.

27. Burke and Schwalbach. "Housing Redlining and Its Lingering Effects on Education Opportunity."

28. Foundation for Excellence in Education, "Education Policy Playbook 2022," Empower Families with Opportunity, 4–5, accessed November 30, 2021, https: //excelined.org/wp-content/uploads/2021/11/ExcelInEd_EducationPolicyPlaybook _2022.pdf.

29. Dahill-Brown, *Education, Equity, and the States*, 114–22.

30. Dahill-Brown, *Education, Equity, and the States*, 111.

31. Kahlenberg and Potter, *A Smarter Charter*, 67.

32. Smarick, *The Urban School System of the Future*, 49–50, 83–102; Hess, *Education Unbound*, 14–16.

33. Smarick, *The Urban School System of the Future*, 69–81.

34. For an argument against local monopolies in service delivery, see Hess, *The Same Thing Over and Over*, 173–77. For an argument in favor of regional charter schools, see Kahlenberg and Potter, *A Smarter Charter*, 167.

35. Brighouse, Ladd, Loeb, and Swift, *Educational Goods*, 136.

36. Bulkley, Marsh, Strunk, Harris, and Hashim, *Challenging the One Best System*; Moe, *The Politics of Institutional Reform*; Osborne, *Reinventing America's Schools*; Hill and Jochim, *A Democratic Constitution for Public Education*; Smarick, *The Urban School System of the Future*; Hess, *Education Unbound*.

37. Harris, *Charter School City*; Moe, *The Politics of Institutional Reform*.

38. Moe, *The Politics of Institutional Reform*; see also Harris, *Charter School City*.

39. Moe, *The Politics of Institutional Reform*, 10–26.

40. In 2021, President Biden proposed a grant program to support school integration. Kalyn Belsha and Matt Barnum, "$100 Million and Many Open Questions: Here's How Biden Is Approaching School Integration," *Chalkbeat*, last modified

June 22, 2021, https://www.chalkbeat.org/2021/6/22/22545227/biden-cardona-school-integration-desegregation-diversity.

41. Karch and Rose, *Responsive States.*

42. Burkam, Lee, and Dwyer, "School Mobility in the Early Elementary Grades: Frequency and Impact from Nationally-Representative Data."

43. Manuela Fonseca and Michelle Horowitz, "State Approaches to Regional Early Childhood Councils," *Center on Enhancing Early Learning Outcomes and PDG TA*, last modified August 2017, http://ceelo.org/wp-content/uploads/2017/08/ceelo_listserv_summary_regionalcouncils_final_web.pdf.

CONCLUSION

1. Hess, *Letters to a Young Education Reformer*, 13–17; Cuban, "A Critique of Contemporary Edu-Giving," in *The New Education Philanthropy*, eds. Hess and Henig, 159; Labaree, *Someone Has to Fail*, 245.

2. For example, Downey, *How Schools Really Matter.*

3. Hess, *The Same Thing Over and Over*, 215–16; Sarason, *The Predictable Failure of Educational Reform*, 13–15.

4. Kuhn, *Fear and Learning in America*, 84.

5. Sarason, *The Predictable Failure of Educational Reform*, 33.

Selected Bibliography

The full bibliography is available online at https://textbooks.rowman.com/education-restated

"19th Amendment to the U.S. Constitution: Women's Right to Vote (1920)." Accessed September 29, 2021. https://www.ourdocuments.gov/doc.php?flash=false&doc=63.

34 C.F.R. §200.3(b)(5); 34 C.F.R. §200.26(a)(1). Accessed July 14, 2021. https://ecfr.federalregister.gov/current/title-34/subtitle-B/chapter-II/part-200.

42 U.S.C. 9831(b)(5). Accessed September 29, 2021. https://www.congress.gov/114/plaws/publ95/PLAW-114publ95.pdf.

42 U.S.C. 9837B(b)(2). Accessed July 14, 2021. https://eclkc.ohs.acf.hhs.gov/sites/default/files/pdf/hs-act-pl-110-134.pdf.

50-State Comparison. "State K-3 Policies." *Education Commission of the States*. Accessed July 14, 2021. https://internal-search.ecs.org/comparisons/state-k-3-policies-05.

Abion, J. Stuart. "School Discipline Is Trauma-Insensitive and Trauma-Uninformed." *Psychology Today*. Last modified January 9, 2020. https://www.psychologytoday.com/us/blog/.

Advance Illinois. "Transforming Teacher Work." Last modified November 2011. https://media.advanceillinois.org/wp-content/uploads/2014/11/04001242/FINAL-Transforming-Teacher-Work.pdf.

Ahmad, Farah Z., and Ulrich Boser. "America's Leaky Pipeline for Teachers of Color." *Center for American Progress*. Last modified May 2014. https://cdn.americanprogress.org/wp-content/uploads/2014/05/TeachersOfColor-report.pdf.

"Integrated Schools: Families Choosing Integration." Accessed September 29, 2021. https://integratedschools.org/.

Index

Index

Acknowledgments

In the early days when the idea for this book was just germinating, a core group of supporters provided invaluable advice and support. Without the encouragement of Jo Anderson, Katie Dealy, and Dana Suskind, this book probably wouldn't have happened. Geoff Nagle, Cristina Pacione-Zayas, and Bradley Tusk also put some wind into the project's sails at key early moments.

The inspiration to write a book in the first place came out of a project on early childhood governance I conducted in 2019–2020, funded by the Heising-Simons Foundation. Rebecca Gomez's support for that project was a key launching point for this one. A project in 2020 supported by Macy Parker and the Silver Giving Foundation helped develop some of the ideas in chapter 2. Cornelia Grumman has been an incredibly supportive partner when it comes to thinking about the relationship between K-12 and early learning.

This is the first book I've ever proposed, so the process of developing a proposal relied on the assistance of many smart colleagues. Jo Anderson, Josh Anderson, Carla Bryant, Tim Daly, Katie Dealy, Amy Dray, John Easton, Paul Goren, Macy Parker, and Emily Krone Phillips all provided insights that contributed meaningfully to the evolution of the project. Maia Connors, David Figlio, Lynn Kagan, Bob Pianta, and Clare Pelino also made recommendations that advanced the proposal process. Rick Hess was a wonderful advocate for the project, assisted by his colleagues Hayley Sanon and R. J. Martin. Dawn Emsellem, Aimee Guidera, and Jennifer Rippner provided terrific insights for the marketing plan. Jo Anderson, Benjamin Boer, Kent Mitchell, and Shelley Taylor helped refer me to some useful sources.

Jo Anderson, Katie Dealy, and Amy Dray read a really early version of the manuscript and provided valuable feedback. I am also grateful for the manuscript reviews provided in fall 2021 by Jo Anderson, Josh Anderson, Benjamin Boer, Laura Bornfreund, Sandy Boyd, Carla Bryant, Tim Daly, John Easton, Larry Frank, Joshua Kaufmann, Geoff Nagle, Darren Reisberg, Bradley Tusk, and Albert Wat. This book is better for their efforts, and of course anything still wrong with it is on me.

Several people provided very specific assistance that shaped the final manuscript. Jacob Bradt provided valuable guidance on readings in behavioral economics. Paul Zavitkovsky conducted key data analysis, which is particularly important to the chapter on accountability. (Paul's analytic skills have been an enormous help to me over many years.) Jamie Brandon was a lifesaver when it came to getting the endnotes in decent shape, and she helped with a lot of manuscript formatting; I don't know how I would have done this without her.

It was a pleasure working with the team at Rowman & Littlefield: Tom Koerner, Kira Hall, and Anna Keyser all made the process feel easy. I am deeply in their debt. Thanks also to Molly Hall for her work on the index.

Education is my family business, and I am deeply grateful to my parents and grandparents for emphasizing its importance—including the importance of learning and debating ideas throughout your life. I think often of my grandfather, Samuel Forsheit, who was a longtime principal in the New York City schools; the influence he had on his children and grandchildren remains substantial to this day. I didn't actually start my career in education policy but was brought into it by Bradley Tusk, and I remain thankful for that.

Over my years in education policy work, I've been fortunate to have many wonderful colleagues and mentors, who have directly and indirectly shaped the arguments in these pages. The actual production of the manuscript wouldn't have been remotely close to possible without the support of my Foresight Law + Policy partners, Reg Leichty and Amy Starzynski.

In addition to professional colleagues, there were many friends who acted as cheerleaders throughout the production process, both in River Forest and around the country (particularly the SBW group). And none of this would have happened without Emily Paster, who offered substantive insights at every stage of the process, as well as enormous ongoing emotional and practical support.

About the Author

Elliot Regenstein is a Chicago-based partner at Foresight Law + Policy. He has extensive experience in state-level policy and advocacy, with a particular focus on early learning; he has also consulted with more than two dozen states on a wide range of education policy topics. Much of his work focuses on how decision-making occurs in state education and early education systems: who is responsible for which decisions, what information they have to support those decisions, and what incentives are acting on key stakeholders. He is a frequent author and speaker on topics including accountability, governance, state data systems, and the connections between early learning and K-12.

Regenstein served as Director of Education Reform for the State of Illinois from 2004 to 2006, and co-chaired the Illinois Early Learning Council from 2004 until April 2009. From 2009 to 2022 he served as chair of the Illinois Early Learning Council's Data, Research, and Evaluation sub-committee, and from 2015 to 2021 he served as chair of the Illinois Longitudinal Data System Governing Board. Regenstein holds a bachelor of arts degree in history from Columbia University and a law degree from the University of Michigan, where he was the executive note editor on the Michigan Law Review. After law school he clerked for the Hon. Kenneth F. Ripple on the United States Court of Appeals for the Seventh Circuit.